Gareth McLean

TAXATION SUMMARY

Terry Cooney, Jim McLaughlin & Joe Martyn

REPUBLIC OF IRELAND   1999/2000

Published by The Institute of Taxation in Ireland,
19 Sandymount Avenue, Dublin 4.

Telephone: (01) 668 8222
Fax: (01) 668 8387
Email: info@taxireland.ie
Website: www.taxireland.ie

First Published 1977
This Edition (23rd) 1999/2000

THE INSTITUTE OF **TAXATION** IN IRELAND

ISBN 0 902565 63 X

© Copyright: The Institute of Taxation in Ireland.   19 Sandymount Avenue, Dublin 4

This book is a summary of the extensive volume of statute and case law in the Republic of Ireland and is not intended as a detailed exposition of that law and practice.

Any views or opinions expressed are not necessarily subscribed to by the Institute.

Neither the Institute nor the authors accept any responsibility for loss or damage occasioned by any person acting or refraining from acting as a result of the material in this book. Professional advice should always be sought before acting on any issue covered in this book.

© Copyright The Institute of Taxation in Ireland 1999

THE INSTITUTE OF TAXATION IN IRELAND

The Institute of Taxation in Ireland was founded in 1967. It has been admitted by the Confederation Fiscale Europeenne (CFE) as a member representing the Republic of Ireland. Under the provisions of the Finance Act 1990, any person who has been admitted as a member of the Institute of Taxation in Ireland has the right to be heard by the Appeal Commissioners and at a rehearing before a Circuit Court Judge (Finance Act 1995). The Institute and its AITI qualification are officially recognised in the State for purposes of the EC Directive of 21 December 1988 regarding Standards for Higher Education Qualifications Awarded on Completion of Professional Education and Training of at least Three Year's Duration.

The objects of the Institute include the promotion of the study of tax law and practice, the making of regular submissions on fiscal matters to the Government and through CFE, to the EU Commission, and the establishment of a high standard of professional ethics for persons engaged in the practice of tax consultancy.

To become an Associate, it is necessary to pass examinations set by the Institute. Designatory letters are AITI and FITI. Fellows, Associates, Members, Student and Subscriber Members of the Institute now number over 5,000, and are drawn mainly from the legal, accounting and banking professions and from the revenue service.

It is possible, outside of the examination system, to participate in many of the benefits of Institute membership by becoming a Subscriber. Full details are available from the Chief Executive, Institute of Taxation in Ireland, 19 Sandymount Ave, Dublin 4. Telephone (01) 66 88 222, Fax (01) 66 88 088/66 88 387 E Mail: info@taxireland.ie Website: www.taxireland.ie

JIM McLAUGHLIN
R.I.P.

Jim McLaughlin died suddenly on 6th March 1999. Jim was President of this Institute in 1986/87 and a partner in Deloitte and Touche.

Jim made a major contribution to "Taxation Summary" since its inception in 1977.

Terry Cooney, Joe Martyn and Paschal Taggart acknowledge the loss of a dear friend and colleague.

May he rest in peace.

FOREWORD

It gives me great pleasure to welcome the 1999/2000 edition of the Taxation Summary. Over the years this book has provided a user friendly and well referenced summary of the various taxes, and has been used by numerous tax practitioners over the years. The size has continued to expand each year and this reflects both upon the continuing commitment of the authors, and of course the growth in the volume of tax legislation.

Sadly, one of the authors, Jim McLaughlin, passed away during the year but his work lives on in this fine publication. Our sincere thanks are due to Jim, Terry Cooney and Joe Martyn.

ADRIAN CRAWFORD
President
Institute of Taxation in Ireland

TABLE OF CONTENTS

CHAPTER 1   INCOME TAX 43

1.1 ADMINISTRATION OF TAX SYSTEM 43
- 1.1.1 Legislation 43
- 1.1.2 Revenue Commissioners 43
- 1.1.3 Fundamental Concepts 43
- 1.1.4 Self Assessment 44
- 1.1.5 Returns 44
- 1.1.6 Surcharge 44
- 1.1.7 Matters of Doubt 44
- 1.1.8 Assessments 45
- 1.1.9 Payment of Income Tax 45
- 1.1.10 Directors 46
- 1.1.11 Appeal Procedures 46
- 1.1.12 Interest on Overdue Tax 49
- 1.1.13 Power of Attachment 49
- 1.1.14 Fixed Charge on Company Book Debts 51

1.2 THE UNIFIED SYSTEM OF PERSONAL TAXATION 52
- 1.2.1 Joint Assessment 52
- 1.2.2 Single Assessment 52
- 1.2.3 Separate Assessment 52
- 1.2.4 Separated Spouses 52
- 1.2.5 Divorced Persons 53

1.3 PERSONAL ALLOWANCES AND RELIEFS 54
- 1.3.1 Personal Allowances 54
- 1.3.2 Age Allowance 56
- 1.3.3 Incapacitated Child Allowance 56
- 1.3.4 Dependent Relative Allowance 57
- 1.3.5 Employed Person Taking Care of Incapacitated Individual 57
- 1.3.6 Blind Persons' Allowance 57
- 1.3.7 Medical Expenses 57
- 1.3.8 Medical Insurance 58
- 1.3.9 Permanent Health Benefit Schemes 58
- 1.3.10 Employee Allowance 58
- 1.3.11 Long Term Unemployed 59
- 1.3.12 Seafarers Allowance 59

Table of Contents

	1.3.13	Rents Paid by Certain Tenants	59
	1.3.14	Fees paid to Private Colleges in the State	60
	1.3.15	Fees paid to EU Colleges	60
	1.3.16	Fees paid for Training Courses	60
	1.3.17	Service Charges	60
	1.3.18	Alarm Systems	61
	1.3.19	Donations/Gifts	61
	1.3.20	Retirement Annuities (a) Tax Relief	61
	1.13.31	(b) Options on Retirement	62
1.4	SMALL INCOME AND AGE EXEMPTIONS		64
	1.4.1	Small Income Exemption	64
	1.4.2	Age Exemption	64
	1.4.3	Marginal Relief	64
1.5	INTEREST PAYABLE		65
	1.5.1	Mortgage Interest	65
	1.5.2	Interest on Loans applied in acquiring shares/lending money to a company	65
	1.5.3	Interest on Loans applied in acquiring an interest in a Partnership	66
	1.5.4	Payment of Interest Net	66
1.6	SCHEDULE C		68
	1.6.1	Exemptions	68
1.7	SCHEDULE D – CASES I and II		69
	1.7.1	Pre-Trading Expenses	70
	1.7.2	Entertainment Expenses	70
	1.7.3	Motor Expenses	70
	1.7.4	Basis of Assessment	71
	1.7.5	Commencement Years	71
	1.7.6	Cessation Years	72
	1.7.7	Period of Computation of Profits	72
	1.7.8	Losses	73
	1.7.9	Withholding Tax on Payments for Professional Services	74
	1.7.10	Ongoing Business	74
	1.7.11	Commencing Business	75
	1.7.12	Cases of Particular Hardship	75
1.8	SCHEDULE D – CASE III		76
	1.8.1	Basis of Assessment	76
1.9	SCHEDULE D – CASE IV		77
	1.9.1	Basis of Assessment	77
1.10	DEPOSIT INTEREST RETENTION TAX		78
	1.10.1	Companies and Pension Funds	78

Table of Contents

	1.10.2	Individuals	78
	1.10.3	Deposit Taker	80
	1.10.4	Returns and Payments	80
	1.10.5	Charities	80
	1.10.6	Repayment to Elderly and Incapacitated Individuals	80
	1.10.7	Non-Resident Depositors	81
1.11	SPECIAL INVESTMENT PRODUCTS		82
	1.11.1	1. Special Investment Policies (SIP)	82
	1.11.2	2. Special Investment Schemes (SIS)	82
	1.11.3	3. Special Portfolio Investment Accounts (SPIA)	83
	1.11.4	Limits on Investment in Special Investment Products	84
1.12	SCHEDULE D – CASE V		85
	1.12.1	Deductions	85
	1.12.2	Capital Allowances	86
	1.12.3	Expenditure on Rented Accommodation	86
	1.12.4	Premiums on Leases	87
	1.12.5	Rents Paid to Non-Residents	88
	1.12.6	Exemption of Income from Leasing of Farm Land	88
	1.12.7	Basis of Assessment	88
	1.12.8	Losses	88
1.13	URBAN RENEWAL – 1986 SCHEME		89
	1.13.1	Expenditure on Commercial Buildings and Structures	89
	1.13.2	Expenditure on Rented Accommodation	90
	1.13.3	Owner / Occupier Residential Accommodation	90
	1.13.4	Double Rent Allowance	91
	1.13.5	Expenditure on Historic Buildings in Urban Renewal Areas	91
1.14	TEMPLE BAR AREA OF DUBLIN		92
	1.14.1	Expenditure on Rented Accommodation	92
	1.14.2	Owner/Occupier Residential Accommodation	93
	1.14.3	Double Rent Allowance	93
	1.14.4	Anti-Avoidance	93
1.15	URBAN RENEWAL SCHEME FROM 1 AUGUST 1994 – DESIGNATED AREA/STREET		94
	1.15.1	Industrial Buildings	95
	1.15.2	Commercial Buildings	95
	1.15.3	Double Rent Allowance	96
	1.15.4	Rented Residential Accommodation	96
	1.15.5	Owner/Occupier Residential Accommodation	97
1.16	URBAN RENEWAL – ENTERPRISE AREAS		98

Table of Contents

1.17		URBAN RENEWAL – RESORT AREAS	100
	1.17.1	Industrial Buildings	100
	1.17.2	Tourism Facilities	100
	1.17.3	Rented Residential Accommodation	102
1.18		URBAN RENEWAL – ISLANDS	104
	1.18.1	Rented Residential Accommodation	104
	1.18.2	Owner/Occupier Residential Accommodation	104
1.19		URBAN RENEWAL - DUBLIN DOCKLANDS	105
	1.19.1	Industrial Buildings	105
	1.19.2	Commercial Premises	105
	1.19.3	Hotels	105
	1.19.4	Balancing Allowances/Charges	105
	1.19.5	Double Rent Allowance	105
	1.19.6	Residential Accommodation	106
1.20		URBAN RENEWAL - 1998-1999 SCHEME	107
	1.20.1	Industrial Buildings	107
	1.20.2	Commercial Premises	107
	1.20.3	Balancing Allowances/Charges	107
	1.20.4	Double Rent Allowance	107
	1.20.5	Rented Residential Accommodation	108
	1.20.6	Owner-occupied Residential Accommodation	108
1.21		RURAL RENEWAL SCHEME - 1998	109
	1.21.1	Industrial Buildings	109
	1.21.2	Commercial Premises	109
	1.21.3	Balancing Allowances/Charges	109
	1.21.4	Double Rent Allowance	110
	1.21.5	Rented Residential Accommodation	110
	1.21.6	Owner occupied Residential Accommodation	110
1.22		SCHEDULE E	111
	1.22.1	Social Welfare Benefits	111
	1.22.2	Basis of Assessment	111
	1.22.3	Deductions	111
	1.22.4	Round Sum Expense Allowances	112
	1.22.5	Benefits-in-Kind	112
	1.22.6	(i) Cars	112
	1.22.7	(ii) Vans	114
	1.22.8	(iii) Accommodation	114
	1.22.9	(iv) Interest Paid at a Preferential Rate	114
	1.22.10	Benefit-in-Kind Exemptions	115
	1.22.11	(i) Works of Art	115
	1.22.12	(ii) Bus/Train Passes	115
	1.22.13	(iii) Childcare Services	116

Table of Contents

	1.22.14	Employee Share Schemes	116
	1.22.15	(i) Rights over Assets	116
	1.22.16	(ii) Share Subscription Schemes	116
	1.22.17	(iii) Approved Profit Sharing Schemes (APSS)	117
	1.22.18	(iv) Employee Share Ownership Trusts (ESOT)	119
	1.22.19	(v) Save As You Earn (SAYE) Share Scheme	121
	1.22.20	Treatment of Unpaid Remuneration	121
	1.22.21	Payments in Connection with the Commencement of Employment	121
	1.22.22	Payments on Retirement or Removal from an Employment	122
	1.22.23	Exemptions	123
1.23		DEEDS OF COVENANT	124
	1.23.1	Covenants from parents to children	124
	1.23.2	Covenants from grandparents to grandchildren	124
	1.23.3	Covenants between other individuals	124
	1.23.4	Other Covenants	125
	1.23.5	Covenants after 5 April 1996	125
1.24		CAPITAL ALLOWANCES	127
	1.24.1	Wear and Tear Allowance	127
	1.24.2	Balancing Allowances and Charges - Plant and Machinery	128
	1.24.3	Writing-Down Allowance - Industrial Buildings	129
	1.24.4	Balancing Allowances and Charges - Industrial Buildings	130
	1.24.5	Lessors	130
	1.24.6	Anti-Avoidance	131
	1.24.7	Expenditure on Dredging	131
	1.24.8	Scientific Research - Capital Expenditure	131
	1.24.9	Expenditure on Patent Rights	131
	1.24.10	Multi-Storey Car Parks	131
	1.24.11	Airports	132
	1.24.12	Hotels, Holiday Camps and Holiday Cottages	132
	1.24.13	Hotel Room Ownership Scheme	133
	1.24.14	Nursing Homes	133
	1.24.15	Private Convalescent Facilities	134
	1.24.16	Childcare Facilities	134
	1.24.17	Student Accommodation	134
	1.24.18	Third Level Institutions	135
	1.24.19	Park and Ride Facilities	135
	1.24.20	Significant Buildings	137
	1.24.21	Restriction of Capital Allowances/Losses	139

Table of Contents

1.25	FARMING TAXATION		141
	1.25.1	Averaging of Farm Profits	141
	1.25.2	Stock Relief	142
	1.25.3	Losses	143
	1.25.4	Discontinued Farm Trades	143
	1.25.5	Pollution Control	143
1.26	SUB-CONTRACTORS		144
	1.26.1	Principal Contractor	144
	1.26.2	Relevant Contract	145
	1.26.3	Gang System	147
	1.26.4	Credit for Tax Deducted	147
	1.26.5	Returns	148
	1.26.6	Payments	148
1.27	EXEMPTIONS		149
	1.27.1	Artists	149
	1.27.2	Patent Royalties	149
	1.27.3	Stallion Services	151
	1.27.4	Forests / Woodlands	152
	1.27.5	Greyhound Stud Fees	152
	1.27.6	Payment in respect of Personal Injuries	152
	1.27.7	Payments made by the Haemophilia HIV Trust	152
	1.27.8	Hepatitis C Compensation	153
	1.27.9	Trusts for permanently incapacitated individuals	153
1.28	RELIEF FOR INVESTMENT IN CORPORATE TRADES (BES)		154
	1.28.1	Qualifying Individual	154
	1.28.2	Qualifying Companies	155
	1.28.3	Company's Limit	157
	1.28.4	Qualifying Trade	158
	1.28.5	Qualifying Shares	158
	1.28.6	Claim for Relief	159
	1.28.7	Withdrawal of Relief	159
	1.28.8	Replacement Capital	161
	1.28.9	Capital Gains Tax	162
	1.28.10	Approved Funds	162
	1.28.11	Spouses	162
1.29	SEED CAPITAL INVESTMENT		163
1.30	INVESTMENT IN FILMS		165
1.31	RESIDENCE OF INDIVIDUALS		168
	1.31.1	Residence	168
	1.31.2	Ordinary Residence	168
	1.31.3	Split Year Residence Relief	168

	1.31.4	Deduction for Foreign Earnings	169
	1.31.5	Cross Border Workers	170
	1.31.6	Seafarers Allowance	170
	1.31.7	Domicile	170
1.32	SECURITISATION OF ASSETS		172
1.33	TRUSTS AND SETTLEMENTS		173
	1.33.1	Foreign Trusts	173
	1.33.2	Surcharge on Undistributed Income	174

CHAPTER 2   CORPORATION TAX 175

2.1	ADMINISTRATION AND FUNDAMENTAL CONCEPTS		175
	2.1.1	Scope of Corporation Tax	175
	2.1.2	Corporation Tax Rates	175
	2.1.3	Residence	176
	2.1.4	Accounting Periods	177
	2.1.5	Self Assessment	177
	2.1.6	Returns	178
	2.1.7	Late Returns	178
	2.1.8	Matters of Doubt	179
	2.1.9	Payment of Corporation Tax	179
	2.1.10	Calculation of Taxable Profits and Allowable Losses	180
	2.1.11	Pre-Trading Expenses	180
	2.1.12	Losses / Management Expenses	180
	2.1.13	Charges on Income	182
	2.1.14	Section 151 Assessments	182
2.2	MANUFACTURING COMPANIES - REDUCED RATE OF 10%		184
	2.2.1	Losses	190
	2.2.2	Exclusions	190
	2.2.3	Time Limit	191
	2.2.4	Anti Avoidance Provisions	191
	2.2.5	Shannon Airport	192
2.3	RESEARCH AND DEVELOPMENT		193
2.4	GROUP RELIEF		195
	2.4.1	Anti-Avoidance	196
2.5	MINING TAXATION		198
	2.5.1	Exploration Expenditure	198
	2.5.2	Rehabilitation Expenditure	199
	2.5.3	Petroleum Companies	199
2.6	CLOSE COMPANIES		200
	2.6.1	Participators and Associates	200

	2.6.2	Certain Expenses for Participators and Associates ...200
	2.6.3	Interest Paid to Directors and Directors' Associates ...200
	2.6.4	Loans to Participators etc. ...200
	2.6.5	Surcharge on Certain Undistributed Income ...201
2.7	SCHEDULE F AND COMPANY DISTRIBUTIONS ...202
	2.7.1	Matters to be treated as Distributions ...202
	2.7.2	"Section 84 Loans" ...203
	2.7.3	Distributions from Manufacturing Profits ...204
2.8	DIVIDEND WITHHOLDING TAX ...206
	2.8.1	General ...206
2.9	FOREIGN ASPECTS ...208
	2.9.1	Foreign Exchange Transactions ...208
	2.9.2	The Euro ...209
	2.9.3	Dividends from a Non Resident Subsidiary ...209
	2.9.4	Unilateral Relief ...210
	2.9.5	Branch Profits ...210
	2.9.6	Companies changing Residence ...211
2.10	ADVANCE CORPORATION TAX ...212
2.11	SPECIAL COMPANIES FOR CORPORATION TAX ...216
	2.11.1	Agricultural and Fishery Co Operatives ...216
	2.11.2	An Bord Pinsean ...216
	2.11.3	Building Societies ...216
	2.11.4	Dublin Docklands Development Authority ...217
	2.11.5	Housing Finance Agency plc ...217
	2.11.6	Irish Horse-Racing Authority ...217
	2.11.7	National Lottery ...217
	2.11.8	National Treasury Management Agency ...217
	2.11.9	Nitrigin Eireann Teoranta (NET) ...218
	2.11.10	Trustee Savings Banks ...218
	2.11.11	Investor Compensation Company Limited ...218
2.12	SPECIAL EMPLOYMENT RELATED RECEIPTS AND PAYMENTS ...219
	2.12.1	Scheme Payments ...219
	2.12.2	Enterprise Trust Limited ...220
	2.12.3	Long Term Unemployed ...220
	2.12.4	Designated Schools ...221
	2.12.5	Eligible Charities ...221
	2.12.6	Renewable Energy Generation ...221
	2.12.7	First Step Limited ...222

Table of Contents

| | 2.12.8 | Scientific Technological Educational and (Investment) Fund (STEIF) | 222 |

CHAPTER 3 DOUBLE TAXATION AGREEMENTS ... 223

3.1	EXISTING DOUBLE TAXATION AGREEMENTS		223
3.2	DOUBLE TAXATION AGREEMENT REPUBLIC OF IRELAND - UNITED KINGDOM		224
	3.2.1	Residence of Individuals	224
	3.2.2	UK Dividends	224
	3.2.3	Repayment of Withholding Tax	225
	3.2.4	Interest	225
	3.2.5	Rents	225
	3.2.6	Business Profits	225
	3.2.7	Royalties	225
	3.2.8	Capital Gains	225
	3.2.9	Salaries, Wages and Directors Fees	225
	3.2.10	Pensions	226
	3.2.11	Charities & Superannuation Schemes	226
	3.2.12	Government Service	226
	3.2.13	Exchange of Information	226
3.3	EU DIRECTIVES		227
	3.3.1	EU Directive No 90/435/EU	227
	3.3.2	EU Directive No 90/434/EU	227

CHAPTER 4 ANTI AVOIDANCE / REVENUE POWERS ... 229

4.1	ANTI AVOIDANCE LEGISLATION		229
	4.1.1	(a) Friendly Societies	229
	4.1.2	(b) Transfer of Assets Abroad	229
	4.1.3	(c) Property Transactions	229
	4.1.4	(d) Industrial and Provident Societies	229
	4.1.5	(e) Exchequer Bills	230
	4.1.6	(f) Bond Washing	230
	4.1.7	(g) Limited Partnerships	230
	4.1.8	(h) Transactions to Avoid Liability to Tax	231
	4.1.9	(i) Capital Distribution Treated as Dividend	231
4.2	REVENUE POWERS		232
	4.2.1	General	232

Table of Contents

	4.2.2	Inspector's right to make enquiries	232
	4.2.3	Power to require production of accounts and books	232
	4.2.4	Production of books and records – Application to High Court	233
	4.2.5	Power to obtain from certain persons particulars of transactions with and documents concerning tax liability of taxpayer	233
	4.2.6	Information from third parties – Application to High Court	233
	4.2.7	PAYE	233
	4.2.8	Subcontractors	233
	4.2.9	DIRT	234
	4.2.10	Inspection of documents and records	234
	4.2.11	Authorised officers and Garda Síochána	235
	4.2.12	Information to be furnished by Financial Institutions	235
	4.2.13	Application to Appeal Commissioners seeking determination that authorised officer is justified in requiring information to be furnished by financial institutions	235
	4.2.14	Application to High Court seeking order requiring information to be furnished by financial institutions	235
	4.2.15	Application to Circuit Court or District Court seeking order requiring information to be furnished by financial institutions	236
	4.2.16	Statement of Affairs	236
4.3	REPORTING REQUIREMENTS		237
	4.3.1	(a) Returns of Certain Information	237
	4.3.2	(b) Off-Shore Funds	238
	4.3.3	(c) Foreign Accounts	238
	4.3.4	(d) Non Resident Companies	239
	4.3.5	(e) Show Tax Reference	240
	4.3.6	(f) Information from Ministers	240
4.4	REVENUE OFFENCES		241
	4.4.1	Revenue Offences Made Public	242
4.5	RESIGNATION OF PROFESSIONAL ADVISORS		243
4.6	TAX CLEARANCE CERTIFICATES		244
	4.6.1	Liquor Licences	244
	4.6.2	Other Licences	244

CHAPTER 5 — CAPITAL ACQUISITIONS TAX 245

- 5.1 CAPITAL ACQUISITIONS TAX 245
  - 5.1.1 Class Thresholds 246
  - 5.1.2 Revised Class Threshold 246
  - 5.1.3 Threshold Amount 247
  - 5.1.4 Indexation 247
  - 5.1.5 Discretionary Trusts 247
  - 5.1.6 Gifts 249
  - 5.1.7 Relief from Double Aggregation 249
  - 5.1.8 Allowance for Prior Tax 249
  - 5.1.9 Surviving Spouses 250
  - 5.1.10 Nephew or Niece of the Disponer 250
  - 5.1.11 Relief in Respect of Certain Marriage Settlements 251
  - 5.1.12 Territorial Limit 251
  - 5.1.13 Disclaimer 251
  - 5.1.14 Joint Tenants 251
  - 5.1.15 Valuation of Agricultural Property 252
  - 5.1.16 Valuation of Shares in Private Companies 253
  - 5.1.17 Valuation of Dwellings taken from Brother/Sister 253
  - 5.1.18 Business Relief 254
  - 5.1.19 Valuation of Limited Interests 255
  - 5.1.20 Free Use of Property 255
  - 5.1.21 Companies 255
  - 5.1.22 Joint Accounts 256
  - 5.1.23 Exemptions 256
  - 5.1.24 Self Assessment 258
  - 5.1.25 Penalties 259
  - 5.1.26 Surcharge 260
  - 5.1.27 Delivery of Returns 260
  - 5.1.28 Interest 261
  - 5.1.29 Accountable Persons 261
  - 5.1.30 Appeals 261
  - 5.1.31 Certificate of Discharge 262
  - 5.1.32 Clearance Certificate 262
  - 5.1.33 Anti-Avoidance 262
- 5.2 PROBATE TAX 263
- 5.3 THE CAT/INHERITANCE TAX DOUBLE TAX AGREEMENT WITH THE UNITED KINGDOM 265
  - 5.3.1 Elimination of Double Taxation 265

Table of Contents

	5.3.2	Time Limit for Credit or Repayment	265
	5.3.3	How to Determine the Country with Subsidiary Rights	265

CHAPTER 6   CAPITAL GAINS TAX 267

6.1	CAPITAL GAINS TAX		267
	6.1.1	Persons Chargeable	267
	6.1.2	Assets	267
	6.1.3	Disposal	268
	6.1.4	Death	268
	6.1.5	Time of Disposal	268
	6.1.6	Husbands and Wives	268
	6.1.7	Divorced Persons	268
	6.1.8	Separate Spouses	269
	6.1.9	Rates of Capital Gains Tax	269
	6.1.10	Reduced Rate of CGT	270
	6.1.11	Computation of Chargeable Gains and Allowable Losses	271
	6.1.12	Indexation	271
	6.1.13	Losses	272
	6.1.14	Part Disposals	273
	6.1.15	Self Assessment	273
	6.1.16	Exemptions and Reliefs	274
	6.1.17	Private Residence	275
	6.1.18	Disposal of Business or Farm	276
	6.1.19	Disposal within the Family of Business or Farm	277
	6.1.20	Replacement of Business and Other Assets	277
	6.1.21	Sale of Shares - Unquoted Company	278
	6.1.22	Compulsory Purchase	280
	6.1.23	Compensation and Insurance Money	280
	6.1.24	Scheme for Retirement of Farmers	281
	6.1.25	Deductions	281
	6.1.26	Interest	281
	6.1.27	Calls on Shares	281
	6.1.28	Rights Issues	282
	6.1.29	Identification of Shares Disposed of with Shares Purchased	282
	6.1.30	Options	282
	6.1.31	Inheritances and Gifts	282
	6.1.32	Liquidations	282
	6.1.33	Reorganisations and Takeovers	283

	6.1.34	Acquisition by a Company of its Own Shares......283
	6.1.35	Assets which have Qualified for Capital Allowances..........285
	6.1.36	Grants 285
	6.1.37	Transfer of a Business to a Company..........286
	6.1.38	Leases..........286
	6.1.39	Trusts 287
	6.1.40	Anti Avoidance 289
	6.1.41	Time Limits 289
	6.1.42	Miscellaneous 289
	6.1.43	Clearance Certificates..........289

CHAPTER 7   RESIDENTIAL PROPERTY TAX....291

7.1	RESIDENTIAL PROPERTY TAX 291	
	7.1.1	Charge 291
	7.1.2	Market Value 292
	7.1.3	Market Value Exemption Limit 292
	7.1.4	Income Limit..........292
	7.1.5	Income 293
	7.1.6	Inflation Relief 293
	7.1.7	Marginal Relief..........293
	7.1.8	Reduction for Children 294
	7.1.9	Returns 294
	7.1.10	Clearance on Sale of Certain Residential Property 294
	7.1.11	Assessment and Payment of Tax..........294
	7.1.12	Interest on Overdue Tax 294
	7.1.13	Overpayment of Tax..........295
	7.1.14	Appeals..........295
	7.1.15	Penalties 295

CHAPTER 8   STAMP DUTIES..........297

8.1	STAMP DUTIES..........297	
	8.1.1	Amnesty 298
	8.1.2	Charge 298
	8.1.3	Conveyance or Transfer on Sale of..........298
	8.1.4	The Crest System..........300
	8.1.5	Letters of Renunciation 300
	8.1.6	Voluntary Dispositions Inter Vivos..........300

Table of Contents

	8.1.7	Where Consideration cannot be ascertained 300
	8.1.8	Valuation of Property Chargeable with Stamp Duty 301
	8.1.9	Anti Avoidance 301
	8.1.10	Deductions in relation to certain Conveyances and Transfers..302
	8.1.11	Transactions between Related Persons...................302
	8.1.12	Transfers between Associated Companies 302
	8.1.13	Leases...303
	8.1.14	Mortgage, Bond, Debenture, Covenant, charged on property within the State..304
	8.1.15	Life Insurance Policies for periods exceeding 2 years..305
	8.1.16	Settlements...305
	8.1.17	Companies' Capital Duty 305
	8.1.18	Levy on Section 84 Loans...306
	8.1.19	Ad Valorem Duty - Exceptions..................................307
	8.1.20	Fixed Rate of Duty 308
	8.1.21	Young Farmers..308
	8.1.22	Transfer on Divorce 309
	8.1.23	Exemptions from Stamp Duties - General 309
	8.1.24	Appeals..311
	8.1.25	Payment of Stamp Duty on Instruments................311
	8.1.26	Interest...312

CHAPTER 9   VALUE ADDED TAX........................313

9.1	VALUE ADDED TAX 313	
	9.1.1	Legislation..313
	9.1.2	European Union Directives 313
	9.1.3	Charge 313
	9.1.4	Supply and Self Supply of Goods............................313
	9.1.5	Amount on which Tax is Chargeable 314
	9.1.6	Intra-Community Acquisitions – Registered Persons 315
	9.1.7	Intra-Community Acquisitions – Unregistered Persons 315
	9.1.8	Non-Taxable Entities 315
	9.1.9	Private Individuals 315
	9.1.10	New Means of Transport..316
	9.1.11	Mail Order and Distance Selling 316

9.1.12	Supplies by VAT-Registered Traders in Ireland	316
9.1.13	Telecommunications Services	316
9.1.14	Transfer of Business	317
9.1.15	Taxable Periods	317
9.1.16	Annual Accounting for VAT	317
9.1.17	Tax Deductible	318
9.1.18	Margin Scheme	318
9.1.19	Agricultural Machinery	319
9.1.20	Auction Scheme	319
9.1.21	Second-Hand Means of Transport	319
9.1.22	Tax Not Deductible	319
9.1.23	Bad Debts	319
9.1.24	Place where Goods Supplied	320
9.1.25	Place where Services Supplied	320
9.1.26	Rates	321
9.1.27	Immovable Goods	321
9.1.28	Option not to Register	324
9.1.29	Farmers	325
9.1.30	Flat Rate Farmer	326
9.1.31	Farm Buildings, Land Reclamation and Land Drainage	326
9.1.32	Repayments to Foreign Traders	326
9.1.33	Retail Export Scheme	326
9.1.34	Supplies to certain Taxable Persons	326
9.1.35	Cash Basis	327
9.1.36	Group Registration	327
9.1.37	Appeals	328
9.1.38	Bankruptcy and Winding Up	328
9.1.39	Unjust Enrichment	328
9.1.40	Time Limits	328
9.1.41	Documentation	328
9.2	ANNEX A ACTIVITIES	330
9.3	ANNEX B SERVICES	331

CHAPTER 10   TAX AMNESTIES 1993 333

10.1	TAX AMNESTIES 1993	333
	10.1.1 Main Amnesty	333
	10.1.2 General Amnesty	334

Table of Contents

APPENDIX — IRISH TAX CASES, INDEX TO 335

1 IRISH TAX CASES, INDEX TO 335
    1.1 Appeals 335
    1.2 Capital Acquisitions Tax 335
    1.3 Capital Allowances 336
    1.4 Capital Gains Tax 336
    1.5 Case III 336
    1.6 Corporation Profits Tax 337
    1.7 Corporation Tax 338
    1.8 Dispositions, Estates, Trusts 338
    1.9 Export Sales Relief 338
    1.10 Land Dealing & Developing 339
    1.11 Liquidations & Receiverships 339
    1.12 Manufacture of Goods 340
    1.13 Married Persons 340
    1.14 Miscellaneous 340
    1.15 Rental Income 341
    1.16 Residential Property Tax 341
    1.17 Schedule E Expenses 342
    1.18 Schedule E Income 342
    1.19 Service Company 343
    1.20 Stock Relief 343
    1.21 Stamp Duty 343
    1.22 Trading Deductions 343
    1.23 Trading Losses 344
    1.24 Trading Miscellaneous 344
    1.25 Trading Receipts 345
    1.26 Value Added Tax 346

INDEX 347

CHARTS — CONTENTS

Income Tax

Chart 1	–	Allowances 1990/91 – 1999/2000
Chart 2	–	Rates/Bands 1990/91 – 1999/2000
Chart 3	–	Exemption Limits
Chart 4	–	PRSI Rates and Levies
Chart 5	–	PAYE Tables
Chart 6	–	Mortgage Interest Relief
Chart 7	–	Motor Vehicles (Passenger) – Restriction of Capital Allowances and Expenses
Chart 8	–	Mileage Rates
Chart 9	–	Subsistence Rates
Chart 10	–	Tax Credits – Irish Dividends
Chart 11	–	Tax Credits – UK Dividends
Chart 12	–	Interest on Overdue Tax/Tax Overpaid
Chart 13	–	Exchange Rates:- IR£/£Stg
Chart 14	–	Specified Amounts
Chart 15	–	Withholding Tax
Chart 16	–	Tax and Interest on Preferential Debts
Chart 17	–	Time Limits

Corporation Tax

Chart 18	–	Rates
Chart 19	–	Manufacturing Relief
Chart 14	–	Specified Amounts
Chart 20	–	Time Limits

Capital Gains Tax

Chart 21	–	Indexation Factors
Chart 14	–	Specified Amounts

Capital Acquisitions Tax

Chart 22	–	Rates
Chart 23	–	Class Thresholds

Probate Tax

Chart 24	–	Exemption Thresholds

Residential Property Tax

Chart 25		(1) Limits – Property & Income
	–	(2) Thresholds for Clearance Certificate
Chart 26	–	Rates – Y/E 5 April 1994

Value Added Tax

Chart 27	–	Fourth Schedule Services
Chart 28	–	Exempted Activities
Chart 29	–	Zero Rate
Chart 30	–	10% Rate
Chart 31	–	12.5% Rate
Chart 32	–	21% Rate

Charts – Contents

Capital Allowances
    Chart 33 – Capital Allowances

Urban Renewal
    Chart 34 – Area Allowances
    Chart 35 – Designated Area/Street from 1.8.94
    Chart 36 – Rental Property

Income Tax Allowance

CHART 1
INCOME TAX ALLOWANCES

	90/91	91/92	92/93	93/94	94/95
Single Person	2,050	2,100	2,100	2,175	2,350
Married Couple	4,100	4,200	4,200	4,350	4,700
Widowed person (in year of bereavement)	4,100	4,200	4,200	4,350	4,700
Widowed person (subsequent years)	2,550	2,600	2,600	2,675	2,850
Widowed person with dependent child (additional)	1,550	1,600	1,600	1,675	1,850
First year after bereavement	–	1,500	1,500	1,500	1,500
Second year after bereavement	–	1,000	1,000	1,000	1,000
Third year after bereavement	–	500	500	500	500
Single Parent – additional	2,050	2,100	2,100	2,175	2,350
Income Limit of Child	720	720	720	720	720
Incapacitated Child	600	600	600	600	600
Income Limit of Child	720	2,100	2,100	2,100	2,100
Dependent Relative allowance	110	110	110	110	110
Income Limit	3,566	3,777	3,877	4,133	4,149
Blind Person	600	600	600	600	600
Both Spouses Blind	1,400	1,400	1,400	1,400	1,400
Age allowance: Single/Widowed Person	200	200	200	200	200
Married	400	400	400	400	400
Employed person taking care of incapacitated person	5,000	5,000	5,000	5,000	5,000
Employee allowance	800	800	800	800	800
PRSI allowance	286	286	286	286	286

CHART 1
INCOME TAX ALLOWANCES

	95/96	96/97	97/98	98/99	99/00 @ Standard Rate 24%	99/00 @ Marginal Rate 46%
Single Person	2,500	2,650	2,900	3,150	4,200	–
Married Couple	5,000	5,300	5,800	6,300	8,400	–
Widowed person (in year of bereavement)	5,000	5,300	5,800	6,300	8,400	–
Widowed person (subsequent years)	3,000	3,150	3,400	3,650	4,200	–
Widowed person with dependent child (additional)	2,000	2,150	2,400	2,650	1,050	500
First year after bereavement	1,500	1,500	1,500	5,000	–	2,650
Second year after bereavement	1,000	1,000	1,000	4,000	–	5,000
Third year after bereavement	500	500	500	3,000	–	4,000
Fourth year after bereavement				2,000	–	3,000
Fifth year after bereavement				1,000	–	2,000
						1,000
Single Parent – additional	2,500	2,650	2,900	3,150	1,050	3,150
Income Limit of Child	720	720	720	720	–	720
Incapacitated Child	600	700	700	800	–	800
Income Limit of Child	2,100	2,100	2,100	2,100	–	2,100
Dependent Relative allowance	110	110	110	110	–	110
Income Limit	4,270	4,440	4,601	4,848	–	5,152
Blind Person	600	700	700	1,000	–	1,500
Both Spouses Blind	1,400	1,600	1,600	2,000	–	3,000
Age allowance: Single/Widowed Person	200	200	400	400	–	400
Married	400	400	800	800	–	800
Employed person taking care of incapacitated person	5,000	7,500	7,500	8,500	–	8,500
Employee allowance	800	800	800	800	1,000	–
PRSI allowance	140	–	–	–	–	–

CHART 2
INCOME TAX RATES AND CUMULATIVE TAX PAYABLE

1990/91

Single/Widow(er)			Tax	Cumulative Income	Tax
6,500	@	30%	1,950	6,500	1,950
3,100	@	48%	1,488	9,600	3,438
Bal	@	53%	–	–	–

Married Couple

13,000	@	30%	3,900	13,000	3,900
6,200	@	48%	2,976	19,200	6,876
Bal	@	53%	–	–	–

1991/92

Single/Widow(er)			Tax	Cumulative Income	Tax
6,700	@	29%	1,943	6,700	1,943
3,100	@	48%	1,488	9,800	3,431
Bal	@	52%	–	–	–

Married Couple

13,400	@	29%	3,886	13,400	3,886
6,200	@	48%	2,976	19,600	6,862
Bal	@	52%	–	–	–

1992/93

Single/Widow(er)			Tax	Cumulative Income	Tax
7,475	@	27%	2,018.25	7,475	2,018.25
Bal	@	48%	–	–	–

Married Couple

14,950	@	27%	4,036.50	14,950	4,036.50
Bal	@	48%	–	–	–

1993/94

Single/Widow(er)			Tax	Cumulative Income	Tax
7,675	@	27%	2,072.25	7,675	2,072.25
Bal	@	48%	–	–	–

Married Couple

15,350	@	27%	4,144.50	15,350	4,144.50
Bal	@	48%	–	–	–

1994/95

Single/Widow(er)			Tax	Cumulative Income	Tax
8,200	@	27%	2,214	8,200	2,214
Bal	@	48%	–	–	–

Married Couple

16,400	@	27%	4,428	16,400	4,428
Bal	@	48%	–	–	–

Income Tax Rates

CHART 2 *continued*

1995/96			Tax	Cumulative Income	Tax
Single/Widow(er)					
8,900	@	27%	2,403	8,900	2,403
Bal	@	48%	–	–	–
Married Couple					
17,800	@	27%	4,806	17,800	4,806
Bal	@	48%	–	–	–
1996/97			Tax	Cumulative Income	Tax
Single/Widow(er)					
9,400	@	27%	2,538	9,400	2,538
Bal	@	48%	–	–	–
Married Couple					
18,800	@	27%	5,076	18,800	5,076
Bal	@	48%	–	–	–
1997/98			Tax	Cumulative Income	Tax
Single/Widow(er)					
9,900	@	26%	2,574	9,900	2,574
Bal	@	48%	–	–	–
Married Couple					
19,800	@	26%	5,148	19,800	5,148
Bal	@	48%	–	–	–
1998/99			Tax	Cumulative Income	Tax
Single/Widow(er)					
10,000	@	24%	2,400	10,000	2,400
Bal	@	46%	–	–	–
Married Couple					
20,000	@	24%	4,800	20,000	4,800
Bal	@	46%	–	–	–
1999/00			Tax	Cumulative Income	Tax
Single/Widow(er)					
14,000	@	24%	3,360	14,000	3,360
Bal	@	46%	–	–	–
Married Couple					
28,000	@	24%	6,720	28,000	6,720
Bal	@	46%	–	–	–

CHART 3
EXEMPTION LIMITS

Single & Widowed	90/91	91/92	92/93	93/94	94/95	95/96	96/97	97/98	98/99	99/00
Under 65 Years	3,250	3,400	3,500	3,600	3,600	3,700	3,900	4,000	4,100	4,100
65 and under 75	3,750	3,900	4,000	4,100	4,100	4,300	4,500	4,600	5,000	6,500
75 and over	4,350	4,500	4,600	4,700	4,700	4,900	5,100	5,200	5,500	6,500

Married Couples	90/91	91/92	92/93	93/94	94/95	95/96	96/97	97/98	98/99	99/00
Under 65 Years	6,500	6,800	7,000	7,200	7,200	7,400	7,800	8,000	8,200	8,200
65 and under 75	7,500	7,800	8,000	8,200	8,200	8,600	9,000	9,200	10,000	13,000
75 and over	8,700	9,000	9,200	9,400	9,400	9,800	10,200	10,400	11,000	13,000

Note: The income limits are increased for each dependent child as follows:

	90/91	91/92	92/93	93/94	94/95	95/96	96/97	97/98	98/99	99/00
First and Second Child	300	300	300	350	450	450	450	450	450	450
Third and Subsequent Child	300	500	500	550	650	650	650	650	650	650

Marginal Relief* rates	53%	52%	48%	48%	40%	40%	40%	40%	40%	40%

*Marginal relief restricts the amount of tax payable to the amount by which total income exceeds the exemption limit, at the above marginal relief rate.

PRSI Rates and Levies

CHART 4
PRSI RATES AND LEVIES

EMPLOYEE – CLASS A1			
	PRSI		LEVIES
	Employer (Income Limit)	Employee (Income Limit)	Employee (Income Limit)
1998/99	12.00% (29,000)	4.5% (24,200)	2.25% (No limit)
1999/00	12.00% (35,000)	4.5% (25,400)	2% (No limit)

Notes: 1998/99 No levies on income of £10,750 pa or less
1999/00 No levies on income of £11,250 pa or less

1998/99 Employers PRSI 8.5% on salaries <£14,040 pa
1999/00 Employers PRSI 8.5% on salaries <£14,560 pa

1998/99
  +   First £100 pw (non cumulative) ie £5,200 pa
1999/00 ignored when calculating employee's PRSI

SELF EMPLOYED			
	INCOME	PRSI (Min)	LEVIES
1998/99	1-24,200 Balance	5% (215) Nil	2.25% 2.25%
1999/00	1-25,400 Balance	5% (215) Nil	2% 2%

Notes: 1998/99 No levies on income of £10,750 pa or less
1999/00 No levies on income of £11,250 pa or less

1998/99
  +   First £20 pw (non-cumulative), ie £1,040 pa is
1999/00 ignored when calculating PRSI (not levies)

Income on which PRSI is calculated is net income after superannuation and capital allowances and does not include benefits in kind. There is no liability to PRSI where reckonable income is below £2,500. This test is applied separately to the income of husband and wife.

PAYE Table Allowances

CHART 5

PAYE TABLE ALLOWANCE FOR SINGLE AND WIDOWED PERSONS

		TABLE ALLOWANCE	1999/2000 24%	46%	40%
TABLE	A	NIL	(14,000–TFA)	Balance	–
	B	6,696	–	Balance	–
	Z	NIL	–	–	ALL

N.B. TABLE A where taxable income* does not exceed £14,000

PAYE TABLE ALLOWANCE FOR MARRIED COUPLES

		TABLE ALLOWANCE	1999/2000 24%	46%	40%
TABLE	R	NIL	(28,000–TFA)	Balance	–
	S	13,392	–	Balance	–
	Z	NIL	–	–	ALL

N.B. TABLE R where taxable income* does not exceed £28,000

TABLE Z is intended for both single people and married couples whose income for the year is only slightly higher than the relevant exemption limit.

Taxable Income means total income less personal allowances and reliefs.

Mortgage Interest Relief

CHART 6
MORTGAGE INTEREST RELIEF

(a) Maximum Allowable

For the year 1998/99, the maximum allowable amounts are as shown hereunder.

	Mortgage Taken Out Prior to 6 April 1994				
	General Ceiling £	Qualifying %	Maximum Qualifying £	Restriction £	Maximum Allowable £
Single Person	2,500	80	2,000	100	1,900
Widow(er)	3,600	80	2,880	100	2,780
Married Couple	5,000	80	4,000	200	3,800
	Mortgage Taken Out on or after 6 April 1994				
	£	%	£	£	£
Single Person	2,500	100	2,500	–	2,500
Widow(er)	3,600	100	3,600	–	3,600
Married Couple	5,000	100	5,000	–	5,000

For the year 1999/00, the maximum allowable amounts are as shown hereunder.

	Mortgage Taken Out Prior to 6 April 1995				
	General Ceiling £	Qualifying %	Maximum Qualifying £	Restriction £	Maximum Allowable £
Single Person	2,500	80	2,000	100	1,900
Widow(er)	3,600	80	2,880	100	2,780
Married Couple	5,000	80	4,000	200	3,800
	Mortgage Taken Out on or after 6 April 1995				
	£	%	£	£	£
Single Person	2,500	100	2,500	–	2,500
Widow(er)	3,600	100	3,600	–	3,600
Married Couple	5,000	100	5,000	–	5,000

Note:
Qualifying interest is relieved at the standard rate.

Mortgage Interest Relief

CHART 6 *continued...*

MORTGAGE INTEREST RELIEF

(b) First Time Buyers

A first-time buyer, who took out a mortgage on or after 6 April 1994 (and who had no previous mortgage interest claim) will qualify for relief on interest paid as follows:

Mortgage Taken Out In	Relief Available	For Years of Assessment
1994/95	100% (subject to General Ceiling)	1994/95 – 1998/99 incl.
1995/96	100% (subject to General Ceiling)	1995/96 – 1999/2000 incl.
1996/97	100% (subject to General Ceiling)	1996/97 – 2000/2001 incl.
1997/98	100% (subject to General Ceiling)	1997/98 – 2001/2002 incl.
1998/99	100% (subject to General Ceiling)	1998/99 – 2002/2003 incl.
1999/00	100% (subject to General Ceiling)	1999/00 – 2003/2004 incl.

Note:
Qualifying Interest is relieved at the standard rate.

Capital Allowances and Expenses on Passenger Motor Vehicles

CHART 7
MOTOR VEHICLES (PASSENGER) – RESTRICTION OF CAPITAL ALLOWANCES AND EXPENSES

PROVIDED FOR USE	RELEVANT LIMIT ALL CARS £
Up to 15.5.1973	No Limit
16.5.1973 - 28.1.1976	2,500
29.1.1976 - 5.4.1986	3,500
6.4.1986 - 27.1.1988	4,000
28.1.1988 - 25.1.1989	6,000
26.1.1989 - 29.1.1992	7,000
30.1.1992 - 26.1.1994	10,000

	NEW CARS* £	SECOND HAND CARS* £
27.1.1994 - 8.2.1995	13,000	10,000
9.2.1995 - 22.1.1997	14,000	10,000
23.1.1997 - 2.12.1997	15,000	10,000
3.12.1997 - 2.12.1998	15,500	10,000
3.12.1998 onwards	16,000	10,000

* Note: In the case of running expenses the increased limits apply to all cars.

Current Civil Service Mileage Rates

CHART 8
CURRENT CIVIL SERVICE MILEAGE RATES EFFECTIVE FROM 1 JANUARY 1996

Annual Mileage		Engine Capacity	
	Under 1138 cc	1138 to 1387 cc	1388 cc and over
		Rate per Mile	
	p	p	p
up to 2000	49.87	57.70	68.20
2001 to 4000	54.98	62.98	75.79
4001 to 6000	29.44	33.38	37.84
6001 to 8000	27.74	31.35	35.31
8001 to 12000	24.33	27.30	30.26
12001 and upwards	20.92	23.25	26.27

Current Civil Service Subsistence Rates

CHART 9

CURRENT CIVIL SERVICE SUBSISTENCE RATES EFFECTIVE FROM 1 JANUARY 1998

Class of Allowances	Night Allowances			Day Allowances	
	Normal Rate	Reduced Rate	Detention Rate	10 hours or more	5 hours but less than 10 hours
	£	£	£	£	£
A	73.18	67.47	36.59	20.74	8.46
B	65.76	56.25	32.89	20.74	8.46
C	55.00	45.51	27.53	20.74	8.46
D	47.58	40.15	23.79	15.66	7.74
E	38.98	32.32	19.47	15.66	7.74

Salary levels corresponding to above classes:-

A - £27,378
B - £15,233 - £27,377
C - £12,515 - £15,232
D - £8,426 - £12,514
E - £10,800

Normal Rate - up to 14 nights
Reduced Rate - next 14 nights
Detention Rate - next 28 nights
Special Rules apply to absences over 56 nights

CHART 10
TAX CREDIT ON DIVIDENDS – Republic of Ireland

Period	Tax Credit Normal Dividend	Tax Credit Manufacturing Dividend
5/4/1976 to 5/4/1978	35/65	N/A*
6/4/1978 to 5/4/1983	30/70	1/18
6/4/1983 to 5/4/1988	35/65	1/18
6/4/1988 to 5/4/1989	32/68	1/18
6/4/1989 to 5/4/1991	28/72	1/18
6/4/1991 to 5/4/1995	25/75	1/18
6/4/1995 to 5/4/1997	23/77	1/18
6/4/1997 to 2/12/1997	21/79	1/18
3/12/1997 to 5/4/1999	11/89	1/18

Note: Tax credits were abolished with effect from 6 April 1999.

CHART 11
TAX CREDITS ON DIVIDENDS – UK

Period	Tax Credit	Tax Credit Repay to R.I.
1979/80 to 1985/86	30/70	15/30
1986/87	29/71	14/29
1987/88	27/73	12/27
1988/89 to 1992/93	25/75	10/25
1993/94 to 1998/99	20/80	5/20
1999/00 et seq	1/9	Nil

Note:
(1) The tax credit is calculated by reference to the net dividend
(2) Repayment to R.I. shareholders is calculated by reference to the tax credit.

CHART 12
(a) INTEREST ON OVERDUE TAX

Rates of Interest		
0.5% per month or part of a month		To 31.7.71
0.75% per month or part of month	From 1.8.71	To 30.4.75
1.5% per month or part of a month	From 1.5.75	To 31.7.78
1.25% per month or part of a month	From 1.8.78	To 31.3.98
1.00% per month on part of a month	From 1.4.98	to date

(b) INTEREST ON TAX OVERPAID

Rates of Interest		
1.50% per month or part of a month	From 6.4.76	To 5.7.78
1.25% per month or part of a month	From 6.7.78	To 26.5.86
1.00% per month or part of a month	From 27.5.86	To 31.7.90
0.60% per month or part of a month	From 1.8.90	To 31.3.98
0.50% per month or part of a month	From 1.4.98	To date

CHART 13
AVERAGE RATES OF EXCHANGE IR£/£Stg.

Year ended	Rate	Year ended	Rate
5.4.1980	.94995	5.4.1990	.9101
5.4.1981	.84582	5.4.1991	.9318
5.4.1982	.81138	5.4.1992	.9288
5.4.1983	.83307	5.4.1993	1.0095
5.4.1984	.80780	5.4.1994	.9737
5.4.1985	.84080	5.4.1995	.9981
5.4.1986	.8441	5.4.1996	1.033
5.4.1987	.9374	5.4.1997	1.023
5.4.1988	.9055	5.4.1998	.9016
5.4.1989	.8527	5.4.1999	.8695

Divide £Stg by these factors to obtain IR£ equivalent

CHART 14
SPECIFIED AMOUNTS (Preliminary Tax)

INCOME TAX

Year of Assessment	%
1990/91 et seq	90 or 100% of p.y.
1986/87 - 1989/90	90
1983/84 - 1985/86	85
1976/77 - 1982/83	80

Note: For the years 1995/96 et seq, 105% of p.p.y. if paying by direct debit.

CORPORATION TAX

AP Ending	%
On or after 6.4.86	90
On or after 6.4.76 - on or before 5.4.86	80

CAPITAL GAINS TAX

Year of Assessment	%
1998/99 et seq.	100
1986/87 - 1997/98	90
1976/77 - 1985/86	80

Retention Tax on Payments for Professional Services

CHART 15
RETENTION TAX ON PAYMENTS FOR PROFESSIONAL SERVICES

The persons who are required to deduct tax from payments for professional services are as follows and include, where any person is a body corporate, any subsidiary resident in the State:

A Minister of the Government.

A local authority within the meaning of section 2(2) of the Local Government Act, 1941.

A body established under the Local Government Services (Corporate Bodies) Act, 1971.

A health board.

The General Medical Services (Payments) Board established under the General Medical Services (Payments) Board (Establishment) Order, 1972 (S.I. No 184 of 1972).

The Attorney General.

The Comptroller and Auditor General.

The Director of Public Prosecutions.

The Commissioner of Valuation.

The Chief Boundary Surveyor.

The Director of Ordnance Survey.

The Revenue Commissioners.

The Civil Service Commissioners.

The Commissioners of Public Works in Ireland.

The Clerk of Dail Eireann.

The Legal Aid Board.

A vocational education committee or a technical college established under the Vocational Education Act, 1930.

Teagasc.

A harbour authority.

An Foras Aiseanna Saothair.

Udaras na Gaeltacha.

The Industrial Development Agency (Ireland).

An Bord Trachtala - The Irish Trade Board.

Shannon Free Airport Development Company Limited.

Bord Failte Eireann.

continued on following page

CHART 15 *continued*

An institution of higher education within the meaning of the Higher Education Authority Act, 1971.

CERT Limited.

The Radiological Protection Institute of Ireland

A voluntary public or joint board hospital to which grants are paid by the Minister for Health in the year 1988/89 or any subsequent year of assessment.

An authorised insurer within the meaning of section 145 of the Income Tax Act, 1967.

An Bord Glas.

An Bord Pleanala.

ACC bank public limited company.

Aer Rianta cuideachta phoibli theoranta.

Arramara Teoranta.

Blood Transfusion Service Board.

Bord na gCon.

Bord Gais Eireann.

Bord Iascaigh Mhara.

Bord na Mona.

Bord Telecom Eireann.

Coillte Teoranta.

Coras Iompair Eireann.

Custom House Docks Development Authority.

Electricity Supply Board.

Housing Finance Agency public limited company.

Industrial Credit Corporation public limited company.

Irish National Petroleum Corporation Limited.

Irish National Stud Company Limited

National Building Agency Limited.

National Concert Hall Company Limited.

An Post National Lottery Company.

Nitrigin Eireann Teoranta.

An Post.

Radio Telefis Eireann.

continued on following page

Retention Tax on Payments for Professional Services

CHART 15 *continued*

Royal Hospital Kilmainham Company.

The Environmental Protection Agency.

Forbairt.

Forfas.

The Irish Aviation Authority.

The National Economic and Social Council.

The National Economic and Social Forum.

The National Road Authority.

Temple Bar Properties Limited

The Irish Film Board.

An educational institution established by or under Section 3 of the Regional Technical Colleges Act 1992 as a regional technical college.

The Dublin Institute of Technology.

Aer Lingus Group public limited company

An Bord Bia

Area Development Management Limited

The Combat Poverty Agency

The Commissioners of Irish Lights

Dublin Transportation Office

The Heritage Council

The Higher Education Authority

The Independent Radio and Television Commission

The Irish Horseracing Authority

The Labour Relations Commission

The Marine Institute

National Rehabilitation Board

National Safety Council

The Pensions Board

The Office of the Director of Telecommunications Regulation

The Law Reform Commission

Northern Regional fisheries Board – Bord Iascaigh Reigiunach an Tuaisceart

The Office for Health Management

Hospital Bodies Administration Bureau

National Social Services Board

National Standards Authority of Ireland

Enterprise Ireland

Dublin Docklands Development Authority

A commission established by the Government or a Minister of the Government for the purposes of providing information to the public in relation to a referendum referred to in Section 1, Article 47 of the Constitution

Office of the Ombudsman

Public Offices Commission

The Office of the Information Commissioner

CHART 16

TAX AND INTEREST AS PREFERENTIAL DEBT *(In winding up of insolvent companies and on appointment, under floating charge, of a receiver)*

Type of tax	Preferential Debt	Legislation
Income Tax	Tax for any twelve months assessed up to 5 April next before "the relevant date" and all interest thereon	Sections 98 and 285 Companies Act 1963
CPT	Do	Do
Corporation Tax	Do	S974 TCA 1997
Capital Gains Tax	Do	S982 TCA 1997
VAT	Tax for the last twelve months ending before "the relevant date"	S62 FA 1976
Interest on VAT	All	Do
PAYE & PRSI	Tax for the last twelve months ending before the "relevant date"	S994 TCA 1997 S995 TCA 1997
Interest on PAYE & PRSI	Do	Do
Deductions on Construction Contracts	Do	S1000 TCA 1997

NOTES

(a) "the relevant date" means
  (i) where the company is ordered to be wound up compulsorily, the date of the appointment (or first appointment) of a provisional liquidator or, if no such appointment was made, the date of the winding-up order, unless in either case the company had commenced to be wound up voluntarily before that date; and
  (ii) Where sub-paragraph (i) does not apply, the date of the passing of the resolution for the winding up of the company.

(b) No preferential debt exists as to (a) Capital Acquisitions Tax, (b) Wealth Tax and (c) interest on these taxes.

(c) Where a person holds a fixed charge on the book debts of a company and the company fails to pay PAYE and VAT, the holder of the fixed charge will on notification from the Revenue Commissioners, become liable to pay the PAYE and VAT.

The amount payable is subject to an overall limit of the amount collected under the fixed charge after the date of notification from the Revenue Commissioners.

(d) PAYE and PRSI includes:
  (i) amounts deducted for the income tax month in which the "relevant date" occurs.
  (ii) amounts which, apart from the provisions of Regulation 31A of the Income Tax (Employments) Regulations 1960 would otherwise have been due to be remitted at the "relevant date".

CHART 17
INCOME TAX TIME LIMITS

(References are to Taxes Consolidation Act 1997 unless otherwise stated)

Section	Topic	Claim etc	Claim to be made within
S930	Error or Mistake	All	Six years of end of year of assessment
S787	Retirement Annuity premiums	Against income of previous year	31 January of following year
S298	Capital allowances on plant and machinery	Lessor	Two years of end of year of assessment
S305	Excess of capital allowances over income from leasing plant or industrial buildings	Set-off of excess against other income of the year of assessment	Two years of end of year of assessment
S381	Trading / Professional Losses	Set-off against other income of year of assessment	Two years of end of year of assessment
S865	Irish repayment claims	All	Ten years of end of year of assessment
S195	Artists, Writers etc.	Exemption from income tax	Year of assessment
S1023	Husbands and wives	Separate assessment	6 July in year of assessment (continues until withdrawn)
S1016	Husbands and wives	Single assessment	Year of assessment (continues until withdrawn)
S43 TMA 1970	UK Repayment claim	All	Six years of end of year of assessment
S503	Investment in corporate trades	Set off against income of year of assessment	Two years of end of year of assessment
S66	Trading etc profits	Second and Third Year Adjustment	On submission of Third Year Return

Rates of Corporation Tax

CHART 18

RATES OF CORPORATION TAX

ACCOUNTING PERIOD	STANDARD RATE	HIGHER ** RATE
1/4/1991 to 31/3/1995	40%	N/A
1/4/1995 to 31/3/1997	38% (First £50,000* @ 30%)	N/A
1/4/1997 to 31/12/1997	36% (First £50,000* @ 28%)	N/A
Y/E 31/12/1998	32% (First £50,000* @ 25%)	N/A
Y/E 31/12/1999	28% (First £100,000* @ 25%)	N/A
Y/E 31/12/2000	24%	25%
Y/E 31/12/2001	20%	25%
Y/E 31/12/2002	16%	25%
YE 31/12/2003 & onwards	12.5%	25%

Note:

* *"Specified amount" see page 175.*

** *Higher rate applies to Case III, Case IV, Case V and income from mining and petroleum activities and dealing in land*

See page 184 with regard to the 10% "Manufacturing Rate".

Manufacturing Relief and Investment in Corporate Trades

CHART 19
MANUFACTURING RELIEF AND INVESTMENT IN CORPORATE TRADES (Section 443 TCA 1997)

Type of Company	10%	RICT
Manufacturing	Yes	Yes
Manufacturing Services	Yes	Yes
90% Related Sales Company	Yes	No
"New" Shannon Company	Yes	Yes
Fish, Engineering	Yes	Yes
Services, Ship Building	Yes	Yes
Data Processing and Computer Software Development Services	Yes	Yes
Services qualifying for IDA Employment Grants	No	Yes
Designated Funds	No	Yes
R & D Company	Yes	No
Financial Services in Custom House Dock Area	Yes	No
Shipping Activities	Yes	Yes
Tourist Activities	No	Yes
Export Sales of Trading Houses	Yes	Yes
Plant Cultivation by "Micro Propagation and Plant Cloning"	Yes	Yes
Factory Ships	Yes	No
Services Re Data Processing	Yes	Yes
Construction and Leasing of Advance Factories	No	Yes
Internationally Traded Service	No	Yes
Film Production for Cinema or TV	Yes	No
Meat Processing in EC approved Factory	Yes	Yes
Fish Processing	Yes	Yes
Remanufacture or Repair of computer equipment or subassemblies	Yes	Yes
Repair or maintenance of Aircraft, Aircraft Engines or Components	Yes	Yes
Service Activities to Ships and Off-Shore Platforms etc	Yes	No
Certain Agricultural or Fishery Society Activities	Yes	No
Newspaper Advertising	Yes	No

CHART 20
CORPORATION TAX TIME LIMITS

(References are to Taxes Consolidation Act 1997 unless otherwise stated)

Section	Topic	Claim etc	Claim to be made within
S307	Plant and Machinery Industrial Buildings	Disclaimer of Initial Allowances	Two years of the end of the accounting period for which the claim arises
S308	Excess Case V Capital Allowances	Against other profits of same accounting period or preceding accounting period	Two years of the end of the accounting period in which the excess arises
S83	Excess management expenses of investment companies	Against franked investment income of same accounting period	Two years of the end of the accounting period in which the excess arises
S396	Trading losses	Against other profits of same accounting period or preceding accounting period	Two years of the end of the accounting period in which the loss is incurred
S399	Case V losses	Against other Case V income of preceding accounting period	Two years of the end of the accounting period in which the loss is incurred
S157	Trading losses	Against franked investment income of same accounting period or preceding accounting period	Two years of end of the accounting period in which the loss is incurred
S429	Group Relief and Consortium Relief	For surrender of trading losses and other amounts eligible for relief	Two years from the end of the accounting period of the surrendering company
S882	New Companies	Advise Inspector of commencement etc	Within thirty days of commencement

CHART 20 *continued*
CORPORATION TAX TIME LIMITS

(References are to Taxes Consolidation Act 1997 unless otherwise stated)

Section	Topic	Claim etc	Claim to be made within
S883	Liability to Corporation Tax	Notification to Inspector	Twelve months from end of accounting period
S239	Income Tax on payments	Returns of payments made under deduction of tax	Within nine months of the end of the accounting period
S239	Income Tax on payments	Remittance of tax deducted	Within six months of the end of the accounting period
S160	Advance Corporation Tax	Against Corporation Tax of preceding accounting period	Two years from the end of the accounting period
S166	Advance Corporation Tax	For Surrender of surplus ACT	Two years from the end of the accounting period

CHART 21
INDEXATION FACTORS FOR CAPITAL GAINS TAX

Year Expenditure Incurred	Multiple for disposals in Year to 5 April:																		
	1983	1984	1985	1986	1987	1988	1989	1990	1991	1992	1993	1994	1995	1996	1997	1998	1999	2000
1974/75	3.342	3.759	4.140	4.397	4.598	4.756	4.848	5.009	5.221	5.355	5.552	5.656	5.754	5.899	6.017	6.112	6.215	6.313
1975/76	2.699	3.035	3.344	3.551	3.714	3.842	3.916	4.046	4.217	4.326	4.484	4.568	4.647	4.764	4.860	4.936	5.020	5.099
1976/77	2.325	2.615	2.881	3.059	3.200	3.309	3.373	3.485	3.633	3.726	3.863	3.935	4.003	4.104	4.187	4.253	4.325	4.393
1977/78	1.993	2.242	2.470	2.623	2.743	2.837	2.892	2.988	3.114	3.194	3.312	3.373	3.432	3.518	3.589	3.646	3.707	3.766
1978/79	1.842	2.071	2.282	2.423	2.534	2.621	2.672	2.760	2.877	2.951	3.059	3.117	3.171	3.250	3.316	3.368	3.425	3.479
1979/80	1.662	1.869	2.059	2.186	2.286	2.365	2.410	2.490	2.596	2.663	2.760	2.812	2.861	2.933	2.992	3.039	3.090	3.139
1980/81	1.439	1.618	1.782	1.893	1.979	2.047	2.087	2.156	2.247	2.305	2.390	2.434	2.477	2.539	2.590	2.631	2.675	2.718
1981/82	1.189	1.337	1.473	1.564	1.636	1.692	1.725	1.782	1.857	1.905	1.975	2.012	2.047	2.099	2.141	2.174	2.211	2.246
1982/83	–	1.125	1.239	1.316	1.376	1.424	1.451	1.499	1.563	1.603	1.662	1.693	1.722	1.765	1.801	1.829	1.860	1.890
1983/84	–	–	1.102	1.170	1.224	1.266	1.290	1.333	1.390	1.425	1.478	1.505	1.531	1.570	1.601	1.627	1.654	1.680
1984/85	–	–	–	1.062	1.111	1.149	1.171	1.210	1.261	1.294	1.341	1.366	1.390	1.425	1.454	1.477	1.502	1.525
1985/86	–	–	–	–	1.046	1.082	1.103	1.140	1.188	1.218	1.263	1.287	1.309	1.342	1.369	1.390	1.414	1.436
1986/87	–	–	–	–	–	1.035	1.055	1.090	1.136	1.165	1.208	1.230	1.252	1.283	1.309	1.330	1.352	1.373
1987/88	–	–	–	–	–	–	1.020	1.054	1.098	1.126	1.168	1.190	1.210	1.241	1.266	1.285	1.307	1.328
1988/89	–	–	–	–	–	–	–	1.034	1.077	1.105	1.146	1.167	1.187	1.217	1.242	1.261	1.282	1.303
1989/90	–	–	–	–	–	–	–	–	1.043	1.070	1.109	1.130	1.149	1.178	1.202	1.221	1.241	1.261
1990/91	–	–	–	–	–	–	–	–	–	1.026	1.064	1.084	1.102	1.130	1.153	1.171	1.191	1.210
1991/92	–	–	–	–	–	–	–	–	–	–	1.037	1.056	1.075	1.102	1.124	1.142	1.161	1.179
1992/93	–	–	–	–	–	–	–	–	–	–	–	1.019	1.037	1.063	1.084	1.101	1.120	1.138
1993/94	–	–	–	–	–	–	–	–	–	–	–	–	1.018	1.043	1.064	1.081	1.099	1.117
1994/95	–	–	–	–	–	–	–	–	–	–	–	–	–	1.026	1.046	1.063	1.081	1.098
1995/96	–	–	–	–	–	–	–	–	–	–	–	–	–	–	1.021	1.037	1.054	1.071
1996/97	–	–	–	–	–	–	–	–	–	–	–	–	–	–	–	1.016	1.033	1.050
1997/98	–	–	–	–	–	–	–	–	–	–	–	–	–	–	–	–	1.017	1.033
1998/99	–	–	–	–	–	–	–	–	–	–	–	–	–	–	–	–	–	1.016

NOTE: No indexation is available for expenditure made within 12 months prior to the date of disposal.

CHART 22
CAPITAL ACQUISITIONS TAX RATES
Position Up To 25 March 1984

There were four separate tables for different classes of relationship, and these were as follows:

TABLE 1
Applicable where the donee or successor is the spouse, child, or minor child of a deceased child, of the disponer

Slice £	Cumulative Slice £	Rate of Tax %	Tax Thereon £	Cumulative Tax £
150,000	150,000	Nil	Nil	Nil
50,000	200,000	25	12,500	12,500
50,000	250,000	30	15,000	27,500
50,000	300,000	35	17,500	45,000
50,000	350,000	40	20,000	65,000
50,000	400,000	45	22,500	87,500
Excess		50		

TABLE II
Applicable where the donee or successor is a lineal ancestor or a linear descendant (other than a child, or a minor child of a deceased child) of disponer.

Slice £	Cumulative Slice £	Rate of Tax %	Tax Thereon £	Cumulative Tax £

(a) the taxable gift of inheritance is taken on or before 31 March 1978.

Slice £	Cumulative Slice £	Rate of Tax %	Tax Thereon £	Cumulative Tax £
15,000	15,000	Nil	Nil	Nil
3,000	18,000	5	150	150
5,000	23,000	7	350	500
10,000	33,000	10	1,000	1,500
10,000	43,000	13	1,300	2,800
10,000	53,000	16	1,600	4,400
10,000	63,000	19	1,900	6,300
10,000	73,000	22	2,200	8,500
15,000	88,000	25	3,750	12,250
15,000	103,000	28	1,200	16,450
15,000	118,000	31	4,650	21,100
15,000	133,000	34	5,100	26,200
15,000	148,000	37	5,550	31,750
15,000	163,000	40	6,000	37,750
15,000	178,000	43	6,450	44,200
15,000	193,000	46	6,900	51,100
15,000	208,000	49	7,350	58,450
Excess		50		

Capital Acquisitions Tax Rates

Slice £	Cumulative Slice £	Rate of Tax %	Tax Thereon £	Cumulative Tax £

(b) The taxable gift or inheritance is taken on or after 1 April 1978

Slice £	Cumulative Slice £	Rate of Tax %	Tax Thereon £	Cumulative Tax £
30,000	30,000	Nil	Nil	Nil
3,000	33,000	5	150	150
5,000	38,000	7	350	500
10,000	48,000	10	1,000	1,500
10,000	58,000	13	1,300	2,800
10,000	68,000	16	1,600	4,400
10,000	78,000	19	1,900	6,300
10,000	88,000	22	2,200	8,500
15,000	103,000	25	3,750	12,250
15,000	118,000	28	4,200	16,450
15,000	133,000	31	4,650	21,100
15,000	148,000	34	5,100	26,200
15,000	163,000	37	5,550	31,750
15,000	178,000	40	6,000	37,750
15,000	193,000	43	6,450	44,200
15,000	208,000	46	6,900	51,100
15,000	223,000	49	7,350	58,450
Excess		50		

TABLE III
Applicable where the donee or successor is a brother or a sister, or a child of a brother or of a sister, of the disponer

Slice £	Cumulative Slice £	Rate of Tax %	Tax Thereon £	Cumulative Tax £

(a) the taxable gift or inheritance is taken on or before 31 March 1978.

Slice £	Cumulative Slice £	Rate of Tax %	Tax Thereon £	Cumulative Tax £
10,000	10,000	Nil	Nil	Nil
3,000	13,000	10	300	300
5,000	18,000	12	600	900
10,000	28,000	15	1,500	2,400
10,000	38,000	19	1,900	4,300
10,000	48,000	23	2,300	6,600
10,000	58,000	27	2,700	9,300
10,000	68,000	31	3,100	12,400
15,000	83,000	35	5,250	17,650
15,000	98,000	40	6,000	23,650
15,000	113,000	45	6,750	30,400
Excess		50		

Capital Acquisitions Tax Rates

(b) The taxable gift or inheritance is taken on or after 1 April 1978

Slice	Cumulative Slice	Rate of Tax %	Tax Thereon	Cumulative Tax
20,000	20,000	Nil	Nil	Nil
3,000	23,000	10	300	300
5,000	28,000	12	600	900
10,000	38,000	15	1,500	2,400
10,000	48,000	19	1,900	4,300
10,000	58,000	23	2,300	6,600
10,000	68,000	27	2,700	9,300
10,000	78,000	31	3,100	12,400
15,000	93,000	35	5,250	17,650
15,000	108,000	40	6,000	23,650
15,000	123,000	45	6,750	30,400
Excess		50		

TABLE IV
Application where the donee or successor does not stand to the disponer in a relationship referred to in Table I, II and III.

Slice £	Cumulative Slice £	Rate of Tax %	Tax Thereon £	Cumulative Tax £

(a) the taxable gift or inheritance is taken on or before 31 March 1978.

Slice	Cumulative Slice	Rate of Tax %	Tax Thereon	Cumulative Tax
5,000	5,000	Nil	Nil	Nil
3,000	8,000	20	600	600
5,000	13,000	22	1,100	1,700
10,000	23,000	25	2,500	4,200
10,000	33,000	30	3,000	7,200
10,000	43,000	35	3,500	10,700
10,000	53,000	40	4,000	14,700
10,000	63,000	45	4,500	19,200
15,000	78,000	50	7,500	26,700
15,000	93,000	55	8,250	34,950
Excess		60		

(b) the taxable gift or inheritance is taken on or after 1 April 1978.

Slice	Cumulative Slice	Rate of Tax %	Tax Thereon	Cumulative Tax
10,000	10,000	Nil	Nil	Nil
3,000	13,000	20	600	600
5,000	18,000	22	1,100	1,700
10,000	28,000	25	2,500	4,200
10,000	38,000	30	3,000	7,200
10,000	48,000	35	3,500	10,700
10,000	58,000	40	4,000	14,700
10,000	68,000	45	4,500	19,200
15,000	83,000	50	7,500	26,700
15,000	98,000	55	8,250	34,950
Excess		60		

Capital Acquisitions Tax Rates

Table from 26 March 1984

Slice	Cumulative Slice	Rate of Tax %	Tax Thereon	Cumulative Tax
Threshold Amount	Threshold Amount +	nil	nil	nil
10,000	10,000	20	2,000	2,000
40,000	50,000	30	12,000	14,000
50,000	100,000	35	17,500	31,500
50,000	150,000	40	20,000	51,500
50,000	200,000	45	22,500	74,000
Balance		55		

Table from 30 January 1991

As regards benefits taken on or after 30 January 1991, the following table applies, and replaces the 1984 table.

Slice	Cumulative Slice	Rate of Tax %	Tax Thereon	Cumulative Tax
Threshold Amount	Threshold Amount +	nil	nil	nil
10,000	10,000	20	2,000	2,000
40,000	50,000	30	12,000	14,000
50,000	100,000	35	17,500	31,500
Balance		40		

Table from 11 April 1994

Slice	Cumulative Slice	Rate of Tax %	Tax Thereon	Cumulative Tax
Threshold Amount	Threshold Amount +	nil	nil	nil
10,000	10,000	20	2,000	2,000
30,000	40,000	30	9,000	11,000
Balance		40		

CAT Class Thresholds / Probate Tax Exemption Thresholds

CHART 23
CAPITAL ACQUISITIONS TAX CLASS THRESHOLDS

Relationship to donor/testator,	Gift or inheritance in										
	1989 or earlier	1990	1991	1992	1993	1994	1995	1996	1997	1998	1999
	£	£	£	£	£	£	£	£	£	£	£
Child or minor child of deceased child or parent where S116 FA 1991 applies	150,000	156,000	161,400	166,350	171,750	174,000	178,200	182,550	185,550	188,400	192,900
Lineal ancestor (other than a parent where S116 FA 1991 applies) lineal descendant (other than a child or minor child of a deceased child), brother, sister, child of brother or sister	20,000	20,800	21,520	22,180	22,900	23,200	23,760	24,340	24,740	25,120	25,720
Any other person	10,000	10,400	10,760	11,090	11,450	11,600	11,880	12,170	12,370	12,560	12,860

CHART 24
PROBATE TAX EXEMPTION THRESHOLDS

	Person dying in						
	1993	1994	1995	1996	1997	1998	1999
Exemption	10,000	10,150	10,390	10,650	10,820	10,980	11,250

Residential Property Tax Limits

CHART 25

(1) RESIDENTIAL PROPERTY TAX LIMITS

	INCOME YEAR ENDED 5 APRIL £	VALUATION AS AT 5 APRIL £
1983	20,000	65,000
1984	22,030	65,622
1985	23,395	66,491
1986	24,468	68,728
1987	25,307	69,971
1988	25,795	74,321
1989	26,654	82,772
1990	27,800	91,000
1991	28,500	96,000
1992	27,500	90,000
1993	28,100	91,000
1994	25,000	75,000
1995	29,500	94,000
1996	30,100	101,000

(2) RESIDENTIAL PROPERTY TAX VALUE THRESHOLD FOR CERTIFICATE OF CLEARANCE

VALUATION DATE*	THRESHOLD £
5 April 1997	115,000
5 April 1998	138,000
5 April 1999	200,000

* The relevant valuation date is the valuation date preceding the date of the contract, or where the date of the contract is 5 April in a year, that date.

CHART 26
RESIDENTIAL PROPERTY TAX RATES FOR YEAR ENDED 5 APRIL 1994

For residential property valued between £75,000 and £100,000 a flat rate of tax was payable as follows:

Valuation not exceeding £	Tax due £
80,000	25
85,000	75
90,000	125
95,000	175
100,000	225

For residential property valued at over £100,000 tax was charged on the excess of the value over £75,000 as follows:

First £25,000	@ 1%	£250.00
Next £50,000	@ 1.5%	£750.00
Balance	@ 2%	—

CHART 27
VAT FOURTH SCHEDULE SERVICES

If Supplier is	and Recipient is	The Place of Supply is	The Person liable for Irish VAT is
Foreign	Irish Business	Ireland	Irish Business Recipient
Foreign	Irish Private	Abroad	No Irish Liability
Irish	Irish Business or Private	Ireland	Irish Supplier
Irish	Business outside Ireland	Abroad	No Irish Liability
Irish	Private in EU	Ireland	Irish Supplier
Irish	Private outside EU	Abroad	No Irish Liability

The above rules are modified where the supplier has an establishment in the country of the recipient.

NOTE: VAT FOURTH SCHEDULE SERVICES include:

Services that are taxed where received viz:

(i) Transfers and assignments of copyrights, patents, licences, trade marks and similar rights;

(ia) Hiring out of movable goods other than means of transport;

(ii) Advertising services;

(iii) Services of consultants, engineers, consultancy bureaux, lawyers, accountants and other similar services, data processing and provision of information (but excluding services connected with immovable goods);

(iv) Acceptance of any obligation to refrain from pursuing or exercising in whole or in part, any business activity or any such rights as are referred to in paragraph (1);

(v) Banking, financial and insurance services (including re-insurance, but not including the provision of safe deposit facilities) in certain circumstances;

(vi) The provision of staff;

(vii) The services of agents who act in the name and for the account of a principal when procuring for him any services specified in paragraphs (i) to (vi).

(viii) Telecommunications services in certain circumstances.

VAT

CHART 28
VAT EXEMPTED ACTIVITIES

The main exempted activities are:

Admission to sporting events.
Circus admissions.
Certain lettings of immovable goods.
Medical, dental and optical services.
Certain agency services.
Insurance services.
Certain banking and stock exchange activities.
Transport of passengers and their baggage.
Betting.
Funeral undertaking.
Certain theatrical and musical performances.
Certain welfare and non-profit making activities.
Management of collective investment undertaking within meaning of S18FA 1989.
Chiropody.
Educational services including pre-school education facilities.
Certain child-care services

CHART 29
VAT ZERO RATE

The main zero-rated goods and services are:

Most food and drink of a kind used for human consumption, most exports of goods and services relating to exports of goods, oral medicine, fertilizers, most articles of personal clothing and footwear suitable for children under 11 years of age, certain services relating to marine safety, certain books and booklets including atlases, certain medical equipment and appliances, certain navigation services.

VAT

CHART 30
VAT 10% RATE

The goods and services liable at this rate are:
Domestic dwellings for which a contract with a private individual has been entered into before 25 February 1993, short term hire of cars under an agreement made before 25 February 1993 and at charges fixed at the time of the agreement, lettings of hotel and holiday accommodation under an agreement made before 25 February 1993 and at charges fixed at the time of the agreement.

CHART 31
VAT 12.5% RATE

The main goods and services liable at this rate are:
Immovable goods, services consisting of the development of immovable goods, concrete and concrete blocks, hotel and holiday accommodation, short term hiring of cars, boats, tents, caravans, mobile homes, tour guide services, fuel for power and heating, coal, peat, timber, electricity, gas, heating oil, hotel and restaurant meals, admissions to cinemas, cabaret, certain live theatrical and musical performances and to certain exhibitions, waste disposal, general agricultural and veterinary services, use of commercial sporting facilities, car driving instruction, care of the human body, general repair and maintenance services, certain imports and supplies of works of art, antiques and collectors' items, certain green fees, brochures, periodicals and newspapers, live poultry and live ostriches, animal insemination services, livestock semen.

CHART 32
VAT 21% RATE

The main goods and services liable at this rate are:
Adult clothing and footwear including materials for their manufacture, household durable and non-durable goods, drink and certain foods, goods for personal use, sport and recreational goods, educational goods, agricultural goods, non-oral medicines, most building materials, office equipment and stationery, most services such as telecommunication services, accountancy services (including farm accountancy services), legal services, advertising services, other goods and services not liable at another rate.

CHART 33
CAPITAL ALLOWANCES

Initial Allowances

Expenditure Incurred	Plant and Machinery	Industrial Buildings	Hotels	Farm Buildings
1.4.71 - 5.4.74	100%	20%	10%	–
6.4.74 - 15.1.75	100%	20%	10%	20%
16.1.75 - 5.4.80	100%	50%	10%	20%
6.4.80 - 31.3.88	100%	50%	10%	Nil
1.4.88 - 31.3.89	*75%	*50%	10%	Nil
1.4.89 - 31.3.91	*50%	*50%	10%	Nil
1.4.91 - 31.3.92	*25%	*25%	10%	Nil
1.4.92 onwards	Nil	Nil	Nil	Nil

* A rate of up to 100% applies to qualifying services companies in the Customs House Docks Area or in the Shannon Customs Free Area, subject to varying time limits.

Writing Down and Wear and Tear Allowances

Expenditure Incurred	Plant and Machinery	Industrial Buildings	Hotels	Farm Buildings
1.4.71 - 5.4.74	Up to 100%	2%	10%	10%
6.4.74 - 15.1.75	Up to 100%	2%	10%	10%
16.1.75 - 1.2.78	Up to 100%	4%	10%	10%
2.2.78 - 5.4.80	Up to 100%	Up to 100%	Up to 100%	10%
6.4.80 - 31.3.88	Up to 100%	Up to 100%	Up to 100%	Up to 30%
1.4.88 - 31.3.89	*Up to 75%	*Up to 75%	Up to 75%	Up to 30%
1.4.89 - 31.3.91	*Up to 50%	*Up to 50%	Up to 50%	Up to 50%
1.4.91 - 31.3.92	*Up to 25%	*Up to 25%	Up to 25%	Up to 25%
1.4.92 - 25.1.94	15%	4%	10%	10%
26.1.94 onwards	15%	4%	15%	15%

* A rate of up to 100% applies to qualifying services companies in the Customs House Docks Area or in the Shannon Customs Free Area, subject to varying time limits.

CHART 34

URBAN RENEWAL AREA ALLOWANCES – 1986 SCHEME

	Dublin Areas	Custom House Docks	Temple Bar	Other Areas
Commercial Property				
Owner Occupier:				
Free Depreciation	50%	100%	100%**	100%
or				
Initial Allowance	25%	50%	50%**	50%
and				
Annual Allowance	2%	4%	4%**	4%
Lessor:				
Free Depreciation	n/a	n/a	n/a	n/a
or				
Initial Allowance	25%	50%	50%**	50%
and				
Annual Allowance	2%	4%	4%**	4%
Qualifying Period	31.07.94	24.01.99***	05.04.99***	31.07.94
Residential Property				
Owner Occupier:	5% p/a for 10 years	Old: 10% pa for 10 years	New: 5% pa for 10 years Old: 10% pa for 10 years	5% pa for 10 years
Lessor:	"Section 23" type relief applies with unrestricted set off against total rental income			
Qualifying Period	As above for each area			
Plant and Machinery				
Accelerated allowances expenditure incurred between 01.04.91 and 01.04.92	25%	25%*	25%	25%
Expenditure incurred after 01.04.92	n/a	n/a*	n/a	n/a

*   For qualifying companies in Customs House Docks and Shannon areas 100% accelerated allowances are available

** This applies for cost of refurbishing existing buildings. For cost of constructing new buildings the allowance is reduced by one half.

*** See page 89 re extensions to 31.12.1999 and 30.06.2000 in the case of Custom House Docks projects and page 92 re extension to 31.12.1999 in the case of residential projects in Temple Bar.

CHART 35

URBAN RENEWAL AREA ALLOWANCES – DESIGNATED AREA/STREET FROM 1.8.1994

	DESIGNATED AREA	DESIGNATED* STREET
INDUSTRIAL PROPERTY		

OWNER OCCUPIER
  Accelerated Allowance
  Initial Allowance
  Annual Allowance
  Maximum
	50%
	25%
	4%
	100%
		50%
		25%
		4%
		100%

LESSOR
  Initial Allowance
  Annual Allowance
  Maximum
	25%
	4%
	100%
		25%
		4%
		100%

COMMERCIAL PROPERTY		

OWNER OCCUPIER
  Accelerated Allowance
  Initial Allowance
  Annual Allowance
  Maximum
	50%
	25%
	2%
	50%
		50%
		25%
		2%
		50%

LESSOR
  Initial Allowance
  Annual Allowance
  Maximum
	25%
	2%
	50%
		25%
		2%
		50%

RESIDENTIAL PROPERTY		

OWNER OCCUPIER
  Construction
  Refurbishment
	5% p.a. (10 yrs)
	10% p.a. (10 yrs)
		Nil
		10% p.a. (10 yrs)

LESSOR
  Construction
  Conversion
  Refurbishment
	100%
	100%
	100%
		Nil
		100%
		100%

DOUBLE RENT ALLOWANCE	YES	NO

*   See page 95 & 96 regarding the restrictions applying to Accelerated Allowance.

CHART 36
RELIEF FOR INVESTMENT IN RENTAL PROPERTY

New Dwellings	*Buildings which qualify*	Construction of NEW dwellings of medium size
	Urban Renewal	
	Custom House Docks Period in which expenditure must be incurred Method of granting relief	25 Jan. 1988 to 24 Jan. 1999 * Against total Case V income
	Temple Bar Area Period in which expenditure must be incurred Method of granting relief	30 January 1991 to 5 April 1999 ** Against total Case V income
	Other Urban Renewal Areas Period in which expenditure must be incurred Method of granting relief	30 January 1991 to 31 July 1997 *** Against total Case V income
	Expenditure which qualifies	Construction cost incl. also development (but not the site or builder's profit)
Conversion to Apartments	*Buildings which qualify*	Conversion to single multi-unit dwelling of a building which waspreviously a single dwelling or not in use as a dwelling
	Urban Renewal	
	Custom House Docks Period in which expenditure must be incurred Method of granting relief	25 Jan. 1988 to 24 Jan. 1999 * Against total Case V income
	Temple Bar Area Period in which expenditure must be incurred Method of granting relief	1 April 1991 to 5 April 1999 ** Against total Case V income
	Other Urban Renewal Areas Period in which expenditure must be incurred Method of granting relief	30 January 1991 to 31 July 1997 *** Against total Case V income
	Expenditure which qualifies	Conversion cost (but not incl. cost of building to be converted or builder's profit)

*   See page 89 re extension to 31.12.1999 and 30.06.2000.
**   See page 92 re extension to 31.12.1999.
*** See page 94 re extension to 30.04.1999.

CHART 36 (concluded)

Refurbishment of Apartments	Buildings which qualify	Refurbishment cost of a building which before and after is in multi-unit dwellings
	Urban Renewal	
	Custom House Docks Period in which expenditure must be incurred # Method of granting relief	25 Jan. 1988 to 24 Jan. 1999 * Against total Case V income
	Temple Bar Area Period in which expenditure must be incurred Method of granting relief	1 April 1991 to 5 April 1999 ** Against total Case V income
	Other Urban Renewal Areas Period in which expenditure must be incurred # Method of granting relief	30 January 1991 to 31 July 1997 *** Against total Case V income
	Expenditure which qualifies	Refurbishment work to render building suitable for use as dwellings - (non-revenue expense nature)
Conversion to Single Dwelling	Buildings which qualify	Refurbishment costs of converting into a single dwelling a building which before that date was not in use as a dwelling
	Urban Renewal	
	Custom House Docks Period in which expenditure must be incurred # Method of granting relief	25 Jan. 1988 to 24 Jan. 1999 * Against total Case V income
	Temple Bar Area Period in which expenditure must be incurred # Method of granting relief	1 April 1991 to 5 April 1999 ** Against total Case V income
	Other Urban Renewal Areas Period in which expenditure must be incurred # Method of granting relief	30 January 1991 to 31 July 1997 *** Against total Case V income
	Expenditure which qualifies	Refurbishment work to render building suitable for use as dwellings - (non-revenue expense nature)

\#   Prior to Finance Act, 1991, expenditure was allowable only against rents from that property
*   See page 89 re extension to 31.12.1999 and 30.06.2000.
** See page 92 re extension to 31.12.1999.
*** See page 94 re extension to 30.04.1999.

CHAPTER 1　　　　　　　　　　　　　　INCOME TAX

1.1 ADMINISTRATION OF TAX SYSTEM

1.1.1 Legislation

The legislation on income tax in the Republic of Ireland is contained in the Taxes Consolidation Act 1997.

1.1.2 Revenue Commissioners

The care and management of direct taxes such as income tax and corporation tax, and of indirect taxes such as customs and excise duty and value added tax, is entrusted to the Revenue Commissioners. The Revenue Commissioners are appointed by the Taoiseach. The Department of the Revenue Commissioners is divided into branches, one of which is the office of the Chief Inspector of Taxes. Inspectors of Taxes are appointed by the Revenue Commissioners and are deployed throughout the country in various tax districts. Responsibility for issuing annual tax returns and for the making of assessments rests with Inspectors of Taxes. Payment of income tax and corporation tax is made through the office of the Collector General, which is another branch of the Revenue Commissioners.

1.1.3 Fundamental Concepts

Year of Assessment - Income tax is charged for a year of assessment, i.e. a year commencing on 6 April in one calendar year and ending on 5 April in the following year.

Total income - This is total income from all sources as computed in accordance with the provisions of the TCA 1997 (it is also called "net statutory income").

Taxable Income - This is total income less personal allowances and reliefs.

Schedules - Income from various sources is grouped for assessment purposes under various schedules. The TCA 1997 contain the rules for measuring the income assessable under the various schedules.

Basis of Assessment - All income is assessable to income tax on a current year basis.

Chapter 1

1.1.4 Self Assessment

Self assessment was introduced for individuals with effect from 1988/89.

1.1.5 Returns

TCA97 s950

Individuals must file a return of income with the Inspector of Taxes each year not later than 31 January in the year after the year of assessment to which the return relates.

However, the 1998 Finance Act proposed that the return filing date be brought forward from 31 January to 30 November in the year following the year of assessment. The effect of this change would be an alignment of the date for filing returns with the date for payment of preliminary tax for the previous tax year (see page 45 re proposed changes to the date for payment of preliminary tax). This change cannot take effect before 1998/99 and then only where the Minister for Finance makes a commencement order.

It should be noted that the 1999 Finance Act was silent on this proposed change.

1.1.6 Surcharge

TCA97 s1084

If a return for a particular year of assessment is not submitted before the "specified date", the tax liability for that year is increased by a surcharge on the amount of tax assessed. This surcharge is calculated on the full tax payable for the year and does not take account of any payments on account.

The surcharge is calculated as follows:-

(a) 5% of the amount of tax subject to a maximum of £10,000 where the return is submitted before the expiry of two months after the specified date, and

(b) 10% of the amount of tax subject to a maximum of £50,000 where the return is not submitted within two months after the specified date.

In the case of new businesses, the surcharge provisions apply from the second filing date only.

1.1.7 Matters of Doubt

TCA97 s955

Where a taxpayer is in doubt as regards a matter to be included in a return, his obligations with regard to the matter will be fulfilled if he draws the Inspector's attention to the matter in question. This provision does not apply where the Inspector or the Appeal Commissioners are of the opinion that the doubt was not genuine and the taxpayer was acting with an avoidance or evasion of tax motive.

1.1.8 Assessments

TCA97 s954

In general, assessments are not made until after a return has been submitted and will be based on the amounts included in the return. Where a person defaults in making a return or the Inspector is dissatisfied with the return, he may make an assessment. A time limit of six years applies to the making of assessments where a full return has been made.

The Inspector may elect not to make an assessment where he is satisfied that the correct tax has been paid. In such cases the taxpayer will be notified by the Inspector of his decision.

1.1.9 Payment of Income Tax

TCA97 s958

Preliminary tax is due on 1 November in the year of assessment.

However, the 1998 Finance Act proposed that the preliminary tax would become payable on 30 November, instead of 1 November in the year of assessment. The effect of this change would be an alignment of the date for payment of preliminary tax with the filing date for the previous tax year (see page 44 re proposed changes to filing date). The change, however, cannot take effect before 1999/2000 and then only where the Minister for Finance makes a commencement order.

It should be noted that the 1999 Finance Act was silent on this proposed change.

In order to avoid any possible interest charges in relation to preliminary tax or any balance of tax payable on an assessment, the taxpayer must pay by the due date for preliminary tax a minimum of:-

(a) 90% of the final tax payable for that tax year - "the 90% rule", or

(b) 100% of the final tax payable for the previous tax year - "the 100% rule". It should be noted that when calculating (b) above:-

— any relief claimed under the business expansion scheme must be ignored and

— any relief for investments in films must be ignored.

Preliminary tax may be paid by means of direct debit. In this instance the taxpayer can base the amount of preliminary tax to be paid on 105% of the tax payable for the pre-preceding year.

When the Preliminary Tax requirements have been met, the balance of tax assessed must be paid on or before 30 April in the year following the year of assessment.

Where the preliminary tax requirements have not been met, the due date for the balance of tax assessed is the date when the preliminary tax is due.

In the case of a couple who are jointly assessed, preliminary tax is based on the couple's liability for the relevant year rather than the individual spouse's liability for that year.

1.1.10 Directors

TCA97 s951

Directors are obliged to make returns of income without being served with notices to do so and the returns may be subject to audit by an Inspector of Taxes.

Directors of shelf companies and directors of certain dormant companies are not, however, required to file returns unless they receive a notice to do so.

Directors who are within the self assessment system are liable to the 10% surcharge (see page 44), if they fail to submit a return of income by the due date. The surcharge applies to the full tax payable for the year, including PAYE deducted.

It should be noted however, that in administering the provisions relating to the submission of returns of income by directors, the Revenue Commissioners have decided that until further notice, returns need not be filed automatically and the surcharge will not, therefore, apply in the case of non-proprietary directors -

(i) who are not otherwise chargeable persons, and

(ii) all of whose income including fees, benefits, distributions etc. has been subject to tax directly or indirectly under PAYE.

In the case of benefits, distributions, etc., it is sufficient for this purpose that such directors supply up to-date details to the inspector of taxes so that the tax is collected by the restriction of tax-free allowances.

Proprietary director means a director of a company who is the beneficial owner of or is able either directly or indirectly to control more than 15% of the ordinary share capital of the company

1.1.11 Appeal Procedures

(a) General

TCA97 s932-s944

A taxpayer aggrieved by an assessment to income tax or corporation tax or by a determination of the Revenue Commissioners in relation to these taxes has the right to appeal against such an assessment or determination. The appeal must be lodged in writing with the Inspector of Taxes within 30 days of the issue of the assessment or determination. If the matter is not subsequently settled by agreement between the Inspector and the taxpayer the appeal will eventually be heard by an Appeal Commissioner.

Appeal Commissioners are appointed by the Minister for Finance.

An application for adjournment of the hearing of an appeal by the Appeal Commissioners may not be refused if made

(a) within 9 months from the end of the tax year to which the assessment relates, or

(b) within 9 months from the date on which the notice of assessment was given to the appellant, whichever of these dates is the earlier.

Where such an application has been refused by the Appeal Commissioners and

(i) the appellant has not made a return of income, or

(ii) the appellant has made a return of income, but all the statements of profits and gains, schedules and other evidence relating to such return have not been furnished by the appellant,

the Commissioners shall make an order dismissing the appeal. They may, however, determine the appeal if they are satisfied that sufficient information has been furnished to enable them to do this. The distinction between dismissal and determination is of the utmost importance as the right of re-hearing of appeals by the Circuit Court is confined to those which have been determined by the Appeal Commissioners. An appellant whose appeal is dismissed by the Appeal Commissioners has the right to appeal to the High Court and to the Supreme Court if he considers that, having regard to the evidence available the dismissal of the appeal was unreasonable. The Revenue Commissioners and taxpayers have the right to take a case on a point of law to the High Court and to the Supreme Court.

The Appeal Commissioners may publish details of their decisions in such cases as they consider appropriate, generally where the point of issue may be of interest to tax practitioners and taxpayers. The identity of the taxpayer involved may not be divulged in such publication.

(b) Self Assessment

The normal appeal procedures apply, but an appeal will not be allowed against an assessment made by reference to the taxpayer's own figures or figures agreed by him, or against a notice of preliminary tax.

Where an estimated assessment is made in the absence of a return, an appeal will be allowed only after the return has been submitted and the tax due on the basis of the return has been paid. The grounds for appeal must be stated in the notice of appeal.

No appeal against the notice of preliminary tax may be made. The taxable person must make a payment of preliminary tax and that amount will displace the tax as shown by the notice.

A person will not be entitled to rely on any ground of appeal at hearing unless it was included in the appeal notice or the Appeal Commissioners or Judge hold that the ground could not have been reasonably stated in the appeal notice.

(c) 1995 Amendments

The 1995 Finance Act introduced additional appeal provisions with effect from 8 June 1995. These are as follows:-

(a) Where an inspector of taxes proposes not to accept a notice of appeal as being valid, he must notify the appellant in writing of his reasons.

(b) A taxpayer will be entitled to appeal directly to the Appeal Commissioners against an inspector's refusal to accept a notice of appeal.

(c) Where an inspector proposes to withdraw a listing of an appeal on the grounds that the appeal may be settled by agreement without recourse to an appeal hearing, he must obtain the agreement of the appellant.

(d) Where a taxpayer feels there is a delay by the inspector in listing an appeal, he will be able to apply directly to the Appeal Commissioners for an early listing.

(e) The grounds on which the Appeal Commissioners may dismiss an appeal are being extended to cover situations of non-cooperation by the appellant with requests for information by the Appeal Commissioners.

(d) Late Appeals

Where a taxpayer fails to lodge an appeal within 30 days of the date of issue of a notice of assessment, the assessment becomes final and conclusive. If, however, the taxpayer was prevented from giving timely notice of appeal due to absence, sickness or other reasonable cause he may apply to the Inspector of Taxes for admission of a late appeal. An application made later than 12 months after the date of the notice of assessment will not be admitted unless the appellant pays the tax charged in the assessment together with accrued interest and submits his return of income and such other information as is necessary to enable the appeal to be determined. Any overpayment of tax arising by reason of the determination of such an appeal will be refunded together with any interest paid thereon. An application for admission of a late appeal will not be entertained in the situations listed below until the relevant action has been completed:

(a) where court proceedings have been initiated for recovery of tax charged in an assessment; or

(b) where a certificate has been issued to a County Registrar or Sheriff in respect of tax charged in an assessment.

Note (1) - Failure to attend or to be represented before the Appeal Commissioners results in the assessment becoming final and conclusive. There is, however, provision for the Appeal Commissioners to re-admit the appeal.

Note (2) - The tax charged in an assessment which has been determined by the Appeal Commissioners becomes payable at the time of determination. This is the position even though an application for re-hearing of the appeal by the Circuit Court has been made.

1.1.12 Interest on Overdue Tax

The rate of interest on overdue tax is 1.00% per month with effect from 1 April 1998 (previously 1.25%) while the rate on overpayments is 0.5% per month (previously 0.6%) – see Chart 12. In cases of fraud or neglect, a penal rate of interest of 2% per month or part of a month is payable.

1.1.13 Power of Attachment

TCA97 s1002

The Revenue Commissioners have power to attach amounts due to a tax defaulter by a third party. The features of the Power of Attachment are as follows:

(a) The Power of Attachment relates to amounts due other than wages and salaries.

(b) The taxes which may be recovered in this manner are income tax, corporation tax, capital gains tax, value added tax, self-employed PRSI, Health contributions, levies employers' PRSI, customs and excise duties, capital acquisitions tax and stamp duty.

(c) The Notice of Attachment will be issued by the Revenue Commissioners to the third party and will show the taxpayer's name and address along with the aggregate of taxes, interest and penalties outstanding.

(d) The debtor who receives the notice must, within 10 days, make a return to the Revenue Commissioners of the amount of debt, if any, owing to the defaulter. Where however the debt exceeds the amount of outstanding taxes etc. it is sufficient to advise a debt equal to that amount.

(e) The recipient of the notice must also pay over to the Revenue Commissioners within the period of 10 days, the amount specified in the Return.

(f) If the amount specified in the Notice is greater than the debt outstanding, the amount of the debt must be paid over. If, however, a further debt becomes due during the "relevant period of the Notice of Attachment" (as defined), a further return and payment must be made within 10 days. This process continues until all outstanding tax etc has been paid.

(g) A "debt" is the aggregate amount of money due by the debtor to the taxpayer at the time of receipt of the Notice of Attachment. It also includes balances (including accrued interest) owing by financial institutions to the taxpayer.

(h) Attachment orders can be placed on joint deposit accounts with financial institutions. Unless evidence to the contrary is produced within 10 days of the notice of attachment, a joint account will be deemed to be held equally for the benefit of each party to the account. Where contrary evidence is produced within the time limit, the amount of the deposit shown to be held by the defaulter will be regarded as a debt due to him and liable to be attached.

(i) Where a Notice of Attachment issues to a debtor, he may not make any disbursements except to the extent:

   (i) that the disbursement will not reduce the debt below the amount of tax etc shown in the Notice, or

   (ii) this disbursement is made pursuant to a Court Order.

(j) A Notice of Attachment cannot include amounts due to the Revenue Commissioners unless a period of one month has expired from the date on which the default commenced, and the Revenue Commissioners have given 7 days' prior notice of the intention to attach the outstanding amount.

(k) A Notice of Attachment may be revoked by the Revenue Commissioners by the issue of a Notice of Revocation where the taxpayer makes good his default.

(l) Copies of Notices of Attachment and Notices of Revocation will be given promptly by the Revenue Commissioners to the taxpayer. In addition, the taxpayer will receive details from the debtor of every payment made to the Revenue Commissioners out of debts due to him, and the Revenue Commissioners will issue receipts to both taxpayer and debtor.

(m) The debtor is indemnified against claims by the taxpayer, and is to be regarded as having made payment to the taxpayer.

(n) The Revenue Commissioners may issue two or more notices of attachment to two or more debtors of the defaulter at the same time. However, the aggregate of the amounts on the notices of attachment must not exceed the total amount of tax defaulted on by the taxpayer.

(o) Any interest on unpaid tax to be collected by attachment is to be specified in the notice of attachment.

1.1.14 Fixed Charge on Company Book Debts

TCA97 s1001

The Revenue Commissioners are entitled to require the person holding a fixed charge on the book debts of a company to pay any relevant amount for which the company is liable (but which it has failed to pay) in respect of certain taxes. The "relevant amount" is defined as any amount which the company is liable to remit to the Collector General in respect of income tax and value added tax. The amount which the holder of the fixed charge (the lender) can be demanded to pay must not exceed the aggregate amount of all moneys etc which the lender has received, directly or indirectly, from the company in payment or part payment of any liabilities due by the company to the lender. Further, only such amounts received by the lender from the company after the date on which he or she is notified by the Revenue Commissioners to make the payment under the Section can be demanded by the Commissioners. The effect of Section 1001 is to reduce the value of the security the lender has obtained by the fixed charge.

It is also provided that the holder of the charge may, within twenty-one days of the creation of the fixed charge, furnish to the Revenue Commissioners the same particulars of the charge which are delivered to the Registrar of Companies. If the holder of the fixed charge does this, it cannot be liable for any relevant amount which the company was liable to pay before the date on which the holder is notified in writing by the Revenue Commissioners. In those circumstances, on receiving notification from the Revenue Commissioners, the holder of the fixed charge may become liable only for payment of any relevant amount which the company subsequently fails to pay.

Chapter 1

1.2 THE UNIFIED SYSTEM OF PERSONAL TAXATION

TCA97
s1015-s1027

The unified system makes no distinction between earned and unearned income. The system provides that having ascertained the income for tax purposes, there are to be deducted the various personal allowances and reliefs to arrive at a figure which represents taxable income. The taxable income is then subjected to rates of tax which graduate from lower to higher levels depending on the taxable income. Rates of tax and cumulative amounts of tax payable on taxable incomes for years from 1990/91 to 1999/00 inclusive are shown in Chart 2.

1.2.1 Joint Assessment

Joint assessment is automatic, unless either spouse gives notice of election for single assessment to the Revenue Commissioners before the end of the tax year. Such notice, when given, continues until withdrawn by the spouse who gave notice. Where a wife is living with her husband, the income of each spouse is taxed as if it were the income of the husband, but with the distinction that the bands of income chargeable at the lower rates are doubled as compared with the single taxpayer.

The assessment may be raised on the wife:

— if the husband and wife jointly elect before 6 July in the year of assessment;

— if they marry in 1993/94 or later and they have not elected nor been deemed to have made an election for the husband to be assessed and for the previous year the income of the wife exceeds that of the husband.

Repayments of tax will be allocated between spouses.

1.2.2 Single Assessment

Where a wife is living with her husband, and an election for single assessment is made, each spouse is treated as a single person with no right of transferring allowances or reliefs between them.

1.2.3 Separate Assessment

A claim may be made for separate assessment of the income tax liability where the joint assessment basis applies. The claim must be made within six months before 6 July in the year of assessment or before 6 July in the following year in the case of marriage.

1.2.4 Separated Spouses

Tax is not deducted at source from legally enforceable maintenance payments. Such payments are deductible for tax purposes in the hands of the payer and chargeable to income tax under Case IV of Schedule D in the hands of the recipient. Both spouses are assessed to income tax as single persons subject to a right of election by separated spouses of a marriage which has not been dissolved or annulled to elect for joint assessment under the provisions of Section 1018. The election for joint assessment may be made only where both spouses are resident in the State.

If the election is made, the husband is assessed to income tax without regard to the maintenance payments and is granted the married man's allowance. If the spouses each have income in their own right, apart from maintenance payments, the income tax applicable to their respective incomes is calculated by the separate assessment procedure but treating the husband's income as undiminished by the maintenance payments. These provisions apply to payments made under maintenance arrangements made after 7 June 1983. In the case of maintenance arrangements made before that date, the new provisions do not apply unless:

(a) a new arrangement is entered into, or

(b) both parties jointly elect in writing and the new provisions apply from the date of (a) or (b)

Where a payment is made for the use or benefit of a child for whom the payer was entitled to child allowance, the payment is:

(a) to be made without deduction of income tax,

(b) to be treated as the income of the payer, and

(c) the payer's income tax liability is to be calculated without any deduction for the payment.

1.2.5 Divorced Persons

In certain circumstances divorced couples may opt for joint assessment for income tax purposes in relation to maintenance payments. Both partners must be resident in the State and remain unmarried. The divorce must have been granted under Section 5 of the Family Law (Divorce) Act, 1996 or if a foreign divorce, it must be recognised as valid in the State.

Chapter 1

1.3 PERSONAL ALLOWANCES AND RELIEFS

The notes which follow are a summary of the conditions under which the personal allowances and reliefs are available. In certain cases a proportion of the allowances and reliefs is available, under the provisions of various double taxation agreements, to individuals not resident in the State (see Chart 1).

In line with the move towards a tax credit system for the tax years 1999/00 onwards, tax relief for certain personal allowances and reliefs is granted at the standard rate only. Please see Chart 1 for the amount of each allowance and the rate at which relief is granted.

1.3.1 Personal Allowances

(a) Married allowance

TCA97 s490

The married allowance is due for the year of assessment, where

(i) a husband and wife are assessed to tax jointly, or

(ii) where the couple are living apart but one is wholly or mainly maintained by the other during the year of assessment and is not entitled in computing the amount of his or her income for tax purposes for that year to make any deduction in respect of sums paid for the maintenance of the other.

Married couples are taxed as single persons in the year of assessment in which the marriage takes place. If the total of the tax paid as single persons exceeds what would have been paid if they were married for the whole year, they will be entitled, on making a joint claim, to repayment. The repayment is calculated by the formula:

$$\frac{A \times B}{12} \text{ - where}$$

A = the tax gained by the election

B = the number of income tax months from the date of marriage to the end of the income tax year (part of a month is treated as a month)

The repayment is allocated proportionately to the tax paid by each. A claim for repayment must be made in writing after the end of the year of marriage and made jointly.

(b) Widowed allowance

TCA97 s462-s463

The widowed allowance is available to a widowed person. A widowed person whose spouse has died in a given tax year is entitled to the widowed person's bereaved in year allowance, for that year only. This allowance is the same as the married person's allowance but is not available to a surviving spouse who is the subject of a joint assessment for the same year.

A widowed person with dependent children is also entitled to:-

(i) the single parent allowance (see below) and

(ii) the following additional allowances:-

— £5,000 in the first year after bereavement

— £4,000 in the second year after bereavement

— £3,000 in the third year after bereavement

— £2,000 in the fourth year after bereavement

— £1,000 in the fifth year after bereavement

In determining whether a child is qualifying or not, the conditions applicable to the single parent allowance (see below) will apply except that there is no restriction in relation to the level of the child's income.

TCA97 s462 (c) Single Allowance

The single allowance is available to other individuals (other than married or widowed).

TCA97 s462 (d) Single Parent Allowance

This allowance may be granted to a person who is not entitled to the married allowance. It is separate from the extra allowance mentioned above which applies to widowed individuals with dependent children. The allowance is granted to either

(i) a widowed person, or

(ii) any other person

who for any year of assessment proves that a qualifying child (as defined below) resided with him or her for the whole or part of that year of assessment.

The relief is not available to an unmarried couple who are living together.

The allowance is granted in addition to the personal allowance so that when the single parent and personal allowances are combined they will equal the married allowance.

A qualifying child for this allowance is a child who:-

(i) is born in the year of assessment, or

(ii) at the commencement of the year of assessment, is under the age of 16 years, or

(iii) if over 16 years of age

— is receiving fulltime instruction at any university, college, school or other educational establishment, or

Chapter 1

- is permanently incapacitated by reason of mental or physical infirmity from maintaining himself, and if he has reached 21 years of age was so incapacitated before reaching that age, or

- is a child of the claimant or a child in the custody of the claimant who is maintained by the claimant at his own expense for the whole or part of the year of assessment.

"Child" includes a step child, a child whose parents have not married, a child who has been informally adopted, and an adopted child, in respect of whom an adoption order under the Adoption Acts 1952 to 1976 is in force.

If the child is entitled in his own right to income exceeding £720 for 1999/2000 (and the single parent has no other qualifying child) the allowance will be restricted by the excess. In calculating the child's income no account is taken of income from scholarships, bursaries or other similar educational endowments.

1.3.2 Age Allowance

TCA97 s464

Claimable by a person where he or his spouse is at least 65 years of age during the year of assessment.

1.3.3 Incapacitated Child Allowance

TCA97 s465

Child allowance is available only in respect of incapacitated children.

The allowance is granted if the claimant proves that he has living at any time during the year of assessment any child who:-

(i) is under 18 years of age and is permanently incapacitated by reason of mental or physical infirmity, or

(ii) if over the age of 18 is permanently incapacitated from maintaining himself, and was so before he reached the age of 21 years, or was in fulltime education at the time he became permanently incapacitated.

The maximum deduction for the tax year 1999/00 (at marginal rate) is £800 for each qualifying child. If the child has income exceeding £2,100 the allowance will be restricted by the amount of the excess. In calculating the child's income no account is taken of income from scholarships, bursaries or other similar educational endowments.

Where an allowance is claimed in respect of a child who has not reached 18 years of age, it is only granted if there is the expectation that, if the child was over 18 years of age, he would be incapacitated from maintaining himself.

Where an allowance is claimed in respect of a child who has reached 18 years of age, it is restricted to the actual amount spent on the maintenance of the child, if this is less than the maximum allowance for the year of assessment.

Where two or more individuals are entitled to relief in respect of the same child, ie where the child is maintained jointly by both persons, each person may claim a proportion of the child allowance relative to the amount expended by him or her on the maintenance of the child.

"Child" includes a stepchild, and a child in respect of whom an adoption order under the Adoption Acts 1952 to 1976 is in force.

It should be noted that a dependent relative allowance cannot be claimed in respect of a child for whom a child allowance has been claimed.

1.3.4 Dependent Relative Allowance

TCA97 s466

Claimable if a person maintains at his own expense:

(a) a relative of his or his wife who is incapacitated by old age or infirmity from maintaining himself, or

(b) his or his wife's widowed mother, or

(c) his son or daughter who is resident with him and upon whom he is dependent by reason of old age or infirmity.

The allowance is reduced by £1 for each £1 by which the income of the person for whom the claim is made exceeds the maximum rate of Old Age Pension payable to a single person (see Chart 1).

1.3.5 Employed Person Taking Care of Incapacitated Individual

TCA97 s467

Claimable by an individual where he/she employs a person to take care of a family member who is totally incapacitated by old age or infirmity.

Where two or more persons employ the carer, the allowance will be apportioned between them. Carers may be employed on an individual basis or through an agency.

1.3.6 Blind Persons' Allowance

TCA97 s468

Claimable by a person where he or his spouse is blind during the year of assessment. Where both husband and wife are blind, an increased allowance is claimable.

1.3.7 Medical Expenses

TCA97 s469

Claimable by a qualified person in respect of health expenses incurred in the provision of non routine health care. The amount claimable is the excess of the cost over £100 for an individual, or over £200 for a family. A qualified person includes not only the claimant

Chapter 1

and his family, but any person for whom dependent relative allowance is claimed.

In the case of expenses incurred on behalf of a dependant relative who has income in his/her own right, in general Revenue take the view that in so far as health expenses are directly or indirectly defrayed out of the dependant's own disposable income, they cannot be regarded as having being defrayed by the claimant.

In calculating the amount of health expenses defrayed in such cases, a deduction should be made of 60% of the dependant relative's old age pension or other similar income.

1.3.8 Medical Insurance

TCA97 s470

Claimable by a person who in the year preceding the year of assessment has made a payment to an authorised insurer under a contract which provides specifically for the payment of actual medical expenses resulting from sickness of the person, his wife, child or other dependants. From 6 April 1996 relief is given at the standard rate of income tax.

1.3.9 Permanent Health Benefit Schemes

TCA97 s471

Premiums and other contributions under permanent health insurance schemes are allowed as deductions for income tax purposes. The amount on which relief is granted is not to exceed 10% of the total income for the year of assessment. Any benefits payable under such schemes are charged to tax under PAYE.

Relief is also available for premia paid to foreign health insurers if the individual first took out the insurance while resident in a member State of the European Union.

1.3.10 Employee Allowance

TCA97 s472

An individual, who is in receipt of emoluments chargeable to income tax under Schedule E, may claim this allowance. In the case of joint assessment and where each spouse is in employment the allowance is available to each spouse.

The allowance is not applicable to emoluments paid by his company to a proprietary director.

The allowance is made to children of proprietary directors and the self-employed who are full-time employees in the business of their parents and where certain conditions are fulfilled. The conditions are:-

(a) PAYE must be operated in respect of the employment, and

(b) the individual's income from the employment must be at least £3,600.

1.3.11 Long Term Unemployed

TCA97 s472A

On taking up a qualifying employment, a long term unemployed individual (unemployed for at least a continuous period of twelve months) may claim, for a three year period, both a tapering personal tax allowance and a tapering tax allowance in respect of each qualifying child. The amounts which may be claimed are:-

	Personal Tax Allowance	Child Tax Allowance
Year 1	£3,000	£1,000 for each qualifying child
Year 2	£2,000	£666 for each qualifying child
Year 3	£1,000	£334 for each qualifying child

The three year period for the employee may commence with either the tax year in which the employment commences or the following tax year.

See page 220 for double deduction available to employers.

1.3.12 Seafarers Allowance

TCA 472B

Seafarers who are absent from the state on a sea-going ship for at least 169 days per year are entitled to a tax free allowance of £5000 per annum.

1.3.13 Rents Paid by Certain Tenants

(a) Persons aged 55 years

TCA97 s473

A person aged 55 years or more, who proves that he has paid rent in the year of assessment in respect of residential premises which was his only, or main residence, is entitled to a deduction of a maximum amount of £1,000 for a single person, £2,000 in the case of a married man assessed jointly and £1,500 for a widowed person. Only payments covering the right to occupy the premises qualify for relief. The relief does not apply to rent paid to certain public authorities, or to rent paid under a tenancy for a period of 50 years or more.

(b) All tenants

All tenants living in private rented accommodation may claim relief in respect of rent paid in the year of assessment at the standard rate. Limits of rent at which the relief will apply are:-

Married couples	£1,000
Widowed person	£ 750
Single person	£ 500

Chapter 1

1.3.14 **Fees paid to Private Colleges in the State**

TCA97
s474-s475

Relief is granted in respect of fees paid by the taxpayer on his own behalf or on behalf of a dependent, insofar as the fees are not met by grants or scholarships. The fees must be paid to a college which is approved by the Minister for Education and must be in respect of an approved undergraduate course of study. Distance education courses in the State provided by colleges outside the State also qualify.

Relief, on similar conditions, is also granted to students who are paying their own fees for approved part-time undergraduate courses of a minimum duration of two years in publicly funded third level institutions and in private colleges which satisfy codes of standards drawn up by the Minister for Education. Fees paid by non-earning spouses, or on their behalf by their spouses, can be set against their spouses taxable income.

The student must not have already obtained a third level qualification. Relief is granted at the standard rate and may not exceed the income tax liability of the taxpayer.

1.3.15 **Fees paid to EU Colleges**

Tax relief at the standard rate is available for fees paid in respect of full-time undergraduate courses in a publicly funded university or similar third level college in any other EU Member State. The courses must be of at least two years duration but courses in medicine, dentistry, veterinary medicine or teacher training do not qualify for the relief. The Minister for Education and Science with the consent of the Minister for Finance, will determine the level of fees which will qualify for the relief. The relief will be given to the person responsible for paying the fees whether on his or her own behalf or on behalf of a spouse or child.

1.3.16 **Fees paid for Training Courses**

TCA97 s476

From a date to be announced by the Minister for Finance relief at the standard rate may be claimed for tuition fees ranging from £250 to £1,000 in respect of approved training courses in the areas of information technology and foreign languages. To qualify for the relief an individual must receive a certificate of competency on completion of the course. The relief will be given to the person responsible for paying the fees whether on his/her own behalf or on behalf of a spouse.

1.3.17 **Service Charges**

TCA97 s477

Relief is granted in respect of local authority service charges which are paid in full and on time by the person liable for them or by another person who resides on the premises to which the service charges relate. Relief is at the standard rate and applies in respect of service charges paid in the preceding calendar year with the maximum qualifying amount for relief being £150.

1.3.18 Alarm Systems

TCA97 s478

A tax allowance of up to £800 is available for expenditure on the installation of intruder alarm systems in the home of a person aged 65 years or over and who lives alone.

Relief is granted at the standard rate and is available for expenditure incurred between 23 January 1996 and 5 April 1998.

The claim may be made either by the person residing in the property or by a relative who incurs the expenditure.

1.3.19 Donations/Gifts

Relief is available (with certain limits) in respect of donations/gifts made to certain approved bodies/charities as follows:-

TCA97 s483
- gifts of money to the State

TCA97 s484
- gifts for education in the Arts

TCA97 s485
- gifts of money to all third level institutions defined in the Higher Education Authority Act, 1971, which are to be used for the purposes of projects approved by the Minister for Education, including the undertaking of research, the acquisition of capital equipment, certain infrastructural development and the provision of facilities designed to increase student numbers in areas of skills needs. Relief applies to both personal and corporate donations with a minimum qualifying donation of £1,000

TCA97 s485A
- gifts to or for the benefit of designated schools. Relief is granted at the standard rate on aggregate gifts of a minimum of £250 and a maximum of £1,000 in a single year of assessment

TCA97 s848
- donations to designated charities

TCA97 s1003
- donation of heritage items

TCA97 s485B
- donations to the Scientific Technological Educational and (Investment) Fund (STEIF)

1.3.20 Retirement Annuities
(a) Tax Relief

TCA97 Ch Pt30

The maximum amount on which tax relief may be claimed in respect of qualifying premiums, for the tax years 1999/2000 et seq is as follows:

Age	% of NET Relevant Earnings
Up to 30 years	15%
30 but less than 40	20%
40 but less than 50	25%
50 years and over	30%

Chapter 1

The 30% limit also applies to individuals who are engaged in specified occupations and professions – primarily sports professionals; irrespective of age.

There is an earnings cap of £200,000 on net relevant earnings. Earning in excess of this amount will not be taken into account in calculating the allowable contribution.

Contributions may be made until an individual reaches 75 years of age.

Accumulated funds can be transferred from one insurer to another.

Where, in any year part of the premium cannot be fully relieved because of the operation of the limits, the part is carried forward and added to the qualifying premium of the following year.

"Net relevant earnings" are earnings from trades, professions and non-pensionable employments, less certain payments and deductions. The earnings of a husband and wife are treated separately for purposes of determining relevant earnings and the relief is available in respect of each spouse with non-pensionable earnings.

Where a qualifying premium is paid after the end of a year of assessment but before 31 January in the year following the year of assessment (the specified return date), it may be treated as paid in the year of assessment. An election for such treatment must be made before 31 January in the year following the year of assessment.

Under Section 45 Finance Act 1998, it was proposed to bring forward the specified return date from 31 January to 30 November (see page 44). The date for payment of qualifying premiums will also be brought forward if the proposed change is implemented.

It should be noted however that the 1999 Finance Act was silent on the proposed change.

1.13.31 **(b) Options on Retirement**

Prior to 6 April 1999, the accumulated pension premiums had to be used to purchase a life annuity.

From 6 April 1999, a number of new options have been introduced for the self employed and proprietary directors on retirement, as follows

- They may take up to 25% of their pension fund tax free and

- Have the remainder of the fund, or £50,000 if less, transferred to an Approved Minimum Retirement Fund (AMRF). However this will not be necessary if the individual has a guaranteed pension (including the State pension) of £10,000 per annum. The amount invested in the AMRF cannot be drawn down until the individual reaches 75 years of age.

- As an alternative to having an amount invested in an AMRF, the individual may opt to have the amount invested in a retirement annuity payable immediately.
- The balance of the funds may be either taken by the individual and taxed at the marginal rate or invested in an Approved Retirement Fund (ARF). Any income or gains earned by an AMRF or ARF are taxed as if they were the income of the individual.
- Where the individual reaches 75 or dies, the AMRF becomes an ARF.
- No further tax is payable on transfers out of an ARF of income or gains accumulated within the ARF.
- Transfers out of the capital originally invested in the ARF, (other than transfers between ARFs), are treated as income of the individual and taxed at the marginal rate.
- The ARF becomes part of the estate of the individual.

A summary of the tax treatment of assets in an ARF, following death is as follows:

ARF inherited by	Income tax due	Capital Acquisitions Tax due
Surviving spouse	No tax due on the transfer to an ARF in the spouses name	No
Children (under 21)	No tax due	Yes*
Children 21 and over	Yes @ 46%	No
Others	Yes @ 46%	Yes*

Death of surviving spouse

Children (under 21)	No	Yes*
Children (over 21)	Yes @ 25%	No
Others	Yes @ 25%	Yes*

Normal Capital Acquisitions Tax thresholds apply.

An ARF or an AMRF must be held by a qualifying fund manager, as listed.

Where a person has purchased a life annuity since 2 December 1998, he/she may opt for the new arrangements, with the agreement of the relevant assurance company.

Chapter 1

1.4 SMALL INCOME AND AGE EXEMPTIONS

TCA97 s187

Exemptions from income tax are available to individuals with small incomes. The exemption limits are increased for individuals aged 65 years or over. Marginal relief applies where the income does not greatly exceed the relevant exemption limit.

The exemption limit is increased by £450 for each of the first two qualifying children that a claimant proves has lived with him/her at any time during the tax year and by £650 per child for each subsequent child.

The definition of a "qualifying child" is the same as for the "Single Parent Allowance" (see page 55) with the exception that there is no income restriction in relation to the child. See Chart 3 for earlier limits.

1.4.1 Small Income Exemption

Total exemption from income tax for the year 1999/2000 is available to an individual under 65 years of age whose "total income" does not exceed the following specified amounts for the year.

- £4,100 in the case of a single, widowed or a married person singly assessed
- £8,200 in the case of a married couple who are jointly assessed

1.4.2 Age Exemption

TCA97 s188

Total exemption from income tax is available to individuals who are aged 65 years or over and whose income for the year 1999/2000 does not exceed the following specified amounts:

Single and widowed (aged 65 or over)	£6,500
Married couples (either spouse aged 65 or over)	£13,000

These limits are increased by the child allowance as outlined above. See Chart 3 for earlier limits.

1.4.3 Marginal Relief

Marginal relief is available where the total income exceeds the above limits, but is less than twice the specified amount. This marginal relief restricts the maximum amount of tax payable to 40% of the amount by which the individual's total income exceeds the exemption limit.

1.5 INTEREST PAYABLE

1.5.1 Mortgage Interest

TCA97
s244-s245

The maximum allowable mortgage interest for individuals for the years 1998/99 and 1999/00 is set out in Chart 6. An individual who sells his only or main residence and acquires another is entitled to claim additional interest on the bridging loan up to the maximum of his marital status class threshold.

1.5.2 Interest on Loans applied in acquiring shares/lending money to a company

TCA97
s248-s252

Relief is given to individuals for interest on loans applied in acquiring shares in or lending money to a qualifying company.

A qualifying company is an unquoted company which is a trading or rental company with Irish rents or an unquoted holding company whose business consists wholly or mainly of holding shares in such trading or rental companies.

The table below shows the relief available.

Investment	Unquoted Trading or Rental Company	Unquoted Holding Company
Full-time director/employee	Unrestricted	Unrestricted
Part-time director/employee	Unrestricted	None

Where the investment in the company is by way of loan, relief is available only if the money lent is used wholly and exclusively for the trade or business of the company or a connected company.

No relief is available where during the period from the making of the loan to the date the interest is paid, the company or any person connected with it makes any loan to the individual or person connected with him, unless such loans are in the ordinary course of business which includes the lending of money.

Where an individual recovers any capital from the company or a connected company without using that amount in reduction of the loan, relief will cease to be given for that amount of the loan.

Capital is treated as being recovered from the company or a connected company where:-

(a) the individual receives value for the sale of any part of the ordinary share capital of the company or of a connected company or consideration by way of repayment of any part of the ordinary share capital, or

(b) the company or a connected company repays the loan or advance, or

(c) the individual receives consideration for the assignment of any debt due to him from the company or from a connected company.

See below re restrictions applying to certain partnerships.

Relief may not be claimed in respect of interest paid on a loan applied in acquiring shares for which BES/Film relief has been claimed.

Relief may not be claimed unless the loan is applied for bona fide commercial purposes and not as part of a scheme or arrangement the main purpose or one of the main purposes of which is the avoidance of tax.

1.5.3 Interest on Loans applied in acquiring an interest in a Partnership

TCA97 s253

Relief is given to individuals for interest on loans applied in purchasing a share in or lending money to a partnership provided the money is used wholly and exclusively for the purposes of the trade or profession carried on by the partnership.

Interest paid on the loan is available for relief if throughout the period from the application of the loan until the interest was paid, the individual personally acts in the conduct of the trade or profession and he has not recovered any capital from the partnership in the period.

Where the individual recovers any capital from the partnership without using the amount recovered in reduction of the loan, relief will cease to be given for that amount of the loan.

Capital is treated as having been recovered where:-

(a) the individual receives consideration for the sale of any part of his interest in the partnership, or

(b) the partnership returns any amount of capital to him or repays any loan made by him, or

(c) the individual receives any consideration for assigning any debt due to him by the partnership.

1.5.4 Payment of Interest Net

TCA97 s246

Where annual interest is paid by companies or where such interest is paid by individuals to persons whose usual place of abode is outside the State, tax at the standard rate should be deducted and paid over to the Revenue.

The following are exceptions to this rule:

(a) Interest paid in the State on an advance from a bank carrying on a bona fide banking business in the State.

(b) Interest paid by such a bank to non residents in the ordinary course of its business.

(c) Interest on any securities in respect of which the Minister for Finance has authorised that payment be made gross, ie Government loan interest.

(d) Interest paid by companies where the Revenue Commissioners have authorised the payment to be made gross, ie Co-op interest.

(e) Interest paid which is a distribution under Section 130.

(f) Interest paid by a qualifying company based in the IFSC to a non resident person.

(g) Interest paid by a company or a collective investment undertaking in the course of a trade or business to companies which are resident in another EU member state or in a country with which Ireland has a double taxation agreement.

1.6 SCHEDULE C

TCA97
s32-s51

Assessments under Schedule C may be made on persons entrusted with the payment of certain interest, annuities, dividends etc, payable out of Public Revenue, and on bankers or dealers who engage in cashing or selling coupons.

1.6.1 Exemptions

There will be no assessment where interest is paid on securities in respect of which the Minister for Finance has authorised that payment be made gross, or where interest is paid by companies which have been authorised by the Revenue Commissioners to make such payments gross.

No tax shall be chargeable in respect of the dividends on any securities of any territory outside the State which are payable in the State to non-residents of the State.

1.7 SCHEDULE D – CASES I and II

Tax is charged on the annual profit or gains arising from any trade (Case I) or from any profession (Case II). The tax treatment of these items is almost identical and therefore they can be considered together. The expression "annual profits or gains" is not defined in the Tax Acts.

TCA97 s3

Trade includes "every trade, manufacture, adventure or concern in the nature of trade". This definition has been held by the courts to embrace profits arising not alone from trading in the normal sense of the word but also from isolated transactions, and activities such as the conducting of professional examinations. Profits from dealing in or developing land are assessable under Case I as are profits from farming.

TCA97 s81

Only deductions authorised by the Tax Acts are allowed in computing the profits of a trade or profession. No deduction is allowed for:

(a) Any expense, not being money wholly and exclusively laid out or expended for the purposes of the trade or profession;

(b) any disbursements or expenses of maintenance of the parties or their families or any sums expended for any other domestic or private purposes;

(c) rent of any dwelling-house except where such part thereof is used for the purposes of the trade or profession;

(d) any sum expended over and above repairs to premises, implements, utensils or articles employed for the purposes of the trade or profession;

(e) any loss not connected with or arising out of the trade or profession;

(f) any capital withdrawn from, or any sum employed or intended to be employed as capital in the trade or profession;

(g) any capital employed in improvements to premises occupied for the purposes of the trade or profession;

(h) any interest which might have been made if any such sums as aforesaid had been laid out at interest;

(i) any debts, except bad debts proved to be such to the satisfaction of the Inspector and doubtful debts to the extent that they are respectively estimated to be bad;

(j) any sum recoverable under an insurance or contract of indemnity;

(k) any annuity or other annual payment payable out of the profits or gains;

(l) any royalty or other sum paid in respect of the user of a patent.

1.7.1 Pre-Trading Expenses

TCA97 s82

An allowance may be claimed in respect of pre-trading expenses in the case of a trade or profession which is set up and commenced on or after 22 January 1997, provided that the expenses:-

(i) were incurred for the purpose of the trade or profession, and

(ii) were incurred within three years of commencement, and

(iii) are not otherwise allowable in computing profits.

Where an allowance is granted for pre-trading expenses, it is treated as if the expenditure was incurred on the date on which the trade/profession commenced.

The pre-trading expenditure which is allowed cannot be used for the purpose of set off against income of the individual other than that arising from the trade or profession in respect of which the expenditure was incurred.

1.7.2 Entertainment Expenses

TCA97 s840

No deduction is granted in respect of any expenses incurred on or after 26 March, 1982 in providing business entertainment. "Business Entertainment" means entertainment of any kind including the provision of accommodation, food and drink or any other form of hospitality in any circumstances whatsoever.

1.7.3 Motor Expenses

TCA97 s376

In the case of motor expenses incurred on or after 2 December 1998 on cars which cost £16,000 or more the allowable expenses are reduced by the lower of (a) one-third of the amount by which the relevant cost of the vehicle exceeds £16,000 and (b) an amount which bears to the qualifying expenses the same proportion as the excess of the cost of the vehicle over £16,000 bears to the cost of the vehicle. The restriction may be expressed by the formula:

$$A \times \frac{B - 16{,}000}{B} \text{ where}$$

A = Qualifying expenses

B = Cost of the vehicle

(See Chart 7 for previous relevant limits)

In the case of a leased vehicle, the list price of which exceeds £16,000 there is a similar restriction with the substitution of the list price of the vehicle for the cost price. In such cases there is a further restriction of the amount of the leasing charges deductible in computing profits. The allowable amount is confined to the proportion of the leasing charges which £16,000 bears to the list price of the vehicle. The allowable amount may, therefore, be expressed by the formula:

$$\frac{D \times 16{,}000}{E} \text{ where}$$

D = Leasing charges

E = List price of the vehicle

The £16,000 limit applies for expenditure incurred on or after 2 December 1998, with the exception that the old limit of £15,000 still applies where the expenditure is under a contract entered into before 2 December 1998 and is incurred within 12 months after that date.

1.7.4 Basis of Assessment

TCA97 s65

Current year basis was introduced with effect from the year of assessment 1990/91. This replaced the preceding year basis which obtained for the years to 1989/90 inclusive, and which is dealt with in previous editions of this book. Where business profits are computed by reference to annual accounts the charge to tax for a year of assessment is based on the profits of an accounting period ending in the year, rather than on the profits of the actual year to 5 April, eg. profits of year ended 31 December 1999 are treated as actual profits of year of assessment 1999/2000.

1.7.5 Commencement Years

TCA97 s66

First year - The profits assessable are those from the date of commencement until the following 5 April.

Second year - The profits assessable are those of the first 12 months' trading. If the actual profits of the second year (based on a 5 April basis) are lower than those of the first 12 months' trading, the difference can be set against the profits of the third year of assessment. When the profits of the third year of assessment are insufficient to absorb the full amount of the difference, any balance can be carried forward as a loss available for set off against profits of subsequent years of assessment.

Chapter 1

For 1998/99 and subsequent years of assessment the basis of assessment is altered to provide that the profits to be assessed in the second year are as follows:-

(a) If there is only one set of accounts made up to a date within that year and these accounts are for a full 12 months, the full amount of the profits of the one year ending on that date;

(b) If the accounts are for less than one year or there are more than one set of accounts made up to a date or dates within that tax year, the full amount of the profits of the one year ending on the later or latest of those dates;

(c) In any other case, the actual profits for the tax year.

Third and subsequent years - The assessment for these years is on a current year basis.

1.7.6 Cessation Years

TCA97 s67

Final year - The assessment is based on the profits from the preceding 6 April to the date of cessation.

Penultimate year - Where the actual profits of the penultimate year of assessment calculated on a 5 April basis exceed the assessed profits calculated on a current year basis, the assessment for the penultimate year is revised to the actual profits.

Where a business commences and ceases within three tax years, the aggregate taxable profits for the three years of assessment may not exceed the profits actually earned in the period. An election for this treatment must be made before the specified return date for the year of cessation.

1.7.7 Period of Computation of Profits

(a) If only one account is made up to a date within the year of assessment and that account is for a period of one year, these accounts will form, as indicated above, the basis of assessment for that year.

(b) If the accounting date is changed, the profits for a year ending on the new date will be adopted.

(c) If more than one set of accounts are made up to different dates in the tax year, the profits for a year ending on the later of those dates will be adopted.

(d) In any other case the assessment will be based on the profits for the year ended 5 April, i.e. the actual year of assessment.

(e) Where there has been a change of accounting date or where two or more sets of accounts are prepared and the rule outlined at (b) or (c) above is adopted, the Revenue can review the assessment for the previous tax year as follows:-

   (i) The review will be a comparison between the assessment for the previous year of assessment and profits of a one year period ending on the corresponding accounting date in the previous year.

   (ii) Where the profits for that year exceed the profits assessed, the Revenue will increase the assessment of the previous year of assessment.

1.7.8 Losses

TCA97 s381-s390

Losses under Cases I and II may be utilised as follows:

Set off against Other Income - the loss incurred in a year of assessment may be deducted from any other income chargeable to tax in that year.

Carry Forward - Any loss not relieved under Section 381 can be carried forward and set-off against the profits of the same trade or profession in subsequent years.

Terminal Loss - Terminal loss relief can be claimed in respect of a loss incurred in the last 12 months of a trade or profession. This loss can be carried back against profits from the same trade or profession "for the three years of assessment last preceding that in which discontinuance occurs". Capital allowances can be used to create or augment the loss.

TCA97 s391

Capital allowances of a year of assessment may be utilised to create or augment a loss. This is subject to the proviso that such capital allowances must first be set-off against any balancing charge assessable in the year of assessment to which they relate. There are provisions also to ensure that capital allowances can be used to create or augment a loss only to the extent that they have not otherwise been effectively relieved.

1.7.9 Withholding Tax on Payments for Professional Services

TCA97
s520-s529

Tax at standard rate is deducted from payments made for professional services by Government Departments, State Bodies, Local Authorities, Health Boards etc.

Services which are regarded as professional services are:

(a) medical, dental, pharmaceutical, optical, aural or veterinary.

(b) architectural, engineering, quantity surveying and related services.

(c) accountancy, auditing, finance and consultancy services.

(d) legal services provided by solicitors and barristers and other legal services.

(e) geological.

(f) training services provided on behalf of FAS.

The bodies who are required to deduct tax are shown at Chart 15. Credit for tax withheld is to be granted as follows:

Corporation Tax:- Against liability of accounting period for which tax is withheld.

Income Tax:- Against liability of the year for which period of withholding tax is credit period. Provision is made for interim refunds which will only be permitted if the Inspector of Taxes considers that hardship would otherwise arise. There are three categories to be considered under this provision:

(a) Ongoing business,

(b) Commencing businesses, and

(c) Cases of particular hardship.

1.7.10 Ongoing Business

It is a condition that the profits for tax purposes of the immediately preceding accounting period must have been agreed and the tax paid.

The interim refund will be restricted by the amount of the liability for the previous year and any other outstanding amounts for VAT, PAYE and PRSI.

1.7.11 Commencing Business

A commencing business would be unable to satisfy the condition at (2) above and in order to cater for this, a formula is provided under which the Inspector may make a refund. The refund will be the lesser of the amounts at (i) and (ii) below:

(i) tax at standard rate on an amount determined by the formula:

$$E \times \frac{A}{B} \times \frac{C}{P} \text{ where}$$

E = Estimated expenses for the basis period
A = Estimated payments from which tax withheld for the basis period
B = Estimated total income for the basis period
C = Number of months covered by claim
P = Number of months in basis period

(ii) The tax withheld

1.7.12 Cases of Particular Hardship

In a case where any of the condition already outlined cannot be fulfilled, the Revenue Commissioners may waive one or more of the conditions. In such circumstances the amount of the refund is at the discretion of the Revenue Commissioners.

Chapter 1

1.8 SCHEDULE D – CASE III

TCA97 s18

Tax is charged under this Case on the following items:

(a) Interest, annuities and other annual payments, excluding bank and certain other deposit interest receivable under deduction of tax.

(b) All discounts.

(c) Profits on securities bearing interest payable out of the public revenue other than such as are charged under Schedule C.

(d) Interest on any securities issued or deemed within the meaning of Section 36 to be issued under the authority of the Minister for Finance, in cases where such interest is paid without deduction of tax.

(e) Income arising from securities outside the State except such income as is charged under Schedule C.

(f) Income arising from possessions outside the State.

For practical purposes the income chargeable under Case III can be broadly summarised under two headings:

(i) Dividends and interest which were not liable to Irish income tax by deduction, regardless of their source.

(ii) Income from foreign possessions such as rental income from foreign property and income from foreign trades and employments.

1.8.1 Basis of Assessment

TCA97 s70

The basis of assessment is the actual basis.

1.9 SCHEDULE D – CASE IV

TCA97 s18

Tax is charged under this Case in respect of any annual profits or gains not falling under any other Case of Schedule D or under any other Schedule.

Examples of items charged under this Case are as follows:

(a) Profits from the sale of a certificate of deposit or of an assignable deposit.

(b) Shares received in lieu of cash dividends.

(c) Income deemed to be that of an individual as a result of a transfer of assets abroad.

(d) Gains from certain disposals of land.

(e) Copyright royalties not chargeable under Case I and II.

(f) Post cessation receipts of a trade or profession.

(g) Certain income from which tax has or is deemed to have been deducted eg annuities, building society interest receivable and bank and certain other deposit interest receivable.

(h) Companies are liable to income tax under Case IV Schedule D in accordance with certain provisions of the Tax Acts. These include:

  (i) distributions made by companies out of capital profits;

  (ii) distributions made by newly resident companies out of profits earned before residence begins;

  (iii) recovery of tax credits previously repaid through loss relief and now being foregone through claiming the loss against profits of subsequent accounting periods.

(i) Profits or gains from an unknown or unlawful source or activity.

(j) Withdrawal of relief on investment in corporate trades.

(k) Liability to corporation tax on dividends on certain preference shares.

(l) Certain disposals of land where there is a right to reconvey.

(m) Interest element included in sale proceeds from certain government stocks.

(n) Income from UCITS and Unit Trusts.

(o) Guaranteed Dividends.

1.9.1 Basis of Assessment

TCA97 s74

The basis of assessment is the actual basis.

Chapter 1

1.10 DEPOSIT INTEREST RETENTION TAX

1.10.1 Companies and Pension Funds

TCA97 s265

Companies and pension funds are permitted to open deposit accounts on which interest is paid without deduction of DIRT.

When such an account is opened a declaration in writing must be completed and signed:-

(i) by a person (referred to as "the declarer") to whom any interest on the deposit is payable by the relevant deposit taker,

(ii) which must be in such form as may be prescribed or authorised by the Revenue Commissioners, including a declaration that the interest is beneficially owned by the company or pension scheme,

(iii) contain details of the beneficial owner's name, address and tax reference number,

(iv) include a certificate by the "appropriate person" that to the best of his knowledge and belief the declaration and the information furnished are true and correct, and

(v) contain such information as the Revenue Commissioners may reasonably require for the purposes of the section.

Where a return is required to be made by a relevant deposit taker in respect of deposit interest on an account where a declaration has been made (as outlined above), that return must include the tax reference number of the person beneficially entitled to the interest.

For the purposes of the declaration, "appropriate person" as far as a company is concerned, is the person appointed as auditor for all the purposes of the Companies Acts 1963 to 1990. For a pension fund it is the administrator or trustee.

1.10.2 Individuals

(i) 20% Rate DIRT Accounts

TCA97 s264

"Special savings accounts" may be opened by individuals on which DIRT is deducted from deposit interest at the rate of 20% and this deduction is treated as satisfying the individual's full liability to tax in respect of the interest and is not included in computing total income for the purposes of the Tax Acts.

Conditions attaching to such an account are:-

(a) It must be designated by the relevant deposit taker as a special savings account.

(b) Funds may not be withdrawn from the account within three months of it being opened.

(c) There must be a minimum period of notice of 30 days in respect of withdrawals.

(d) Fixed rates of interest must not apply to the account for a period in excess of 24 months.

(e) The amount deposited (including interest added) must not exceed £75,000 at any time (provided the person does not hold any other special savings products).

(f) The account holder must be over the age of 18.

(g) The account must be in the name of the person beneficially entitled to the deposit.

(h) Except in the case of a married couple, the account must not be a joint account.

(i) An individual, subject to the exception for married couples, can only have one special savings account at any one time.

(j) Married couples may hold an account separately in their own names or one or two joint accounts. Each of the two accounts, be they single or joint, can have a maximum balance of £50,000.

A person opening a special savings account must make a declaration to the deposit taker in such a manner as is required by the Revenue Commissioners. This declaration requires the following:-

- That the required conditions in relation to the deposit are met.
- Show the full name and address of the individual beneficially entitled to the interest.
- An undertaking from the individuals that if they cease to meet the qualifications, they will notify the deposit taker.
- Any other information which the Revenue Commissioners may reasonably require.
- The forms signed by the person.

The deposit taker must keep and retain for a period of six years, a register of all declarations made.

All monies held in special savings accounts are subject to the same terms.

(ii) Standard Rate DIRT Accounts

DIRT deducted at the standard rate from interest on accounts of individuals, other than special savings accounts, is regarded as satisfying the individuals full liability to tax in respect of that interest. However, the interest is included in computing total income for the purposes of the Tax Acts.

Chapter 1

1.10.3 Deposit Taker

DIRT is deducted by a "relevant deposit" taker who is:

TCA97 s256

(a) A person who holds a licence under Section 9, Central Bank Act, 1971, or a person who holds a licence or similar authorisation under the law of any other Member State of the EC which corresponds to a licence granted under Section 9, or

(b) A building society within the meaning of the Buildings Societies Act 1989, or a society established in accordance with the law of any other Member State of EC.

(c) A Trustee Savings Bank within the meaning of the Trustee Savings Bank Acts, 1863 to 1979.

(d) The Agricultural Credit Corporation plc.

(e) The Industrial Credit Corporation plc.

(f) The Post Office Savings Bank.

(g) The ICC Investment Bank Limited.

The following are not regarded as relevant deposit takers:

(a) Credit Unions
(b) Friendly Societies
(c) Industrial & Provident Societies
(d) Investment Trust Companies
(e) Unit Trusts

1.10.4 Returns and Payments

TCA97 s258

Deposit takers are, subject to certain exceptions, obliged to account for DIRT on an annual basis in respect of all relevant interest accrued but not actually paid or credited by them in a year of assessment.

1.10.5 Charities

TCA97 s266

Charities are exempt from the retention tax. The charity must make a declaration in writing to the deposit taker that it is entitled to the charitable exemption. The declaration must be made before the interest can be paid without deduction of the retention tax. The charity must establish its entitlement to the exemption from the retention tax with the Revenue Commissioners before the deposit taker can pay the interest gross. Where, however, an exempted charity suffers retention tax, it may claim a repayment.

1.10.6 Repayment to Elderly and Incapacitated Individuals

TCA97 s267

Repayment of retention tax may be made to an individual who is not liable or fully liable to income tax and who satisfies the Revenue Commissioners that:-

(a) at some time during the tax year he or his spouse was aged 65 years or more, or

(b) throughout the tax year or from some date during the tax year he or his spouse was or became permanently incapacitated by reason of mental or physical infirmity from maintaining himself or herself.

1.10.7 Non-Resident Depositors

TCA97 s263

Deposit accounts held by non-residents are exempt from the retention tax. A declaration must be made to the appropriate bank before interest can be paid without retention tax.

Chapter 1

1.11 SPECIAL INVESTMENT PRODUCTS

1.11.1 1. Special Investment Policies (SIP)

TCA97 s723
TCA97 s839

SIP are operated by life assurance companies. The policies are issued in respect of "special investment funds". Such a fund's cumulative expenditure must include a minimum of 55% on Irish ordinary shares and a minimum of 10% in respect of Irish companies with a market capitalisation of less than £200M. Income and gains of the special investment funds are subject to corporation tax at the rate of 20%, with effect from 6 April 1999. The conditions attaching to SIP are as follows:

(i) The payments made by an individual in respect of the policy or policies must not exceed £75,000.

(ii) The policy may be issued to and owned only by an individual over the age of 18.

(iii) The policy may be issued only to the individual who is beneficially entitled to all amounts (apart from mortality cover) payable under the policy.

(iv) Except in the case of a married couple, the policy may not be a joint policy.

(v) A person taking out a SIP must sign a declaration indicating that he complies with all of the necessary conditions. This declaration will also contain any other information which the Revenue Commissioners may feel reasonable to require.

(vi) On the maturity of a SIP, the individual has no further liability to income tax or capital gains tax.

(vii) Investment in SIP is subject to certain limits in the overall context of investments in special investment products.

1.11.2 2. Special Investment Schemes (SIS)

TCA97 s737
TCA97 s839

SIS are operated by authorised Unit Trust Schemes. Holdings in such schemes are referred to as "special investment units". Expenditure on trust assets must include a minimum of 55% in respect of Irish equities and a minimum of 10% in respect of Irish companies with a market capitalisation of less than £200M. Income and gains of SIS are taxed at the standard rates of income tax and capital gains tax and then reduced so that the effective rate of charge for both taxes is 20% with effect from 6 April 1999. Special Investment Units may only be issued to individuals subject to certain conditions:

(i) Aggregate payments for units must not exceed £75,000.

(ii) Units may only be sold to and owned by individuals over the age of 18;

> (iii) Except in the case of a married couple, an individual owning units of an authorised unit trust scheme may not buy or own such units of another authorised unit trust scheme;
>
> (iv) A married couple may buy and jointly own units of one or two authorised unit trust schemes but may not otherwise buy or own such units in any scheme either individually or jointly.

A person acquiring these units must sign an approved declaration in a form prescribed by the Revenue Commissioners which contains the full name and address of the individual beneficially entitled together with the amount paid.

Holders of units will have no personal liability to income tax or capital gains tax.

Where units are sold at a loss in any year of assessment and interest is earned in respect of those units in the following year of assessment, the loss will not be allowed until that following year of assessment.

Investment in SIS is subject to certain limits in the overall context of investment in Special Investment Products.

1.11.3 3. Special Portfolio Investment Accounts (SPIA)

TCA97 s838
TCA97 s839

SPIA are operated by designated stockbrokers and are confined to Irish stock-market products. Expenditure on these products must include a minimum of 55% in respect of Irish equities and a minimum of 10% in respect of Irish companies with a market capitalisation of less than £100M.

Income and gains accruing to investments in SPIA are taxed at 20% with effect from 6 April 1999, and the tax is deducted and payable by the stockbroker.

The amount of money invested by any individual in an equity investment account must not exceed £75,000.

The definition of qualifying shares also includes shares quoted on the Developing Companies Market (DCM). The existing limit in respect of the total investment which can be made by an individual in a SPIA is increased by the lesser of £10,000 and the amount invested by the SPIA in shares of companies quoted on the DCM. These increased limits apply to SPIAs opened on or before 5 April 2000.

The individual investor will have no personal liability to tax in respect of his investments in these accounts.

Where securities are sold at a loss in any year of assessment, and interest is earned in respect of those securities in the following year of assessment the loss will not be allowed until that following year of assessment.

Investment in SPIA is subject to certain limits in the overall context of investments in Special Investment Products.

1.11.4 Limits on Investment in Special Investment Products

TCA97 s839

There are now four different types of special investment products:-

Special Savings Accounts (deposit accounts) - SSA.
Special Investment Policies (assurance policies) - SIP.
Special Investment Schemes (units) - SIS.
Special Portfolio Investment Accounts (equities) - SPIA.

An individual can invest a maximum of £75,000 in one, or a combination of, the above products.

The entitlements of a married couple saving and investing jointly are effectively double the entitlements of an individual.

The declaration which each individual has to complete must include details of any other investments held either in his own name or jointly with his spouse. Any subsequent acquisitions must be notified in writing to the person to whom the declaration was made.

1.12 SCHEDULE D – CASE V

TCA97 s18

Tax is charged under Case V in respect of rents from any premises in the State.

1.12.1 Deductions

TCA97 s97

In arriving at the chargeable income the following expenses may be deducted from the gross rents receivable.

(i) Rent payable on the property.

(ii) Rates payable on the property.

(iii) Goods provided and services rendered in connection with the letting of the property.

(iv) Repairs, insurance, maintenance and management of the property.

(v) Interest on money borrowed to purchase, improve, or repair the property. Interest paid prior to the first letting is not allowable.

TCA97 s248A

No relief is available for interest on money employed on or after 23 April 1998 in the purchase repair or improvement of residential premises.

This restriction does not apply where the property is acquired before 31 March 1999 under a contract evidenced in writing entered into before 23 April 1998. Neither does it apply to interest on borrowed money employed on or after 23 April 1998 in the improvement or repair of a residential premises which in the 12 months to 23 April 1998 was a rented residential premises and which was owned on 23 April 1998 by the person in receipt of the rental income.

No restriction applies for interest on borrowed money employed in connection with certain premises in designated resort areas, designated rural development areas or where planning permission, applied for before 23 April 1998, restricts the use of the premises to short-term residential use not exceeding 2 months at any one time.

In the case of foreign properties the restriction applies from 2 May 1998.

The restriction applies where at any time on or after 23 April 1998 a person turns a sole or main residence into rented accommodation. The restriction applies from the date of the change of use.

TCA97 s284

(vi) Capital allowances (see below).

TCA97 s328

(vii) Expenditure on rented accommodation (see below).

Chapter 1

1.12.2   **Capital Allowances**

TCA97 s284

Capital allowances (wear and tear) may be claimed for the years 1997/98 et seq in respect of capital expenditure incurred on the provision of machinery or plant (fixtures and fittings) where:-

1. the expenditure is incurred wholly and exclusively in respect of a house which is used solely as a dwelling which is or is to be let as a furnished house, and

2. the furnished house is provided for renting or letting on bona fide commercial terms on the open market.

The allowances available are 15% of the expenditure incurred for the first six years and 10% in the seventh year.

Any rental losses which arise due to a claim for capital allowances may only be carried forward against future rental income.

1.12.3   **Expenditure on Rented Accommodation**

TCA97 s325-s329

Expenditure incurred in the period 25 January 1988 to 31 July 1994 (excluding certain designated areas) on the construction, refurbishment or conversion of a house or flat for letting is allowable as a deduction against the rental income from the property or other properties.

The relief applies to new, refurbished or converted property, measuring between 35 and 125 square metres in the case of a house and 30 to 90 square metres in the case of a flat which, without having been used for owner occupation, is let by its owner to a tenant on an arms length basis.

A certificate of reasonable cost provided by the Department of Environment is required in the case of expenditure on conversion of the cost of the house or flat built by the person who lets them.

The expenditure which qualifies for relief and the method of granting relief is shown at Chart 36.

A clawback of relief will arise where the property ceases to be a qualifying premises or the lessor's interest passes to another party (including on death) within ten years of the first letting of the premises under a qualifying lease. Where a clawback occurs the original relief may be claimed by the new owner but cannot exceed the price paid by the new owner.

If the property is sold after the qualifying ten year period, and provided that all the qualifying conditions have been met during that period, the original owner will continue to be entitled to any unutilised allowances i.e. the allowances do not travel with the property.

The property must be let under a qualifying lease which means the following conditions must be satisfied:-

(i) The lease must be a genuine rental agreement with regular payments by way of rent only.

(ii) The tenant cannot be granted an option to buy at less than market value.

Where a qualifying unit is erected by a speculative builder and sold to an investor who lets the property, the site cost together with a proportion of the builders profit will not be allowable as qualifying expenditure. Qualifying expenditure is arrived at by applying the formula:

$$\text{Purchase Price} \times \frac{\text{Builder's Development Cost}}{\text{Builder's Site Cost} + \text{Builder's Development Cost}}$$

The following is an example of how to compute qualifying expenditure:

	£
Cost of Site	5,000
Site Development Costs	2,000
Building Costs	20,000
Builders Profit	3,000
Purchase Price	30,000

Qualifying expenditure is, therefore, as follows:

$$£30,000 \times \frac{(£2,000 + £20,000)}{(£5,000 + £2,000 + £20,000)} = £24,444$$

1.12.4 Premiums on Leases

TCA97 s98

Where a premium is received on the granting of a lease of less than 50 years duration a portion of the premium is treated as rent and assessed in the first year. The assessable portion of the premium is calculated as follows:

$$\text{Assessable Portion} = P \times \frac{51 - N}{50} \quad \text{where -}$$

P = Amount of the premium and

N = The amount of each complete period of 12 months in the term of the lease.

Provided the lessee uses the premises for the purpose of a trade or profession or where he lets the premises he will receive an annual deduction, in computing his profits, for the portion of the premium assessable on the lessor divided by the number of years of the lease.

Chapter 1

1.12.5 Rents Paid to Non-Residents

TCA97 s1041

Rents payable directly to persons whose usual place of abode is outside the State must be paid under deduction of tax at standard rate, and the tax paid over to the Revenue Authorities.

1.12.6 Exemption of Income from Leasing of Farm Land

TCA97 s664

Exemption from income tax is granted in respect of certain leasing income obtained by a lessor of agricultural land. The conditions attaching to the relief are:-

(a) The income must arise from the leasing of farmland

(b) The lease must be in writing and for a definite term of 5 years or more

(c) The land must be leased to an individual who is not connected with the lessor and who uses the farm land leased for the purpose of a trade of farming carried on solely by him or in partnership.

(d) (i) The land must be leased by an individual who is aged 55 years or more, or who is permanently incapacitated by reason of mental or physical infirmity from carrying on a trade of farming and

 (ii) has not, after 30th January 1985 leased the farm land from a connected person on terms which are not at arms length.

For any qualifying lease entered into on or after 23 January 1996, the limits are:-

£6,000 for a lease of 7 years or more

£4,000 for a lease of between 5 and 7 years

The leasing income of a husband and wife is treated separately for the purposes of the relief, whether they are jointly assessed or not.

1.12.7 Basis of Assessment

TCA97 s75

The basis of assessment is the actual basis.

1.12.8 Losses

TCA97 s384

Case V losses incurred in a year of assessment can be carried forward and set off against Case V profits for any subsequent year of assessment.

TCA97 s105

Anti-avoidance measures exist to prevent the carry forward of losses against future rental income where those losses arise out of interest payments becoming due for a period during which the property is not occupied for the purpose of a trade or as a residence.

1.13 URBAN RENEWAL – 1986 SCHEME

TCA97
s339-s350

Relief from income tax and corporation tax is available, in connection with the redevelopment of the Custom House Docks area and the Temple Bar area in Dublin together with certain designated areas in Cork, Dublin, Galway, Limerick, Waterford, Athlone, Castlebar, Dundalk, Letterkenny, Tralee, Kilkenny, Wexford, Tullamore, Sligo, Ballina, Bray, Carlow, Clonmel, Drogheda, Ennis, Portlaoise and Longford.

1.13.1 Expenditure on Commercial Buildings and Structures

TCA97
s339-s350

Capital allowances similar to the allowances available for industrial buildings (see Chart 35) are available in designated areas in respect of capital expenditure on the construction or refurbishment of commercial premises (eg offices, shops, leisure and car parking facilities, cinemas, theatres etc).

(a) **Designated areas outside Dublin**

The allowances available are as follows:

Owner occupier	- Up to 100% free depreciation
Lessors	- 50% initial allowance
	- 4% annual allowance

The relief applies to expenditure incurred up to 31 July 1994 and in certain circumstances up to 31 December 1994.

(b) **Customs House Docks Area and Tallaght (Dublin)**

TCA97
s322-s329

The allowances available are similar to those available in the designated areas outside Dublin (see above).

With regard to Tallaght (Dublin), the time limit for claiming reliefs runs for the same period as for the designated areas outside Dublin (see above).

With regard to the Custom House Docks area the time limit runs from 25 January 1988 to 24 January 1999. However, the expiry date has been extended to 31 December 1999, and 30 June 2000 where 51% of the expenditure has been incurred before 31 December 1999. These extensions are subject to approval of the EU Commission and will come into effect by Ministerial Order once EU approval is secured.

(c) **Dublin Designated Areas other than the Custom House Dock Area and Tallaght (Dublin)**

TCA97
s339-s350

The allowances available are reduced to one half of the allowances available in the areas outside Dublin, ie

Owner occupier	- Up to 50% Free Depreciation
Lessors	- 25% Initial Allowances
	- 2% Annual Allowance

The time limit for claiming these allowances runs for the same period as for the designated areas outside Dublin (see above).

(d) Temple Bar

TCA97
s330-s338

The allowances available in Temple Bar are dealt with separately on page 92.

The period for which commercial buildings in designated areas must be retained in order to avoid the imposition of a balancing charge for capital allowances purposes, is 13 years, in respect of disposals made on or after 6 May 1993.

1.13.2 Expenditure on Rented Accommodation

TCA97
s346-s350

Certain reliefs (formerly known as Section 23 Relief) are available for expenditure incurred on the provision of rented residential accommodation within the designated areas. The qualifying conditions and reliefs are set out in Sections 346-348. In general the qualifying expenditure will be allowed against the rental income from the property in question and from all other properties. The reliefs available are the same in all designated areas and the time limits for claiming the relief are as follows:

TCA97
s346-s348

(i) All designated areas other than Custom House Dock Area and Temple Bar

Relief is available for expenditure incurred on or before 31 July 1994.

TCA97
s325-s328

(ii) Customs House Dock Area

Relief is available for expenditure incurred on or before 24 January 1999. (See page 89 re extensions to 31 December 1999 and 30 June 2000.

1.13.3 Owner/Occupier Residential Accommodation

TCA97 s349

Individuals who are owner occupiers are entitled to an annual deduction from their income of 5% of the amount of the qualifying expenditure incurred by them in respect of qualifying premises for a period of ten years. The qualifying premises must be newly constructed or refurbished within the time limits outlined above. Qualifying expenditure is arrived at after deduction of any sum the individual received directly or indirectly from the State or any board established by the State, or any public or local authority.

If the qualifying expenditure in relation to qualifying premises is incurred by two or more persons, the Inspector of Taxes has powers to apportion the expenditure between the taxpayers. There is a right of appeal against the Inspector's decision to the Appeal Commissioners and if necessary to the Circuit Court. For each year that the allowance is granted, the qualifying premises must remain the individual's only or main residence.

1.13.4 Double Rent Allowance

TCA97 s345

This relief applies to all designated areas and the Customs House Docks area and is in respect of an industrial building which is deemed to be an industrial building by virtue of Section 323. A double rent deduction is allowed in computing the trading profits of a trade or profession for tax purposes.

The building must be let under a bona fide commercial lease to an unconnected person.

However, in order to exclude rent paid between persons who become connected after the lease has been entered into, any rent payable between connected persons will not qualify for the allowance, in the case of leases entered into on or after 21 April 1997.

The allowance will not be granted in respect of qualifying leases entered into on or after 6 May 1993, where the claimant or persons connected with the claimant, own other property which is subject to a claim for double rent allowance, unless it can be shown that the lease was not taken out for the sole or main reason of obtaining the double rent allowance.

The allowance is for a period of ten years commencing on the date on which the rent in respect of the premises is first payable. The relief cannot exceed the rent payable.

In order to qualify for the relief in respect of rents paid on or after 25 April 1992, qualifying capital expenditure must be incurred on the construction or refurbishment of the building in the qualifying period of the urban renewal relief scheme.

In the case of leases entered into on or after 6 May 1993, where the premises has been refurbished, the double rent allowance is only granted provided the capital expenditure on refurbishment equals at least 10% of the market value of the building immediately before the expenditure was incurred.

Where a qualifying lease is entered into on or after 21 April 1997, a rent payable between connected persons will not qualify for the double rent allowance.

1.13.5 Expenditure on Historic Buildings in Urban Renewal Areas

TCA97 SCh32 Para20

An individual may claim relief for expenditure incurred on repairing, restoring or maintaining a building which is occupied by him as his sole or main residence. The building must be determined by the Commissioners of Public Works to be a building which is of significant scientific, historical, architectural or aesthetic interest.

The relief applies to expenditure incurred between 24 May 1989 and 31 July 1994 and is offset as follows:-

> 25% of expenditure in the year of assessment in which it is incurred, and 5% per annum in the succeeding five years.

Chapter 1

1.14 TEMPLE BAR AREA OF DUBLIN

TCA97
s330-s338

The Temple Bar area of Dublin which falls between Westmoreland Street, Dame Street, Lord Edward Street and the river Liffey is part of the Urban Renewal areas.

The period within which qualifying expenditure must be incurred is from 30 January 1991 to 5 April 1999. However, this period has been extended to 31 December 1999, in the case of residential projects only provided 50% of the total cost of such projects was incurred on or before 5 April 1999.

The approval of Temple Bar Renewal Limited is required in respect of the expenditure incurred.

The reliefs available are:

For expenditure on the construction of commercial buildings (other than multi-storey car parks), industrial buildings allowances are available as follows:-

Owner occupier	up to 50% Free Depreciation or
	25% Initial Allowance
	2% Annual Allowance
	Maximum 50%
Lessors	25% Initial Allowance
	2% Annual Allowance
	Maximum 50%

For expenditure on the construction of multi-storey car parks and for qualifying refurbishment expenditure on existing buildings allowances are available as follows:

Owner occupier	up to 100% Free Depreciation or
	50% Initial Allowance
	4% Annual Allowance
	Maximum 100%
Lessors	50% Initial Allowance
	4% Annual Allowance
	Maximum 100%

For existing buildings on which refurbishment expenditure is incurred, the capital allowances are also given in respect of the purchase price of the building, but only if the amount of the refurbishment expenditure equals or exceeds the purchase price or, if lower, the market value of the building on 1 January 1991.

1.14.1 Expenditure on Rented Accommodation

TCA97
s334-s336

Reliefs are available for expenditure incurred on the provision of rented residential accommodation within Temple Bar. The qualifying conditions and reliefs are set out in Sections 334-336.

Income Tax

1.14.2 Owner/Occupier Residential Accommodation

TCA97 s337

Where expenditure is incurred by an individual on the construction of a qualifying premises used or to be used as his sole or main residence, an allowance equal to 5% of the construction expenditure is given for each of the first 10 years.

For expenditure incurred by an individual on the refurbishment of a qualifying premises, used or to be used as his sole or main residence, an allowance equal to 10% of the expenditure is given for each of the first 10 years. The allowance is also given on the purchase price of the building, but only if the amount of the refurbishment expenditure equals or exceeds the purchase price or, if lower, the market value of the building at 1 January 1991.

1.14.3 Double Rent Allowance

TCA97 s333

A person carrying on a trade or profession in a qualifying premises paying rent under a qualifying lease is entitled to a double rent allowance for 10 years (see page 91). This relief applies to both commercial premises and to industrial buildings. It is a condition of the relief that the building is one on which qualifying construction or refurbishment expenditure has been incurred in the relevant period.

1.14.4 Anti-Avoidance

Capital allowances arising out of an investment through a scheme or arrangement which provides facilities for the public, or a section of the public, to share income or gains arising from the acquisition are restricted to set off against rental income only.

The restriction does not apply to a scheme or an arrangement which, in the opinion of the Revenue Commissioners, is in accordance with a practice for the sharing of such income or gains which commonly prevailed in the State in the 5 years up to 30 January 1991 and the participants in which qualified for relief by way of set off of the capital allowances against income other than income from the building concerned.

Chapter 1

1.15 **URBAN RENEWAL SCHEME FROM 1 AUGUST 1994 – DESIGNATED AREA/STREET**

TCA97
s339-s350

An Urban Renewal Scheme applies for designated areas and streets in Dublin, Cork, Limerick, Waterford, Galway, Athlone, Ballina, Ballinasloe, Bray, Carlow, Castlebar, Clonmel, Drogheda, Dundalk, Dungarvan, Ennis, Enniscorthy, Kilkenny, Killarney, Letterkenny, Longford, Mallow, Monaghan, Mullingar, Navan, Nenagh, Newbridge, Portlaoise, Roscommon, Sligo, Tralee, Tullamore, Wexford, Wicklow.

The qualifying period commenced on 1 August 1994 and ended on 31 July 1997. However, the expiry date was extended to 31 July 1998 for projects in respect of which the relevant local authority can certify that at least 15% of the total cost of the project had been incurred before 31 July 1997.

The expiry date was further extended to 31 December 1998 provided the following conditions were met:-

(1) A certificate is obtained from the local authority in writing, that not less than 15% of the total cost of the expenditure on the building or structure had been incurred before 31 July 1998; and

(2) An application for planning permission had been received by the Planning Authority not later than 1 March 1998; and

(3) Where expenditure had not been fully incurred before 31 July 1998, the relevant authority gives a certificate, in writing, stating that in its opinion:

(a) The person had on 31 July 1997 a reasonable expectation that the expenditure would be incurred in full before 31 July 1998; and

(b) Failure to incur the expenditure was for bona fide commercial reasons due to a significant extent to a delay outside the direct control of the person including an unanticipated delay in obtaining planning permission or a fire certificate or legal proceedings in completing the acquisition of the site or the failure of a building contractor to fulfil his/her obligations or the need to respect any archaeological site or remains.

It should be noted that the Certification Guidelines issued by the Department of Environment in relation to the extension to 31 December 1998 (dated 13 February 1998) state that "a developer must make a formal application, in writing, to the relevant local authority as soon as practicable. The latest date for the receipt of applications was 31 March 1998."

A further extension from 31 December 1998 to 30 April 1999 applies in the case of residential projects only, which had previously been extended to 31 December 1998 and where the relevant local authority had issued a certificate certifying that at least 50% of the total residential cost of the project was incurred before 31 December 1998.

Income Tax

1.15.1 Industrial Buildings

TCA97 s341

(a) Designated Area

Expenditure incurred on the construction or refurbishment of a qualifying building qualifies for the following allowances:

Owner occupier	Up to 50% Free Depreciation or
	25% Initial Allowance
	4% Annual Allowance
	Maximum 100%
Lessors	25% Initial Allowance
	4% Annual Allowance
	Maximum 100%

A qualifying building is one in use for the purpose of a trade carried on in a factory, mill or similar premises or let on bona fide commercial terms.

(b) Designated Street

Allowances similar to those at (a) may be claimed on refurbishment expenditure on a building in existence on 1 August 1994 and which fronts onto a designated street.

However in order to qualify for the accelerated allowances, matching expenditure which qualifies for relief as expenditure on the conversion or refurbishment of residential premises must be incurred on the building. Where the refurbishment expenditure on the industrial element of the building exceeds the expenditure on the residential accommodation, no accelerated capital allowances may be claimed on the excess. However, the annual 4% allowance may be claimed on the excess.

A clawback of allowances cannot arise once 13 years have elapsed from the time the premises were first used as an industrial building.

1.15.2 Commercial Buildings

TCA97 s342

(a) Designated Area

Expenditure incurred on the construction or refurbishment of a qualifying building qualifies for the following allowances:

Owner occupier	Up to 50% Free Depreciation or
	25% Initial Allowance
	2% Annual Allowance
	Maximum 50%
Lessor	25% Initial Allowance
	2% Annual Allowance
	Maximum 50%

Chapter 1

A qualifying building is one in use for the purposes of a trade or let on bona fide commercial terms, whether or not it is in use for the purposes of a trade.

Office accommodation in the county boroughs of Dublin, Cork, Limerick, Galway and Waterford is excluded from the definition of a commercial building except where the capital expenditure in relation to the office development is less than 10% of the total capital expenditure of the entire building. Office accommodation in all other areas qualifies as commercial.

(b) Designated Street

Allowances similar to those at (a) may be claimed for refurbishment expenditure on a building in existence on 1 August 1994, and which fronts onto a designated street.

However in order to qualify for the accelerated allowances, matching expenditure which qualifies for relief as expenditure on the conversion or refurbishment of residential premises must be incurred on the building. Where the refurbishment expenditure on the commercial element of the building exceeds the expenditure on the residential accommodation, no accelerated capital allowances may be claimed on the excess.

A clawback of allowances cannot arise once 13 years have elapsed since the premises were first used as a commercial premises.

1.15.3 Double Rent Allowance

TCA97 s345

A double rent allowance may be claimed by lessees of certain industrial and commercial premises, similar to the existing double rent allowance under the old Urban Renewal Relief (see page 91). The allowance applies to premises in designated areas only.

The allowance may also be claimed for rent paid for a building or structure used for the purposes of the trade of hotel keeping. However, the deduction is dependent on the lessor disclaiming the entitlement to capital allowances.

1.15.4 Rented Residential Accommodation

TCA97 s346-s350

(a) Construction

Expenditure incurred on the construction of rented accommodation in a designated area only may be claimed as a deduction against the rental income from the premises or other rental income. The maximum floor size is 90 square metres for a flat/maisonette or 125 square metres in respect of expenditure incurred on or after 12 April 1995, and 125 square metres for a house. The relief may be claimed over a ten year period.

Income Tax

The property must be let on an arm's length basis. A clawback of the relief arises where the property ceases to be a qualifying premises or the ownership of the lessor's interest passes to another party, within the ten year period. Where a clawback occurs, the original relief granted may be claimed by the new owner but cannot exceed the price paid by the new owner.

(b) **Conversion**

Expenditure incurred on the conversion into rented residential accommodation of buildings situated in designated areas or fronting onto designated streets may be claimed as a deduction against the rental income from the premises or other rental income. Conversion expenditure is only allowed to the extent that it is attributable to qualifying residential units.

(c) **Refurbishment**

Expenditure incurred on the conversion into rented residential accommodation of buildings situated in designated areas or fronting onto designated streets, may be claimed as a deduction against rental income from the premises or other rental income. The premises must before and after refurbishment contain two or more residential units.

A certificate of reasonable cost from the Minister of the Environment is required in respect of the conversion, refurbishment or reconstruction of rented residential accommodation.

1.15.5 Owner/Occupier Residential Accommodation

TCA97 s349

Expenditure incurred by an individual on the construction or refurbishment of owner/occupier residential accommodation in a designated area or on the refurbishment of such accommodation in a designated street may be claimed for income tax purposes.

An annual deduction of 5% (in the case of construction expenditure) and 10% (in the case of refurbishment expenditure) may be claimed. The deduction is allowed against total income. Site costs and any State or local authority grants or payments are excluded from expenditure. The relief may be claimed annually for 10 years.

The dwelling must be occupied as the sole or main residence of the individual who must be the first owner/occupier after the expenditure has been incurred. In the case of construction expenditure, the maximum floor size for a flat or maisonette is 90 square metres or 125 square metres in respect of expenditure incurred on or after 12 April 1995, and for a house 125 square metres. In the case of refurbishment expenditure, the maximum floor size for any property is 125 square metres.

There is no clawback of relief where the owner ceases to occupy or own the premises.

Chapter 1

1.16   URBAN RENEWAL – ENTERPRISE AREAS

TCA97 s339
TCA97 s343

Section 343 provides for tax allowances for "enterprise areas" in Dublin, Cork, Galway and Wexford and provision is also included in the Section for the designation by order of areas immediately adjacent to seven regional airports as enterprise areas. The airports in question are those at Cork, Donegal, Galway, Kerry, Knock, Sligo and Waterford. The designation order will be made by the Minister for Finance after consultation with the Minister for Transport, Energy and Communications. An "enterprise area" is an area designated under the urban renewal scheme by the Minister for Enterprise & Employment. The allowances are available on the construction or refurbishment of premises used by qualifying companies carrying on qualifying trading operations in these areas.

In the case of areas designated under the 1995 Finance Act, the qualifying period commenced retrospectively on 1 August 1994 and ended on 31 July 1997 and runs in conjunction with the 1994 Urban Renewal Scheme (see page 94). However, the expiry date was extended to 31 December 1998 for projects in respect of which a local authority can certify that at least 15% of the total cost of the project had been incurred before 31 July 1997.

In the case of areas designated under the 1997 Finance Act, the qualifying period is 1 July 1997 to 31 December 1999 and for the areas adjacent to the regional airports, from the date specified in the designation order until 31 December 1999.

The Minister for Enterprise & Employment must certify that a company is a qualifying company and the company must be either a manufacturing company liable to the 10% rate of corporation tax, or a company engaged in qualifying internationally traded service activities and has been approved for financial assistance under a scheme administered by Forfas, Forbairt, Industrial Development Agency (Ireland), or Údarás na Gaeltachta.

TCA97 s339
TCA97 s343

The service activities eligible are:- data processing, software development, technical and consulting, commercial laboratory, healthcare, research and development, media recording, training, publishing, financial, administrative headquarters, and in the case of the areas adjacent to the seven regional airports, freight forwarding and certain allied services.

The allowances, which may be claimed in respect of either industrial or commercial buildings are as follows:-

Owner occupier	Up to 50% free depreciation or 25% initial allowance*, plus 4% annual allowance Maximum 100%
Lessors	25% initial allowance* plus 4% annual allowance Maximum 100%

Note: The initial allowance is 50% in Airport Enterprise Areas in respect of expenditure incurred on or after 1 January 1998

Tenants who lease new or refurbished premises in respect of which allowances have been claimed will be entitled to double rent allowance and rates remission. The termination dates for entering into qualifying leases for double rent allowances are as follows:

(i) Enterprise Areas – Finance Act, 1995 – leases entered into on or before 31 July 1999;

(ii) Enterprise Areas – Finance Act, 1997, – leases entered into on or before 31 December 1999;

(iii) "Airport" Enterprises Areas – no double rent relief available.

(iv) Multi-storey car parks – 31 July 1997 or 30 June 1998 where the relevant local authority had certified by 30 September 1998 that 15 per cent of the total cost of the project had been incurred before 1 July 1998. Since the definition of a qualifying lease is one entered into within the qualifying period or within one year of the end of such period, leases in respect of multi-storey car parks can be granted up to 30 July 1998 or 30 June, 1999.

A clawback of allowances cannot arise once 13 years have elapsed from the time the premises were first used as a qualifying building, or in the case of refurbishment, 13 years after the expenditure was incurred.

Chapter 1

1.17 URBAN RENEWAL – RESORT AREAS

TCA97 s351-s359

Section 351 provides for a scheme of tax reliefs aimed at promoting the renewal and improvement of certain resort areas. The areas in question are Achill, Arklow, Ballybunion, Bettystown/Laytown/Mosney, Bundoran, Clogherhead, Clonakilty, Courtown, Enniscrone, Kilkee, Lahinch, Salthill, Tramore, Westport and Youghal.

TCA97 s351

The qualifying period commenced on 1 July 1995 and ended on 30 June 1998. However, the expiry date was extended to 30 June 1999 where the local authority gave a certificate, in writing, before 30 September 1998, that the person constructing, converting or refurbishing the building has satisfied them that not less than 15% of the total cost of the building or structure (including site cost) has been incurred by 30 June 1998.

A further extension from 30 June 1999 to 31 December 1999 applies where at least 50% of the total expenditure was incurred on or before 30 June 1999 and a certificate to that effect has been issued by the relevant local authority on or before 30 September 1999.

1.17.1 Industrial Buildings

TCA97 s352

Expenditure on the construction or refurbishment of certain industrial buildings or structures, namely hotels, holiday camps and holiday cottages registered with Bord Failte Eireann qualifies for the following allowances:-

Owner occupier	Up to 75% Free Depreciation or 50% Initial Allowance, and 5% Annual Allowance Maximum 100%
Lessors	50% Initial Allowance 5% Annual Allowance Maximum 100%

In the case of refurbishment expenditure, the reliefs are available only if the expenditure incurred is not less than 20% of the market value of the building or structure immediately before the expenditure was incurred.

1.17.2 Tourism Facilities

TCA97 s353

Similar allowances to those outlined above under the heading "Industrial Buildings" are available for expenditure incurred on the construction or refurbishment of buildings or structures in use in the operation of "qualifying tourism facilities". These include tourist accommodation facilities which are registered or listed under the Tourist Traffic Acts, eg B & B accommodation and such other classes of facilities as may be approved by the Minister for Tourism and Trade. A list of both the qualifying tourist accommodation facilities and non-accommodation tourism facilities is set out below.

Qualifying Tourist Accommodation Facilities:

— Hotels

— Guesthouses

— Caravan and camping sites

— Holiday hostels

— Youth hostels

— Holiday camps

— Holiday cottages

— Holiday apartments

— Bed and breakfast establishments

Qualifying Non-Accommodation Tourism Facilities:

— Leisure/sports facilities (eg swimming, water sports, tennis, squash, golf, angling, equestrian).

— Marina, mooring and breakwater facilities.

— Indoor/outdoor adventure and amusement centres/parks.

— English/Irish language schools.

— Theme/Interpretative Centres/Parks.

— Tourist information facilities.

— Craft exhibition and demonstration centres.

— Entertainment facilities, eg theatres, bowling alleys, amusement arcades (excluding activities licensed under the 1956 Gaming and Lotteries Act).

— Restaurants/cafes.

— Licensed premises, including existing retail outlets which are an integral part of and are located in the premises.

— Car hire operations.

— Car parks.

— Retail outlets which are an integral part of and located in tourist buildings qualifying under Sections 47 and 48 of the 1995 Finance Act.

— Existing heritage buildings with public access (improvements to).

— Existing activities listed under the 1956 Gaming and Lotteries Act (improvements to).

A clawback of allowances cannot arise where the building or structure is retained for at least 11 years after its construction or after

Chapter 1

the refurbishment has been carried out and provided the building or structure remains registered or listed during the 11 year period.

TCA97 s355 In the case of holiday cottages, holiday apartments and other self catering accommodation, Section 355 restricts the allowances available as follows:-

(i) both the double rent allowance and capital allowances cannot apply, and

(ii) capital allowances can only be offset against rental income, including rental income from other sources, or against the income from the trade of operating holiday cottages, apartments or self-catering accommodation where a trade is being carried on.

However the above restrictions will not apply where certain steps had been taken before 5 April 1996 in relation to the planning or development of such cottages, apartments or self catering accommodation.

TCA97 s354 Tenants carrying on a trade or profession in a qualifying building will be entitled to a double rent allowance for 10 years (see page 91).

1.17.3 Rented Residential Accommodation

TCA97 s356-s359 Allowances similar to those available under Sections 325-329 (formerly "Section 23") may also be claimed for expenditure incurred on the construction, conversion or refurbishment of certain rented residential accommodation. Similar provisions to those applying to Sections 325-329, also apply in relation to the size of qualifying premises, qualifying leases, retention of property for 10 years, clawback of allowances etc.

Qualifying premises means a house, the site of which is wholly within a resort area, which is used solely as a dwelling and the total floor area of which is not less than 30 square metres and not more than 125 square metres where the house is a self contained flat, or not less than 35 square metres and not more than 125 square metres in any other case.

However, additional provisions have been introduced to ensure that qualifying premises are available primarily for letting to tourists. A premises will not be a qualifying premises unless:-

(i) it is used primarily for letting to and occupation by tourists with or without prior agreement, and

(ii) it is used and occupied for no other purpose during the months April to October in each year.

In addition, the house must not be let or leased to or occupied by any person for more than two consecutive months at any one time or for more than six months in any year. A register of lessees of the house must also be maintained.

The allowance available is 100% of the expenditure incurred exclusive of site costs and relief may be claimed against all rental income.

In the case of expenditure on conversion and refurbishment only that part of expenditure incurred on the conversion or refurbishment of a building into qualifying units is allowable. Conversion or refurbishment expenditure relating to part of a building other than qualifying units, is excluded from the relief.

The allowance in respect of expenditure on refurbishment will only apply, in the case of a building which, before and after the refurbishment, contains one or more residential unit and the expenditure must be certified by the Minister for the Environment to have been necessary to ensure the suitability as a dwelling of any residential unit in the building.

Chapter 1

1.18   **URBAN RENEWAL – ISLANDS**

TCA97
s360-s365

Sections 360-365 provide for a scheme of incentives aimed at encouraging persons to reside on a number of designated islands off the south and west coasts of Ireland. The islands in question are in the administrative counties of Cork, Donegal, Galway, Limerick, Mayo and Sligo.

The qualifying period commenced on 1 August 1996 and ends on 31 July 1999.

However, the expiry date has been extended to 31 December 1999 where at least 50% of the total cost of the project has been incurred on or before 31 July 1999 and a certificate to that effect, has been issued by the relevant local authority on or before 31 October 1999.

1.18.1   **Rented Residential Accommodation**

Relief is available for 100% of the cost of construction, conversion or refurbishment expenditure against the rental income from that building. In the case of refurbishment, the building must, before and after refurbishment, contain two or more residential units. The maximum floor area is 125 sq metres for any type of dwelling. A certificate of reasonable cost from the Minister for the Environment is required in respect of the conversion, refurbishment or reconstruction expenditure.

The property must be let under a qualifying lease for a minimum period of twelve months.

A clawback of relief will arise where the property ceases to be a qualifying premises or the lessor's interest passes to another party within a ten year period. Where a clawback occurs the original relief may be claimed by the new owner but cannot exceed the price paid by the new owner.

1.18.2   **Owner/Occupier Residential Accommodation**

An owner/occupier may claim a deduction of 5% of the cost of construction or refurbishment of owner occupied residential accommodation. Qualifying expenditure for this purpose is exclusive of site costs and all state or local authority grants or payments. The individual who incurs the expenditure on construction or refubishment must be the first owner and first occupier of the dwelling after the expenditure has been incurred. The relief may be claimed in each of the first ten years of the life of the dwelling following construction or refurbishment provided that the dwelling is the sole or main residence of the individual.

The floor area must not exceed 125 sq metres and a certificate of reasonable cost from the Minister for the Environment is required in respect of the expenditure. There is no clawback of relief where the owner ceases to occupy or own the dwelling at any time after first occupation. There is no allowance available to a second owner.

Income Tax

1.19 URBAN RENEWAL - DUBLIN DOCKLANDS

TCA97
s366-s372

Sections 366-372 provide for a scheme of incentives for the Dublin Docklands Area. The areas which may benefit are outlined in the Dublin Docklands Development Authority Act 1997. The qualifying period for incurring expenditure is 1 July 1997 to 30 June 2000.

1.19.1 Industrial Buildings

TCA97 s368

Expenditure incurred on the construction or refurbishment of a qualifying industrial building qualifies for the following allowances

Owner occupier	Up to 100% Free Depreciation or
	50% Initial Allowance
	4% Annual Allowance
	Maximum Allowance
Lessors	50% Initial Allowance
	4% Annual Allowance
	Maximum 100%

Refurbishment expenditure only qualifies if it is equal to or more than 10% of the market value of the building before refurbishment.

1.19.2 Commercial Premises

TCA97 s369

Allowances at the same rates as for industrial buildings (see above) may be claimed on the cost of construction or refurbishment of commercial premises including multi-storey car parks and offices.

There is however provision for the above allowances to be reduced to one half. This will occur where a Ministerial Order designating an area as a qualifying area makes specific provision for halved allowances.

1.19.3 Hotels

TCA97 s370

Hotels do not benefit from the accelerated allowances. Relief is available at 15% per annum for 6 years and 10% in year 7 for construction/refurbishment expenditure.

Capital allowances or double rent allowances may be claimed in respect of a hotel, but not both.

1.19.4 Balancing Allowances/Charges

TCA97 s369

A building may be sold after 13 years without suffering a clawback of allowances.

1.19.5 Double Rent Allowance

TCA97 s370

A double rent allowance for ten years is available to lessees for rent paid under a lease of a building in respect of which capital allowances have been claimed (see page 91).

Chapter 1

1.19.6 **Residential Accommodation**

TCA97 s371 Owner occupiers may claim a deduction of 5% per annum for 10 years in respect of newly constructed residences and 10% per annum for 10 years in respect of the cost of refurbishment of such residences. Relief is only available by reference to the work which actually takes place in the qualifying period.

1.20 URBAN RENEWAL - 1998-1999 SCHEME

TCA97 s372B

The 1998 Finance Act together with the Urban Renewal Act 1998, provide for a new scheme of incentives for certain urban areas.

A total of 43 towns and cities have been designated on the basis of Integrated Area Plans (IAPs) submitted by local authorities.

The qualifying periods for these incentives are as follows:-

Residential premises	1 March 1999 to 28 February 2002
Industrial/Commercial premises	Awaiting approval from EU Commission under State Aid rules

1.20.1 Industrial Buildings

TCA97 s372C

Expenditure incurred on the construction or refurbishment of a qualifying industrial building will qualify for the following allowances:-

Owner occupiers	Up to 50% Free Depreciation or 25% Initial Allowance 4% Annual Allowance Maximum 100%
Lessors	25% Initial Allowance 4% Annual Allowance Maximum 100%

Refurbishment expenditure only qualifies if it is equal to or more than 10% of the market value of the building before refurbishment.

1.20.2 Commercial Premises

TCA97 s372D

Allowances at the same rates as for industrial buildings (see above) may be claimed in respect of expenditure incurred for the construction or refurbishment of qualifying commercial buildings.

However the amount of expenditure which qualifies for allowances is restricted to 50% of the qualifying expenditure.

1.20.3 Balancing Allowances/Charges

A clawback of allowances will not occur on an event arising more than 13 years after the building was first used or more than 13 years after the expenditure on refurbishment was incurred.

1.20.4 Double Rent Allowance

TCA97 s372E

A double rent allowance is available to lessees for rent paid under a qualifying lease of a building in respect of which capital allowances have been claimed. In the case of hotels, the double rent allowance is

Chapter 1

only available if the person entitled to the capital allowances disclaims those allowances.

1.20.5 Rented Residential Accommodation

TCA97 s372F — "Section 23" type relief is granted against all rental income for expenditure incurred on the cost of construction (excluding site cost) of rented residential accommodation.

TCA97 s372G — Relief is granted against all rental income for expenditure on the conversion into rented residential accommodation of a building which had not previously been in use as a dwelling or the conversion into two or more houses of a building which, prior to the conversion, had not been in use as a single dwelling.

1.20.6 Owner-occupied Residential Accommodation

TCA97 s372I — Relief is granted by way of deduction from total income of the owner occupier of an amount equal to 5% of construction expenditure and 10% of refurbishment expenditure incurred on owner-occupied residential accommodation. The individual incurring the expenditure must be the first owner and occupier of the property after the expenditure has been incurred.

The relief may be claimed in each of the first 10 years of the life of the dwelling following construction or refurbishment provided that the dwelling is the sole or main residence of the individual.

1.21 RURAL RENEWAL SCHEME - 1998

TCA97 s372L

The 1998 Finance Act provided for a new scheme of incentives targeted at the Upper Shannon Region – covering all of the counties of Leitrim and Longford and certain parts of Cavan, Roscommon and Sligo.

The qualifying periods for these incentives are as follows:-

Residential Premises

Lessors	1 June 1998 to 31 December 2001
Owner Occupiers	6 April 1999 to 31 December 2001
Industrial/Commercial premises	Awaiting approval from EU Commission under State Aid rules

1.21.1 Industrial Buildings

TCA97 s372M

Expenditure incurred on the construction or refurbishment of qualifying industrial buildings, including piers and jetties will qualify for the following allowances:-

Owner Occupiers	Up to 50% Free Depreciation or 25% Initial Allowance 4% Annual Allowance Maximum 100%
Lessors	25% Initial Allowance 4% Annual Allowance Maximum 100%

Refurbishment expenditure only qualifies if it is equal to or more than 10% of the market value of the building before refurbishment.

1.21.2 Commercial Premises

TCA97 s372N

Allowances at the same rates as for industrial buildings (see above) may be claimed in respect of expenditure incurred on the construction or refurbishment of qualifying commercial premises, including certain infrastructural projects such as the provision of sewerage facilities, water supplies or roads for public purposes where these have been approved by a local authority.

However, the amount of expenditure which qualifies for allowances is restricted to 50% of the qualifying expenditure.

1.21.3 Balancing Allowances/Charges

A clawback of allowances will not occur on an event arising more than 13 years after the building is first used or more than 13 years after the expenditure on refurbishment was incurred.

Chapter 1

1.21.4 **Double Rent Allowance**

TCA97 s372O A double rent allowance for 10 years is available to lessers for rent paid under a qualifying lease of a building on which allowances have been claimed.

1.21.5 **Rented Residential Accommodation**

TCA97 s372P;
TCA97 s372Q "Section 23" type relief is granted against all rental income for the cost of construction (excluding site costs) of rented residential accommodation. Relief is granted against all rental income for the cost of conversion into rented residential accommodation of a building which had not previously been in use as a dwelling or the conversion into two or more houses of a building which, prior to the conversion had not been in use as a dwelling, or had been in use as a single dwelling.

TCA97 s372R Relief is granted against all rental income for expenditure incurred on refurbishment of a building which before and after refurbishment contains one or more residential units.

Leases must be for a minimum of 3 months and the accommodation must be the sole or main residence of the lesee throughout the period of the lease.

1.21.6 **Owner occupied Residential Accommodation**

Owner occupiers of residential accommodation may claim a deduction of 5% per annum for 10 years in the case of construction expenditure and 10% per annum for 10 years in the case of refurbishment expenditure.

The individual incurring the expenditure must be the first owner and occupier of the dwelling after the expenditure has been incurred and the dwelling must be the sole or main residence of the individual.

1.22 SCHEDULE E

The income chargeable under Schedule E consists, in general, of the emoluments of all offices and employments, together with pensions and annuities. Expenses allowances and benefits in kind, as well as ex-gratia payments and other compensation payments are assessable under Schedule E. Emoluments paid in respect of an office or employment either before its commencement or after its cessation are liable to income tax under Schedule E.

1.22.1 Social Welfare Benefits

TCA97 s126

Certain social welfare benefits are deemed to be profits or gains arising from an employment and are taxable as follows:

    from 6.4.93   Disability/injury benefit*

    from 6.4.94   Unemployment/pay related benefit*

* From 6 April 1995, the first £10 pw of unemployment benefit and all payments in respect of child dependants are excluded from the taxation of unemployment benefit and disability benefit.

* Disability benefit payable for 18 days (3 weeks) in the tax year 1997/98 and 36 days (6 weeks) in subsequent years is exempt from tax.

Payments made under systematic short time working arrangements are exempt.

1.22.2 Basis of Assessment

TCA97 s112

All income assessable under Schedule E is assessed on the actual income of the year of assessment, regardless of whether taxed under PAYE or not.

1.22.3 Deductions

TCA97 s114

The deductions available in computing income for Schedule E purposes are confined to expenses incurred wholly, exclusively and necessarily in the performance of the duties of the office or employment. There is no deduction for expenses incurred in placing an individual in a position to perform the duties of the office or employment eg travel from home to place of employment. No deduction is allowed in respect of entertainment expenses.

TCA97 s284

In addition to the deduction for expenses, there is an allowance for wear and tear on any wasting asset used by an individual in the course of performing the duties of his office or employment, eg private motor car.

Chapter 1

1.22.4 **Round Sum Expense Allowances**

Where a round sum payment is made, the employer is obliged to deduct income tax under PAYE. The employee must then make a claim to the Inspector of Taxes justifying the expenses as having been incurred wholly, exclusively and necessarily in the performance of the duties of the office or employment. In certain circumstances the Inspector of Taxes may agree to dispense with the necessity to deduct income tax and thus avoid the procedure of an annual claim to expenses.

1.22.5 **Benefits-in-Kind**

Benefits-in-kind are assessable under Schedule E as a perquisite of an office or employment. All directors of bodies corporate are assessable on benefits-in-kind as well as employees whose emoluments, including any benefit-in-kind and before deducting relief for any expenses, amount to £1,500 or more per annum, are also assessable.

Where an asset owned by an employer is provided for the private use of a director or employee for free or less than full consideration, the benefit-in-kind is computed on the annual value of the use of the asset in addition to current expenditure incurred by the employer in connection with the asset. The main areas under which assessments to benefits-in-kind arise are as follows:

1.22.6 **(i) Cars**

TCA97 s121

(a) the benefit-in-kind is the amount by which the cash equivalent of the benefit of the car for the year exceeds the aggregate of the amounts which the employee makes good to the employer in respect of the cost of providing or running the car.

(b) For the years 1992/93 et seq, the cash equivalent is calculated by the formula:

30% x OMV where

OMV = The original market value of the car, ie its retail price before registration in the State.

(c) The figure of 30% is reduced by the following:

(i) 4.5% OMV where no part of the cost of the fuel used in the course of the private use of the car by the employee is borne by the employer.

(ii) 3% OMV where no part of the cost of the insurance of the car is borne by the employer.

(iii) 3% OMV where no part of the cost of repairing and servicing of the car is borne by the employer.

(iv) 1% OMV where no part of the cost of the road tax is borne by the employer.

(d) Where business mileage exceeds 15,000 the cash equivalent as calculated above is reduced by applying the percentages set out in the following table.

Business Mileage		Percentage Charge
Exceeding Miles	Not Exceeding Miles	
15,000	16,000	97.5
16,000	17,000	95
17,000	18,000	90
18,000	19,000	85
19,000	20,000	80
20,000	21,000	75
21,000	22,000	70
22,000	23,000	65
23,000	24,000	60
24,000	25,000	55
25,000	26,000	50
26,000	27,000	45
27,000	28,000	40
28,000	29,000	35
29,000	30,000	30
30,000		25

(e) From 6 April 1996, if an employee elects in writing to the Inspector of Taxes, the benefit in kind attributable to the company car may be reduced by 20% provided the employee completes at least 5,000 business miles and spends more than 70% of his working time away from the employer's business premises.

The employee must work on average at least twenty hours each week and keep a log book which must record the following:-

- mileage

- nature and location of business transacted, and

- amount of time spent away from employer's business premises.

Employers must sign the log book to confirm to the best of their knowledge and belief that the details are correct.

(f) Cars included in car pools are treated as not having been available for the private use of employees if all of the following conditions are satisfied:

(i) The car is made available to, and actually used by, more than one employee and in the case of each of them it is made available to him by reason of his employment, but is

Chapter 1

not ordinarily used by any one of the employees to the exclusion of the others

(ii) Any private use by each employee is incidental to other use.

(iii) The car is not normally kept overnight at or in the vicinity of any of the employees' homes.

1.22.7 **(ii) Vans**

Where an employee has the private use of a van, the benefit in kind is, in practice, calculated as follows:

$$\text{Benefit in Kind} = C \times \frac{\text{Annual Private Mileage}}{\text{Total Annual Mileage}} \quad \text{Where}$$

C = Annual value (cost of vehicle x 12.5%) plus total running expenses.

1.22.8 **(iii) Accommodation**

TCA97 s118

Where the employer makes living or other accommodation available for a director or employee the benefit in kind is the amount which could reasonably be expected to be obtained on a yearly letting if the tenant paid tenant's rates and if the landlord undertook to bear the cost of repairs, insurance and any other expenses necessary to command that rent. Where the living accommodation is owned by the employer the amount referred to is, in practice, calculated as 8% of the current market value of the accommodation. In addition any other current expenses borne by the employer in relation to the living accommodation form part of the benefit.

Any amount made good to the employer by the director or employee is deducted in arriving at the benefit in kind.

1.22.9 **(iv) Interest Paid at a Preferential Rate**

TCA97 s122

A preferential loan is a non arms-length loan made to an employee by his/her employer. The employee is subject to income tax on the interest benefit as determined by the excess of the specified rate over the preferential rate. The specified rates are 6% in respect of loans which are qualifying home loans and 10% in all other cases.

An interest free loan will be deemed to have arisen where there is an unpaid balance due on the allotment of shares to employees or directors by the employing company. If any unpaid balance is written off in favour of the director or employee the amount written off is deemed to be a taxable emolument.

Where such shares are sold at a price above market value the excess is treated as a taxable emolument.

Where an individual is taxed in respect of preferential interest on a house mortgage, the figure is deemed to be interest paid for tax purposes and is an allowable deduction subject to the marital status class limit of that individual. Where an employee has a loan from his employer and the loan is released or written off in whole or in part, the amount written off is assessed to tax under Schedule E or Case III Schedule D. This charge to tax is also deemed to be interest paid. Details of Preferential Loans made or released or of interest waived should be included in the P35 return.

1.22.10 Benefit-in-Kind Exemptions

A number of benefits are specifically exempt from income tax as follows:-

1.22.11 (i) Works of Art

TCA97 s236

Where a company incurs expenses in connection with an art object owned by the company and which is on loan to a director or employee and displayed in a significant building or approved garden (see page 137), owned or occupied by that director or employee, no benefit-in-kind arises.

An art object is any work of art or a scientific collection which is determined by the Minister for Arts, Culture and the Gaeltacht to be an object which is intrinsically of significant national, scientific, historical or aesthetic interest and to which the Revenue Commissioners consider reasonable access for viewing has been afforded. This access must be similar to that afforded to significant buildings (see page 137) and the exemption may be withdrawn where the Revenue Commissioners consider that reasonable access has not been afforded.

The exemption applies for the years 1994/95 et seq. There is however provision that the exemption from benefit-in-kind may be claimed back as far as 1982/83 once the individual can show to the Revenue Commissioners that reasonable access and viewing facilities were provided to the public on the same basis as access was afforded to the significant building or approved garden in which the object was kept.

1.22.12 (ii) Bus/Train Passes

TCA97 s118

Any benefit-in-kind arising from the provision of an annual or monthly bus or train pass by an employer to an employee or director is exempt from income tax. The exemption will only apply in respect of a bus/train pass issued in respect of a scheduled licensed passenger transport service.

Chapter 1

1.22.13 **(iii) Childcare Services**

TCA97 s118

Any benefit arising from certain childcare services provided by employers to employees on a free or subsidised basis is exempt from income tax. The exemption will apply where the childcare service is either provided on premises which are made available by the employer alone, or where the employer provides the service jointly with other participants (e.g. other employers) on premises made available by one or more participants in the joint scheme. In such circumstances the employer must be wholly or partly responsible for both financing and managing the service. In addition, the childcare service must meet requirements of the Childcare (Pre-School Services) Regulations, 1996.

1.22.14 **Employee Share Schemes**

There are a number of schemes operated by employers whereby shares in the employer company are allocated to employees, or whereby employees are given options to acquire shares in the employer company, as follows:-

1.22.15 **(i) Rights over Assets**

TCA97 s128

A charge to tax arises on the date of exercise of rights over assets (including options) by reference to the difference between the market value of the asset at that date and the price paid for the asset together with the price paid for the right. If the right is capable of being exercised later than 7 years after it has been obtained, a tax charge is also imposed on the date the right is granted by reference to the difference between the value of the right and the price which is paid for it. Any income tax paid at this stage may be set off against income tax payable when the right is exercised. In addition any amount assessable to income tax is deemed to be part of the cost for capital gains tax purposes.

1.22.16 **(ii) Share Subscription Schemes**

TCA97 s479

Where an eligible employee of a qualifying company subscribes for eligible shares in the company, he is entitled, in estimating the amount of his total income for the year of assessment in which the shares are issued, to a deduction of an amount equal to the amount of the subscription. The maximum deduction for the years 1996/97 et seq is £5,000. The conditions for this relief are as follows:

(a) The individual subscribes for the shares.

(b) The deduction is granted for the tax year in which the shares are issued.

(c) The individual takes up new ordinary shares in the company.

(d) The shares are issued in a company which is resident and incorporated in the State and is a trading company or a holding company.

(e) Where the individual sells the shares within 3 years of the date of acquisition, any income tax relief granted is withdrawn by reference to the tax year in which it was originally given. If however the sale takes place between 4 and 5 years of acquisition only 75% of the relief will be withdrawn.

(f) The relief will not be withdrawn where the employee ceases employment with the particular company, where he ceases to be a resident or where he ceases to be a full-time employee.

(g) An amount equivalent to the tax deduction granted is excluded from the base cost of the asset in calculating capital gains tax liability on the sale of the shares.

1.22.17 (iii) Approved Profit Sharing Schemes (APSS)

TCA97
s509-s518

In general, the purposes of APSS's are as follows:-

(a) To give companies a tax deduction, subject to certain restrictions, for the costs of providing shares for employees for the purposes of profit sharing schemes and for the costs of running the schemes.

(b) To give the recipient employee exemption from income tax on the grant to him of shares up to certain limits.

(c) To grant the employee favourable income tax treatment on any growth in the value of the shares

The main features of such schemes are:

(a) The scheme must be established under a trust deed and the scheme and trust deed must be approved by the Revenue Authorities.

(b) The costs to a company in setting up a scheme, in providing shares for employees under a scheme and the running costs thereof are, subject to certain limitations, tax deductible.

(c) Although trustees must hold the shares, they are appropriated to employees. An employee is exempt from income tax on shares received to the value of £10,000 for the tax years 1995/96 et seq.

Subject to certain conditions, this may be increased, on a once off basis, to £30,000 in respect of shares which previously had been held in an ESOT as security for borrowings by the ESOT. In particular the shares in question must have been so held in the ESOT for a minimum period of 10 years.

Trustees are not liable to capital gains tax on the appropriation of shares, or on the sale of shares on the open market and to the extent that such proceeds are used to repay monies borrowed by those trustees including the payment of interest on such borrowings.

(d) The employee must hold the shares for more than three years in order to avoid an income tax penalty. If the shares are sold within three years, income tax is charged at 100% of the value of the shares.

If within the three year period the employee ceases to be an employee of the company, or has reached pensionable age as defined in Section 2, Social Welfare (Consolidation) Act 1993, income tax is charged at 50% of the value of the shares.

However, with effect from 27 March 1998 this holding period will not apply where shares pass or are transferred from an employee share ownership trust (ESOT) to an approved profit sharing scheme (APSS) provided the following conditions are met:-

(i) immediately prior to the transfer, the ESOT had held the shares for at least three years; and

(ii) the participating employee must have been a beneficiary of the ESOT for the three year period ending on the date on which the shares are transferred.

Where the conditions are met, the participants will be able to dispose of his or her shares without any income tax implications immediately he or she receives them through the APSS.

Where the shares are held for a period of less than three years in an ESOT, the holding period in the APSS for the exemption to apply will be reduced proportionately.

(e) Scheme shares may, subject to certain conditions, be subject to a restriction imposed by a company's Articles of Association requiring employees to dispose of shares on leaving the company.

(f) A disposal of shares is treated as a disposal by the employee for purposes of capital gains tax. Any amount assessed to income tax is not deducted in computing capital gains.

(g) While the trustees hold the shares the employee is absolutely entitled to the shares as against the trustees and he is also entitled to any dividends which arise thereon.

(h) Participation in the scheme is determined on the following basis:

(i) Participation in the scheme is open to every full-time director or full time and part time employee who has been such for a qualifying period (which must not exceed 3 years).

(ii) Shares may be appropriated only to an individual who, at the time is (or was within the preceding 18 months or 15 years, where certain conditions are met) a director or employee.

(iii) Shares may not be allotted to any individual who has a material interest (more than 15 per cent of the ordinary shares) in the company where it is a close company.

(iv) All participating directors or employees must be eligible to participate on similar terms.

(i) The shares must be ordinary shares of the company and must be quoted on a recognised Stock Exchange, or, if not so quoted, be shares in a company which is either controlled by a company whose shares are so quoted or be shares in a company not under the control of another company.

(j) An APSS may not be approved by the Revenue Commissioners unless they are satisfied that it is not intended solely to confer benefits on the directors and higher paid employees of a group of companies. In addition, the Commissioners may not approve an APSS if they consider that there are features in the scheme which would act as a disincentive to employees of the company to participate in the scheme.

1.22.18 (iv) Employee Share Ownership Trusts (ESOT)

TCA97 s519

The main features of ESOTs are as follows:-

(a) The ESOT must be established by a company (the founding company) which must not be controlled by another company, and it must extend to all companies which the founding company controls. However with regard to ESOTs approved on or after 27 March 1998, the founding company has the option of selecting the companies it wants to include in the ESOT.

(b) Three alternative forms of trustees are provided for, ie majority employee representation, a paritarian trust with equal company/employee representation or a single corporate trustee with equal company/employee representation on the board of directors.

(c) All employees and full-time directors of the founding company or a group company who have been such for a qualifying period of not more than 3 years, and are chargeable to tax under Schedule E, must be eligible to be beneficiaries under the ESOT. However, a company at its discretion may include other employees, eg foreign based employees.

(d) Former employees and directors (within 18 months of their departure or 15 years where certain conditions are met) may also be included.

Chapter 1

(e) Employees and directors cannot be beneficiaries if they have, or had within the previous 12 months, a material interest (ie 5% of the ordinary share capital) in the company.

(f) The functions of the trustees must be to acquire shares in the founding company (either out of contributions from the company or borrowings) for distribution to beneficiaries.

(g) Shares must be transferred to beneficiaries by the trustees within 20 years of their acquisition by the trustees.

(h) Sums of money received by the trustees (eg from the founding company, dividends, etc) must be spent, normally within 9 months, on one or more qualifying purposes. With effect from 27 March 1998 the trustees are exempt from income tax arising on such income, if and to the extent that the income is spent by the trustees within the qualifying period, for one or more qualifying purposes. The trustees will, however, not be entitled to any tax credit in relation to exempt dividends.

(i) Shares or sums (or both) must be offered to all beneficiaries of the ESOT and the transfers be made at the same time on similar terms.

(j) An ESOT may not be approved by the Revenue Commissioners unless they are satisfied that it is not intended solely to confer benefits on the directors and higher paid employees of a group of companies.

The reliefs available are as follows:-

(i) A company may claim a deduction for corporation tax purposes for -

   (a) the costs (legal etc) of setting up an approved ESOT, and

   (b) contributions to the trustees of an approved ESOT where the company, or a company it controls, has employees who are beneficiaries under the ESOT and the contributions are expended by the trustees during the "expenditure period" on one or more "qualifying purposes".

(ii) dividends received by trustees of an approved ESOT in respect of securities held by them will not be liable to the surcharge under Section 805 in respect of undistributed income, and

(iii) the transfer of securities by the trustees of an approved ESOT to trustees of an approved profit sharing scheme will be exempt from capital gains tax in respect of any chargeable gain arising on such transfer.

1.22.19 (v) Save As You Earn (SAYE) Share Scheme

There are two aspects to this scheme – an approved savings-related share option scheme and a certified contractual savings scheme. The latter scheme is used to fund the purchase of shares allocated to employees under the former scheme.

In brief the SAYE scheme allows employees to save a part of their after tax salaries – between £10 and £250 per month over a three year period and at the end of this period the savings can be used by the employees to purchase shares in their employers company.

The shares can be purchased at a discount of 25% of their market value at the beginning of the three year savings period. No charge to income tax arises on the purchase at this discounted price.

TCA97 s519A Where an individual obtains a right to acquire shares in his/her employing company or a group company, no tax will be chargeable in respect of the receipt or exercise of that right except in certain circumstances where the option is exercised within 3 years of being obtained.

TCA97 s519B The cost of establishing a savings related share option scheme is allowed as a deduction for corporation tax purpose.

Any terminal bonus or interest earned on an individuals' savings is exempt from tax, including DIRT.

TCA97 s519C Contractual savings schemes must be with "qualifying savings institutions" as listed.

TCA97 Sch 12A Certain conditions must be complied with in order for a savings-related share option scheme to be approved by the Revenue Commissioners. These conditions govern the type of company eligibility, type of shares, exercise of rights, acquisition of shares and the share price.

1.22.20 Treatment of Unpaid Remuneration

TCA97 s996 Remuneration which is allowed as a deduction in computing the Schedule D profits of an employer, but which has not been paid within 6 months of the end of his accounting period, is deemed to have been paid on the last day of the accounting period. This remuneration is, therefore, subject to the PAYE regulations regarding the collection of tax and the charging of interest on unpaid PAYE.

1.22.21 Payments in Connection with the Commencement of Employment

Whether payments in connection with the commencement of an employment (commonly referred to as "inducement payments") are taxable under Schedule E as an emolument of the new office or employment depends on the facts of each particular case. As a general rule, it may be said that the payment will be an emolument

Chapter 1

of the new employment where the payment is made under the terms of a contract of service or is in effect made in consideration of future services to be rendered to the new employer. The payment may not be taxable, however, where it can be shown that the payment is in fact compensation for the loss of some right as a result of taking up the new employment.

1.22.22 **Payments on Retirement or Removal from an Employment**

TCA97 s201

Where a payment not otherwise chargeable to income tax is made in connection with the termination of an office or employment, tax is to be charged only on the excess of the payment over the higher of (i) the basic exemption and (ii) an amount entitled the Standard Capital Superannuation Benefit calculated by the formula:

$$\frac{A \times N}{15} - L \quad \text{where}$$

A = One year's average of the remuneration for the last 3 years of service.

N = Number of complete years of service.

L = Any tax-free lump sum received or receivable under an approved superannuation scheme.

With regard to payments made on or after 1 December 1998, the basic exemption is £8,000 together with £600 for each complete year of service in the employment in respect of which the payment is made.

Where the Standard Capital Superannuation Benefit does not give a favourable result the basic exemption may be increased by a maximum figure of £4,000 if the following conditions are met:

(i) The claimant has never previously made a claim for a reduction or elimination of tax liability arising out of the receipt of a lump sum payment taxable under the provisions relating to such payments.

(ii) Any tax-free lump sum benefit received or receivable under an approved superannuation scheme relating to the employment does not exceed £4,000. Where an amount of less than £4,000 is received or receivable the basic exemption will be less that amount. Refunds of pension contributions taxable @ 10% or 25% are treated as taxed amounts and are therefore ignored.

Tax payable on the termination payment is the lower of the following:

(i) Income tax calculated on the basis of treating the lump sum (after deducting the exempt amount as mentioned above) as extra income earned in the year of assessment in which retirement etc occurs.

(ii) Income tax calculated on the basis of taxing the lump sum payment (after deducting the exempt amount) at a rate obtained by dividing the total tax payable for the five years of assessment immediately prior to the year of retirement etc by the taxable income of those five years. The extra tax payable on this basis is expressed by the formula:

$$P \times \frac{T}{I} \text{ where}$$

P = The lump sum payment after deduction of the exempt amount.

T = Tax liability on income of the previous five years of assessment.

I = Taxable income of the previous five years of assessment.

1.22.23 Exemptions

The exemptions from the charge to tax under Schedule E are:

(a) Payments made in connection with the termination of an office or employment by the death of the holder or made on account of injury to or disability of the holder.

(b) Payments made in connection with restrictive covenants before 24 April 1992.

(c) Payments from pension schemes where the contribution by the employer was assessed as emoluments.

(d) Payments to approved pension schemes.

(e) Certain allowances to members of the Defence Forces.

(f) Allowances to widows of members of the British Armed Forces in respect of children.

(g) Allowances under certain Army Pension Acts.

(h) Childrens allowances under Social Welfare Acts.

(i) Payments to Commonwealth representatives.

(j) Payments to Consular representatives

(k) Scholarship income. (A benefit in kind may arise in certain circumstances.)

(l) Statutory redundancy payments.

(m) Certain payments in respect of thalidomide children.

(n) Lump sum payments made to employees under certain company restructuring schemes involving agreed pay restructuring.

Chapter 1

1.23 DEEDS OF COVENANT

The relief available for 1994/95 and later years is as follows:-

1.23.1 Covenants from parents to children

Minor child	No tax relief is available for covenants in favour of a minor child, ie under 18 years.
Adult child	Tax relief applies for 1994/95 and 1995/96 only, subject to 5% of total income. Total income is defined as an individual's gross income less certain deductions eg mortgage interest. No relief is available for payments made after 5 April 1996.
Permanently incapacitated adult child	Unrestricted tax relief will continue for all years for covenanted payments to permanently incapacitated adult children.

1.23.2 Covenants from grandparents to grandchildren

Minor grandchild	For "existing" covenants, ie those in existence prior to 8 February 1995, tax relief subject to the 5% income restriction, applies for 1994/95. There is no relief available for 1995/96 or later years, unless the grandchild is incapacitated, where unrestricted relief is available.
	No relief is due on "new" covenants ie those entered into on or after 8 February 1995.
Adult grandchild	Tax relief applies for 1994/95 and 1995/96 only, subject to the 5% income restriction.
Permanently incapacitated grandchild	Unrestricted tax relief will continue for all years for covenanted payments to permanently incapacitated grandchildren, regardless of age.

1.23.3 Covenants between other individuals

Minor	Unrestricted tax relief applies for 1994/95 only on existing covenants. No relief is available for 1995/96 or later years on an existing covenant. No relief is due for new covenants.
Permanently incapacitated minor	Unrestricted tax relief will continue for all years for covenanted payments to permanently incapacitated minors.
Adult individual	Tax relief applies for 1994/95 and 1995/96 only, subject to the 5% income restriction as follows:

	(i) if the covenant is new the restriction will apply for both 1994/95 and 1995/96, and
	(ii) if the covenant is an existing covenant the restriction will apply for 1995/96 only.
Person 65 and over	Tax relief will continue for all years, subject to a 5% income restriction as follows:
	(i) if the covenant is new the restriction will apply for 1994/95 and later years, and
	(ii) if the covenant is an existing covenant the restriction will apply for 1995/96 and later years.
Permanently incapacitated adult individual	Unrestricted tax relief will continue for all years for covenants in favour of permanently incapacitated individuals.

1.23.4 Other Covenants

Tax relief applies to covenants for research and teaching of natural sciences and to certain bodies for the promotion of human rights for all years subject to the 5% income restriction as follows:-

(i) if the covenant is new, the restriction will apply for all years, and

(ii) if the covenant is an existing covenant the restriction will apply only from 1995/96.

1.23.5 Covenants after 5 April 1996

TCA97 s792

The only covenants that will be recognised for tax purposes after 5 April 1996 will be those paid to:-

(i) persons who are permanently incapacitated,

(ii) a permanently incapacitated minor child if paid by a person other than the parent,

(iii) persons who are aged 65 years or over,

(iv) a university or college for the purposes of research or the teaching of the natural sciences, and

(v) certain bodies established for the promotion of human rights.

The foregoing provisions could cause hardship. Accordingly, if the Revenue are satisfied that hardship arises, certain covenants in favour of children will continue to qualify for relief up to the year 2000. There are two classes of covenants affected:

(i) those entered into before 6 April 1993, and

(ii) covenants replacing, and entered into immediately after the expiration of a covenant entered into before 6 April 1993 in favour of an individual who is not the covenantor's child.

To qualify for the extended period, certain conditions must be satisfied.

All of the above covenants will be restricted to 5% of the covenantor's total income, with the exception of covenants in favour of permanently incapacitated persons where unrestricted relief is available.

1.24 CAPITAL ALLOWANCES

Capital allowances are granted for "chargeable periods" - accounting periods in the case of companies liable to corporation tax and years of assessment in the case of other persons liable to income tax. All capital allowances are granted by reference to events occurring in an accounting period (companies) or in a basis period for a year of assessment (other persons).

1.24.1 Wear and Tear Allowance

Plant and Machinery

TCA97 s285

This is an allowance for the wear and tear of plant and machinery in use for the purpose of a trade, profession, vocation, or employment at the end of a basis or accounting period.

For chargeable periods ending on or before 5 April 1996, the calculation of the allowance depends on the date the plant and machinery was provided for use, as follows:-

Pre 1.4.92: In the first period of claim, the allowance is calculated by reference to the cost of the item less grants. In subsequent periods, the allowance is calculated by reference to the cost as reduced by grants and allowances for previous periods, ie the written-down value.

Post 1.4.92: The allowance is calculated at an annual rate of 15% on the straight line basis over six years and the final 10% in year seven. This applies to both new and second hand items of plant and machinery, other than vehicles suitable for the conveyance by road of persons or goods or the haulage by road of other vehicles. In the case of such vehicles, the reducing balance method described above continues to apply.

For chargeable periods ending on or after 6 April 1996, the allowance is an annual rate of 15% (straight line) in the case of all plant and machinery (other than motor vehicles) no matter when provided. In the case of such plant and machinery provided for use before 1 April 1992, the rate of 15% will apply to the written down value of those items. For motor vehicles, the 20% reducing balancing method continues to apply. (See Chart 33)

Where the expenditure is incurred before 6 May 1993, grants from the State, any Board established by Statute or any public or local authority are deducted. Where the expenditure is incurred on or after 6 May 1993, all grants are deducted.

Plant and machinery includes computer software or the right to use such software for the purposes of a trade.

Chapter 1

Motor Vehicles

TCA97
s373-s376

The rate of wear and tear allowances which is applied to motor vehicles is usually 20%. The wear and tear allowances on new passenger motor cars provided on or after 2 December 1998 and costing more than £16,000 are computed as though the cars had cost £16,000. (See Chart 7 for previous relevant limits.) However, the new ceiling of £16,000 does not apply to expenditure incurred within twelve months from 2 December 1998 under a contract entered into before that date. In this instance allowances must be calculated by reference to the previous limits which also apply to existing and second-hand cars.

The restriction by reference to cost of £16,000 etc does not apply to motor cars in use in a taxi or car hire business. In addition, the annual rate of wear and tear on such cars is 40%.

1.24.2 Balancing Allowances and Charges - Plant and Machinery

TCA97 s288

Balancing allowances and/or charges may arise when one or more of the following events occur in a period:

(a) an item of plant and machinery on which initial or writing-down allowance was granted is sold (see earlier editions for meaning of initial allowance); or

(b) such an item ceases permanently to be used for the purposes of the trade or profession; or

(c) the trade or profession ceases.

TCA97 s289

Where the sale proceeds realised on an item are less than its written-down value a balancing allowance arises on the difference.

Where the sale proceeds exceed the written-down value a balancing charge arises on the difference. The balancing charge cannot exceed the aggregate of initial and wear and tear allowances previously obtained on the item. For purposes of computing balancing allowances and charges, the treatment of grants obtained on the purchase of an item will depend on whether the grants were taken into account in calculating wear and tear and/or initial allowances in the first instance. Where the grants were ignored in the first instance, they are treated on disposal of the item as capital allowances obtained, and are deducted from the written-down value. The calculation of the balancing allowance or charge is made by reference to the resultant figure. In a case where this resultant figure is negative, it is administrative practice to confine the balancing charge to the amount of the sale proceeds arising on the disposal. In situations where the grants have been deducted in computing wear and tear and/or initial allowances, the written-down value will reflect the deduction and the balancing charge arising on the disposal will be confined to the amount of the sale proceeds. The overriding limit on the balancing charge continues to be the aggregate of initial and wear and tear allowances previously obtained on the item.

Transfers at Written-Down Values - Subject to certain conditions items qualifying for capital allowances may be transferred for tax purposes at their tax written-down values. In this way no balancing allowance or charge arises on the transfer. In computing a balancing allowance or charge on a subsequent disposal by the transferee, the allowances claimed by the transferor are taken into account.

TCA97 s290

Withheld Balancing Charge - A taxpayer may, for tax purposes elect to reduce the cost of the replacement of an item by any balancing charge arising on the disposal of the item. When the replacement is disposed of, any balancing allowance or charge arising will take account of the balancing charge previously withheld.

1.24.3 Writing-Down Allowance - Industrial Buildings

TCA97 s272

This is an allowance granted to a person who at the end of a basis or accounting period holds the "relevant interest" in an industrial building (as defined) in use for the purpose of a trade carried on by him.

The allowance is granted with effect from 1 April 1992 at 4% per annum of the capital expenditure incurred on the construction of industrial buildings exclusive of grants. See Chart 33 for allowances claimable in earlier years and special rates applying to farm buildings and hotels.

Where free depreciation had been claimed prior to 1 April 1992, the 4% allowance will be applied to the balance of expenditure not claimed by means of free depreciation.

A purchaser of a qualifying building may claim the allowance (where applicable) provided that the previous owner(s) does not claim allowances and it is acquired within one year of first use. However, the amount in respect of which allowances may be claimed depends on whether or not the seller is a person who carries on a trade of the construction of buildings.

Where the expenditure on the construction was incurred by a non-builder, the person who acquires the building is deemed to have incurred construction expenditure on the date the purchase price is payable equal to the lower of:-

(a) the actual construction expenditure, or

(b) the net price (as defined) paid by him.

If the seller is a builder, allowances may be claimed on the net price which in effect includes part of the builder's profit.

Chapter 1

The net price paid is:-

$$B \times \frac{C}{C+D} \quad \text{where:}$$

B = the purchase price

C = the construction expenditure

D = the site cost

TCA97 s268 Expenditure incurred on or after 23 April 1996 on industrial buildings situated outside the State does not qualify for any allowances. However, certain transitional provisions apply in the case of certain foreign hotel projects, the deadline for completion of which is 30 September 1998.

TCA97 s268 The allowance is extended to expenditure incurred on or after 25th January 1984 on laboratories used wholly or mainly for mineral analysis in connection with the exploration for, or the extraction of, minerals (including oil and natural gas).

1.24.4 Balancing Allowances and Charges - Industrial Buildings

TCA97 s274 In general these follow on the same lines as for plant and machinery. No balancing allowance or charge can arise as a result of any event occurring more than 50 years after the building was first used, where the expenditure on the building was incurred prior to 16th January 1975. Where the expenditure was incurred on or after 16th January 1975, the period is 25 years. In the case of hotels the period is 50 years for expenditure incurred in the period 30th September 1956 to 31st December 1959, 10 years in the period 1 January 1960 to 25 January 1994 and 7 years for all subsequent periods.

No balancing allowances arise on the sale of an industrial building where the seller and buyer are connected with each other or it appears that the sole or main object of the transaction was to obtain the balancing allowance.

1.24.5 Lessors

TCA97 s403 In general lessors deriving income from the leasing of plant and machinery or industrial buildings are entitled to the same capital allowances as those who purchase and use such items in their own businesses.

However a number of restrictions are in place on the set-off of capital allowances arising in the case of certain leases of plant and machinery. These restrictions effectively "ring fence" capital allowances within the leasing trade. Exclusion from these restrictions applies in the case of certain companies operating in Shannon or the IFSC.

1.24.6 Anti-Avoidance

TCA97 s289

There are anti-avoidance provisions designed to prevent the obtaining of a tax advantage through transactions in plant and machinery or industrial buildings carried out other than at arms length.

1.24.7 Expenditure on Dredging

TCA97 s303

There are reliefs on expenditure incurred on or after 30 September 1956 on "the removal of anything forming part of or projecting from the bed of the sea or of any inland water". The expenditure must be for the purposes of a qualifying trade. The reliefs are:

Initial Allowance 10%
Annual Allowance 2%

1.24.8 Scientific Research - Capital Expenditure

TCA97 s764

The full amount of the expenditure is deductible as a trade expense for the period in which the expenditure is incurred.

1.24.9 Expenditure on Patent Rights

TCA97 s755

Subject to certain restrictions an allowance of one-seventeenth of the cost is granted for the period in which the expenditure is incurred and for the 16 subsequent chargeable periods.

1.24.10 Multi-Storey Car Parks

TCA97 s344

Certain capital allownaces are available on expenditure incurred on the construction or refurbishment of certain multi-storey car parks, where the relevant local authority certifies that the car park has been developed in accordance with criteria laid down by the Minister for the Environment.

The qualifying period commenced on 1 July 1995 and ended on 30 June 1998. However, the expiry date was extended to 30 June 1999 where the local authority gave a certificate, in writing, before 30 September 1998, that not less than 15% of the total cost of the multi-storey car park (including site cost) had been incurred by 30 June 1998.

A further extension from 30 June 1999 to 31 December 2000 applies where at least 15% of the total cost of the project was incurred before 30 June 1999 and a certificate to this effect has been obtained from the relevant local authority. This extension does not apply in the case of multi-storey car parks within the county boroughs of Cork or Dublin (i.e. within the Cork or Dublin Corporation jurisdictions).

Chapter 1

The allowances available are:-

Owner Occupier	Up to 50% Year 1 Maximum 50%*
Lessors	Up to 25% Year 1 2% annual allowance Maximum 50%*

*These allowances have been increased from 50% to 100% with effect from 1 August 1998, in cases where double rent relief is not available (see below).

Tenants of multi-storey car parks in respect of which capital allowances have been claimed are entitled to a double rent allowance.

The latest date for entering into qualifying leases in respect of multi-storey car parks was 31 July 1998.

However, this deadline was extended to 30 June 1999 where 15% of the total cost of the project was incurred on or before 30 June 1998.

As double rent allowance is no longer available (apart from the cases referred to in the preceding paragraph) the capital allowances available in respect of multi-storey car parks has been increased from 50% to 100% with effect from 1 August 1998.

Where the double rent allowance is available on leases entered into after 31 July 1998, the maximum allowance remains at 50%.

In the case of refurbishment, capital allowances will be available only if the amount expended on the refurbishment equals at least 20% of the site-exclusive market value of the car park immediately before the refurbishment

1.24.11 Airports

TCA97 s268

Capital expenditure incurred on or after 27 March 1998, on buildings used for the management or operation of an airport, such as terminal buildings etc, will qualify for an industrial buildings allowance of 4% per annum. The tax life of such buildings is 25 years.

Allowances are also available in respect of existing airport buildings or structures with effect from 27 March 1998, on a net figure based on the original cost less the amount of capital allowances that would have been granted had those buildings qualified before 27 March 1998.

1.24.12 Hotels, Holiday Camps and Holiday Cottages

TCA97 s272

Capital expenditure incurred on or after 27 January 1994 on any building or structure in use as a hotel or holiday camp registered with Bord Failte qualifies for an annual industrial buildings

Income Tax

allowance of 15% for the first six years and 10% in the seventh year. Registered holiday cottages qualify for an allowance of 10% per annum. (See page 100 re holiday cottages in Resort Areas).

TCA97 s405 Where the expenditure is incurred on or after 24 April 1992 on the construction or acquisition of a holiday cottage, industrial building allowances will only be allowed against income from that cottage or the trade for which the holiday cottage is used. This restriction does not apply to expenditure incurred before 6 April 1993 where, before 24 April 1992 either –

(a) a building contract for the construction of the holiday cottage was entered into, or

(b) a land purchase (or lease) contract was entered into for the construction of the holiday cottage and a planning application for its construction was received by a planning authority.

1.24.13 Hotel Room Ownership Scheme

TCA97 s409 Anti-avoidance legislation exists to counteract any room ownership schemes entered into in connection with a hotel investment by a hotel partnership, whereby the partners claim capital allowances on their investment in the hotel and at the end of the tax life of the hotel, each partner receives a room or suite in the hotel.

Capital allowances are denied in respect of an investment in a hotel, by a partnership, where a room ownership scheme is in existence. It applies to hotel investments, the capital expenditure in respect of which is incurred on or after 26 March 1997. Transitional provisions apply in cases where contracts were entered into or planning permission was received prior to 26 March 1997.

1.24.14 Nursing Homes

TCA97 s268;
TCA97 s272;
TCA97 s274

Capital expenditure incurred on or after 3 December 1997, on the construction, extension or refurbishment of buildings used as private, registered nursing homes and on the conversion of an existing building into such a nursing home qualifies for capital allowances at the rate of 15% per annum for six years and 10% in year 7.

The nursing home must be registered with a health board under the Health (Nursing Homes) Act 1990.

The tax life of such buildings is 10 years and allowances will be clawed back if the building ceases to be a qualifying nursing home within 10 years.

The allowances are subject to the £25,000 limit per annum on the amount of allowances which an individual passive investor can claim against non-rental income. (see page 139)

Chapter 1

1.24.15 Private Convalescent Facilities

TCA97 s268
TCA97 s272
TCA97 s274

Capital expenditure incurred on or after 2 December 1998 on the construction, extension and refurbishment of a private convalescent facility qualifies for capital allowances at the rate of 15% per annum for the first 6 years and 10% in year 7.

The allowances also apply to expenditure incurred on the conversion of an existing building into a private convalescent facility.

The facilities are to be used as an alternative to hospital care for patients recovering from acute hospital treatment and must be approved by the relevant health board. Such approval will be subject to meeting certain requirements and standards which will be specified in guidelines to be published by the Minister for Health and Children with the consent of the Minister for Finance.

The tax life of such buildings is 10 years and allowances will be clawed back if the building ceases to be a qualifying convalescent facility within 10 years.

1.24.16 Childcare Facilities

TCA97 s843A

Capital expenditure incurred on or after 2 December 1998, on the construction, extension and refurbishment of a building or part of a building used as a childcare facility qualifies for capital allowances at the rate of 15% per annum for the first 6 years and 10% in year 7.

The allowances also apply to expenditure incurred on the conversion of an existing building or part of a building for use as a childcare facility.

The premises must meet the required standards for such premises as provided in the Childcare Act 1991 and must be in use for the purpose of providing:-

(i) A pre-school service, or

(ii) A pre-school service and a day care or other service to cater for children other than pre-school children.

The premises must not include any part of a building or structure in use as, or as part of a dwelling-house.

The tax life of such buildings is 10 years and allowances will be clawed back if the building ceases to be a qualifying childcare facility within 10 years.

1.24.17 Student Accommodation

TCA97 s380

Capital expenditure incurred in the period between 1 April 1999 and 31 March 2003 on the construction, conversion or refurbishment of rented residential accommodation for third level students, qualifies for "Section 23" type relief.

Income Tax

The relief provides for a deduction of 100% of the construction, conversion or refurbishment expenditure, which may be off-set against all rental income – whether derived from the premises in question or from other lettings.

The buildings must conform with guidelines issued by the Minister for Education and Science. These guidelines deal with various features of the scheme, including the institutions which qualify, conditions relating to the standards and location of accommodation and the categories of students whose accommodation will be covered.

The accommodation must be provided within an 8km radius of the main campus and must be approved by the relevant college.

There will be a clawback of allowances where the premises are sold within 10 years and a subsequent purchaser can claim the original allowances on a premises where a clawback arises.

1.24.18 Third Level Institutions

TCA97 s843

Capital expenditure incurred on construction of certain buildings used for the purposes of third level education and the provision of machinery and plant qualifies for capital allowances, subject to certain conditions.

The premises must be in use for the purposes of third level education provided by an "approved institution" (as defined) and must be let to that institution. In addition, the approved institution must have raised at least 50% of the cost of the total expenditure before construction begins, and that expenditure must be approved by the Minister for Education with the consent of the Minister for Finance.

Allowances also apply to projects funded by the Research and Development Fund announced by the Minister for Education and Science in November 1998.

Allowances are granted at the rate of 15% per annum for the first 6 years and 10% in year 7 and may be claimed in respect of expenditure incurred between 1 July 1997 and 31 December 2002. No balancing charge will arise after seven years from the period when the premises were first used.

1.24.19 Park and Ride Facilities

TCA97 s372

Various capital allowances are available in respect of qualifying expenditure incurred on park and ride facilities in the larger urban areas.

Park and ride facilities are defined as a building or structure served by a bus or train service with the purpose of providing, for members of the public intending to continue a journey by bus or rail without preference for any particular class of person and on payment of an appropriate charge, parking space for mechanically propelled vehicles. It also includes any area under, over or immediately adjoining any qualifying park and ride facility.

The scheme is subject to guidelines to be issued by the Minister for the Environment and Local Government and the local authorities empowered to certify areas for park and ride facilities are, Cork, Dublin, Galway, Limerick and Waterford Corporations, Dun Laoghaire/Rathdown, Fingal, Kildare, South Dublin and Wicklow County Councils and the Urban District Councils in Kildare, Meath and Wicklow.

The qualifying period is from 1 July 1999 to 30 June 2002 and the allowances available are as follows:

(a) **Park & Ride Facilities**

Expenditure incurred on the construction or refurbishment of qualifying park and ride facilities, qualifies for the following allowances

Owner Occupier	100% Free Depreciation or
	50% Initial Allowance
	4% Annual Allowance
	Maximum 100%
Lessor	50% Initial Allowance
	4% Annual Allowance
	Maximum 100%

In the case of refurbishment expenditure, the allowances are available only if the expenditure is not less than 10% of the value of the premises before refurbishment.

The tax life of such facilities is 13 years.

(b) **Commercial Premises**

Expenditure incurred on the construction or refurbishment of certain commercial premises located on the site of a park and ride facility qualifies for the same allowances as shown above for park and ride facilities.

However the total mount of capital expenditure which qualifies for allowances is restricted, so that, only expenditure which, when combined with expenditure on any residential accommodation at a park and ride facility, does not exceed 50% of the total allowable expenditure at the facility, will qualify for relief.

(c) **Rented Residential Accommodation**

Expenditure incurred on the construction of certain rented residential accommodation located on the site of a park and ride facility qualifies for "Section 23" type relief. The relief is a deduction of 10% of the construction expenditures against all rental income whether it arises from the premises in question or from other lettings.

There is an overall limit on the amount of expenditure which will qualify for this relief, so that, only expenditure which, when combined with any expenditure on owner-occupier accommodation at a park and ride facility, does not exceed 25% of total allowable expenditure at the facility, will qualify for relief.

(d) **Owner-occupied Residential Premises**

Relief is available for expenditure incurred on the construction of owner-occupied residential accommodation located on the site of a park and ride facility.

A deduction of 5% of the expenditure incurred may be claimed by the owner occupier as a deduction from total income, for 10 years provided the dwelling is the sole or main residence of the individual.

There is an overall limit on the amount of expenditure which will qualify for this relief, so that, only expenditure which, when combined with any expenditure on "Section 23" accommodation at a park and ride facility, does not exceed 25% of the total allowable expenditure at the facility, will qualify for relief.

1.24.20 Significant Buildings

TCA97 s482

Relief from income tax is available to the owner or occupier of an "approved building" for certain expenditure incurred on or after 6 April 1982 on the repair, maintenance or restoration of that building or garden. The relief is allowed by treating the expenditure as if it were a loss in a separate trade carried on by the owner or occupier, and relief may be claimed under the normal sections applying to an individual who has incurred a Case I or Case II of Schedule D loss. For the tax years 1995/96 et seq any unutilised portion of the "loss" may be carried forward for a period of up to 2 years.

An Approved Building is defined as a building within the State which is determined

— by the Commissioners of Public Works in Ireland, to be a building which is intrinsically of significant scientific, historical, architectural or aesthetic interest, and

— by the Revenue Commissioners to be a building to which reasonable access is afforded to the public.

The question of reasonable access is decided in each individual case, however the following are the minimum requirements:

— access to the whole or a substantial part of the building is allowed at the same time;

— access is allowed annually for sixty days (of which forty days must be in the period from 1 May to 30 September) in a reasonable manner and at reasonable times for periods at least averaging 4 hours a day.

— the charge levied (if any) is reasonable.

Relief will not be granted in respect of expenditure incurred in a chargeable period beginning on or after 23 May 1994 unless the claimant can prove that he/she has provided Bord Failte with the details of the dates and times which the building is open to the public by 1 January in:-

(a) the chargeable period for which the claim is made, and

(b) in each of the five chargeable periods immediately preceding the chargeable period in which the claim is made or if shorter, each of the chargeable periods since 23 May 1994.

This information must be given to Bord Failte on the understanding that it may be published for the promotion of tourism.

Relief will not be granted for any chargeable period prior to the one in which the application for approval of the building is made to the Revenue Commissioners.

Relief is only allowed for expenditure not already relieved under any other provisions of the taxes acts, or re-imbursed to the individual by a grant or other means. Either the Office of Public Works or the Revenue Commissioners may withdraw their determinations at any time if they feel the building ceases to qualify, which may give rise to a clawback of relief granted in the five year period prior to revocation.

The relief also applies to:-

(i)   expenditure incurred on or after 6 April 1993, on the cost of maintenance or restoration of an "approved garden". An approved garden is a garden, not attached to an approved building, which has been determined to be of significant horticultural, scientific, historical, architectural or aesthetic interest.

(ii) buildings which are in use as tourist accommodation facilities for at least six months in any calendar year, of which four months must be in the period 1 May to 30 September. To qualify the building must be approved by Bord Failte as a guest house and the Board must be notified of the opening times of the guest house.

(iii) expenditure of up to an aggregate of £5,000 pa on:-

(a) the repair, maintenance or restoration of an "approved object", in an approved building or garden subject to the objects being on display in the approved building or garden for a period of at least two years from the year in which the relief for the contents is claimed.

(b) the installation, maintenance or replacement of a security alarm system, and

(c) the provision of public liability insurance for an approved building or garden.

An approved object is an object (including a picture, sculpture, book, manuscript, piece of jewellery, furniture or other similar object) or a scientific collection which is owned by the owner or occupier of the approved building.

Relief for a chargeable period in respect of expenditure incurred on or after 12 February 1998 will be limited to the amount of that expenditure attributable to the actual work carried out during that chargeable period.

1.24.21 Restriction of Capital Allowances/Losses

TCA97 s409A;
TCA97 s409B

In the case of passive investors, the amount of capital allowances on qualifying buildings which can be set off against non-rental income, is restricted to £25,000 in any tax year. There is no restriction on the amount which can set off against rental income. The restriction does not apply to companies, owner operators and active partners.

In the case of a partnership, where an individual is not an active partner and capital allowances have been used under Section 392, to create or augment a loss in the partnership, the amount of the loss which may be set against other income is based on the formula:-

$$A + £25,000, \text{ where}$$

A = the amount of profits or gains of the individual trade in the year of loss before the capital allowances are taken into account

Where an individual is a partner in two or more partnership trades, then those partnership trades in which he is not an active partner are deemed to be a single partnership trade.

The restriction applies to all types of commercial premises, including multi-storey car parks, which attract capital allowances under the various existing tax incentive schemes and the proposed new Urban and Rural Renewal Scheme.

Capital allowances on hotels are ring fenced and may be set off only against rental income in the case of individual investors. This restriction does not apply to owner operators or companies, or to certain hotels located in counties Cavan, Donegal, Leitrim, Mayo, Monaghan, Roscommon or Sligo.

Chapter 1

Transitional arrangements have been provided for where certain commitments were made prior to 3 December 1997. Accordingly the restrictions outlined above will not apply where before 3 December 1997:-

1. In the case of construction, the foundation of the building was laid in its entirety;

2. In the case of refurbishment, work up to the value of 5 per cent of the total cost of the refurbishment was carried out;

3. The building was provided for the purposes of a project approved for grant assistance by an industrial development agency within a period of two years ending on 3 December 1997;

4. An application for planning permission on the building had been received by a planning authority before 3 December 1997;

5. The individual can prove to the Revenue Commissioners that a detailed plan had been prepared and that discussions had taken place with the planning authority before 3 December 1997 and that this can be supported by an affidavit or statutory declaration by the planning authority and the expenditure is incurred by the person entitled to the capital allowances under an obligation entered into before 3 December 1997 or before 1 May 1998 pursuant to negotiations which were in progress before 3 December 1997;

6. Obligations will be treated as having been entered into before 3 December 1997 only if there was an existing and binding contract, in writing, under which the obligation arose;

7. Negotiations pursuant to which the obligation was entered into shall not be regarded as having been in progress unless preliminary commitments or agreements in writing, were entered into before that date.

1.25 FARMING TAXATION

TCA97
s654-s664

All farming carried on by individuals, with the exception of certain market gardening and other activities, is liable to income tax under Case I of Schedule D.

1.25.1 Averaging of Farm Profits

TCA97 s657

An individual may elect that his farming profits chargeable to income tax are to be computed by reference to an average of the profits arising in each of the preceding three years. Where an election for averaging is made, the election remains in force for all future years, except where the individual decides to opt out of the averaging system.

Losses - Where losses are taken into an averaging calculation and the result of that calculation is a loss, one-third of the loss is available for relief against other income under Section 381 or for carry forward under Section 382.

Capital Allowances - Capital Allowances are not subject to averaging.

Stock Relief - As Stock Relief is treated as if it were a trading expense, profits for averaging purposes are the profits after deduction of Stock Relief.

Opting Out of Averaging - The individual may opt out of the averaging system only if he was charged to tax on the average basis for each of the three years of assessment immediately preceding the year for which he wishes to revert to the normal year basis.

If he wishes to revert to the normal year basis, no amendment is made in the average basis assessment for the last average year but the two years prior to the last average year are reviewed and if the existing assessment for either or both year(s) is less than the amount of the assessment for the last average year, an additional assessment for the difference is made for the year(s) affected.

Cessation - Where all farming carried on by an individual ceases, the normal cessation provisions are applied irrespective of an election for the average basis.

Time Limits - The Time Limit within which an election for the average basis may be made is within 30 days of the date of the notice of assessment to income tax on farming profits. Notification of opting out of the averaging system must be given on or before 31 January in the year following the year of assessment.

1.25.2 Stock Relief

TCA97
s665-s669

Individuals or companies carrying on the trade of farming may deduct 25% of any increase in stock values in a chargeable period or period of account as a trading expense incurred in that period.

The relief cannot increase or create a loss. Excess capital allowances or unused losses may not be carried forward from or before a period in which stock relief is claimed. The relief must be claimed in writing on or before the return filing date for the period to which it relates. The relief is available for individuals up to the year of assessment 2000/2001 and in the case of companies for accounting periods ending on or before 5 April 2001.

In the case of "young trained farmers", as defined, who become such qualifying farmers between 6 April 1999 and 5 April 2001, the tax relief available is 100% of any increase in stock values. This special relief will apply for a period of four years.

Special provisions apply to commencements and certain other situations where opening stock may not be at a realistic value. In such circumstances the Inspector of Taxes is entitled to treat the farmer as having trading stock of such value as appears to him to be reasonable and just.

Special treatment applies to profits resulting from the disposal of livestock due to statutory disease eradication measures. This special treatment is broadly as follows:-

— profits arising from the disposal of cattle herds due to statutory disease eradication schemes are excluded in computing income for tax purposes for the accounting period in which the livestock depopulation takes place. Such profits are deemed to arise in two equal instalments in each of the next two accounting periods, and

— in lieu of the normal 25% stock relief, a farmer will be allowed to elect for stock relief of 100% in the two year deferral period. This stock relief will be capped having regard to the amount re-invested in replacement stock.

This special treatment is available in the case of total cattle herd depopulation arising from statutory disease eradication schemes. Where the disposal is due to brucellosis, a farmer is treated as having disposed of an entire herd where under the brucellosis eradication rules he disposes of all eligible animals, together with any other animals that must be disposed of in accordance with those rules.

1.25.3 Losses

TCA97 s662

Relief for farm losses against other income is claimable only where the farming is carried on, on a commercial basis with a view to the realisation of profits. The relief will only be available for three consecutive years and in special cases, four consecutive years.

If there is no other income, or if relief is denied because of the three/four year rule losses may be carried forward for set off against future farming profits.

1.25.4 Discontinued Farm Trades

TCA97 s656

A farmer ceasing to trade and a successor to that trade may jointly elect to transfer trading stock at book value.

1.25.5 Pollution Control

TCA97 s659

Farm pollution control allowances are available to a farmer who has a farm nutrient management plan in place in respect of his farm and who incurs necessary capital expenditure for the control of pollution on certain buildings and structures.

The relief applies to expenditure incurred between 6 April 1997 and 5 April 2000. There is an accelerated allowance in year one of 50% of expenditure incurred up to a maximum expenditure of £20,000 (ie a maximum first year allowance of £10,000). With effect from 6 April 1998 the limit of £20,000 is increased to £30,000 (giving a maximum first year allowance of £15,000). The balance of expenditure is written off over the next seven years in accordance with the normal wear and tear capital allowances rules, ie 15% per annum for 6 years and 10% in the final year.

Chapter 1

1.26 SUB-CONTRACTORS

TCA97 s531

There are special rules relating to payments made by principal contractors to sub-contractors in respect of relevant contracts, forestry operations and meat processing operations. The principal contractor must deduct tax at 35% from such payments and remit this to the collector general unless the sub-contractor produces a certificate authorising the receipt of the amount without deduction of tax (Form C2). The sub-contractor's Inspector of Taxes (acting on behalf of the Revenue Commissioners) will issue such a certificate of authorisation if he is satisfied that:-

(a) The applicant is or is about to become a sub-contractor engaged in the business of carrying out relevant contracts.

(b) The business is or will be carried on from a fixed place of business and has or will have such equipment, stock and other facilities as in the opinion of the Revenue Commissioners are required for the purposes of the business.

(c) Proper books and records will be kept in relation to the business.

(d) The applicant has paid all his due taxes and delivered all necessary returns and supplied all information requested by his Inspector of Taxes for the "qualifying period", which includes the period from the beginning of the tax year to the date the application for Form C2 is made to the Inspector.

Where the contractor has been resident outside the State during the qualifying period and applies for a Form C2, he/she must satisfy the Revenue that he/she has complied with the tax obligation of the country in which he/she were resident during the qualifying period.

(e) There is good reason to expect that the applicant will keep proper books and records in the future.

If the Inspector of Taxes refuses, for any reason, to issue Form C2, the sub-contractor can apply to the Revenue Commissioners who have powers to issue the certificate even though they may not be satisfied on one or more of the conditions. A sub-contractor has a right of appeal against a refusal by the Revenue Authorities to issue the certificate.

1.26.1 Principal Contractor

A principal contractor is defined as one of the following:

(a) A person who, in respect of the whole or any part of the construction operations to which the contract relates is himself the contractor under another construction contract.

(b) A person carrying on a business which includes the erection of buildings or the manufacture, treatment or extraction of materials for use whether used or not in construction operations.

(c) A person who is connected with a company carrying on such a business as is mentioned in paragraph (b) (a person being regarded for the purposes of this paragraph as being so connected if he would be regarded for the purposes of Section 639 as being so connected).

(d) A local authority, a public utility society within the meaning of Section 2, Housing Act 1966 or a body referred to in paragraphs 1 or 2 of Section 12 (2)(a) or Section 19 or 45 of that Act.

(e) A Minister of State.

(f) Any Board established by or under statute.

(g) A person who carries on any gas, water, electricity, hydraulic power, dock, canal or railway undertaking.

(h) A person carrying on a business of meat processing operations in an establishment approved and inspected in accordance with the European Communities (Fresh Meat) Regulations 1987 (S.I. No 254 of 1987) and with effect from 6 October 1998

- in an establishment approved and inspected in accordance with the European Communities (Fresh Poultry Meat) Regulations 1996 (SI No 3 of 1996) and

- a person carrying on a business which includes the loading, hauling, cleaning and grading operations in the meat and poultry industries.

(i) A person carrying on a business which includes the processing (including cutting and preserving) of wood from thinned or felled trees in sawmills or other like premises on the supply of thinned or felled trees for such processing.

1.26.2 Relevant Contract

A relevant contract means a contract between a sub-contractor and a principal contractor where the sub-contractor is liable as follows:-

(a) to carry out relevant operations; or

(b) be answerable for the carrying out of such operations by others; or

(c) to furnish his own labour or the labour of others in the course of such operations i.e. employment agencies.

Chapter 1

Where a person is an employee of the principal contractor a "Relevant Contract" does not exist between them. PAYE is operated on payments to the employee in the normal way.

Relevant operations are any of the following:

(i) The construction, alteration, repair, extension, demolition or dismantling of buildings or structures.

(ii) The construction, alteration, repair, extension, or demolition of any works forming or to form part of land including walls, roadways, power lines, aircraft runways, docks and harbours, railways, inland waterways, pipelines, reservoirs, watermains, wells, sewers, industrial plant and installations for purposes of land drainage.

(iii) The installation in any building or structure of systems of heating, lighting, air conditioning, sound proofing, ventilation, power supply, drainage, sanitation, water supply, burglar or fire-protection.

(iv) The external cleaning of buildings (other than cleaning of any part of a building in the course of normal maintenance) the internal cleaning of buildings and structures so far as carried out in the course of their construction, alteration, extension, repair or restoration.

(v) Operations which form an integral part of or are preparatory to or are for rendering complete such operations such as are described above including site clearance, earth moving, excavation, tunnelling and boring, laying of foundations, erection of scaffolding, site restoration, landscaping, and the provision of roadways and other access works.

(vi) Operations which form an integral part of or are preparatory to or are for rendering complete the drilling or extraction of minerals, or natural gas or the exploration or exploitation of natural resources.

(vii) The haulage for hire of materials, machinery or plant for use whether or not in any of the aforesaid construction operations.

(viii) Forestry operations which include:-

   (a) the planting, thinning, lopping or felling of trees in woods, forests or other plantations, eg the maintenance of woods, forests and plantations and the preparation of land, including woods or forests which have been harvested for planting.

   (b) the haulage or removal of thinned, lopped or felled trees;

(c) the processing (including cutting or preserving) of wood from thinned, lopped or felled trees in sawmills or other like premises;

(d) the haulage for hire of materials, machinery or plant for use, whether used or not, in any of the aforesaid operations;

(ix) "Meat processing operations" which include:-

(a) the slaughter of cattle, sheep or pigs;

(b) the division (including cutting or boning), sorting, packaging (including vacuum packaging) or branding of, or the application of any other similar process to the carcasses, or any part of the carcasses, of slaughtered cattle, sheep or pigs;

(c) the application of methods of preservation (including cold storage) to the carcasses, or any part of the carcasses, of slaughtered cattle, sheep or pigs;

(d) the loading or unloading of the carcasses, or any part of the carcasses of slaughtered cattle, sheep or pigs at any establishment where any of the operations referred to in paragraphs (a), (b) and (c) are carried on.

1.26.3 Gang System

A relevant contract is deemed to exist between the principal contractor and each member of a gang. The principal contractor making a payment to a group or gang must consider the tax status of each individual member of that group or gang and make payment in full or deduct tax accordingly from each element of the payment. Individual gang members must give the principal contractor details of the amount due to them.

1.26.4 Credit for Tax Deducted

The gross amount receivable under the contract is included in the computation of the profit of the sub-contractor and he is entitled to credit for, or repayment of, the tax suffered. During the course of a year of assessment the sub-contractor may apply for repayment of the tax deducted in that year on a monthly basis. The repayment will be confined to the amount of the tax suffered which appears to the Revenue Commissioners to exceed the proportionate part of the amount of tax for which the sub-contractor is estimated to be liable for that year of assessment. Any amount outstanding in respect of VAT, PAYE, PRSI and capital gains tax will however be deducted from the amount of the repayment.

Chapter 1

1.26.5 **Returns**

The Revenue can require principal contractors to make returns of all deductions made within 9 days of the end of the Income Tax month and the tax deducted must be paid over to the Revenue.

1.26.6 **Payments**

Where a person to whom a C2 has been issued wishes to receive payments without deduction of tax, the C2 must be produced in person to the principal contractor who then applies to Revenue for a payments card. On receipt of the payments card, the principal contractor may make payments without deduction of tax. The requirement for the subcontractor to produce the C2 in person may be relaxed in two circumstances

(i) Where the subcontractor has nominated a bank account to Revenue into which all payments are to be made by principal contractors, the principal will be entitled to apply for a payments card without having seen the subcontractor's C2. The subcontractor will have to notify the principal of details of his or her C2 and of the nominated bank account and the principal will have to undertake to make all payments directly into that bank account.

(ii) Where the principal contractor already holds a payments card in relation to a subcontractor and the contract in relation to which the payments card was issued is ongoing at the end of the tax year, the principal will be allowed to apply for a payments card for the following year without having seen the subcontractor's C2 for that year.

1.27 EXEMPTIONS

1.27.1 Artists

TCA97 s195

Certain earnings of individuals who are determined by the Revenue Commissioners to have produced a work or works generally recognised as having cultural or artistic merit are exempted from Irish income tax.

"A Work" is defined as an original and creative work, whether written, composed or executed as the case may be, which falls into one of the following categories:

(a) A book or other writing.

(b) A play.

(c) A musical composition.

(d) A painting or other like picture.

(e) A sculpture.

The exemption applies to an individual only. The relief will be granted to a person who has written, composed or executed the work or works jointly with another individual. The individual must be resident in Ireland and not resident elsewhere, or ordinarily resident and domiciled in Ireland and not resident elsewhere. If the Revenue Commissioners accept that the claim to exemption is valid, any profits or gains arising to the claimant from the publication, production or sale, as the case may be, of the work or works or a work of his in the same category as that work and which would, apart from the exemption, be included in an assessment under Case II of Schedule D, are to be disregarded for all purposes of the Tax Acts. There are detailed rights of appeal.

A formal claim for exemption must be made on a special claim form Artists 1 or 2 depending on the category of the claim, and the exemption will only apply from the tax year in which the claim is made. It should be noted that, notwithstanding the exemption granted or claimed for any year, a return of total income from all sources must be made for each year.

The Arts Council and the Minister for Arts, Culture and the Gaeltacht have drawn up guidelines for the correct operation of this provision.

1.27.2 Patent Royalties

TCA97 s234

The exemption from income tax afforded to individuals in respect of income arising from a qualifying patent (with the exception of those mentioned below) has been phased out completely with regard to patent income arising on or after 6 April 1994.

Chapter 1

Income from a qualifying patent, paid on or after 11 April 1994, is exempt where the royalty or other sum is paid in respect of:-

(i) a manufacturing activity of a company or of an incorporated enterprise, whether that activity is carried on in the State or elsewhere, or

(ii) a "non manufacturing" activity, to the extent that the income arises from bona fide "third party" payments, ie where the payer and payee of the royalty are not connected. Connected persons include spouses, in-laws, relatives, trustees, partners and companies controlled by another person or persons.

The exemption available under paragraph (i) above is restricted in the case of connected persons, to an amount which would have been payable if the payer and the beneficial recipient were independent persons acting at arms length. This restriction applies in respect of royalties paid on or after 23 April 1996.

The exemption from income tax also applies to dividends paid out of "manufacturing royalties" and bona fide "third party" exempt royalties in respect of "eligible shares" in a patent company.

Eligible shares are shares which are:

—fully paid up

—carry no preferential right to dividends or assets on a winding up and no preferential right to be redeemed

—are not subject to any different treatment from the treatment which applies to all shares of the same class.

The exempt or non exempt status of distributions made out of royalty income received by a company on or after 28 March 1996 depends on the source of the exempt royalty income and may be summarised as follows:-

(a) Royalty income received from unconnected persons:-

distributions to shareholders are fully exempt.

(b) Royalty income received from connected persons:-

distributions to shareholders are exempt up to the amount of the "aggregate expenditure" "on research and development incurred by the company. Aggregate expenditure includes expenditure incurred by the company, its group companies and companies under common ownership, in that accounting period and the two previous accounting periods.

The restriction on the amount of tax free distributions can be avoided, where the Revenue Commissioners are satisfied that the royalty income is from a qualifying patent in respect of an invention which:-

(a) involved radical innovation; and

(b) was patented for bona fide commercial reasons and not primarily for the purposes for avoiding liability to taxation.

The Revenue Commissioners, after considering the evidence, which the recipient submits to them and after consultation (if any) as may seem to them to be necessary with such persons as in their opinion may be of assistance to them, will determine the portion of the distribution which may be exempt from tax.

The recipient will be notified of the determination in writing and will have the right of appeal to the Appeal Commissioners within 30 days.

A qualifying patent is a patent covering an invention for which the research, planning, processing, experimenting, testing, devising, designing or developing was carried out in the State.

"Income from a qualifying patent" means any royalty or other sum paid in respect of the user of the invention to which the qualifying patent relates and includes any sum paid for the grant of a licence to exercise rights under such patent.

"Resident of the State" means any person who is resident in the State for income tax or corporation tax purposes and who is not resident elsewhere.

1.27.3 Stallion Services

TCA97 s231

The following income is exempt from tax:-

(i) income arising to the owner (or part owner) of a stallion which is ordinarily kept on land in the State from the sale of services, or the rights to such services, of mares within the State, or

(ii) income arising to the part owner of a stallion, which is ordinarily kept on land outside the State, from the sale of services (or rights to services) of mares by the stallion. However the part owner must carry on in the State a trade which consists of or includes bloodstock breeding, and it must be shown to the satisfaction of the Inspector that the part owner acquired the stallion and held it primarily for the purpose of the service of mares owned or partly owned by the part owner of the stallion in the course of his trade.

Chapter 1

1.27.4 Forests / Woodlands

TCA97 s232

Profits or gains arising from the occupation of woodlands managed on a commercial basis and with a view to the realisation of profits are not to be taken into account for any purpose of the Income Tax Acts.

The tax free status of income so exempted is preserved when dividends are paid out of such income.

Losses incurred in the occupation of woodlands managed on a commercial basis with a view to the realisation of profits may not be claimed under Section 381.

1.27.5 Greyhound Stud Fees

TCA97 s233

Income arising from greyhound stud fees is exempt from tax on the same basis as income from stallion services outlined above. The exemption applies for the tax years 1996/97 et seq in the case of income tax and for accounting periods ending on or after 6 April 1996 in the case of corporation tax.

1.27.6 Payment in respect of Personal Injuries

TCA97 s189

Any payments made to, or in respect of, an individual by a Court or under "out of Court" settlements in respect of damages received for personal injury, where the individual is permanently and totally incapacitated by reason of mental or physical infirmity from maintaining himself as a result of such injury are exempt from income tax.

In addition, any income, including rental income arising from the investment of such a payment is exempt from tax and is disregarded in computing total income. However, the amount of any such income must be included in a return of total income.

The exemption only applies where the income arising from the investment of the payment is the "sole or main" income of the individual concerned. The Revenue Commissioners accept "sole or main" as being more than 50%. They also accept that an invalidity pension from the Department of Social Welfare is disregarded for the purposes of calculating whether the investment income is the sole or main income of the individual, provided the injury or disability which gave rise to the payment of the Social Welfare Benefit/Pension is the same injury or disability which gave rise to the payment of the compensation.

1.27.7 Payments made by the Haemophilia HIV Trust

TCA97 s190

Payments in the nature of income made by the Haemophilia HIV Trust to, or in respect of, beneficiaries under the Trust are disregarded for all purposes of the Tax Acts.

1.27.8 Hepatitis C Compensation

TCA97 s191

Compensation payments made by the Tribunal set up by the Minister for Health on 15 December 1995 or received through the courts are exempt from income. Any investment income arising from the compensation is also exempt from income tax provided, that the income is the individuals sole or main income and the person is permanently and totally incapacitated. The exemption applies to individuals who have been diagnosed positive for Hepatitis C antibodies or Hepatitis C virus where they received the blood transfusion or blood product within the State.

1.27.9 Trusts for permanently incapacitated individuals

TCA s189A

Income arising to the trustees of a trust which has been set up for the benefit of a permanently incapacitated individual and funded by subscriptions from the general public, is exempt from tax for the tax years 1997/98 et seq.

The income paid by the trustees to the incapacitated individual is also exempt from tax.

In order for the above exemptions to apply, the income arising to or being paid by the trustees, must be the sole or main income of the incapacitated individual.

The identity of the incapacitated person must be known to the subscribers and the total amount subscribed must not exceed £300,000 and no one person can make a subscription of more than 30% of the total subscriptions.

Chapter 1

1.28 RELIEF FOR INVESTMENT IN CORPORATE TRADES (BES)

TCA97 s488-s508

The relief applies to shares issued on or after 6 April 1984. The scheme runs until 5 April 2001. The relief is only available to individuals who subscribe for new ordinary shares.

Relief is given as a deduction from total income and the maximum amount which qualifies for relief in any one tax year is £25,000. Where relief cannot be obtained due to an insufficiency of income, the unrelieved amount may be carried forward and claimed as a deduction in future years, subject to the overall limit of £25,000.

The relief may be granted through the PAYE system. The minimum amount which can be invested in any one company during a tax year is £200. This restriction does not apply where the investment is made through a designated fund.

If the investment is made through a designated fund and the shares are issued in the year of assessment following the year in which the investment was made in the fund, the individual may elect for relief in the earlier year.

1.28.1 Qualifying Individual

TCA97 s493

The individual must not be connected with the company during a period starting with the incorporation of the company (or if later, two years before the shares are issued) and ending five years after the shares are issued. In determining whether an individual is connected with the company, it is necessary to take into account any interest held by his associates. Associates do not include spouses or relatives.

In addition, an individual will be regarded as connected with the company if he, or an associate of his, is any of the following:

(a) A partner of the qualifying company or of any subsidiary of the company.

(b) A director or employee of the qualifying company or of any subsidiary of the company who, during the five years after the date the eligible shares are issued, received any "non-armslength" payment from the company or any subsidiary. Non-armslength payments do not include the following:-

   (i) Payment or reimbursement of travelling or other expenses wholly exclusively and necessarily incurred by them in the performance of their duties.

   (ii) Interest at a reasonable rate on money lent to the company.

   (iii) Normal dividends.

   (iv) Payment for goods at arm's length.

Income Tax

(v) Payment for services rendered which is taken into account for the purpose of Case I or II of Schedule D.

(c) The owner of, or entitled to own, in excess of 30% of the company's issued ordinary share capital and loan capital. This restriction is removed where the issued share capital does not exceed £150,000 with effect from 6 April 1993 and £250,000 with effect from 6 April 1994.

(d) The individual has control of the qualifying company within the meaning of Section 11.

(e) The individual has at any time in the five year relevant period had control within the meaning of Section 11 of another company which has, since that time and before the end of that relevant period, become a subsidiary of the qualifying company.

(f) The individual directly or indirectly possesses or is entitled to acquire any loan capital of a subsidiary of the qualifying company.

(g) The individual, if not already connected with the qualifying company under any of the foregoing rules, subscribes for shares in the company as part of any arrangement which provides for another person to subscribe for shares in another company, but only if the individual or any other individual who is a party to the arrangement is connected with that other company.

1.28.2 Qualifying Companies

In order for the individual to obtain tax relief, the investment must be made in a qualifying company. The company must be incorporated in the State and for a period of three years from the date the shares are issued (or if later, three years from the company commencing to trade) the company must satisfy a number of conditions which include the following:

(a) The company must be resident in the State.

(b) The company must not be quoted on a Stock Exchange. For this purpose a company trading on the Unlisted Securities Market is regarded as quoted.

(c) The company must not have a group connection with another company unless it has subsidiaries which would also all fulfil the required conditions.

However with effect from 6 April 1997, companies can enter both the Developing Companies Market (DCM) of the Irish Stock Exchange and similar or corresponding markets in other EU Member States without its status as a BES qualifying company being affected, provided that it enters the DCM before or at the same time as it first enters one of the other EU unlisted markets.

(d) The company must be carrying on (or intend to carry on) a qualifying trade on a commercial basis, principally in the State, or be a company whose business consists wholly of:-

   (i) The holding of shares or securities of, or the making of loans to one or more qualifying subsidiaries; or

   (ii) Both the holding of shares or securities, or the making of such loans and the carrying on principally in the State of one or more qualifying trades.

The company will not be a qualifying company in the following circumstances.

(a) If an individual has acquired a controlling interest in the company's trade after 5th April 1984; and

(b) For a five year period beginning two years before the later of the date on which the shares were issued or the date the company began to trade, he has, or had, a controlling interest in another trade; and

(c) The trade carried on by the company or a substantial part of it:-

   (i) Is concerned with the same or similar types of property or provides the same or similar services as the other trade; or

   (ii) Serves substantially the same or similar outlets or markets as the other trade.

For the purpose of this prohibition, an individual has a controlling interest in a trade:

(a) In the case of a trade carried on by the company if:-

   (i) He controls the company.

   (ii) The company is a close company and he or an associate of his is a director of the company and the beneficial owner of, or able directly or through the medium of other companies or by any other indirect means, to control more than 30% of the ordinary share capital of the company.

   (iii) Not less than 50% of the trade could be regarded as belonging to him.

(b) In any other case, if he is entitled to not less than 50% of the assets used for, or the income arising from the trade.

From 6 April 1997, the definition of "qualifying company" has been extended to include a company quoted on the Developing Companies Market either prior to or subsequent to its qualifying for BES relief.

1.28.3 Company's Limit

With effect from 3 December 1997, the maximum amount which may be raised by a company through the issue of eligible shares is £250,000. Previous issues of eligible shares by the company or group of companies are aggregated in calculating the £250,000.

However, certain transitional arrangements apply for companies where proposals to raise BES funds were well advanced before 3 December 1997. Companies which satisfy the conditions set out in the transitional arrangements may still raise up to the old limit of £1m.

Where companies are associated (within the meaning of the following paragraph), the maximum amount that can be raised under the scheme by all such associated companies is £250,000. Where £250,000 has already been raised by the associated companies no further amounts can be raised by the applicant company under the scheme. Where the amounts previously raised by the associated companies (including the applicant company) is less than £250,000, the applicant company may only raise an amount equal to the difference between the amounts so raised and £250,000.

A company will be associated with another company where it could reasonably be considered that:-

(i) both companies act in pursuit of a common purpose, or

(ii) any person or group(s) of persons, having a reasonable commonality of identity, have or had the means or power, either directly or indirectly, to determine the trading operations carried on or to be carried on by both companies, or

(iii) both companies are under the control of any person or group(s) of persons having a reasonable commonality of identity.

The subsidiaries of companies are also taken into account for the purposes of the above rules with effect from 28 March 1996.

The following are the only exceptions to the limit of £250,000:-

(i) an exchange facility established in the Custom House Docks Area where the amount which can be raised is limited to £100,000.

(ii) Companies raising funds under the associated Seed Capital Scheme, the limit is £500,000 of which a maximum of £250,000 may be raised under the BES.

(iii) Companies raising funds used solely in connection with the construction and leasing of an advance factory building where the limit is £1m.

Chapter 1

1.28.4 **Qualifying Trade**

A qualifying trade is one consisting wholly or mainly of the following operations:-

(a) The manufacture of goods and certain other trades within the meaning of Section 443. The company must therefore claim and be entitled to the 10% rate of corporation tax.

(b) The rendering of services in the course of a service undertaking in respect of which an employment grant was made by the IDA, or which has received grant aid from Udaras na Gaeltachta.

(c) Tourist traffic undertakings.

(d) Qualifying shipping activities.

(e) The export sale of Irish manufactured goods by a special trading house.

(f) Construction and leasing of advance factories promoted by local community groups.

(g) The cultivation of plants in the State as defined by Section 443.

(h) Certain research and development activities.

(i) The cultivation of horticultural produce in greenhouses.

(j) The production, publication, marketing and promotion of qualifying musical recordings.

(k) Trading activities on an exchange facility established in the Custom House Docks Area.

If the company is not carrying on a trade at the time the shares are issued, it will be regarded as carrying on a trade if it has expended at least 80% of the money subscribed for the shares on research and development which is connected with an undertaking with a view to the carrying on of the trade, and begins to carry on the trade within three years after that time. In all other cases, the company must commence trading within two years from the date of issue of the shares.

Where the company carries on qualifying trading operations and other trading operations, the total amount receivable from sales made and services rendered in the course of qualifying trading operations must not be less than 75% of the total amount receivable by the company from all sales made and services rendered.

1.28.5 **Qualifying Shares**

The shares eligible for relief must be fully paid ordinary shares. During a five year period commencing with the date on which they were issued, the shares must not carry a present or future preferential right to dividends or to the company's assets on its winding up and no present or future preferential right to be redeemed. No relief is available on shares issued after 12 April 1989 which are the subject of either a put or call option at a price other than their market value at the date at which the option is exercised.

The shares must be issued for the purpose of raising money for a qualifying trade which is being carried on by the company or which it intends to carry on.

The company must provide satisfactory evidence to the Revenue Commissioners that the money was used for any of the following purposes.

(a) Enabling the company, or enlarging its capacity, to undertake qualifying trading operations.

(b) Enabling the company to engage in research and development, the acquisition of technological information and data, the development of new or existing services or products, or the provision of new products or services.

(c) Enabling the company to identify new markets and to develop new and existing markets for the products and services.

(d) Enabling the company to increase its sale of products or provision of services.

In all cases the money must be used with a view to the creation or maintenance of employment in the company.

1.28.6 Claim for Relief

The claim for relief must be made within two years of the end of the year of assessment in which the shares are issued.

A claim for relief must be accompanied by a certificate from the company certifying that the conditions for the relief have been satisfied.

1.28.7 Withdrawal of Relief

Where an individual receives any value from the company during a period beginning with the incorporation of the company (or if later, two years before the issue of the shares) and ending five years after the issue of the shares, the amount of the relief granted on the shares will be reduced by the value received.

An individual receives value from the company in the following situations.

(a) (i) The company repays, redeems or repurchases, any of its share capital or securities which belong to the individual; or

(ii) It makes any payment to him for giving up his right to any of the company's share capital or any security on its cancellation or extinguishment.

(b) The company repays any debt to the individual other than a debt which was:

(i) An ordinary trade debt incurred by the company; or

(ii) Any other debt which was incurred by the company on or after the earliest date on which the subscription for the shares in respect of which the relief is claimed, otherwise than in consideration of the extinguishment of a debt incurred before that date.

(c) The company makes to the individual any payment for giving up his right to any debt or its extinguishment other than:

(i) A debt in respect of a payment of the kind mentioned earlier in connection with directors or employees.

(ii) A debt in respect of reasonable remuneration for services rendered and which are taken into account under Case I or II of Schedule D.

(iii) A debt in respect of the payment for the supply of goods which does not exceed their market value.

(d) The company releases or waives any liability of the individual to the company or discharges, or undertakes to discharge any liability of his to a third party.

(e) The company makes a loan or advance to the individual.

(f) The company provides a benefit or facility for the individual.

(g) The company transfers an asset to the individual for no consideration or for a consideration less than its market value, or acquires an asset from him for a consideration exceeding its market value.

(h) The company makes to him any other payment except a payment of the kind mentioned in connection with payments to directors or employees, or a payment in discharge of an ordinary trade debt.

An individual will also receive value from the company if any person who would be regarded as connected with the company:-

(a) purchases any of its share capital or securities which belong to the individual; or

(b) makes any payment to him for giving up any right in relation to the company's share capital or securities.

The relief available to an individual may be reduced or eliminated if, at any time during the relevant period, the company repays, redeems or repurchases any or its share capital which belongs to any member, other than:-

(a) the individual; or

(b) another individual whose relief is thereby reduced; or

(c) makes any payment to such member for giving up his right to any of the company's share capital on its cancellation or extinguishment.

The amount of any value received from the company is subtracted from the ordinary share capital in determining whether or not the subscribed amount exceeds the permitted 30% interest in the company.

1.28.8 Replacement Capital

An individual is not entitled to relief in respect of any shares in a company where at any time in the relevant period the company or any of its subsidiaries:

(a) Begins to carry on as its trade or as part of its trade, a trade which was previously carried on at any time in the relevant period otherwise than by the company or any of its subsidiaries; or

(b) Acquires the whole or greater part of the assets used for the purposes of a trade so previously carried on.

These provisions apply where the individual is either the person who owned more than one half of the trade at any time during the relevant period or the person who has controlled another company which previously carried on the trade.

An individual is not entitled to relief in respect of any shares in the company where:-

(a) The company comes to acquire all the issued share capital of another company at any time in the relevant period; and

(b) The same person controlled or controls both companies.

An individual who has been granted relief, must notify the Inspector of Taxes within 60 days of an event occurring which causes the relief to be withdrawn.

The company must give similar notification of an event occurring which causes the company to cease to be a qualifying company. Withdrawal of the relief will be by means of an assessment under Case IV of Schedule D.

1.28.9 Capital Gains Tax

If a gain arises on disposal, the individual will be liable to capital gains tax in the normal way, the tax relief obtained being disregarded. If the shares are sold at a loss, the loss is reduced by the amount of the relief obtained. Where relief has been granted on some shares in an individuals combined holding, the shares sold must be identified with shares for which relief has been granted on a first-in, first-out basis.

Where there has been a re-organisation of share capital and a bonus issue is made, the bonus shares are treated as also having obtained the relief.

1.28.10 Approved Funds

Investment through a designated fund is permitted. The Revenue Commissioners will approve a fund as a designated fund provided certain conditions are satisfied.

1.28.11 Spouses

The relief is available to each spouse, subject to availability of income in his/her own right.

1.29 SEED CAPITAL INVESTMENT

TCA97
s488-s508

The Business Expansion System (BES) also provides income tax relief for investment by certain individuals in new companies.

Individuals who satisfy certain conditions may obtain income tax relief for investment in new ordinary shares in a newly incorporated company, which is engaged in a BES type activity or in certain research and development activities.

With effect from 6 April 1995, a sum of up to £125,000 subscribed for shares in the new company will be relieved against the total income of the individual for any of the five years immediately preceding the year in which the investment is made. The maximum relief in any one tax year is £25,000.

The investment in the new company may be made in two stages with the second stage being made before the end of the second tax year following the tax year in which the first investment was made.

To qualify for the relief, the individual must:-

(a) be a full-time employee or a full-time director with the new company at any time up to six months after the end of the tax year in which the business is established;

(b) derive not less than 75% of his total income from Schedule E sources, income from other sources not being more than £15,000 in each of the three years of assessment preceding the year of assessment immediately prior to the year of assessment in which the employment commences;

(c) not have possessed or have been entitled to acquire more than 15% of the ordinary share capital, loan capital or voting power of a company other than a seed capital company except where the individual owns more than 15% of only one other company provided:-

   (i) the company's turnover in each of the three accounting periods prior to the accounting period which the investment is made in the seed capital company did not exceed £100,000 and

   (ii) the company is a trading company other than a company trading in land or financial services.

(d) acquire at least 15% of the issued ordinary share capital of the seed capital company and retain that 15% for two years from the date of the investment or from the date on which the company commences to trade whichever is later.

An individual will not be regarded as ceasing to comply with the employment and shareholding conditions where the company is

Chapter 1

wound up or dissolved for bona fide commercial reasons and not as part of a tax avoidance scheme.

The new company must be carrying on trading operations of a BES nature which have been certified by an industrial agency, Bord Failte or a County Enterprise Board, to be a bona fide new venture having the potential for the creation of employment. It must be eligible to be grant aided by the agency or Bord Failte as appropriate. The value of the company's interest in land and buildings (excluding fixtures and fittings) must not be greater than half the value of its total assets. It must deal on an arms-length basis in any transactions with the individuals previous employer company during a period of 3 years from commencement of operations.

1.30 INVESTMENT IN FILMS

TCA97 s481

Relief is provided for an investment made in a qualifying film company.

The main provisions are as follows:-

(i) Section 481 finance is permitted in respect of:-

   (a) up to 60% of the total production costs for films with a budget of £4m or less.

   (b) between 50% and 60% of the total production costs for films with a budget of between £4m and £5m.

   (c) up to 50% of the total production costs for films with a budget of over £5m.

   (d) The overall limit for Section 481 finance is £7.5m. However, where more than half of the finance is subscribed by corporate investors in respect of one film, the maximum amount which can be raised is £15m, provided application for certification is made on or after 26 March 1997.

   The limits at (a) - (d) above are increased by 10% in the case of:-

   — "off-season" film productions, ie those productions where principal photography commences between the beginning of October and the end of January.

   — films where post production work is carried out wholly or mainly in the State and an application for certification was made on or after 26 March 1997.

(ii) Relief may be claimed on investments made between 23 January 1996 and 5 April 2000 by individuals and companies.

(iii) Individuals may claim relief on investments of up to £25,000 in any one tax year. Where relief cannot be obtained due to an insufficiency of income, the unrelieved amount may be carried forward and claimed in the following year (see (v) below).

(iv) Investors (individual or corporate) may offset 80% of the investment in a qualifying film at their marginal tax rate.

(v) There is a total annual investment limit of £8m for a company and its connected companies, in relation to any period of twelve months ending on an anniversary of 22 January 1997. However, a corporate investment in any one film company cannot exceed £3m in respect of investments made on or after 23 March 1997, and where in a twelve month period, the total of investments made by a company and its connected companies exceeds £3m, the excess can only be invested in film projects with a budget of less than £4m.

Chapter 1

(vi) Where shares in a qualifying company are retained for more than 1 year, the relief claimed on the investment is ignored for capital gains tax purposes on a subsequent disposal of the shares. A loss on disposal is restricted by the amount of the relief.

(vii) Investments must be made directly by the investor into a qualifying company and such a company may only make one qualifying film.

(viii) Relief is only available in respect of investments in share capital.

(ix) An investment cannot be made in a film company before the Minister for Arts, Culture and the Gaeltacht has indicated that a satisfactory application for certification of a film has been received.

(x) The certificate to be issued by the Minister for Arts, Culture and the Gaeltacht shall specify such conditions as the Minister may consider proper and in particular it will specify the percentage of the total production cost of the film which can be met by Section 481 investments.

(xi) Tax relief is available from the date of commencement of principal photography. The certificate to be issued by the Minister for Arts, Culture and the Gaeltacht will contain a requirement that the film company inform the Minister when principal photography has commenced.

(xii) A certificate will not be granted where the film production has commenced before the film company has made an applicaiton to the Minister.

(xiii) A film company is not permitted to include in its name the words "Ireland", "Irish", "Eireann", "Eire" or "National".

(xiv) the term "film" has been defined so as to fall within the categories of film which are eligible for certification. These categories of films are included in guidelines issued by the Minister.

The qualifying film company must be incorporated and resident in the State and not resident elsewhere. In general, at least 75% of the work on the production of the film must be carried out in the State and not more than 60% of the cost of production may be obtained from investor companies qualifying for relief under this section.

With effect from 6 May 1993 however, where this 75% rule is not met, and provided that not less than 10% of the production work is carried out in the State, the Minister for Arts, Culture and the Gaeltacht can waive the 75% requirement and provide the film making company with a certificate, stating that the film may be treated as a qualifying film for the purposes of the relief. In any such case, and where less than 60% of the production work is carried out in the State, the percentage of the cost of producing the film met by Section 481 investments cannot be in excess of the percentage of production work which is carried out in the State.

Prohibitions exist regarding payments by the qualifying company to the investor company or individual.

Chapter 1

1.31 RESIDENCE OF INDIVIDUALS

1.31.1 Residence

TCA97 s819-s824

An individual is resident in the State in a tax year if he spends:-

(a) 183 days in the State in that year, or

(b) 280 days in aggregate in that tax year and the preceding tax year.

Notwithstanding (b) above, an individual who is present in the State for 30 days or less in a tax year will not be treated as resident for that year unless he elects to be resident.

A day will only count if the individual is present in the State at the end of the day.

1.31.2 Ordinary Residence

TCA97 s820

An individual is ordinarily resident in the State from commencement of the fourth tax year if he has been resident for each of the three preceding tax years.

An individual leaving the State will not cease to be ordinarily resident until he has been non-resident for three continuous tax years.

Where an individual is not resident in the State, but ordinarily resident, he will be subject to Irish tax on Irish source income and foreign income excluding income derived from a trade or profession, no part of which is carried on in the State, or from an office or employment, all the duties of which are performed outside the State. The first £3,000 of foreign investment income in any year is exempt.

1.31.3 Split Year Residence Relief

TCA97 s822

With effect from 6 April 1994, for the purposes of a charge to tax on employment income, where an individual is resident in Ireland for a tax year and he was not resident in the preceding year, and he satisfies the Revenue that he is in Ireland with the intention and in such circumstances that he will be resident for the following year, he will be deemed to be resident for that year only from the date of arrival.

Similarly, where an individual is resident for a tax year and he satisfies the Revenue that he is leaving other than for a temporary purpose with the intention and in such circumstances that he will not be resident for the following year, he will be regarded as resident up to the date of his departure.

Where an individual is treated as resident for part of a year the employment income which arises or, in the case of an individual taxed on the remittance basis on his employment income, the amounts received in the State, will be treated as income arising or amounts received for a year of assessment in which the individual is resident in the State. Income arising, or amounts remitted in the remaining part of the year will be treated as arising or received in a year in which the individual is not resident.

1.31.4 Deduction for Foreign Earnings

TCA97 s823

Certain individuals who spend substantial periods working outside the State may claim a deduction for the portion of their employment income related to the duties exercised outside the State. The following requirements apply:-

(i) the individual must be resident in the State,

(ii) the individual must have at least "90 qualifying days" in a tax year or a period of twelve months spanning two tax years. Qualifying days are defined as days of absence from the State which are substantially devoted to the performance of the employment and are one of at least 14 consecutive days on which the individual is absent from the State and which, taken as a whole, are substantially devoted to performance of his duties,

(iii) the individual must be a director of a trading or professional company or in an employment which is not funded by the State and which is not an employment with a board, authority or other similar body established under Statute, and

(iv) the split year of residence does not apply.

The deduction is calculated by the formula:

$$\frac{D \times E}{365} \quad \text{Where}$$

D = the number of qualifying days in the year of assessment.

E = the employment income concerned.

The deduction does not apply to U.K. employment income, income from employments exercised in the U.K. or where the individual is taxed on a remittance basis.

Employment income does not include severance payments, share options, benefits-in-kind etc accruing to an employee on or after 10 March 1999.

Non-resident individuals from other EU Member States with income subject to Irish tax may claim personal allowances proportionate to the amount of income subject to Irish tax. Where the income subject to Irish tax is more than 75% of total income, full personal allowances apply.

Chapter 1

1.31.5 **Cross Border Workers**

Income tax payable in the State for 1998/99 et seq on employment income from a country with which Ireland has a double tax treaty is reduced by the proportion which the employment income bears to total income.

The relief is not claimable where the seafarer allowance or the foreign earnings deduction is claimed.

The conditions under which the relief may be claimed are:-

(a) The employment is held outside the State in a country with which Ireland has a double tax treaty;

(b) The employment is held for a continuous period of 13 weeks;

(c) The employment must not be with the Government or an authority set up by the State or under Statute;

(d) The duties of the employment must be performed wholly outside the State (incidental duties performed in the State are regarded as performed outside the State);

(e) The income must be taxed in the other country; and

(f) The employee must be at least one day per week in the State.

1.31.6 **Seafarers Allowance**

TCA97 s472A

Seafarers are entitled to a deduction of £5,000 from employment income on a sea-going ship (excluding fishing vessels) where the seafarer is at sea on a voyage to or from a foreign port for at least 169 days in a tax year. A mobile or fixed installation in foreign waters may be treated as a foreign port for this purpose.

The allowance may not be claimed in any year in which a seafarer claims the foreign earnings deduction or the remittance basis or split year rules apply.

The foreign earnings deduction has been amended for seafarers to provide that where a seafarer is outside Ireland for a continuous period of 14 days and during that period visits a port in the United Kingdom and also visits a port other than in the United Kingdom or Ireland, the foreign earnings deduction may be claimed as if the UK visit were a qualifying period.

1.31.7 **Domicile**

TCA97 s71

The principle of domicile is a matter of international law and broadly refers to the country which an individual considers as his natural home. It is not therefore determinable in the same manner as residence or ordinary residence.

An individual acquires a domicile of origin at his birth and this is normally that of the father. This domicile of origin is retained unless the individual takes steps to acquire a domicile of choice. Such steps would normally entail a positive indication of a change of citizenship, the making of a will under the laws of the place adopted as the new domicile, disposing of property in the place where the domicile of origin arises etc.

The Domicile and Recognition of Foreign Divorces Act 1985 provides, that the domicile of married women is to be determined in the same way as that of any other adult.

In the case where the individual is not domiciled in the State or being a citizen of the State not ordinarily resident in the State, he is liable to tax only on so much of his foreign income as is remitted to or enjoyed in any form in the State. In this connection there are anti avoidance provisions to prevent the use of "back to back" loans. (These provisions apply only to individuals ordinarily resident in the State.) UK income is not dealt with on the remittance basis.

Chapter 1

1.32 SECURITISATION OF ASSETS

TCA97 s110

Securitisation is an arrangement under which a bank or building society sells off a portfolio of its mortgages to investors such as pension funds or life assurance companies. It is provided that the company acquiring the qualifying assets is brought into charge under Case I of Schedule D on the basis that it is carrying on a trade. The provisions ensure that the existing tax treatment is continued in the event of securitisation, normal trade expenses and the treatment of bad and doubtful debts and the recovery of debts already deducted are the same as for the original lender.

TCA97 s110

The securitisation rules apply to a much wider range of assets in the case of a securitisation vehicle which is an IFSC certified company.

The income, profit or gains of a body designated under the Securitisation (Process of Certain Mortgages) Act, 1995 is exempt from certain taxes being income tax, corporation tax and capital gains tax.

1.33 TRUSTS AND SETTLEMENTS

TCA97 s791
Where a settlor has power to enjoy the income of his settlement, or where the settlor or his wife has power of revocation, all the income of the settlement will be deemed to be his income for tax purposes.

TCA97 s792
Where the settlor divests himself absolutely of his capital into a settlement he will not be charged to tax on any income arising to the settlement.

TCA97 s795-s746
The income of a settlement created by a living parent in favour of his children, who are under 18 and unmarried, is deemed to be the income of the parent for tax purposes, unless the settlement is irrevocable and accumulating.

1.33.1 Foreign Trusts

A trust which, apart from the residence of an approved Irish trustee, has no Irish connection is not regarded as resident in Ireland for tax purposes and therefore neither its income or gains arising from asset transactions will be liable to taxation in Ireland.

A "foreign trust" is a trust in respect of which:

- the settlor and the beneficiaries are not resident, ordinarily resident or domiciled in the State;

- the assets are situated outside the State, with the exception of an operating bank account in the State held by a trustee solely for the purposes of processing transactions in relation to assets situated outside the State;

- the income arises from sources outside the State;

- the trustees, other than certain Irish resident trustees which satisfy specified conditions, are not resident, ordinarily resident or domiciled in the State.

The conditions to be satisfied by an Irish resident trustee are that the trustee must be:

1. (a) a trustee of an authorised Unit Trust, (under the Unit Trust Act, 1990),

    (b) a trustee of an authorised collective investment undertaking (under the European Communities (UCITS) Regulations, 1989),

    (c) in the opinion of the Central Bank, an appropriate person to be a trustee,

    (d) a licensed bank,

Chapter 1

2. authorised by the Central Bank to engage in the management of trusts in the course of its business, and

3. carrying on a business which includes the management of trusts.

1.33.2 Surcharge on Undistributed Income

TCA97 s805

Trustees are liable to tax at the standard rate on settlement income. Where there is undistributed settlement income, there is an additional 20% surcharge. If the distributable income of the settlement is distributed within the year of assessment, or within 18 months of the end of the year of assessment, the surcharge does not apply. In computing the distributable income the expenses of the trustees, which are properly chargeable to income are allowable deductions. Undistributed income of a charity or of an approved pension scheme is not liable to the surcharge.

CHAPTER 2   CORPORATION TAX

2.1 ADMINISTRATION AND FUNDAMENTAL CONCEPTS

2.1.1 Scope of Corporation Tax

TCA97 s4

All companies resident in the State and all non resident companies which carry on a trade in the State through a branch or agency, subject to specific exceptions, are liable to corporation tax.

TCA97 s882

A company which commences to carry on a trade, profession or business is obliged to deliver a written statement within thirty days of commencement to the Revenue Commissioners containing such information as the name of the company, its registered office, the name of the secretary and the nature of the trade, profession or business.

The penalty for not submitting such a statement is £500 on the company and £100 on the secretary. If judgement is given and a statement is still outstanding then a further penalty of £50 per day is payable.

An Inspector of Taxes has the power to make corporation tax assessments on any company whether it is resident in the State or not.

The appeal provisions that exist for income tax purposes also apply for corporation tax purposes (see page 46).

2.1.2 Corporation Tax Rates

TCA97 s21

With effect from 1 January 1999, the standard rate of corporation tax is 28%. Previous rates are set out in Chart 18.

A reduced rate of 10% applies to manufacturing companies (see page 184).

TCA97 s22

A reduced rate of 25% applies to the first £100,000 (referred to as the "specified amount") of a company's income in the year ending 31 December 1999 (excluding income qualifying for the 10% rate). Previous rates are set out in Chart 18. The following points should be noted in relation to this reduced rate:-

(i)   The specified amount is determined by the formula:-

$$50,000 \; \frac{N}{12} \; \times \; \frac{1}{A} \; \text{where}$$

N = the number of months in the accounting period, and

A = one plus the number of associated companies which the company has in the accounting period.

Chapter 2

(ii) Associated companies may, subject to certain conditions, jointly elect to allocate the specified amount between them in such manner as they specify.

(iii) The specified amount is reduced pro-rata in the case of accounting periods of less than 12 months duration.

(iv) Capital gains do not qualify for the reduced rate.

The standard rate of corporation tax for trading income is to be reduced on a phased basis, to 12½% as follows:

Y/E 31.12.1999	28%
Y/E 31.12.2000	24%
Y/E 31.12.2001	20%
Y/E 31.12.2002	16%
Y/E 31.12.2003 et seq.	12½%

For the years ending 31 December 2000 et seq, a corporation tax rate of 25% will apply to certain income of companies including income chargeable under Case III, Case IV, Case V, income from working minerals, petroleum activities and dealing in or developing land, other than construction operations.

The 10% rate will continue to apply to manufacturing income until such time as title to that rate expires, at which stage such income will be taxable at 12½% (See page 184).

2.1.3 Residence

TCA97 s24-s25

Prior to the publication of the Finance Act 1999, the residence of a company was determined not by the place of incorporation but by where the central management and control actually resides. The key factors to be considered in determining where the central management and control resides are:-

(a) Location of Directors' Meetings

(b) Location of Shareholders' Meetings

(c) Location of Head Office of the Company

(d) Location of Statutory Books, Company Seal

(e) Where major contracts are negotiated and policy determined

All companies incorporated in the State after 11 February 1999 are resident for tax purposes and all companies incorporated prior to that date, are resident for tax purposes from 1 October 1999. However the link between incorporation and residence will not apply where:

- the company or a related company carries on a trade in the State, and either the company is ultimately controlled by persons resident in EU Member States or countries with which Ireland has a tax treaty, or the company or a related company are quoted companies.

or

- the company is regarded as not resident in the State under a tax treaty between Ireland and another country.

2.1.4 Accounting Periods

TCA97 s27

Corporation Tax is chargeable in respect of the taxable profits of a company for an accounting period. An accounting period commences whenever a company:-

(a) commences to carry on a trade

(b) becomes resident in the State

(c) acquires its first source of income, or

(d) is being wound up.

An accounting period ends on the occasion of any of the following:

(a) On the expiration of twelve months from the beginning of the accounting period.

(b) On an accounting date of the company, or, if there is a period for which the company does not make up accounts, the end of that period.

(c) On the company beginning or ceasing to trade or to be, in respect of the trade or (if more than one) of all the trades carried on by it, within the charge to Corporation Tax.

(d) On the company beginning or ceasing to be resident in the State.

(e) On the company being wound up.

2.1.5 Self Assessment

TCA97 s951

The self assessment system applies to companies with effect from 1 October 1989. To enable the system to work efficiently, it is necessary to ensure as far as possible that a company can satisfy its tax obligations by filing a return containing all necessary information to finalise its liability for an accounting period and by making one payment of tax unless a liability to advance corporation tax (ACT) arises, where two payments may be necessary.

Chapter 2

2.1.6 Returns

TCA97 s951

A company must submit a return of profits, chargeable gains and other particulars to the Inspector of Taxes not later than 9 months from the end of the accounting period to which the return relates.

2.1.7 Late Returns

TCA97 s1084

Where a company's tax return is not submitted to the Inspector of Taxes before the return filing date, the company is penalised by way of a surcharge and a restriction on the use the company may make of certain reliefs and allowances, as outlined below:

(a) Surcharge

Where a company's return is not submitted before the filing date, the tax liability for that period is increased by a surcharge on the amount of the tax assessed. The rate of surcharge applicable is 10% for accounting periods ending on or before 5 April, 1995.

For accounting periods ending on or after 6 April 1995, the surcharge is as follows:-

(a) 5% of the amount of tax subject to a maximum of £10,000, where the return is submitted before the expiry of two months after the specified date, and

(b) 10% of the amount of tax subject to a maximum of £50,000 where the return is not submitted within two months after the specified date.

(b) Restriction of Allowances and Reliefs

TCA97 s1085

Where a company fails to submit a tax return for accounting periods ending between 1 April 1992 and 5 April 1995 on time, there is an effective 50% restriction on the use the company may make of certain reliefs and allowances. With regard to accounting periods ending on or after 6 April 1995 the restrictions are graded and capped as follows:-

Where the delay in filing is less than two months, reliefs and allowances are to be restricted by 25% subject to a maximum in each case of £25,000, or £10,000 in the case of the offset of advance corporation tax.

Where the delay is two months or more, reliefs and allowances are to be restricted by 50%, subject to a maximum in each case of £125,000, or £50,000 in the case of the offset of advance corporation tax.

The following are the reliefs and allowances which are restricted:-

- set off for excess Schedule D Case IV and Schedule D Case V capital allowances against total profits.

- set off for trading losses against total profits in current year and carry back to prior year;

- carry back of Schedule D Case V deficiency against Schedule D Case V income of previous accounting period;
- refund of tax credit on franked investment income;
- entitlement to reverse claim for refund under section 25 (1);
- entitlement to reverse claim under section 26 (1) (refund of tax credit on franked investment income by use of trading losses and terminal losses in case of financial concerns);
- entitlement to group relief. This includes:

    entitlement to make group payments without withholding tax;

    group loss relief;

    consortium relief
- entitlement to carry back ACT against mainstream corporation tax of previous accounting period;
- surrender of ACT to another group company.

In the case of any of the reliefs which involve groups of companies (eg loss relief or surrender of surplus ACT) it is a condition that both the surrendering company and the claimant company should each have submitted their tax returns on time.

2.1.8 Matters of Doubt

TCA97 s955

Where a taxpayer is in doubt as regards a matter to be included in a return, his obligations with regard to the matter will be fulfilled if he draws the Inspector's attention to the matter in question. The provision does not apply where the Inspector or the Appeal Commissioners are of the opinion that the doubt was not genuine and the taxpayer was acting with an avoidance or evasion of tax motive.

2.1.9 Payment of Corporation Tax

TCA97 s958

Corporation tax is payable in one instalment six months after the end of the accounting period or within one month of the making of the assessment if that date is later. Where the payment falls after the 28th day of a particular month, the tax must be paid on or before the 28th day of that month.

The same dates apply for the payment of preliminary corporation tax. In order to avoid any possible interest charges in relation to the payment of preliminary tax, a company must pay at least 90% of its ultimate liability by the due date. Where adequate preliminary tax has been paid on time and an assessment is subsequently raised, to recover any balance of tax due, the balance must be paid within one month of the date of the assessment.

Chapter 2

2.1.10 Calculation of Taxable Profits and Allowable Losses

TCA97 s76

Corporation Tax is charged on the profits of a company, ie income and chargeable gains.

Except as otherwise provided in the Corporation Tax Act income must be calculated in accordance with income tax principles. Income is calculated under the different Schedules and Cases appropriate to Income Tax.

The provisions of the Capital Gains Tax Act 1975 apply to chargeable gains of companies. Gains or losses are calculated in the normal way.

Where "Development Land" is disposed of any gain arising is assessed to Capital Gains Tax.

2.1.11 Pre-Trading Expenses

TCA97 s82

An allowance may be claimed in respect of pre-trading expenses in the case of a trade or profession which is set up and commenced on or after 22 January 1997, provided that the expenses:-

(i) were incurred for the purpose of the trade or profession, and

(ii) were incurred within three years of commencement, and

(iii) are not otherwise allowable in computing profits.

Where an allowance is granted for pre-trading expenses, it is treated as if the expenditure was incurred on the date on which the trade/profession commenced.

A deduction may also be claimed in respect of certain pre-trading charges.

The pre-trading expenditure which is allowed cannot be used for the purpose of set off against income of the company other than that arising from the trade of profession in respect of which the expenditure was incurred.

2.1.12 Losses / Management Expenses

TCA97 s396

Trading losses are computed in the same manner as trading profits. A trading loss can be

(a) Set off against other profits before charges in the same accounting period.

(b) Set off against profits before charges of the preceding accounting period of corresponding length, if the company carried on the trade in that period.

(c) Set off against future profits of the same trade unless the loss has been otherwise utilised.

Losses under the other Cases of Schedule D and capital losses may be utilised as follows:

TCA97 s396	CASE III (Trading)	Carry forward only against future Case III profits.
TCA97 s399	CASE IV	Carry forward only against Case IV profits.
TCA97 s399	CASE V (Rents)	Carry back to previous accounting period of same length and source and forward against future Case V profits.
TCA97 s308	CASE V (Excess Capital Allowances)	Same as trading losses.
TCA97 s78	CAPITAL LOSSES	Carry forward only against future capital profits.
TCA97 s653	CAPITAL LOSSES (Development Land)	Set against other capital profits of same accounting period or forward against future capital profits or development land profits.
TCA97 s397	Terminal loss relief arises where a company incurs a loss in its last twelve months trading and claims to carry back against income from the same trade in the preceding three years the loss incurred in the last twelve months. Terminal loss relief will be given only where all other claims for loss relief have been made.	
TCA97 s83	If Management Expenses exceed the profits of a resident investment company the excess may be carried forward for set off against profits of a subsequent period.	
TCA97 s157	Trading losses can be off set against franked investment income received in the current accounting period or in the preceding accounting period of equal length, resulting in a repayment of the tax credit.	
	If the company subsequently decides to avail of these losses, which were relieved at the standard rate, against future profits liable at a higher rate, it can do so under the provisions of Section 157. The Revenue will clawback the income tax repaid by an assessment under Case IV of Schedule D.	
TCA97 s663	Relief for losses incurred by a company in farming or market gardening is restricted in that the farming must be carried on a commercial basis. To enable losses to be set off against other income, it would be necessary for the company to make a profit every fourth year, or, in exceptional circumstances, every fifth year.	
TCA97 s400	In a company reconstruction, the successor company can take over the accumulated trading losses of the predecessor company provided 75% of the shareholders in the successor company were shareholders in the predecessor company in the three year period, one year before and two years after the reconstruction.	

Chapter 2

TCA97 s401 — The carry forward of accumulated trading losses of a company will be disallowed where there has been both a change of ownership of the company and a major change in the nature or conduct of the trade carried on.

2.1.13 Charges on Income

TCA97 s243 — Income tax at the standard rate should be deducted by companies from certain interest payments, patent royalties, annuities and other annual payments. These payments are known as charges and are not allowable as an expense in computing income for corporation tax purposes; they are, however, deductible from the corporation tax profit figure (ie the income plus chargeable gains figure). Where there is an excess of charges in any year, the excess can be carried forward and set off against future profits of the same trade. Excess charges can, however, be utilised to augment a terminal loss. (See page 190 for restrictions applying in the case of "10%" activities.)

TCA97 s239 — Any income tax deducted from charges must be paid over to the Revenue within six months of the end of the company's accounting period. However where the company has received income under deduction of tax it may deduct the income tax suffered from the income tax owed and pay the balance to the Collector General. Where the income tax suffered exceeds the income tax owed, the excess is allowed as a deduction from the corporation tax payable.

2.1.14 Section 151 Assessments

TCA97 s239 — In respect of accounting periods ending on or after 6 April 1990, the requirement on companies to make a return and pay over to the Revenue, any income tax deducted from certain payments within six months of the end of the accounting period, was changed as follows:

(a) A return of payments must be made at the same time as the return of profits (ie nine months after the end of the accounting period) and

(b) the income tax due is treated as corporation tax payable for the company's accounting period, (ie six months after the end of the accounting period).

TCA97 s240 — Where a company makes payments under deduction of tax in a period which is not an accounting period of the company, both the return of such payments and the tax deducted must be made within six months of the end of the accounting period.

TCA97 s241 — Companies not resident in the State, but which carry on trade in the State are subject to the same conditions as are set out under Section 239 above for accounting periods ending on or after 6 April 1990.

The income tax payments which are deemed to be payments of corporation tax by virtue of Section 239 are not to be taken into account in calculating relief under the 10% corporation tax rules.

TCA97 s884 When required by notice, a company must furnish a return within the time limit stipulated in the notice, of the following:

(i) The profits of the company, specifying the sources of income, any capital gains or losses and particulars of all charges on income.

(ii) Distributions received with related tax credits.

(iii) Payments made under deduction of income tax.

(iv) A list of loans to participators.

Chapter 2

2.2 MANUFACTURING COMPANIES - REDUCED RATE OF 10%

TCA97
s442-s457

A reduced rate of corporation tax applies to manufacturing companies in respect of income arising from the sale of goods manufactured in the State. The Corporation Tax rate applicable to the sale of manufactured goods is:

Period	Normal CT Rate	Reduction Factor	Manufacturing Rate
1/4/1991 to 31/3/1995	40%	3/4	10%
1/4/1995 to 31/3/1997	38%	28/38	10%
1/4/1997 to 31/12/1997	36%	26/36	10%
1/1/1998 to 31/12/98	32%	22/32	10%
1/1/1999 to 31/12/1999	28%	18/28	10%

Agreement has been reached between the Irish Government and the EU Commission with regard to the phasing out of the 10% manufacturing rate and profits which are at present taxed at 10% will be taxed at 12½% from 1 January 2003, with the following exceptions:

(i) Companies which carried on a manufacturing trade at 23 July 1998 will continue to be taxed at 10% until 31 December 2010 and

(ii) Companies which were not carrying on a manufacturing trade at 23 July 1998, but which were approved by a government grant agency on or before 31 July 1998 will continue to be taxed at 10% until 31 December 2010.

(iii) IFSC Companies

Where certified operations were approved, on or before 31 July 1998, the 10% rate will apply until 31 December 2005 and where certified operations were approved after 31 July 1998, the 10% rate will apply until 31 December 2002.

(iv) Shannon Airport Zone

Where certified operations were approved on or before 31 May 1998, the 10% rate will apply until 31 December 2005 and where certified operations were approved after 31 May 1998, the 10% rate will apply until 31 December 2002.

Corporation Tax

TCA97 s448 The reduced rate applies to profits derived from goods manufactured and sold by the company. Other goods sold by the company are referred to as merchandise. The Corporation Tax payable is reduced by the formula:

$$\text{Corporation Tax} \times \frac{\text{Sales of Goods}}{\text{Sales of Goods and Merchandise}} \times \frac{\text{Income from Goods* and Merchandise}}{\text{Total Income*}} \times \text{Reduction Factor}$$

* Income less charges as deducted against 10% manufacturing income.

TCA97 s443 "Goods" are defined in Section 443 and mean goods manufactured in the State in the course of a trade by a company which, for the relevant accounting period, is the company claiming relief in relation to the trade. However, where:

(a) there are two companies one of which manufactures goods and the other of which sells them in the course of its trade, and

(b) one of the companies is a 90% subsidiary of the other or both companies are 90% subsidiaries of a third company, any goods manufactured within the State by one of the companies shall, when sold in the course of its trade by the other company, be deemed to have been manufactured within the State by the other company. 90% means where the parent company must be entitled to 90% of any distribution of profits and 90% of the assets on a winding up.

The definition of goods does not include goods sold by retail unless they are sold:

(a) to a person who carries on a trade of selling goods of a class to which the goods sold to him belong, or

(b) to a person who uses goods of that class for the purposes of a trade carried on by him, or

(c) to a person, other than an individual, who uses goods of that class for the purposes of an undertaking carried on by him

The term manufacturing is extended to include the subjecting of commodities or materials belonging to another person to a process of manufacture within the State. Such services are regarded as manufacture of goods and the amount receivable from them is treated as an amount receivable from the sale of goods.

In addition to conventional manufacturing the following activities also qualify for the 10% manufacturing relief:

(a) Fish produced on a fish farm within the State.

(b) Mushrooms cultivated within the State. This activity ceases to come within the scope of the 10% rate in respect of accounting periods beginning on or after 1 June 1994.

(c) Repairing of ships carried out within the State.

185

(d) Design and planning services the work on the rendering of which is carried out in the State in connection with chemical, civil, electrical or mechanical engineering works executed outside the territories of the Member States of the European Communities.

(e) From 13 April 1984, Computer Services ie data processing services and/or software development services, the work on the rendering of which is carried out in the State in the course of a service undertaking in respect of which an employment grant was made by the IDA under S2 of the Industrial Development (No.2) Act 1981.

From 6 April 1989 the definition of "Computer Services" is extended to include technical or consultancy services which relate to data processing services and/or software development services, the work on the rendering of which is carried out in the State in the course of a service undertaking for which an employment grant was made by the Industrial Development Authority.

Where a grant for such Computer Services is made by the Shannon Free Airport Development Company Ltd or by Udaras na Gaeltachta, such services will be regarded as the manufacture of goods with effect from 1 January 1988.

(f) Qualifying shipping activities, ie the carriage of cargo and passengers on sea going ships which are Irish owned and registered or which are leased from foreign lessors without a crew. Losses and capital allowances arising from qualifying shipping trades cannot be offset against profits and income other than against another qualifying shipping trade. The 10% manufacturing relief applies for the period 1 January 1987 to 31 December 2000.

Manufacturing relief is granted to fishing vessels where the fish are subjected to a manufacturing process on board the qualifying ship, and to the letting or charter of a qualifying ship for qualifying purposes. It is also granted where a qualifying ship is used for transporting supplies or personnel to a mobile or fixed rig, platform vessel or installation of any kind at sea involved in hydrocarbon exploration and development -

where

(i) the operation of the ship

and

(ii) the crew of the ship remain under the direction and control of the company.

Such companies do not qualify for investment in corporate trades relief and are subject to the leasing restrictions under S40 FA 1984.

(g) Income of Trading Houses.

A trading house is a company carrying on a trade which consists solely of the sale by wholesale on the export market of goods manufactured in the State.

(h) Cultivation of plants by the process known as micro propagation or plant cloning.

(i) Repair or maintenance of aircraft, aircraft engines or components within the State.

(j) The production of a film for exhibition to the public in cinemas or on television or for training or documentary purposes provided that not less than 75 per cent of the work on its production is carried out in the State.

(k) Meat processed within the State, including that owned by the Intervention Agency, in an establishment approved and inspected in accordance with the European Communities (Fresh Meat) Regulations 1987. For any accounting period beginning on or after 1 April 1990 there shall be excluded from the definition of manufacture any goods sold into an intervention agency and shall exclude from the definition of manufacture any goods sold to a person which are subsequently sold to the intervention agency.

(l) Fish Processing carried on in the State.

(m) The remanufacture or repair of computer equipment or of subassemblies within the State, where such equipment or subassemblies were originally manufactured by that company or a connected company.

(n) Activities carried on by an agricultural or fishery society where:

- its trade consists wholly or mainly of the selling by wholesale of goods which have been acquired from its members;
- its members have already qualified for manufacturing relief in respect of the processing of these goods; and
- all, or the majority of its members are themselves agricultural or fishery societies.

(o) The purchase of milk by an agricultural society from its members and the subsequent sale of that milk to a certified qualifying company.

A qualifying company is one carrying on a trade which consists wholly or mainly of the manufacture of specified milk products, or is certified by the Minister for Agriculture, Food and Forestry as a qualifying company for the purposes of the section, notwithstanding that the trade does not consist wholly or mainly of the manufacture of milk products. In the latter case, the milk manufacturing activity will be regarded as a separate trade. This treatment will not apply, however, if the company's trade consists mainly of the application of a process of pasteurisation of milk. The Minister may issue a qualifying certificate where he is satisfied that a company has carried on or is intending to carry on the milk manufacturing trade for a period of at least three years.

Certificates remain in force for two years but may be revoked by the Minister at any time.

(p) The production of a newspaper, which is published at least fortnightly for sale to the public, regardless of whether the production company prints the newspaper or not. The relief applies to both the income from the sale of the newspaper and to the income from advertising services provided in the course of the production of the newspaper.

TCA97 s446 (q) Certain trading operations carried out in the Customs House Docks Area as follows:

The Customs House Docks Area is as defined in Section 322. To qualify for the relief the company must obtain a certificate from the Minister for Finance. The Minister has to certify that such trading operations as specified in the certificate are relevant trading operations for the purpose of the Section. The relief applies from the date specified in the certificate until 31 December 2005 unless the certificate is revoked because the company fails to set up in the Customs House Docks Area, or where it fails to comply with any of the conditions set out in the certificate. The Minister must give notice of the revocation in writing.

The Minister will not certify that a trading operation is a relevant trading operation unless:

(a) it is carried on within the Customs House Docks Area,

(b) the Minister is satisfied that it will contribute to the development of the area as an international financial business area,

(c) it falls within one or more of the following classes of trading operations

  (i) the provision for persons not ordinarily resident in the State of services, in relation to transactions in foreign currencies, which are of a type normally provided by a bank in the ordinary course of its trade,

(ii) the carrying on behalf of persons not ordinarily resident in the State of international financial activities including, in particular,

  (1) global money management

  (2) international dealings in foreign currencies and in futures, options and similar financial assets which are denominated in foreign currencies

  (3) dealings in bonds, equities and similar instruments which are denominated in foreign currencies, and

  (4) insurance and related activities

(iii) the provision for persons not ordinarily resident in the State of services of, or facilities for processing, control, accountancy, communication, clearing, settlement, or information storage in relation to financial activities,

(iv) the development or supply of computer software for use in the provision of the services at (iii) above or for the reprocessing, analysing or similar treatment of information in relation to financial services, or

(v) the carrying on of operations which are similar to, or ancillary to, any of the operations described in the foregoing paragraphs, in regard to which the Minister is of the opinion that they will contribute to the use of the area as an international financial services centre,

(vi) dealing in commodity futures or commodity options on behalf of persons not ordinarily resident in the State,

(vii) the income and gains arising to a Foreign Life Assurance company or Foreign Unit Trust business located in the IFSC on investments located outside the State.

(viii) The provision of management services to collective investment undertakings, the investors in which are non resident and the provision of services ancillary to such management services.

Any reference to a service or facility provided for an activity carried on, on behalf of a person not ordinarily resident in the State will not qualify to the extent that it is provided for any part of the non resident's trade which is carried on in the State.

Where a company, because of circumstances, cannot immediately locate in the Custom House Docks Area a certificate will be granted provided the company within a certain time limit moves into the area.

Chapter 2

2.2.1 Losses

TCA97 s455

Section 455 imposes a restriction or "ring fence" on loss and allowances attributable to "10 per cent" trading activites. From 1 April 1992 such losses and allowances may only be set against "10 per cent" income in the current and previous accounting periods and carried forward for set-off against "10 per cent" income in subsequent accounting periods. There are certain exceptions to this rule in the case of an IFSC company or where the loss is created by capital allowances due under certain projects approved by the IDA in the two-year period ended 31 December 1988.

Similarly where a company incurs a charge (eg royalties, interest etc) in the course of a 10 per cent activity the amount of relief available for that charge is restricted to the income arising from the 10 per cent activity.

See page 196 for the position relating to "10 per cent" losses and group relief.

2.2.2 Exclusions

TCA97 s443

Sales of manufactured goods to the Intervention Agency are specifically excluded from the 10% relief, and for the purpose of this exclusion the sale of goods to a person other than the Intervention Agency shall be deemed to be a sale to the Intervention Agency if, and to the extent that, these goods are ultimately sold to the Intervention Agency.

Sales of goods from mining and construction operations are specifically excluded from the 10% relief. However, companies carrying on such activities which also manufacture goods in course of the same trade may be entitled to relief on a just and reasonable basis.

For any relevant accounting period beginning on or after the 1st April, 1990 the following activities are not regarded as manufacturing:

(i) Processes applied to any product, produce or material acquired in bulk for sale or distribution such as: dividing, cutting, drying, mixing, sorting, packaging, branding, testing or purifying.

(ii) The application of methods of preservation, pasteurisation or maturation to any foodstuffs.

(iii) The preparation of food or drink for human consumption where it is intended to be consumed at or about the time it is prepared.

(iv) Improving or altering any articles or materials without imposing on them a change in their character.

(v) Repairing, refurbishing, reconditioning or restoring articles or materials.

(vi) Except where a company sells goods manufactured by a closely connected company, no company will be entitled to manufacturing relief if it does not carry out the process for which the relief is being claimed.

2.2.3 Time Limit

TCA97 s448

A claim for manufacturing relief must be lodged before the date on which the assessment for the accounting period becomes final and conclusive.

2.2.4 Anti Avoidance Provisions

TCA97 s453

Section 453 deals with transactions between associated persons and effectively substitutes arm's length prices for artificial prices in respect of dealings between connected persons. These rules apply in the following cases:

(1) If a buying company is making a claim and buys from another person (the seller) and

    (a) the seller has control over the buyer, or the seller being a body corporate or partnership, the buyer has control over the seller or some other person has control over both the seller and the buyer, and

    (b) the price in the transaction is less than that which might have been expected to obtain if the parties to the transaction had been independent parties dealing at arm's length,

the income or losses of the buyer and the seller are computed for any purpose of the Taxes Acts as if the price in the transaction had been that which would have obtained if the transaction had been a transaction between independent persons dealing as aforesaid.

(2) Where a company claiming relief sells goods to another person (the buyer) and

    (a) the buyer has control over the seller or, the buyer being a body corporate or partnership, the seller has control over the buyer or some other person has control over both the seller and the buyer, and

    (b) the goods are sold at a price greater than the price which they might have been expected to fetch if the parties to the transaction had been independent parties dealing at arm's length, the income or losses of the buyer and the seller are computed, for any purpose of the Taxes Acts, as if the goods had been sold by the seller to the buyer for the price which they would have fetched if the transaction had been a transaction between independent persons dealing as aforesaid.

Control is defined as having the meaning assigned to it by Section 11.

2.2.5 Shannon Airport

TCA97 s445

Certain trading operations of a qualified company carried on within the airport qualify for the manufacturing companies' tax rate of 10%. This will expire on 31 December 2005. The Minister for Finance will give a certificate certifying that such operations qualify for this rate if they fall within one or more of the following classes of trading operations.

(a) Repair or maintenance of aircraft.

(b) Trading operations in regard to which the Minister is of the opinion, after consultation with the Minister for Transport, that they contribute to the use or development of the airport.

(c) Trading operations which are ancillary to any of those operations described in the foregoing paragraphs or to any operation consisting, apart from this section, of the manufacture of goods.

A condition of the relief is that the operations must be derived from an "initial investment" within the principles of Articles 92/94 of the EU Treaty.

2.3 RESEARCH AND DEVELOPMENT

TCA97 s766

A manufacturing company may claim tax relief on incremental expenditure on research and development incurred in a three year period beginning on 1 June 1995. A period cannot be a relevant period if it commences on or after 1 June 1999.

The research and development project must be certified by Forbairt.

The relief is a quadruple deduction for the incremental expenditure incurred subject to an upper limit of £175,000 and the exclusion of the first £25,000 of such expenditure.

Prior to the passing of the Finance Act 1996, the base expenditure for determining the level of incremental expenditure in any year is the higher of the expenditure:-

(i) in the base period (ie the period of 12 months immediately before the 3 years), or

(ii) any earlier year within the three year period.

That rule was relaxed in respect of any relevant period commencing on or after 1 June 1996, so as to determine relief with reference to a fixed base level of expenditure, ie the expenditure incurred in the base period. The excess of the expenditure in each of the three years over that fixed base level will, after deducting £25,000 in each year, qualify for relief.

Example:

Year	Expenditure £000	Qualifying Expenditure*	
		Old Scheme	New Scheme
Base	100	–	–
Year 1	170	70	70
Year 2	165	–	65
Year 3	200	30	100

(*before reduction of the first £25,000)

Prior to the Finance Act 1996, companies which were grant aided in respect of research and development expenditure in the relevant or base period were denied any relief. Section 766 relaxes this rule as follows:-

(i) a company or group will now only be disqualified from any allowance for a relevant period in respect of research and development if grant aid at a level exceeding £50,000 is received in that relevant period.

(ii) where a company or group is not disqualified from relief in respect of a relevant period under the above rule, the expenditure to be taken into account in computing the relief is limited to expenditure which is not grant aided.

The limits apply on a group basis in the case of group companies. Where a company obtains relief under this heading it will not be entitled to raise BES funds in that period.

2.4 GROUP RELIEF

TCA97
s410-s429

Group relief may be claimed where one member of a group of companies is entitled to surrender its trading loss to another member of the same group. To be a member of a group of companies, the following conditions have to be satisfied:

(a) Both companies must be resident in the State and one company must be a 75% subsidiary of the other company, or both companies must be 75% subsidiaries of a third company which is also resident in the State.

However, for accounting periods ending on or after 1 July 1998, the condition that all companies must be resident in the State has been amended so that group and consortium (see below) relief, and the ability to make certain payments gross, are available where all companies are resident in the EU.

Loss relief however, is restricted to losses incurred in a trade in respect of which the company is within the charge to corporation tax in the State.

(b) The parent company must be beneficially entitled to not less than 75% of the profits available for distribution to the equity holders.

(c) The parent company must be beneficially entitled to not less than 75% of the assets available for distribution to the equity holders on a winding up.

It is not necessary for the claimant company to make a claim for the full amount of trading losses available and therefore two or more group or consortium companies may make a claim in respect of the same surrendering company for the same accounting period.

Similarly, an investment company which has an excess of management expenses for an accounting period may surrender the excess to a fellow group member. Excess charges may also be surrendered within a group of companies. Claims for group relief must be made by the claimant company within two years from the end of the surrendering company's accounting period to which the claim relates.

The surrendering company must also notify the Inspector of Taxes of its consent to surrender the relief.

Group relief is also available to members of a consortium where the loss making company is owned by a consortium. A consortium is one where five or fewer companies own between them all the ordinary share capital of a trading company or of a holding company whose business consists wholly or mainly in the holding of shares in trading companies which are its 90 per cent subsidiaries. The loss

Chapter 2

making company cannot be more than a 75% subsidiary of any member of the consortium.

Inter group charges are paid gross.

TCA97 s420 Losses, excess capital allowances or excess charges on income of a company liable at a 10% rate of tax can only be surrendered to another group or consortium company which is also liable at a 10% rate of tax.

The two exceptions to this rule are

(i) surrenders to or from companies carrying on a trade within the IFSC area and

(ii) for the duration of export relief, this restriction will not apply where the last claim to relief from CT by a company in respect of manufacturing income was a claim for ESR.

TCA97 s617 Sales of assets between companies within a Group are treated as if the transaction gives rise to a no profit/no loss situation. Companies within a group may also claim "roll over" relief (see page 277) where one company disposes of certain assets and another company within the group reinvests within the time limit. Where roll over relief has been claimed within a group and the company with the new asset leaves the group, the "roll over" deferral comes to an end.

2.4.1 Anti-Avoidance

(i) Company leaving a Group

TCA97 s423 Where a company leaves a group, after having received an asset by way of inter-group transfer, it incurs a chargeable gain on the asset. The gain is calculated by reference to the date at which the original owner company acquired the asset.

These provisions do not apply where:-

(i) the asset was acquired by the company leaving the group prior to 6 April 1974, or

(ii) the asset has been held by the company leaving the group for more than 10 years, or

(iii) the company leaves the group by reason of it or any other company being wound up. This exclusion will apply only where a company ceases to be a member of a group on or after 28 March 1996 by way of a winding up or dissolution, which is for bona fide commercial reasons and must not be part of a scheme or arrangement the main purpose or one of the main purposes of which is the avoidance of tax, or

(iv) two or more companies which themselves form a sub group, leave together and the asset had earlier been transferred between them. However, where the companies leave the group on or after 23 April 1996, and

a dividend has been paid or a distribution made by one of those companies to a company which is not one of those now leaving the group; and

this dividend or distribution has been paid wholly or partially out of profits which derive from the disposal of an asset by one of the companies to another, then

the amount of the dividend paid, or distribution made, to the extent that it comes out of those profits, shall be deemed for Capital Gains Tax purposes to be part of the consideration received by the member of the group making the disposal. Thus the amount which the company receives together with such a dividend constitutes the proceeds of the disposal.

(ii) Company entering a Group

TCA97 s626A

The "pre-entry losses" of a company joining a group on or after 1 March 1999 cannot be used to offset subsequent capital gains within the group. The company entering the group will, however, be able to use such losses in the same way that it could have, had it never joined the group.

(iii) Depreciatory Transactions

TCA97 s621

Certain anti avoidance provisions may be invoked where a loss arises on the disposal of a group company and the loss has arisen as a result of a depreciatory transaction. Such transactions may include the movement of assets or the payment of dividends.

Any loss arising under these circumstances will be reduced by such an extent as appears to the Inspector of Taxes to be just and reasonable.

(iv) "Loss Buying" of trading losses

TCA97 s401

Trading losses cannot be carried forward where there is a change in ownership and a major change in the nature or conduct of the trade.

Chapter 2

2.5   **MINING TAXATION**

TCA97
s670-s683

The main features of mining taxation are:-

Scheduled minerals

Mine Development Allowance

Exploration Expenditure

Allowance for expenditure on abortive exploration

Expenditure incurred by one member of a group of companies may, by election, be deemed to be the expenditure of another member.

Investment allowance of 20% on new plant purchased on or after 6 April 1974 (with the exception of cars, lorries etc)

Annual mineral depletion allowance on capital expenditure in acquiring after 31 March 1974, a scheduled mineral asset entitling one to work deposits of schedule minerals.

Where after 31 March 1974 a person sells any scheduled mineral asset the net proceeds are to be brought into charge to tax.

In respect of a marginal mine, the tax chargeable on the profits of that mine may be reduced to such amount (including nil) as the Minister for Finance may specify.

2.5.1   **Exploration Expenditure**

An "Exploration Company" is one whose business consists primarily of exploring for scheduled minerals.

Exploring for scheduled minerals means the carrying on in the State of any of the following activities in relation to scheduled minerals:-

(i)   Searching for deposits,

(ii)   Testing deposits,

(iii)   Winning access to deposits,

(iv)   The systematic searching for areas containing scheduled minerals,

(v)   Searching by drilling or other means,

but the definition excludes operations for developing or working a qualifying mine.

For as long as a company is an exploration company which does not carry on a trade of working a qualifying mine and incurs expenditure on exploring for scheduled minerals, it shall be deemed to be carrying on a trade of working a qualifying mine coming within the charge to corporation tax when it first incurs capital expenditure.

Where such companies incur expenditure on or after 1 April, 1990 the following provisions apply:-

(i) Unsuccessful exploration expenditure can be carried forward for set-off against mining income indefinitely.

(ii) Allowances due to an exploration company may be transferred to its 100 per cent parent or subsidiary company. If such a transfer is made a claim for Group Relief cannot also be made.

(iii) Should an exploration company which is deemed to be carrying on a trade of working a qualifying mine commence to actually work a qualifying mine it may carry forward any unused losses of the deemed trade against income of the actual trade providing there is no change in ownership about the time actual trading begins.

2.5.2 Rehabilitation Expenditure

An allowance is available for expenditure incurred on the rehabilitation of the site of a qualifying mine following the closure of the mine. Where the rehabilitation expenditure is incurred after cessation of the trade of working a qualifying mine it will be treated as incurred on the date of cessation of the trade and, accordingly, an allowance will be made in respect of that expenditure in the chargeable period in which the trade ceases.

2.5.3 Petroleum Companies

TCA97
s684-s697

A special rate of corporation tax of 25% applies to income arising from petroleum leases. Special features are:-

- Separation of trading activities
- 25% rate of corporation tax
- Ring fence on losses arising in a petroleum activity as well as losses from another trade
- Ring fence on group relief for losses
- Ring fence on capital gains tax losses
- Restrictions on relief for interest
- Restrictions on set-off of advance corporation tax
- Capital allowances on development and exploration expenditure
- Surrender of the benefit of the deduction for exploration expenditure to an associated company
- Relief for additional expenditure on abandonment of exhausted oil fields
- Rules for valuation of petroleum in certain circumstances
- Deferral of capital gains tax on certain disposals and exchanges

Chapter 2

2.6 CLOSE COMPANIES

TCA97 s430

Broadly speaking, a close company is a company which is under the control of five or fewer participators or under the control of its directors.

2.6.1 Participators and Associates

TCA97 s433

A participator in a company is a person having a share or interest in the company's capital or income, whilst an individual's associates include his spouse, his partners and direct relatives.

2.6.2 Certain Expenses for Participators and Associates

TCA97 s436

Where a close company incurs expense in providing a benefit of any kind for a participator or an associate of a participator of the company, who is not a director or employee of the company, and without that person paying for it, the company will be deemed to have made a distribution (See Schedule F and Company Distributions) equal to the amount of that expense. The expense will therefore not be allowed in computing the company's profits for tax purposes. The recipient of the benefit will be deemed to have received a dividend of the grossed up amount which will be liable to higher rates of income tax if applicable.

2.6.3 Interest Paid to Directors and Directors' Associates

TCA97 s437

Interest paid to directors and directors' associates in excess of a specified limit (13%) will in certain circumstances be treated as a distribution with the same consequences as outlined above for Section 436.

2.6.4 Loans to Participators etc

TCA97 s438

Most loans to participators or their associates are deemed to be annual payments made under deduction of income tax but are not considered as charges under Section 243. The company is obliged to pay over income tax at a rate of 24/76ths of the loan to the Revenue Commissioners. If the loan or part of it is repaid the company is entitled to reclaim the proportionate part of the tax originally paid over. If such a loan is released or written off the grossed up amount of the loan will be regarded as income of the borrower in the year in which the loan is written off and the tax paid over will cease to be recoverable by the company.

There is an exception to these provisions where a loan of not more than £15,000 is made to a participator or his associate who is a director or employee of the close company or of an associated company. The loan must satisfy the following conditions:

(a) the aggregate of the loans made to the borrower or his spouse by the close company or its associated companies must not exceed £15,000 and

(b) the borrower works full time in the close company or in an associated company, and

(c) the borrower together with his associates must not directly or indirectly control more than 5% of the ordinary share capital of the company.

If the borrower together with his associates acquires more than 5% of the ordinary share capital of the company the loan outstanding at that time will be regarded as an annual payment with the usual implications.

2.6.5 Surcharge on Certain Undistributed Income

TCA97
s440-s441

A surcharge of 20% is chargeable on a close company which does not distribute its after tax investment income or rental income within 18 months of the end of the accounting period. However where the undistributed income figure is £500 or less the surcharge is not applied and for amounts slightly over £500 there is marginal figure. There is no surcharge on undistributed trading income.

The 20% surcharge also applies to service companies and in respect of accounting periods ending on or after 1 April 1995 is calculated as 20% of:-

— ½ of distributable income, plus

— ½ of distributable investment and estate income, less

— any distributions made for the period.

With regard to accounting periods ending on or after 1 April 1996, the 20% surcharge has been reduced to 15% in respect of the trading or professional income but investment and rental income is still subject to the 20%.

The same £500 exemption and marginal relief referred to above also apply in the case of service companies.

Chapter 2

2.7 SCHEDULE F AND COMPANY DISTRIBUTIONS

TCA97 s136

Schedule F charges to income tax on an actual basis dividends and other liable distributions received by individuals. Dividends paid between 6 April 1976 and 5 April 1999 were paid net but attracted a tax credit (See Chart 10). An individual was liable to income tax on both the net dividend and the related tax credit at his marginal rate less a deduction for the tax credit. Tax credits were abolished with effect from 6 April 1999 at which time a dividend withholding tax was introduced (see page 206).

2.7.1 Matters to be treated as Distributions

TCA97 s130

The following are some of the matters which constitute distributions under corporation tax legislation.

(a) Dividends paid by a company including a capital dividend.

(b) Any distribution out of assets in respect of shares, except any part of it which represents a repayment of capital. Acquisition by a company of its own shares in certain circumstances is excluded (See page 283).

(c) Redemption of bonus shares and bonus debentures.

(d) Sale of assets by a company at an undervalue or purchase of assets by a company at overvalue.

(e) (i) interest on loans with rights of conversion into shares or securities,

(ii) interest the rate of which depends on the results of the company,

(iii) interest paid to a non resident parent or associate company where there is at least a 75% ordinary shareholding relationship. In such a case the existence of a double taxation agreement can be advantageous.

Such interest will not however be a distribution and will be allowed as a deduction in computing profits if

(i) it is paid by a qualifying company within the IFSC or Shannon.

(ii) it is paid to a company which is resident in a country with which Ireland has a Double Tax Treaty, with certain exceptions eg United Kingdom.

(iii) the paying company makes an election in writing to the Inspector with the company's returns of profit for the period to have it so treated.

Distributions made in a winding up are not chargeable under Schedule F.

2.7.2 "Section 84 Loans"

TCA97 s133

There are exceptions in the case of certain loans of a type mentioned at (e) (i) and (ii).

All new loans made after 19 December 1991 must satisfy the following conditions:

(i) the borrower commenced to trade after 31 January 1990 or the trade is one in relation to which the borrower was committed to the creation of additional employment under a business plan approved by one of the grant-giving bodies;

(ii) the trade of the borrower was included in a list prepared by the IDA and approved by the Minister for Industry and Commerce and Minister for Finance before 25 March 1992 specifying the amount of borrowing considered essential for the success of the trade. The amount specified is to be treated as reduced (with certain exceptions) by the amount of any relevant principal advanced or treated as advanced, to a borrower and the reduced amount is then treated as the amount specified on the list.

(iii) the borrower does not carry on relevant trading operations in the IFSC.

Where on or after 6 May 1993 the repayment period of an existing "Section 84" loan is extended, the lender will be treated as having received repayment of the "Section 84" loan and as having advanced a new non-"Section 84" loan in its place.

Currency exchange gains which are connected with "Section 84" loans denominated in a foreign currency are taxed as income from the sale of manufactured goods. In addition, gains and losses on such "Section 84" loan are treated as profits or gains or losses of the borrowers trade in the course of which the loans are used.

No domestic sourced loans in a foreign currency will qualify from 30 January 1991, where the interest rate on the loan exceeds 80% of DIBOR. This limit will not apply to:

(I) Loans drawn down before 30 January 1991, where the rate of interest on that date exceeded 80% of DIBOR, provided that the rate does not exceed that which would apply if the loan was in the same currency, both at the time the interest is paid and on 30 January 1991.

(ii) Loans on the IDA list made on or after 30 January 1991, but before 20 December 1991, provided that the rate does not exceed a rate approved by the Minister for Finance or, if lower, the rate applicable to the currency in which the loan was advanced.

Chapter 2

(iii) Loans on the IDA list made on or after 20 December 1991, provided that the rate does not exceed a rate approved by the Minister for Finance.

"Section 84" loans drawn down on or after 11 April 1994 have a time limit of seven years, while loans drawn down before that date will cease to qualify as "Section 84" loans on 11 April 2001. Where certain "Section 84" loans were repaid prematurely before 7 December 1993 a replacement loan for such a loan will only be a qualifying loan up to the scheduled repayment date of the original loan.

2.7.3 Distributions from Manufacturing Profits

TCA97
s147-s151

The formula below sets out the amount of the manufacturing dividend paid by a company. The formula determines the manufacturing dividend paid for an accounting period in the proportion which the company's manufacturing distributable income for the period bears to its total distributable income for the period. The formula is

$$Y \times \frac{(A-B)+E-U}{(R-S)+T-W} \quad \text{where}$$

Y = the distribution made by the company.

A = the amount of the company's 10% manufacturing relieved income for the accounting period.

B = the reduced corporation tax attaching to the income at "A".

E = the amount of any manufacturing dividends received in the accounting period.

R = The total amount of the company's income finally charged to corporation tax for the period excluding chargeable gains but including exempt income.

S = the corporation tax attributable to the income at "R", after manufacturing relief and export sales relief.

T = the total of all distributions received in the accounting period.

U = the amount of 10% distributions included in W.

W = the amount of all distributions made before 6 April 1989 treated as made for an accounting period for which the distribution Y is to be treated as made.

The formula to determine the distributable income of the company is

$$(R - S) + T - W$$

The distributable manufacturing income is determined by the formula

$$(A - B) + E$$

A company which makes a distribution out of manufacturing profits on or after 6 April 1989 may by notice in writing to the Inspector within 6 months from the end of the accounting period in which the distribution is made nominate the accounting period for which it is paid. This is provided:

(i) the nominated accounting period is within nine years of the payment date

and

(ii) the distribution or part thereof does not exceed the undistributed income of the company for that accounting period at the date of payment.

The company will not be entitled to state that the distribution was made for the accounting period in which it was actually paid unless it is one of the following:

(a) An interim dividend paid before 6 April 2002.
(b) A "Section 84" distribution.
(c) A preference share funding distribution.
(d) A distribution of the accounting period in which the company commences or ceases to be within the charge to corporation tax.
(e) It should be noted that where a company pays an interim dividend it is not entitled to claim that it is a distribution made for the accounting period in which it is made where:

   (i) the company would have to use estimation in order to determine the amount of the dividend which was a specified dividend under the provisions of Section 147, or

   (ii) the payment of the interim dividend would assist the company in arrangements whereby the company could attach different rates of tax credit to dividends paid on similar shareholdings.

The above election applies to dividends paid on or after 1 June 1994 out of income, regardless of whether it is 10%, export sales relief, Shannon exempt or other income.

Chapter 2

2.8 DIVIDEND WITHHOLDING TAX

2.8.1 General

In his budget speech of 2 December 1998 the Minister for Finance stated the following:-

> "since owners of capital in the form of shares would benefit from the reduced corporation tax rate on profits, I believe it right that the government should accordingly take action to ensure that the tax due on dividends is paid to the Exchequer. The existing tax credit on dividends will be abolished as and from 6 April next under measures taken in my first Budget. In effect this means that after 5 April the onus of payment of tax on dividends received by individuals will rest on self assessment and income declaration by shareholders.
>
> I propose, therefore, to introduce on and from 6 April 1999 a withholding tax at the standard rate of income tax on dividends paid to individuals resident in the State and certain non residents. This tax will have to be deducted from dividends before they are paid out. Those individual shareholders liable to tax at the higher rate will be required as before to declare their dividend income in their tax returns and to pay the balance of income tax due to the Exchequer".

As stated by the Minister this change has been introduced in the context of the phasing in of the reduced rates of corporation tax and is intended to claw back some of the revenue foregone through the introduction of the reduced rates. The imputation system of corporation tax which was designed to prevent, in some degree, the payment of double taxation on the same profits has now been abandoned and income tax will be payable on the gross amount of the dividend declared with a deduction against tax liability being granted in respect of the tax withheld on payment of the dividend.

The new provisions can be summarised as follows:

TCA97
Pt 6, Ch 8A

(a) Tax at the standard rate applies to distributions (including scrip dividends and non cash distributions) made by an Irish resident company on or after 6 April, 1999.

(b) This applies to all distributions including those payable out of exempt income.

(c) A recipient who is liable to tax on a distribution, such as an Irish resident individual, can claim an off-set for the tax withheld against his tax liability. Where the withholding tax exceeds the tax liability, the balance will be refunded.

(d) Exemption is granted to an Irish resident company, a pension scheme, a qualifying employee share ownership trust, a collective investment undertaking and a charity.

(e) Exemption is also granted to residents of tax treaty countries, residents of EU Member States, companies not resident in the State which are ultimately controlled by residents of tax treaty countries or EU Member States and companies the principal class of shares of which are substantially and regularly traded on a recognised stock exchange in such countries or Member States.

(f) A declaration in the prescribed form and any other evidence required must be provided to establish entitlement to the exemption.

(g) Where exempt status is established payment can be made in full directly to the shareholder or through an "authorised intermediary".

(h) There are provisions for a "withholding agent" to pay distributions and withhold tax on behalf of the company.

(i) The withholding tax must be paid over to the Revenue on or before the 14th day of the month following the month in which the distribution was made.

(j) With effect from 6 April 1999 the treatment of shares received in lieu of cash dividends is amended in line with the introduction of the dividend withholding tax. The effect of the amendment is that the company issues a number of shares which has a value, at the date of distribution, equal to the cash foregone, reduced by an amount equal to income tax at the standard rate on the amount of cash foregone. The distributing company must pay over the notional income tax deducted to the Collector General in the normal way. Where the distributing company is quoted the shareholder is taxed on this type of distribution under Schedule F and, where the company is unquoted, under Schedule D, Case IV. The taxable amount is the full amount of the cash foregone and credit is given for the withholding tax paid by the company.

(k) A statement showing the tax withheld must be supplied to the shareholder in all cases. These details can be supplied on the dividend counterfoil.

(l) Penalties and fines are imposed for the non operation or incorrect operation of the withholding tax provision.

(m) Section 153 TCA 1997 currently provides for an effective exemption from the charge to Irish income tax for all non resident persons in respect of distributions made by Irish resident companies. With effect from 6 April 1999 this exemption will apply only to a person (other than a company) who is resident for tax purposes in another EU Member State or in any tax treaty country and who is neither resident nor ordinarily resident in the State and certain other non resident companies.

Chapter 2

2.9 FOREIGN ASPECTS

2.9.1 Foreign Exchange Transactions

TCA97 s79;
TCA97 s402

As the taxation of international financial transactions is beyond the scope of this summary the authors would refer readers to the Tax Administration Liaison Committee's publication on this subject entitled "Taxation of International Financial Transactions in Ireland". However the following sets out the major changes for corporation tax purposes, of the treatment of foreign exchange gains and losses related to corporate borrowings for the purposes of a trade.

Prior to the passing of the 1994 Finance Act, tax law effectively ignored foreign exchange gains and losses arising in respect of long term borrowings. Such borrowings were deemed to be capital liabilities and therefore the exchange gains or losses arising on them were ignored in the computation of trading profits. Since the borrowings are not regarded as assets for capital gains tax purposes, gains or losses arising did not give rise to chargeable gains or losses. However, the matching losses and gains on hedging instruments were charged to tax, thereby producing anomalous tax results.

Section 56 Finance Act 1994 brought the foreign exchange gains and losses on both trade borrowings and related hedging contracts into the computation of a company's trading income for tax purposes to the extent that those gains and losses have been properly credited or debited to the company's profit and loss account.

These accounting entries are brought into the computation of income for tax purposes regardless of whether they represent realised or unrealised gains and losses and also regardless of whether the trade borrowing is characterised as a "revenue" or "capital" item for tax purposes.

Hedging gains and losses are to be excluded in the computation of the company's chargeable gains. In addition, since gains and losses arising on holdings of foreign currency for trade purposes are also brought into the computation of income, they too are excluded from the computation of chargeable gains.

The above provisions apply in respect of accounting periods beginning on or after 1 January 1995.

The treatment of hedging instruments in respect of trade borrowings outlined above, was extended to hedging instruments designed to remove exchange rate risks in relation to the corporation tax liability of a company in respect of accounting periods ending on or after 1 April 1996. Accordingly gains or losses which arise on such instruments are not chargeable gains or allowable losses

Certain provisions also exist to deal with the computation of capital allowances and loss relief due to a trading company which has a "functional currency" other than Irish pounds. For accounting periods commencing on or after 1 January 1994, such a company may compute its capital allowances in that foreign currency. Where the company incurs capital expenditure in a currency other than its functional currency, it must translate that expenditure into the functional currency equivalent at the rate of exchange at the time the expenditure was incurred and must compute the capital allowances due by reference to that functional currency amount.

In the case of a company which has losses in the functional currency it may carry them forward in that currency and convert them into Irish Pounds as and when they are used.

2.9.2 The Euro

Section 47 and Schedule 2 of the 1998 Finance Act provide amendments to cater for the change in currency of the State to the Euro on 1 January 1999. These amendments, however, do not take effect until such time as the Minister for Finance, by order, appoints.

2.9.3 Dividends from a Non Resident Subsidiary

TCA97 s222

An Irish resident company may claim to have relevant dividends received from a 51% non resident subsidiary after 6 April 1988 excluded from its income chargeable to corporation tax, if the following conditions are fulfilled:

(a) The Minister of Finance has approved the company's investment plan and issues a certificate covering the amount of the relevant dividend.

(b) The foreign subsidiary is resident in a country with which Ireland has a Double Taxation Treaty.

(c) The relevant dividends are applied by the company for the purpose of the approved investment plan within one year before the date on which the dividends are received in the State and two years after that date.

An "Investment Plan" means a plan of a company resident in the State which is directed towards the creation or maintenance of employment in the State from trading operations carried on in the State.

Where all or part of the relevant dividends are not used for the purposes of the investment plan, the Minister may withdraw the relief.

The claim for relief should be made in writing and submitted with the company's return of profits for the period in which the relevant dividends are received in the State.

There are two important adjustments, effective from 1 January 1991, to the provisions outlined above, namely:

1. The company's investment plan can now be submitted to the Minister for Finance one year after the commencement of its implementation where there is reasonable cause for the delay, and

2. The Revenue Commissioners can extend the period in which the dividends may be applied for the purposes of the approved investment plan in that they need not necessarily be applied one year before and two years after the date of receipt as set out in (c) above.

2.9.4 Unilateral Relief

TCA97 Sch24

A company resident in the State which receives a dividend from a "25% subsidiary" which is resident in a territory with which Ireland does not have a double tax treaty will be entitled to reduce Irish tax on the dividend by any withholding tax paid in that territory on the dividend and by an appropriate part of the foreign tax on the income underlying the dividend.

A company resident in the State which receives a dividend from its "25% subsidiary" resident in a country with which Ireland has a double tax treaty or otherwise, which subsidiary has itself subsidiaries, will be entitled to reduce the Irish tax by an appropriate amount of withholding tax and underlying tax borne by those subsidiaries and their subsidiaries. This is conditional on the company paying the dividend being a 25% subsidiary of the company to which it pays the dividend and being connected with the ultimate Irish parent company.

The Finance Act 1999 introduced new measures on double tax relief as follows:

(a) Where an Irish resident company receives a dividend from a subsidiary in a tax treaty country and the double tax relief available to it under the treaty is less generous than unilateral relief the company may claim the unilateral relief.

(b) Tests on whether companies are "related" or "connected" are based with effect from 6 April 1999 on voting rights rather than ordinary share capital for the purposes of unilateral relief and double tax relief.

2.9.5 Branch Profits

TCA97 s847

Section 847 provides for the exemption from corporation tax and capital gains tax of income and gains from a foreign branch in the case of a company meeting certain conditions.

The conditions include that a company resident in the State has an investment plan which involves the investment by it of substantial permanent capital in the State for the purposes of the creation, before a date specified in the plan, of substantial new employment in the State and that the maintenance of the employment created will be dependent on carrying on trading operations through foreign branches. The Minister for Finance must be satisfied that the plan is an investment plan and must certify that the company is a qualifying company. Guidelines will be drawn up for determining what is substantial new employment and what is a substantial permanent capital investment.

2.9.6 Companies changing Residence

TCA97
s627-s629

Where a company ceases to be resident in the State on or after 21 April 1997, it is deemed to have disposed of and reacquired all of its assets immediately before the event of changing residence, at their market value at that time, even though no actual disposal has taken place. However, assets which continue to be used in Ireland by a branch or agency of the company are not subject to the above provision.

In addition, the above provision will not apply where the company is ultimately owned by a foreign company, ie a company controlled by persons resident in a country with which Ireland has a double taxation treaty.

Roll over relief will only apply to assets disposed of prior to changing residence if their replacements acquired after that time are similarly used in Ireland by a branch or agency of the company.

Where a company which transfers residence is a 75% subsidiary of an Irish resident company, then both companies may elect in writing within two years of the change of residence, to have the deemed disposal and its resulting tax charge deferred.

A charge to capital gains will in those circumstances crystallise only if:-

(i)   within 10 years the assets are actually disposed of, or

(ii) the company ceases to be a 75% subsidiary of the other, or

(iii) the Irish resident parent itself changes its residence.

In the event of non payment of tax arising under provisions as outlined above, the Revenue Commissioners may collect the tax due from any Irish resident group company or controlling director of the company.

Chapter 2

2.10 ADVANCE CORPORATION TAX
(Abolished from 6 April 1999)

TCA97
s159-s172

Where an Irish resident company makes a distribution on or after 9 February 1983, it is liable to pay advance corporation tax (ACT). The amount of the ACT is, equal to the tax credit attaching to the distribution.

ACT paid by a company can be set off, against the company's corporation tax liability for the accounting period in which the distribution is made. It can however only be set off against corporation tax on the company's income, and not against corporation tax arising on the company's capital gains.

Where a company's ACT liability exceeds the corporation tax charged on its income for an accounting period, the surplus ACT may be set off against the corporation tax on the company's income of an earlier accounting period ending within the previous twelve months. The claim for set off of the surplus must be made within two years of the end of the accounting period in which the surplus arose. If a company cannot set off its ACT liability fully, either in the period in which the distribution is made, or in the appropriate earlier period, the balance of ACT can be carried forward indefinitely and set off against corporation tax on the company's income for future accounting periods.

An Inspector of Taxes may make any necessary assessments to recover the balance of corporation tax due where a company has erroneously overclaimed ACT.

In computing its liability to ACT a company may deduct the tax credits on distributions received in the accounting period from the tax credits arising on distributions made in that period. If the tax credits on distributions received by the company exceed the tax credits on distributions made, no liability to ACT arises and the excess credits can be carried forward to future accounting periods.

The tax credits attaching to distributions made before 9 February 1983 cannot be taken into account as they were not subject to ACT. Where a company obtains payment of a tax credit under Section 157 the credit cannot be set off for ACT purposes against tax credits on the distributions made by the company.

Where a company obtains payment of a tax credit in respect of a distribution received by it, and later the tax credit is recoverable by an assessment under Case IV Schedule D because the company elects to set off the losses to greater benefit against its taxable profits, the tax credit will be reinstated as a deductible tax credit, for the accounting period in which the recovery is made, in arriving at the company's liability to ACT in respect of its distributions in that period.

Where a company has availed of relief under Section 162 and has carried forward to a later accounting period its excess tax credits in respect of distributions received by it, this excess will be set off against the ACT payable in respect of distributions made in the later accounting period, before the set off of tax credits in respect of distributions received in that accounting period.

Payment of dividends between members of a group of companies must be made without accounting for ACT. A group for purposes of this exemption is composed of:-

— An Irish resident company which is a 51% subsidiary of another Irish resident company;

— Two Irish resident companies both of which are 51% subsidiaries of another Irish resident company.

— A trading or holding company owned by a consortium, the members of which include the company receiving the dividend.

A company is a 51% subsidiary of another company if and so long as more than 50% of its ordinary share capital is owned directly or indirectly by that other company.

However, it is possible for the companies involved to elect to actually pay the ACT. The election must be made by the paying company and before the due date for payment of the ACT.

Distributions of profit deemed to arise for tax purposes on shares being bought back, redeemed or repaid by the issuing company, are also included in the exemption from advance corporation tax outlined above, provided the other requirements in respect of a group or consortium relationship are met.

Where a company has paid ACT in respect of dividends paid by it in an accounting period, and the company does not wish to carry back or forward the ACT paid, the surplus ACT may be surrendered in whole or in part to one or more companies which are members of the same group (see conditions for Group Companies page 186).

Both companies must be in the required group relationship throughout the surrendering company's accounting period. If, however, the accounting periods of the two companies do not coincide, the date of the recipient company's notional payment of ACT is determined as follows:

(a) If the surrendered ACT was paid in respect of one dividend only, or of dividends, all of which were paid on the same date, the recipient company will be treated as having paid ACT (equal to the surrendered amount) in respect of a distribution made by it on the date on which the dividends were paid.

Chapter 2

(b) If the surrendered ACT was paid in respect of dividends paid on different dates, the surrendered amount will be apportioned by reference to the formula

$$\frac{A}{B} \quad \text{where}$$

A = the amount of the tax credit attaching to the dividend paid on each relevant date.

B = the total amount of the tax credits attaching to dividends paid in the accounting period.

Where an amount of ACT is surrendered, the recipient company is deemed to have paid an amount of ACT equal to the surrendered amount and the ACT is deemed to have been paid on the respective dates on which the dividends giving rise to the ACT were paid.

A company which has received surplus ACT from a surrendering group company cannot carry the surrendered ACT back against the corporation tax liability of the previous accounting period. It can, however, set off the surrendered ACT against its corporation tax liability of the current period before setting off its own surplus ACT, which can be carried back to the previous accounting period.

A claim for surrender of ACT by a recipient company to a surrendering company must be made within two years after the end of the accounting period to which the claim relates. Any ACT surrendered can be paid for by the recipient company and this payment is exempt from corporation tax provided the payment does not exceed the amount of ACT surrendered.

Section 167 is an anti-avoidance section introduced to counteract one company acquiring another company which has surplus unused ACT. The rules are similar to those which apply where a company which has unused trading losses at the date of purchase and can be summarised as follows:

(a) Where within any period of three years there is both a change of ownership of a company and a major change in the nature of conduct of the trade or business carried on by the company; or

(b) at the time of the change of ownership, the company's trade or business has become small or negligible,

Surplus ACT arising in an accounting period beginning before the change of ownership cannot be carried forward to an accounting period ending after the change of ownership. For this purpose the accounting period in which the change of ownership takes place, is treated as two accounting periods, the first ending with the change, the second beginning with the change.

A company which is a 75 per cent subsidiary of a non-resident parent company can pay a dividend to its parent company without the imposition of advance corporation tax provided that the parent company is resident in a country with which Ireland has a double taxation agreement.

Advance corporation tax will not arise where a company, owned by a consortium which includes non-resident companies, makes a distribution on or after 23 April 1996 to the consortium members, provided that the non-resident members are resident in a country with which Ireland has a double taxation agreement. A company is owned by a consortium if it is at least 75 per cent owned by five or fewer companies, each of which has a beneficial ownership of between 5 per cent and 75 per cent of the ordinary share capital.

ACT does not apply to certain "Section 84" loans which were already in existence on 9 February 1983 or were entered into within four months of that date so long as negotiations were in progress on that date.

A company must make a return to the Collector General within nine months of the end of the accounting period in which distributions are made or received by it. Any ACT payable has to be paid within six months from the end of the relevant period. Where the payment falls after the 28th day of a particular month, the tax must be paid on or before the 28th day of that month.

It is not necessary for an assessment to be made in order to collect ACT due, but an assessment can be made if the tax is not paid before the due date or if the Inspector is not satisfied with the return. The normal appeal procedures will apply in respect of ACT assessments as for corporation tax assessments.

Interest is chargeable at the rate of 1.00% per month or part of a month from the due date until payment. The payment on account procedures which apply to corporation tax do not apply to ACT assessments. The penalties for failure to make a return or for making an incorrect return for corporation tax purposes equally apply for ACT purposes.

A loss making company paying "Section 84" loan interest on or after 25 May 1993, is liable to ACT at the rate of 1/18th of the interest paid. This is the same rate that would apply if the company had income from its manufacturing activities. Where such a company pays interest between 1 January 1992 and 25 May 1993 the company and the recipient of the interest may elect in writing for the lower rate of ACT to apply to that interest.

A company, which is an investment company within the meaning of Part XIII of the Companies Act 1990 and operating from the IFSC, may claim to be exempted from ACT arising out of its redemption of shares and securities.

Chapter 2

2.11 SPECIAL COMPANIES FOR CORPORATION TAX

2.11.1 Agricultural and Fishery Co Operatives

TCA97 s443

Co-operatives were largely exempt from corporation tax prior to 1992.

The exemption ceased from 1 April 1992 and the co-operatives concerned are subject to corporation tax in the same manner as any other company. From 1 April 1992 the activities of agricultural and fishery co-operatives can be divided into three separate categories:

(i) manufacturing activities which qualify for the 10% rate under the definition of manufacturing as existed prior to 1992;

(ii) the two categories of activity for which manufacturing relief has been specifically introduced in the case of agricultural and fishery co-operatives as dealt with in Section 443.

(iii) other categories of activity which would have been exempt under the previous regime but which do not qualify for manufacturing relief.

Losses incurred prior to 1 April 1992 are available for set-off against future trading income under Section 396 to the same extent as they would have been available if the co-operative had been subject to tax at all times. The co-operative is deemed to have made any claims which it could have made under Section 396 in the period prior to 1 April 1992. This means that it is assumed to have already used up any losses which it could have used against exempt income but it will not be assumed to have claimed such "exempt losses" against other income or gains prior to 1 April 1992.

2.11.2 An Bord Pinsean

TCA97 s220

Profits arising to An Bord Pinsean are exempt from corporation tax.

2.11.3 Building Societies

TCA97 s703
Sch16

Where a building society converts to a company the following taxation provisions apply:

A. Commencement/Cessation

(i) The trade of the society is not treated as permanently discontinued and the trade of the successor company is not treated as having commenced.

(ii) Financial assets and financial trading stock are shown in the accounts of the successor company at their cost to the society.

B. Capital Allowances

The conversion does not give rise to a balancing allowance or charge.

C. Capital Gains

(i) The conversion of the society into the successor company does not give rise to a charge to capital gains tax. Assets acquired by the company are deemed to have been acquired at the date and cost at which they were acquired by the Society.

(ii) Where members of the society receive shares in priority to others or for no consideration or at a reduced value they are regarded as having obtained an option.

(iii) Where a member of the Society receives shares in the successor company, he is treated as having acquired the shares for the actual consideration given or for no consideration.

2.11.4 Dublin Docklands Development Authority

TCA97 s220

Profits and gains arising to the Authority are exempt from corporation tax.

2.11.5 Housing Finance Agency plc

TCA97 s218

Income arising from the business of making loans and advances under the Housing Finance Agency Act 1981 is exempt from Corporation Tax. Investment income arising to the Agency is also exempt.

2.11.6 Irish Horse-Racing Authority

TCA97 s220

Income and gains of the Irish Horse-Racing Authority, Irish Thoroughbred Marketing Limited and Tote Ireland Limited are exempt from corporation tax and capital gains tax.

2.11.7 National Lottery

TCA97 s220

Profits arising to a company authorised to hold the National Lottery are exempt from corporation tax.

2.11.8 National Treasury Management Agency

TCA97 s230

Profits arising to the National Treasury Management Agency are exempt from Corporation Tax.

Capital gains arising to the agency are also exempt from tax under the provisions of Section 610.

Any interest annuity or other annual payments paid by the agency are paid without deduction of income tax.

Chapter 2

2.11.9 **Nitrigin Eireann Teoranta (NET)**

TCA97 s217

Any income arising to NET from the supply of natural gas to Irish Fertiliser Industry Limited for the period from 1 January 1987 to 31 December 1999 is exempt from corporation tax provided the natural gas is purchased from Bord Gais Eireann.

2.11.10 **Trustee Savings Banks**

TCA97 s704
Sch17

Provision is made to deal with the taxation consequences of mergers under the Trustee Savings Banks Act, 1989. These main provisions are:-

(a) Amalgamation.

On the amalgamation of two or more Trustee Savings Banks, the merged bank and the former banks will be treated as the same person.

(b) Reorganisation

(i) Unused trading losses of a company controlled by the Minister cannot be set off against profits of a company not controlled by the Minister.

(ii) The acquisition of Financial Assets and Financial Trading Stock from the Trustee Savings Banks by the successor will be treated as having been acquired at their cost to the original bank.

(iii) The reorganisation from Trustee Savings Banks to Companies will not give rise to a Balancing Allowance or Charge.

(iv) Unused Capital Allowances, carried forward by the Trustee Savings Banks, cannot be utilised by the successor company.

(v) Trustee Savings Banks will not be liable to Capital Gains Tax, as the transfer will be deemed to give rise to neither a gain nor a loss.

(vi) For subsequent disposals by the successor company, it will be deemed to have acquired the assets at the same time and at the same cost at which it was acquired by the Trustee Savings Banks.

2.11.11 **Investor Compensation Company Limited**

TCA97 s219B

The Investor Compensation Company Limited is exempt from corporation tax, capital gains tax and DIRT.

Corporation Tax

2.12 SPECIAL EMPLOYMENT RELATED RECEIPTS AND PAYMENTS

2.12.1 Scheme Payments

TCA97 s226   Payments to employers under the following schemes are disregarded for all purposes of the Taxes Acts:

(a) Employment Incentive Scheme.

(b) Employment Maintenance Scheme.

(c) Employers' Temporary Subvention Fund.

(d) Employers' Employment Contributions Scheme.

(e) Employment grants under Section 2, Industrial Development (No 2) Act 1981.

(f) Enterprise Allowance Scheme of Minister of Labour.

(g) The Enterprise Scheme of An Foras Aiseanna Saothair.

(h) Employment grants under Section 10(5)(a), Udaras na Gaeltachta Act 1979 (paid on or after 1 April 1993).

(i) Employment grants under Section 21(5)(a) Industrial Development Act 1986, as amended (paid on or after 1 April 1993).

(j) An Bord Trachtala under the Market Development Fund, and

(k) An Foras Aiseanna Saothair (FAS) under the Employment Subsidy Scheme.

(l) From 1 April 1995, certain employment grants made by Udaras na Gaeltachta, IDA Ireland and Forbairt to medium/large industrial undertakings under the schemes known, respectively, as:-

— "Deontais Fhostaiochta o Udaras na Gaeltachta do Ghnothais Mhora/ Mheanmheide Thionscaliocha", and

— "Scheme Governing the Making of Employment Grants to Medium/Large Industrial Undertakings"

(m) From 6 April 1996, the following payments made to employers in respect of new employment provided by them:-

— The Back to Work Allowance Scheme,

— A scheme to be established by the Minister for Enterprise and Employment and administered by FAS for the purpose of promoting the employment of individuals who have been unemployed for three years or more,

— Operating Agreements between the Minister for Enterprise and Employment and the County Enterprise Boards,

Chapter 2

- The EU Leader II Community Initiative (1994 to 1999),
- The Area Partnerships Scheme administered by Area Development Management Limited under the EU Operational Programme for Local, Urban and Rural Development,
- The Special European Union Programme for Peace and Reconciliation in Northern Ireland and the Border Counties of Ireland,
- The Joint Northern Ireland/Ireland INTERREG Programme 1994 to 1999, or
- Initiatives of the International Fund for Ireland.
- The Shannon Free Airport Development Limited (Amendment) Act, 1970.

(n) From 6 April 1997 payment made to employers under:-

- The employment support scheme which is administered by the National Rehabilitation board, and
- The Pilot Programme for the Employment of People with Disabilities which is administered by the Rehab Group.

2.12.2 Enterprise Trust Limited

TCA97 s88

Companies may claim tax relief from corporation tax for donations made to the Enterprise Trust Limited. This company was set up by various employers' bodies in response to Section VII of the Programme for Economic and Social Progress which has the objective of implementing a community response in particular local areas to long-term unemployment. A company which makes a gift between 1 April 1992 and 31 December 2002 is entitled to treat the payment as a trading expense or as an expense of management, as appropriate. The total donations received by Enterprise Trust Limited may not exceed £5m in any of the years 1999 to 2002.

In order to be allowable, gifts must be between £500 and £100,000 in any year.

2.12.3 Long Term Unemployed

TCA97 s88A

Employers may claim a double deduction in respect of certain emoluments paid to employees who were long-term unemployed.

The employment must be a "qualifying employment" and the emoluments must be payable to a "qualifying individual".

The double deduction may be claimed against trading or professional profits in respect of:-

1. Emoluments paid to the qualifying employee in the first thirty six months of the employment, and

2. The employer's PRSI contribution on those emoluments.

See page 59 for allowances available to employee.

2.12.4 Designated Schools

TCA97 s485A

Companies may claim tax relief on donations to, or for the benefit of designated schools. Relief applies to aggregate gifts of between £250 and £10,000 given to any one designated school in an accounting period, subject to an overall limit of £50,000 or 10% of the company's profits where gifts are given to more than one school.

2.12.5 Eligible Charities

TCA97 s486A

An eligible charity is one authorised by the Revenue Commissioners and which has been granted exemption from tax for 3 years prior to its application for authorisation. Authorisation is conferred by way of certificate of eligibility which will be effective for a period of up to 5 years and which can be renewed. The most important conditions and restrictions which apply to this relief are as follows:-

- Relief will only be given where the donation to any single charity by a company is not less than £250 and will not be given in respect of the excess of donations over £10,000 in any 12 months accounting period. The upper limit of relief for donations from a single company to all charities in such an accounting period is the lesser of £50,000 or 10 per cent of the company's profits.

- The donation must be in cash and no conditions may attach to it.

- No benefit may be received by the company or anyone connected with the company in return for the donation.

The Minister for Finance may require any eligible charity to publish such information, including accounts, as the Minister deems proper. In addition, provision is made to allow the Minister for Justice, Equality and Law Reform, at some future date, to impose conditions in relation to the authorisation of eligible charities. Eligibility for the relief may be withdrawn by the Revenue Commissioners if the various conditions are not complied with.

2.12.6 Renewable Energy Generation

TCA97 486B

A company investing in a renewable energy project may, subject to certain conditions, obtain a deduction in computing taxable profits. This scheme will come into effect by the making of an Order by the Minister for Finance which would be valid for a period of 3 years. Clearance from the European Commission is required.

The relief will operate as follows:-

- A deduction from company profits may be obtained for an investment in new ordinary shares in a company setting up a renewable energy project.
- Such renewable schemes are in wind, hydro and biomas technology.
- The maximum amount which may be funded under this project is 50% of the capital expenditure. This figure excludes land and is net of grants. There is an overall limit of Ir£7.5m on any project.
- An individual company or group of companies may not invest more than Ir£10m per annum in such projects.

The shares when issued must be held for a period of 5 years, otherwise the relief will be withdrawn.

2.12.7 First Step Limited

TCA97s486

Companies may claim tax relief for donations made to First Step Limited, a company established for the purposes of assisting job creation by supporting enterprise in areas of high unemployment. Donations between £500 and £100,000 made by a company in an accounting period from 1 June 1993 to 31 December 2002 qualify for relief.

2.12.8 Scientific Technological Educational and (Investment) Fund (STEIF)

TCA97 s485B

Companies (and individuals) may claim tax relief on gifts of up to a maximum of £1,000, made to STEIF, in any one accounting period (year of assessment).

CHAPTER 3 DOUBLE TAXATION AGREEMENTS

3.1 EXISTING DOUBLE TAXATION AGREEMENTS

Ireland has entered into comprehensive double taxation agreements with:

Australia	Malaysia*
Austria	Mexico
Belgium	Netherlands
Canada	New Zealand
Cyprus	Norway
Czech Republic	Pakistan
Denmark	Poland
Estonia	Portugal
Finland	Russia
France	South Africa
Germany	South Korea
Hungary	Spain
Israel	Sweden
Italy	Switzerland
Japan	United Kingdom
Latvia	United States of America
Lithuania	Zambia
Luxembourg	

Not yet in force.

Chapter 3

3.2 DOUBLE TAXATION AGREEMENT REPUBLIC OF IRELAND - UNITED KINGDOM

(As applicable to residents of Republic of Ireland)

A double taxation agreement based on the model OECD Agreement was ratified in June 1976. This has been amended by protocols signed in October 1976, November 1994 and November 1998.

The agreement is based on the "credit' method of allowance for tax payable in the country of non residence. The main features of the agreement are:

3.2.1 Residence of Individuals

Article 4

To determine in which of the two countries an individual is resident for the purposes of the treaty the following series of tests is applied:

(a) where has the individual his permanent home or the centre of his vital interest, or

(b) where has the individual his habitual abode, or

(c) of which State is the individual a national.

If any one of the foregoing tests can be positively applied, the residence of the individual is determined as being in the particular country.

Should all these tests fail to produce a positive answer, the final decision is left to be agreed between the Revenues of each country.

The concept of "double residence" is effectively removed by the operation of these provisions.

3.2.2 UK Dividends

Article 11

Dividends received from a UK company by an Irish resident are taxable in Ireland. They may also be taxable in the UK but subject to the following

(a) The tax charged in the UK cannot exceed 5% of the gross amount of the dividend if the beneficial owner is a company which controls directly or indirectly 10% or more of the paying company's voting power

(b) In all other cases the tax charged in the UK cannot exceed 15% of the gross amount

Where the Irish Authorities certify that such dividends are not liable to Irish taxation (e.g. in the case of superannuition schemes etc.) they will also be exempt from UK taxation.

Double Taxation Agreements

3.2.3	**Repayment of Withholding Tax**
Article 11	Individuals resident in Ireland may be entitled to repayment of part of the withholding tax. The amount repayable will be dependent upon the personal reliefs and allowances claimable in the United Kingdom and the proportion which the United Kingdom income bears to the total world income.
3.2.4	**Interest**
Article 12	Taxable only in Ireland for individuals resident in Ireland. United Kingdom tax deducted from interest is repayable in full.
3.2.5	**Rents**
Article 7	Taxable in the United Kingdom with a right to set off the United Kingdom tax against the tax payable in Ireland on the same income.
3.2.6	**Business Profits**
Article 8	Taxable only in Ireland unless there is a permanent establishment in the United Kingdom when the profits applicable to the permanent establishment will be taxed in the United Kingdom. Any tax payable in the United Kingdom will be available as a credit against the tax payable in Ireland on the same profits.
3.2.7	**Royalties**
Article 13	Taxable only in Ireland.
3.2.8	**Capital Gains**
Article 14	An Irish resident earning capital gains in the United Kingdom is normally taxable in Ireland alone. There are some exceptions to this

  (a) Gains derived by an Irish resident from the alienation of immovable property in the United Kingdom or from certain shares deriving the greater part of their value from such shares may also be taxed in the United Kingdom.

  (b) Gains from the alienation of business property of a permanent establishment may also be taxed in the United Kingdom.

3.2.9	**Salaries, Wages and Directors Fees**
Articles 15 and 16	Salaries, wages and directors fees paid from the United Kingdom are liable to tax under PAYE in the United Kingdom. Any tax so paid is available as a credit against the tax paid on the same income in Ireland (there are circumstances where the remuneration may be taxable in the state of residence only).

3.2.10 Pensions

Article 17

(a) Other than Government pensions: Taxable only in Ireland.

(b) State pensions and remuneration: Taxable only in the United Kingdom unless the recipient is a sole national of Ireland when tax is payable also in Ireland with a right to set off the United Kingdom tax paid against the Irish tax payable on the same income.

3.2.11 Charities & Superannuation Schemes

Article 14A

Such bodies continue to be exempt from tax in appropriate circumstances.

3.2.12 Government Service

Article 18

Salaries, wages and other similar remuneration, other than a pension, are taxable only in Ireland. They may, however, be taxable in the United Kingdom if the services are rendered there by a resident of the United Kingdom who is also a United Kingdom national.

3.2.13 Exchange of Information

Article 25

Provision is made for the exchange of information as is necessary for the carrying out of the convention which is expressed to be for the avoidance of double taxation and the prevention of fiscal evasion with respect to taxes on income and capital gains.

3.3 EU DIRECTIVES

3.3.1 EU Directive No 90/435/EU

TCA97 s831

The provisions of this Directive on dividends and distributions paid by subsidiary companies are applied by Section 831. The directive applies to the distributions between companies with a 25% shareholding relationship. Member States may alternatively by means of bilateral agreements apply a 25% holding of voting rights criterion for parent/subsidiary status. The purpose of these provisions is to grant credit for tax paid on profits in EU Member States out of which distributions are made to companies in other Member States. To qualify for this treatment the foreign company must be resident in an EU country and at least 25% of its share capital must be owned directly by a company from another Member State.

Where a parent/subsidiary relationship exists and the subsidiary pays a distribution other than a distribution in a winding up to the parent the Directive requires the following reliefs to be given:-

1. The parent company's State must either exempt the distribution received from the charge to tax (the exemption method) or else give credit against tax charged for any foreign withholding tax deducted from the distribution and for underlying tax suffered by the subsidiary on the profits out of which the distribution was paid (the credit method).

2. The subsidiary's State must not deduct withholding tax from the distribution.

3. The parent company's State must not deduct withholding tax from the distribution.

3.3.2 EU Directive No 90/434/EU

The purpose of this directive is to remove tax barriers to mergers, divisions, transfers of assets and exchanges of shares between companies from different member States. In general terms it achieves this by deferring any capital gains tax which would arise at the time of the merger etc. Sections 583-584 contain the necessary legislation to deal with exchanges of shares.

Mergers and divisions (as defined in the Directive) cannot occur under Irish company law and accordingly no tax legislation is possible.

The chapter, therefore, deals with transfers of assets in the main and, broadly speaking, allows the following transactions to take place without corporation tax or capital gains tax implications:

Chapter 3

(a) The transfer of a trade or part of a trade by one company to another in exchange for shares in the latter company which then carries on that trade as a branch of its activity. Both companies must be EU member States companies.

(b) The transfer of trading assets by an Irish subsidiary to its 100% parent within the EU.

(c) The transfer of development land in the course of a scheme of reconstruction or amalgamation.

(d) The transfer of development land within a group.

The relevance of (c) and (d) is that previously transactions in development land gave rise to a tax charge in these situations as Irish tax law did not allow a deferral of gains on development land or similar transactions between Irish resident companies.

CHAPTER 4   ANTI AVOIDANCE / REVENUE POWERS

4.1 ANTI-AVOIDANCE LEGISLATION

The principal anti avoidance provisions are:

4.1.1 (a) Friendly Societies

TCA97 s211

Restriction of exemption for Friendly Societies to those which satisfy the Revenue Commissioners that they are "bona fide" societies.

4.1.2 (b) Transfer of Assets Abroad

TCA97 s806

Prevention of tax avoidance by an individual ordinarily resident in the State of liability to tax by means of transfers of assets by virtue or in consequence of which either alone or in conjunction with associated operations income becomes payable to persons, eg a tax haven company, resident or domiciled outside the State.

The legislation provides that the income of the non resident or non domiciled person is to be treated as the income of the resident individual unless he proves that the transfer was not for the purpose of avoiding liability to tax and was a bona fide commercial transaction.

Finance Act 1998 amends the provision by extending it to transfers made by individuals resident in the State. It also applies irrespective of when the transfer was made but only to income arising after 12 February 1998.

The Revenue Commissioners have substantial powers to obtain information in connection with any transfer of assets abroad.

4.1.3 (c) Property Transactions

TCA97 s639-s647

Prevention of avoidance involving gains from (real) property transactions or transactions in shares deriving value from real property.

4.1.4 (d) Industrial and Provident Societies

TCA97 s438

Loans or advances made on or after 23 May 1983 to participators or their associates by a registered industrial or provident society are deemed to be annual payments made under the deduction of tax. The society is therefore obliged to pay over income tax at a rate of 24/76ths of the loan to the Revenue Commissioners (see loans to participators etc page 200).

Chapter 4

4.1.5 (e) Exchequer Bills

TCA97 s45-s48

Exemption does not apply in respect of the excess of the amount received on redemption over the issue price of Exchequer Bills and Agricultural Commodity Intervention Bills issued after 25 January 1984 unless a tender for them was submitted on or before that date.

4.1.6 (f) Bond Washing

TCA97 s815

A person who transfers or sells certain securities is to be treated for taxation purposes as having received the interest which has accrued to the date of sale. The securities referred to are those exempted from capital gains tax under the provisions of Section 607, and stocks, bonds and obligations of any government, municipal corporation, or other body corporate. Shares of a company within the meaning of the Companies Act 1963, or similar body, are excluded.

The provisions do not apply:

(a) where the security has been held by the same owner for a continuous period of at least two years, or

(b) where the vendor is a dealer in securities, the profits of whose trade are assessed to tax under Case I Schedule D, or

(c) where the transfer or sale is between a husband and wife at a time when they are treated as living together for income tax purposes. (The combined period of ownership of the spouses is taken into account for the purpose of the two year rule), or

(d) where the security is one, the interest on which is treated as a distribution under the Tax Acts.

4.1.7 (g) Limited Partnerships

TCA97 s1013

In respect of limited partnerships set up after 22 May 1985, the right of the limited partners to set off losses and capital allowances arising out of the partnership trade against their other income is restricted to the amount of their contribution to the limited partnership trade.

Losses and capital allowances arising from contributions to limited partnerships by limited partners on or after 24 April 1992 will only be available for setoff against profits or gains arising from the partnership trade and will not be available against the total income of the limited partner.

Similar restrictions apply in the case of partnership whose activities include producing, distributing or holding films or video tapes or exploring for or exploiting oil and/or gas resources. A partner in such a partnership who does not work for the greater part of his/her time on the day to day management or conduct of the partnership trade will be subject to restrictions in respect of the use of losses, capital allowances and certain interest payments.

4.1.8 (h) Transactions to Avoid Liability to Tax

TCA97 s811

If the Revenue Commissioners form an opinion that a transaction is a "tax-avoidance transaction", they will notify each person, undertaking such a transaction, of this, state the amount of tax that they consider the person is attempting to avoid and how they propose to recharacterise the transactions for tax purposes to counteract the avoidance. In examining the transaction, the Revenue Commissioners may look at both the substance and outcome of the transaction and of related transactions and not merely the form.

The Revenue Commissioners will not regard a transaction as a tax-avoidance transaction if it was made with a view to the realisation of profits in the course of business and was not primarily to avoid tax, or if the transaction was undertaken to obtain the benefit of a tax incentive, provided that the transaction would not result in a misuse or abuse of the incentive.

Anyone receiving such a notice from the Revenue Commissioners may lodge an appeal within 30 days. The appeal procedure will be in the form normally applying to Income Tax appeals.

The section applies to any transaction completed on or after 25 January 1989. It also applies to transactions carried out on or before that date if the transaction would reduce any charge or assessment to tax which could not fall due earlier than 25 January 1989 and to transactions which would generate a refund which would not be payable earlier than that date.

4.1.9 (i) Capital Distribution Treated as Dividend

TCA97 s817

Where a shareholder disposes of shares in a close company without significantly reducing his percentage shareholding in the company, the proceeds of sale will be treated as a receipt assessable under Schedule F. The close company will be regarded as having made a distribution of an equivalent amount.

An exemption applies in the case of bona fide disposals of shares which are not part of any scheme or arrangement to avoid tax.

Chapter 4

4.2 REVENUE POWERS

4.2.1 General

Chapter 4, Part 38 of the TCA 1997 provides for certain Revenue Powers. The Finance Act 1999 substituted existing powers under sections 900, 901, 902, 907 and 908 by new powers and it provided for additional powers contained in sections 902A, 904A, 906A and 908A. In addition, it also amended the provisions of sections 905 and 909.

Given the exceptional nature of these extended powers, the Revenue have issued a Statement of Practice (SP-Gen 1/99) setting out the approach that they will adopt in using these powers and they have also published Guidance Notes and Instructions for Revenue staff, which are available to taxpayers and their advisors.

A brief summary of Revenue powers, is as follows:

4.2.2 Inspector's right to make enquiries

TCA97 s899

This section enables an inspector to verify the accuracy of information provided by –

- persons acting as agents in respect of rents
- Ministers, Health Boards, Local Authorities, etc in respect of rents paid
- fees or commissions paid for services
- persons in receipt of income on behalf of others
- nominee holders of securities
- intermediaries in relation to UCITS
- persons in relation to Third Party Returns

Interest paid by banks without deduction of tax is outside the scope of this section.

4.2.3 Power to require production of accounts and books

TCA97 s900

This section gives power to an authorised officer to require a person to produce, or make available books etc. and furnish information etc. relevant to the person's tax liability.

An "authorised officer" is an inspector or other Revenue officer authorised in writing for the purpose of this section by the Revenue Commissioners.

A person carrying on a profession cannot be required to disclose any information or professional advice of a confidential nature given to a client.

Anti Avoidance / Revenue Powers

4.2.4	**Production of books and records – Application to High Court**
TCA97 s901	This section gives power to an authorised officer to apply to a judge of the High Court for an order seeking production or availability of books etc. and information etc. from a person, which are relevant to the person's tax liability. A person carrying on a profession shall not be required to disclose any information or professional advice of a confidential nature given to a client.

4.2.5 Power to obtain from certain persons particulars of transactions with and documents concerning tax liability of taxpayer

TCA97 s902 This section gives power to an authorised officer, when enquiring into the tax liability of any person, to seek from a third party books etc. or information etc. relevant to the tax liability of the person subject to enquiry (who will be given a copy of the notice served on the third party).

4.2.6 Information from third parties – Application to High Court

TCA97 s902A An authorised officer can apply to a judge of the High Court for an order seeking books etc. and information from a third party that are relevant to the tax liability of a person, including a group or class of persons. Before such an application is made the authorised officer must have the consent of a Revenue Commissioner. A person carrying on a profession shall not be required to disclose any information or professional advice of a confidential nature given to a client.

4.2.7 PAYE

TCA97 s903 Similar powers, as outlined above, exist in relation to the operation of PAYE. These include the power:

- to enter and search any premises which is connected with the operation of PAYE;
- to examine, remove and retain records, and
- to seek explanations from all persons on the premises other than customers or clients.

4.2.8 Subcontractors

TCA97 s904 The Revenue Commissioners also have extended powers in relation to the supervision and monitoring of the subcontractors legislation.

An authorised officer may, at all reasonable times, enter any premises where he has reason to believe:-

(a) that relevant operations are being carried on;

(b) that any person is making or has made payments to a subcontractor in connection with the performance by the subcontractor of a relevant contract in relation to which that person is principal;

(c) that any person is or was in receipt of such payments;

(d) that records are or may be kept in those premises.

He may require the principal or sub-contractor or any employee or any other person providing bookkeeping, clerical or other administrative services to the principal or subcontractor who is on that premises to produce any records which he requires for the purpose of that enquiry.

If he has reason to believe that any of the records which have not been produced to him are on those premises, he can search the premises.

He can examine, copy, take extracts from, remove or retain any records for a reasonable period for the further examination thereof or for legal or criminal proceedings.

The authorised officer may require the principal or subcontractor or any employee or any other person providing bookkeeping, clerical or other administrative services to the principal or subcontractor to give all reasonable assistance including providing information, explanations and furnishing documents.

4.2.9 DIRT

TCA97 s904A

This section gives power to an authorised officer to audit the DIRT returns of a relevant deposit taker i.e. banks etc.

4.2.10 Inspection of documents and records

TCA97 s905

This section gives power to an authorised officer to enter premises where any trade or profession is carried on at a reasonable time and to search for and inspect records relevant to tax liability. The authorised officer is empowered to remove the records for examination and to require certain persons at the premises to render all reasonable assistance. A search may be conducted at a private residence only where the officer has been invited to enter the house by the occupier or on foot of a warrant by the District Court.

TCA97 s905A

This section also gives power to an authorised officer to carry out an on-site audit of a financial institution.

Furthermore under this section, as amended, application can be made to a judge of the District Court for the issue of a search warrant in relation to any premises. The judge can issue such a warrant if satisfied on information given on oath, that there are reasonable grounds for suspecting that there has been a failure to comply with the tax legislation, which failure is seriously prejudicial to the proper assessment or collection of tax and that records that are material to such assessment or collection are likely to be kept at the premises concerned.

4.2.11 Authorised officers and Garda Síochána

TCA97 s906

This section gives power to an authorised officer who is authorised to enter premises to carry out inspection duties to bring with him/her a member or members of the Garda Síochána. If the Revenue officer is obstructed or interfered with, the Gardaí has the power of arrest without warrant.

4.2.12 Information to be furnished by Financial Institutions

TCA97 s906A

This section gives power to an authorised officer to issue a notice to a financial institution requiring it to make available for inspection books etc. or to furnish information relevant to a person's tax liability. The person subject to inquiry will be given a copy of the notice. Before such a notice is issued by an authorised officer the consent of a Revenue Commissioner is required.

4.2.13 Application to Appeal Commissioners seeking determination that authorised officer is justified in requiring information to be furnished by financial institutions

TCA97 s907

This section gives power to an authorised officer to apply to the Appeal Commissioners for consent to issue a notice to a financial institution requiring it to make available for inspection books etc., or to furnish information relevant to a person's tax liability (including a group or class of persons and a person who is claiming exemption from DIRT on the basis of non-residence in the State). Before such an application is made the authorised officer must have the consent of a Revenue Commissioner.

4.2.14 Application to High Court seeking order requiring information to be furnished by financial institutions

TCA97 s908

This section gives power to an authorised officer to apply to a judge of the High Court for an order seeking from a financial institution access to books etc. or information relevant to a person's tax liability (including a group or class of persons and a person who is claiming exemption from DIRT on the basis of non-residence in the State.) Application can also be made by the authorised officer for an order of the Court to freeze assets of a person in the custody of the financial institution Before an application to the High Court is made by an authorised officer under this section, he or she must have obtained the consent of a Revenue Commissioner.

Chapter 4

4.2.15 Application to Circuit Court or District Court seeking order requiring information to be furnished by financial institutions

TCA97 s908A

This section gives power to an authorised officer to apply to a judge of the Circuit Court or of the District Court for an order authorising the officer to inspect and take copies of bank records for the purpose of investigating a Revenue offence. A judge may make such an order if he or she is satisfied that on information given on oath that there are reasonable grounds for suspecting that an offence which would result in serious prejudice to the proper assessment or collection of tax is being, has been, or is about to be committed and that there is material in the possession of the financial institution which is likely to be of substantial value in the investigation of that offence. Before an application is made by an authorised officer under this section, he or she must have obtained the consent of a Revenue Commissioner

4.2.16 Statement of Affairs

TCA97 s909

An Inspector of Taxes may by notice in writing, require a person who has delivered a return of income tax or capital gains tax and his spouse if they are living together, to provide a statement of affairs within a specified period. The statement of affairs should include all assets wherever situated to which the taxpayer and his spouse are beneficially entitled and all liabilities for which they are liable on a specified date.

Where a person is chargeable to tax in a representative capacity, he may be required to provide a statement of all the assets and liabilities of the person in respect of which he is chargeable. Similarly a person chargeable as a trustee may be required to provide a statement of all the assets and liabilities comprised in the trust.

Assets acquired otherwise than at arm's length must be identified and the name and address of the disposer provided.

Anti Avoidance / Revenue Powers

4.3 REPORTING REQUIREMENTS

4.3.1 (a) Returns of Certain Information

TCA97 s894

The self assessment system applies to "third party" returns. These are returns:

(a) by letting agents and managers of premises. The return must contain the following:-

  (i) the full address of all such premises;

  (ii) the name and address of every person to whom such premises belong;

  (iii) a statement of all rents and other such payments arising from such premises, and

  (iv) such other particulars relating to all such premises as may be specified in the notice.

(b) of fees and commissions paid. With regard to these returns it should be noted:-

  (i) Government departments and State bodies are included in the category of persons who must make returns under the section;

  (ii) in addition to other particulars the tax reference number of the payee must be included on the return. This means that the administrative burden of ascertaining each person's tax number will be transferred from the Revenue to the "third party";

  (iii) the return is to include details of payments made on behalf of any other person;

  (iv) no return will be required in respect of payments totalling less than £500 to any one person.

(c) of interest paid or credited without deduction of tax,

(d) of income received belonging to others. No return is required where the income received in respect of any one person does not exceed £500.

(e) by nominee holders of securities.

(f) by certain intermediaries in relation to UCITS.

The onus is on the "third party" concerned to make the return without any notice being served by the Inspector of Taxes.

The return must be submitted by the normal filing date ie within 9 months of the end of the accounting period for a company or by 31 January following the year of assessment in the case of an individual.

Chapter 4

The returns mentioned above with the exception of returns of interest paid and credited, may be subject to audit by the Inspector of Taxes.

4.3.2 (b) Off-Shore Funds

TCA97 s896

Financial institutions, consultants and other intermediaries who assist Irish residents in acquiring a material interest in certain off-shore funds are obliged to report the matter to the Revenue Commissioners on an automatic basis. The Irish resident investors are also obliged to report such acquisitions on their annual returns of income. Section 743 lists the off-shore funds to which these reporting requirements apply.

4.3.3 (c) Foreign Accounts

TCA97 s896

Reporting requirements are imposed on Irish intermediaries who assist or act in opening such accounts and on the taxpayer concerned.

An intermediary, who assists or acts for an Irish resident in relation to the opening of a foreign account is obliged to supply to the Inspector of Taxes the following information:

(i) the full name and permanent address of the resident;

(ii) the resident's tax reference number;

(iii) the name and address of the person with whom the account was opened;

(iv) the date on which the account was opened.

A resident who requests an intermediary to provide him with a service in relation to the opening of a foreign bank account must furnish to the intermediary the details which the intermediary is required to include in the above return. The intermediary is also obliged to take all reasonable care (including, where necessary, the requesting of documentary evidence) to confirm that the details furnished are true and correct.

The intermediary must supply the above information to the Inspector of Taxes on or before the normal return filing date, ie 31 January following the end of the year of assessment for an individual or within 9 months of the end of the accounting period in the case of a company.

A resident is obliged also to forward the following information to the Inspector of Taxes within three months of the opening of a foreign account;

(i) name and address of the person with whom the account was opened;

(ii) the date on which it was opened;

(iii) the amount of the initial deposit;

(iv) name and address of any Irish intermediary.

Where a resident fails to deliver this information within the three month time-limit the resident's tax return for the relevant income tax year or chargeable period will be deemed not to have been filed on time and consequently the 10% surcharge for late filing will apply.

The section also provides for penalties on both the intermediary and the resident in connection with the above information.

4.3.4 (d) Non Resident Companies

TCA97 s882

Companies which are incorporated in the State but not resident for tax purposes (see page 176) and companies which are neither incorporated nor resident in the State but carry on a trade there must supply the Revenue Commissioners with the following information:-

Incorporated but not Resident

(i) the territory in which it is resident

(ii) if treated as being non-resident by virtue of the fact that it is ultimately controlled by residents of the EU or a tax treaty country and the company or a related company is trading in the State, to identify the company trading in the State.

(iii) if treated as being non-resident under the terms of a tax treaty, to identify

(iv) where the company is controlled by a quoted company, the name and address of the quoted company, and

(v) in any other case the ultimate beneficial owners of the company.

Neither incorporated or resident but carrying on a trade

(i) The address of the company's principal place of business in the State.

(ii) The name and address of the agent, manager, factor or the representative of the company; and

(iii) The date of commencement of the company's trade, profession or business.

The above requirements apply to new companies incorporated on or after 11 February 1999 and to companies incorporated before that date from 1 October 1999.

Where a company fails to make a return of the information outlined above or to pay any penalty arising, the penalty can be recovered from the company secretary or where the company secretary is not an Irish resident individual from an Irish resident director of the company.

The information must be supplied within thirty days of:-

— the company commencing to carry on a trade, profession or business, wherever carried on, or

— any time at which there is a material change in information previously delivered by the company, or

— when requested to do so by an Inspector of Taxes.

4.3.5 (e) Show Tax Reference

TCA97 s885

Persons carrying on a profession, or a trade consisting solely of the supply of services, must show one of their tax reference numbers on invoices, credit notes, debit notes, receipts, accounts, vouchers and estimates relating to amounts of £5 or more. "Tax reference number" means either a tax serial number or a VAT registration number.

4.3.6 (f) Information from Ministers

TCA97 s910

The Revenue Commissioners have power to request any Minister to provide them with such information in the possession of the Minister in relation to payments made by the Minister to such persons or classes of persons as the Revenue Commissioners may specify in the notice. The 1999 Finance Act extended this power to payments made by statutory bodies.

4.4 REVENUE OFFENCES

TCA97 s1078

Section 1078 contains very wide provisions relating to the topic of revenue offences, the main details of which are set out below.

(1) A person shall, without prejudice to any other penalty to which he may be liable, be guilty of an offence under this Section if, after the date of the passing of this Act, he:

   (a) knowingly or wilfully delivers any incorrect return, statement or accounts or knowingly or wilfully furnishes any incorrect information in connection with any tax

   (b) knowingly aids, abets, assists, incites or induces another person to make or deliver knowingly or wilfully any incorrect return, statement or accounts in connection with any tax

   (c) claims or obtains relief or exemption from, or repayment of, any tax, being a relief, exemption or repayment to which, to his knowledge, he is not entitled

   (e) knowingly or wilfully fails to comply with any provision of the Acts requiring:-

     (i) the furnishing of a return of income, profits or gains, or of sources of income, profits or gains, for the purposes of any tax

     (ii) the furnishing of any other return, certificate, notification, particulars, or any statement or evidence, for the purposes of any tax

     (iii) the keeping or retention of books, records, accounts or other documents for the purposes of any tax, or

     (iv) the production of books, records, accounts or other documents, when so requested, for the purposes of any tax,

   (cc) knowingly or wilfully, and within the time limits specified for their retention, destroys, defaces, or conceals from an authorised officer -

     (i) any documents, or

     (ii) any other written or printed material in any form, including any information stored, maintained or preserved by means of any mechanical or electronic device, whether or not stored, maintained or preserved in a legible form, which a person is obliged by any provision of the Acts to keep, to issue or to produce for inspection.

   (f) fails to remit certain income tax or value added tax or

(g) obstructs or interferes with any officer of the Revenue Commissioners, or any other person, in the exercise or performance of powers or duties under the Acts for the purposes of any tax.

(2) A person guilty of an offence under this Section shall be liable

(a) on summary conviction to a fine of £1,000 which may be mitigated to not less than one fourth part thereof or, at the discretion of the court, to imprisonment for a term not exceeding 12 months or to both the fine and the imprisonment, or...

(b) on conviction on indictment, to a fine not exceeding £100,000 or at the discretion of the court, to imprisonment for a term not exceeding 5 years or to both the fine and the imprisonment.

(3) Notwithstanding the provisions of any other enactment, proceedings in respect of an offence under this Section may be instituted within 10 years from the date of the commission of the offence or incurring of the penalty (as the case may be).

Penalties for non compliance with the measures outlined in above range from £1,000 to £1,200.

4.4.1 Revenue Offences Made Public

TCA97 s1086

The Revenue Commissioners may publish any number of lists of persons or companies who have been convicted of tax offences or who have made back duty settlements with the Revenue Commissioners during a year. Publication of back duty settlements is confined to those cases where the amount of the settlement is £10,000 or more and where a full voluntary disclosure had not been made.

Anti Avoidance / Revenue Powers

4.5 RESIGNATION OF PROFESSIONAL ADVISORS

TCA97 s1079

Auditors and tax advisors are obliged to cease to act for a company in certain circumstances. The features of these provisions are as follows:

(1) An auditor or tax advisor (referred to as a relevant person), who in the course of his or her normal work for a client company becomes aware of certain material tax offences committed by the company, is obliged to communicate particulars of the offences to the company and request it to either rectify the situation or report the offences to the Revenue Commissioners within six months after the communication. If the company does not do so the relevant person is obliged to cease to act for the company as auditor or as tax adviser and not to so act for a period of 3 years or until the matter has been rectified, if that is earlier. An auditor who is required to resign under the section must notify the company of his or her resignation and send a copy of the notification to the Revenue Commissioners.

(2) The main offences are making an incorrect return, failure to make a return (except where a return has been made in one of the last three years), false claims to relief and issuing false documents.

(3) Penalties for failure to comply with the section consist of, in the case of summary conviction, a fine of £1,000 which can be mitigated to £250 and, in the case of conviction on indictment, a fine not exceeding £5,000 or imprisonment of up to 2 years, or both.

(4) The requirement to cease to act for the company will not prevent a person from acting in the preparation for, or conduct of, legal proceedings which are extant or pending 6 months after the time at which the offences are required to be communicated to the company.

(5) The measure provides that it will be a good defence against a prosecution under the section for a relevant person to show that he or she would not have been aware of the offences by the company if the person had not been assisting or advising the company in preparing for legal proceedings. It also provides indemnity for a relevant person who complies with his or her obligations under the section.

Chapter 4

4.6 TAX CLEARANCE CERTIFICATES

4.6.1 Liquor Licences

TCA97 s1094

A licensee must obtain a tax clearance certificate from the Collector General before a retail liquor licence can be obtained or renewed. A clearance certificate will be issued where the applicant has complied with all obligations imposed by the Tax Acts, and the Value Added Tax Act 1972 in relation to:-

(i) the payment or remittance of taxes, interest and penalties required to be paid or remitted under the Acts, and

(ii) the delivery of returns.

It is necessary for the beneficial holder of the licence to apply for the tax clearance certificate. This means that a nominee holder of a licence cannot apply for it.

Where a licence is transferred and the predecessor is connected with the successor then the affairs of both the predecessor and the successor must be in order before a certificate will be issued. This provision also applies in the case of licences which had elapsed within the previous 5 years when they had been beneficially held by a person other than the current applicant.

Connected persons in the case of a partnership means the other partners and in the case of a company any shareholder who owns or controls (directly or indirectly) more than 50% of the ordinary share capital of the company.

An applicant has a right of appeal against the Collector General's refusal to issue a clearance certificate. However, this right does not apply where tax arrears are the reason for the refusal.

4.6.2 Other Licences

The tax clearance procedure outlined above is extended to the following activities,

Vendors of hydrocarbon oil and liquid petroleum gas

Wholesalers of spirits, beer and wine

Bookmakers

Gaming licence holders

Auctioneers (in respect of their licence, auction permits or house agent permits)

CHAPTER 5   CAPITAL ACQUISITIONS TAX

5.1 CAPITAL ACQUISITIONS TAX

The Capital Acquisitions Tax Act 1976 introduced a gift tax on every taxable gift taken on or after 28 February 1974, and also an inheritance tax in respect of every taxable inheritance taken on or after 1 April 1975. There are three stages in the evolution of capital acquisitions tax (CAT) which began as a very restricted disponer/beneficiary tax, and finally ended up as a full accessions tax.

CAT is charged at progressive rates on a successive slice system. Rates of CAT since inception are set out in Chart 22. Gifts are liable to CAT @ 75% of the rate applicable to inheritances.

Stage 1 - Originally there were four different tables of rates which applied for different classes of beneficiaries depending on their relationship to the person from whom the gift/inheritance (benefit) was received. Benefits taken from one disponer by one beneficiary are aggregated inter se. Aggregation is the important factor in arriving at the amount of tax chargeable on any particular benefit. A later benefit is taxed at a higher rate of tax than an earlier benefit, when both benefits aggregate. Under the earlier system, benefits taken from different disponers did not aggregate.

Stage 2 - Under the provisions of Section 102 Finance Act 1982, the scope of aggregation was widened. Benefits from all disponers were aggregated provided those benefits were taxed under the same appropriate table of rates. For example, benefits taken by a beneficiary from both his father and mother were aggregated while a benefit taken by the same beneficiary from his uncle did not aggregate with the benefits taken from his parents.

It was also provided that all benefits taken prior to 2 June 1982 were to be ignored for aggregation purposes.

Stage 3 - Under the provisions of Section III Finance Act 1984, a system of full aggregation of all benefits taken by any beneficiary from all disponers was introduced.

The tables of rates applicable during stages 1 and 2 are set out in Chart 22. Each of those tables of rates has a fixed threshold or a nil band which is based on the consanguinity of the disponer to the beneficiary. Aggregation rules were readily applied when aggregation was confined to a single table. Even when the system of aggregation was widened at stage 2, the aggregation rules were still confined to a single table. However, when a full accessions tax system was introduced in stage 3 and all benefits taken by a beneficiary from any disponer were aggregated, a single table of

Chapter 5

rates applied and a new format of consanguinity relief was introduced. Features of stage 3 which apply to benefits taken on or after 26 March 1984 are as follows:

(a) There are three class thresholds replacing the four previous tax free thresholds.

(b) There is only one table of rates.

(c) All benefits received since 2 June 1982 are aggregated.

(d) Benefits received prior to 2 June 1982 are ignored and are not aggregated.

FA99 s201
(e) In relation to gifts on inheritances taken on or after 2 December 1998 benefits received prior to 2 December 1988 are not aggregated.

5.1.1 Class Thresholds

The 1984 Finance Act introduced a class threshold which corresponded generally to the old nil bands of the old tables. There are three class thresholds:

Class (a)
£150,000 where the beneficiary is on the day the benefit is taken the spouse, child or minor child of a deceased child of the disponer.

It should be noted since 30 January 1985 an inheritance taken by the spouse of the disponer is exempt and as and from 31 January 1990 a gift taken by the spouse of a disponer is also exempt.

Section 107 of the Finance Act 1991 applies Class (a) threshold to an inheritance (but not a gift) taken by a parent of the disponer where the inheritance is an absolute interest and is taken on the date of death of the disponer. This relief is back dated to 2 June 1982.

Class (b)
£20,000 where the beneficiary is on the day the benefit is taken a lineal ancestor, a lineal descendant (other than a child or a minor child of a deceased child), a brother, a sister, or a child of a brother or of a sister, of the disponer.

Class (c)
£10,000 where the beneficiary on the day the benefit is taken is not entitled to either a Class (a) or a Class (b) threshold.

N.B. See Chart 23 re indexation of class thresholds.

5.1.2 Revised Class Threshold

The four nil bands in the original tables of rates are replaced by one nil band called the threshold amount. The threshold amount is arrived at from the class thresholds. The class threshold of each

Capital Acquisitions Tax

benefit in an aggregate is given a revised class threshold which is the lesser of the following:

(a) The class threshold applicable to that benefit, and

(b) The total of the taxable values of all taxable benefits to which the class threshold at (a) above applies and which benefits are included in the aggregate. This is subject to the proviso that where the revised class threshold is less than the smallest of the class thresholds that apply in relation to all of the taxable benefits included in the aggregate, the revised class threshold is that smallest class threshold.

5.1.3 Threshold Amount

The threshold amount is the greatest of the revised class thresholds that apply in relation to all of the taxable benefits included in any aggregate. It is the amount of the aggregate on which tax is charged at nil rate.

5.1.4 Indexation

Section 128, Finance Act 1990 provided that in respect of any taxable benefit taken in 1990 and subsequent years the threshold amounts of both the old and the new aggregates were to be indexed in accordance with the consumer price index. The indexation factors are as follows:-

Year	Factor	Year	Factor
1990	1.040	1995	1.188
1991	1.076	1996	1.217
1992	1.109	1997	1.237
1993	1.145	1998	1.256
1994	1.010	1999	1.286

As and from 1994 the position is reversed in accordance with the provisions of Section 145, Finance Act 1994. With regard to taxable benefits taken on or after 11 April 1994 the indexation factor is applied to the class threshold and not to the threshold amount (see Chart 23).

Computations

Detailed examples of the operation of these provisions are contained in the Institute's "Capital Acquisitions Tax" by John F. Condon and Jim Muddiman.

5.1.5 Discretionary Trusts

FA90 s129;
FA92 s224;
FA94 s143

Chapter 1, Part V Finance Act 1984 imposed a once off charge on the property of new and existing discretionary trusts. It is provided that where, on or after 25 January 1984, property is or becomes subject to

Chapter 5

a discretionary trust, the trust will be deemed to have taken an inheritance. A charge to tax will not arise, however, until

(a) The disponer is deceased, and

(b) none of the principal objects of the trust is under the age of 25 years (see below).

Section 22 FA 1992 provided that where property is or becomes subject to a discretionary trust on or after 31 January 1993 the test at (b) above will apply when the last principal object of the trust attains the age of 21.

Section 143 Finance Act 1994 increased the initial once-off charge from 3% to 6% with effect from 11 April 1994. It also provided for a full refund of the increase in the charge, if, within 5 years of the death of the disponer or, in the case of a trust with principal objects, within 5 years of the youngest reaching 21 years of age, all property within the trust has been transferred absolutely to the beneficiaries.

Principal Objects - These are defined as such objects of the trust as are for the time being:

(a) The spouse of the disponer.

(b) The children of the disponer.

(c) The children of a child of the disponer where such child predeceased the disponer.

Exemptions - Exemption from this tax is granted to any discretionary trust which has been created exclusively for any of the following purposes:

(a) For public or charitable purposes in the State or Northern Ireland.

(b) (i) For the purposes of certain superannuation schemes.

    (ii) From 5 April 1990 a sponsored superannuation scheme will only qualify where it contains no object other than to benefit employees.

FA85 s65   (c) For the purposes of a registered Unit Trust Scheme.

(d) For the benefit of an individual for the reason that such individual is because of age, improvidence or physical, mental or legal capacity, incapable of managing his own affairs.

(e) For the purposes of providing for the upkeep of a house or garden referred to in Section 39, Finance Act 1978.

General - Apart from the above provisions, the transfer of property into a discretionary trust is not a taxable disposition for gift or inheritance tax purposes. When, however, a beneficiary receives a distribution of either income or capital from a discretionary trust,

CAT may become payable depending on the relationship between the disponer and the beneficiary.

The following are exempt from the 6% discretionary trust tax:-

(a) Property which on the termination of the discretionary trust is taken by the State.

(b) The notional interest on interest free loans deemed to be benefits under the provisions of Section 31 of Capital Acquisitions Tax Act 1976.

FA86 s102-s108; FA92 s225
The Finance Act, 1986 as amended introduced an annual levy of 1% on the assets held by discretionary trusts which were affected by the provisions of the Finance Act, 1984, ie where:-

(a) the disponer is dead, and

(b) none of the principal objects of the trust is under the age of 21 years (previously 25 years).

The 1% levy applies to property which has become subject to a discretionary trust on 5 April in any year from 5 April 1986 onwards. The 1% levy is not payable in the same year as the 6% charge. In order to facilitate compliance and collection costs, the values of real property and non quoted shares agreed for one chargeable date may, subject to certain limitations, apply to the following two chargeable dates.

Section 225 Finance Act, 1992 provides that on and from 5 April 1994 the 1% levy applies as soon as the last of the principal objects of the trust attains the age of 21 years (reduced from 25 years).

5.1.6 Gifts

CATA76 Para6 Sch2;
CATA76 s3
The rate of tax applicable to a gift is 75% of that referable to an inheritance. Where a donor dies within two years of making a gift the gift is regarded as an inheritance and the full rates of tax apply. The date of the gift is the date the beneficiary becomes beneficially entitled in possession.

5.1.7 Relief from Double Aggregation

FA85 s61
As and from 2 June 1982 where the same property is chargeable to capital acquisitions tax more than once on the same event it shall not be included more than once in any aggregate for the purpose of computing tax.

5.1.8 Allowance for Prior Tax

FA85 s62
Where capital acquisitions tax is chargeable more than once in respect of the same property on the same event, the net tax payable on an earlier event will be allowable as a credit against tax on the later event.

Chapter 5

FA85 s63;
FA88 s66

Capital gains tax payable by reference to an event which gives rise to a charge to capital acquisitions tax is available for credit against such capital acquisitions tax. This applies from 30 January 1985. If on or after 6 April 1988 gift tax or inheritance tax is charged on a property and the same event constitutes a disposal for capital gains tax purposes, the CGT payable, if any, shall be deducted from the net gift tax or inheritance tax as a credit against same, provided that the amounts deducted shall be equal to the lesser of the net gift tax or inheritance tax or CGT.

5.1.9 Surviving Spouses

CATA76 Para8 Sch2

Surviving spouses are deemed to have the same relationship as their deceased spouses where benefits are received from a relation of the deceased person. For example, the normal class threshold between a father in law and his daughter in law is Class (c). However, if her husband dies before the disponer, the class threshold is Class (a) as she becomes a child of the disponer for CAT purposes.

5.1.10 Nephew or Niece of the Disponer

FA89 s83 Para9 Sch2

If a nephew or niece of the disponer has worked substantially on a full time basis for the period of five years ending on the date of the gift or the date of the inheritance in carrying on, or assisting in the carrying on of the trade, business or profession or the work of or connected with the office or employment of the disponer, and the gift or inheritance consists of property used in connection with the trade, business or profession, or of shares in a company owning such property, then the nephew or niece will enjoy a Class (a) threshold as if he or she was a child of the disponer. In relation to gifts or inheritances taken on or after 1 May 1989 except gifts or inheritances taken under a discretionary trust, the following conditions apply:

Where the gift or inheritance consists of property used in connection with the business, trade or profession of the disponer and the donee or successor works

(i) more than 24 hours per week for the disponer at a place where the business etc is carried on

or

(ii) more than 15 hours as above where the business etc is carried on exclusively by the disponer, spouse of the disponer, and the donee or successor.

Where the gift or inheritance consists of shares in a private trading company controlled by the disponer of which he is a director, and the donee or successor works

(i) more than 24 hours per week at a place where the business etc of the company is carried on or

(ii) more than 15 hours per week for the company as above where the business etc is carried on exclusively by the disponer, any spouse of the disponer and the donee or successor.

5.1.11 Relief in Respect of Certain Marriage Settlements

FA81 s46

This was introduced to give relief in the case of marriage settlements satisfying the following conditions:-

(a) There must have been a disposition made prior to 1 April 1975, and

(b) the settlor must be a grandparent of the donee or successor, and

(c) the expressed consideration for the disposition must have been the marriage of the parents of the donee or successor.

If the above conditions are satisfied and there is a termination of the parents interest and the donee or successor becomes entitled in possession, then the donee or successor will enjoy a Class (a) threshold as if he or she was a child of the disponer.

5.1.12 Territorial Limit

FA93 s6, s12, s122;
FA93 s124

There is a territorial limit to the extent to which gifts and inheritances are taxable. The entire property comprised in the gift or inheritance is taxable where, at the time of the gift or inheritance:

(a) The disponer is domiciled in the State, or

(b) The proper law of the disposition is the law of the State. If neither of these criteria applies only so much of the gift or inheritance as is situate in the State at the date of the gift is liable to tax. As and from 18 June 1993 gifts and inheritances of foreign assets taken from a foreign domiciled person under a disposition governed by Irish law are not taxable.

5.1.13 Disclaimer

CATA76 s13

A successor is entitled to disclaim his or her right to an inheritance, or his or her legal rights under Part IX of the Succession Acts. Such disclaimer is not a disposition for the purpose of the CAT Act and therefore does not give rise to a claim for inheritance tax on the original inheritance nor to a claim for gift tax on the benefit conferred by the disclaimer. The ultimate beneficiary however, takes a taxable inheritance from the deceased.

5.1.14 Joint Tenants

CATA76 s14

The liability to inheritance tax in respect of an inheritance taken by persons as joint tenants is the same in all respects as if they took the inheritance as tenants in common in equal shares.

Chapter 5

5.1.15 Valuation of Agricultural Property

FA80 s19, s83;
FA82 s100;
FA91 s114;
FA93 s128;
FA94 s141;
FA95 s158;
FA96 s122;
FA97 s134

Normally the tax is based on the market value of the property comprised in the gift or inheritance and allowance is given for all liabilities, costs and expenses that are properly payable out of the taxable gift or inheritance. However, where the donee or successor is a farmer within the meaning of the Act, the market value of all agricultural property passing on or after 23 January 1997 is reduced by 90%. Relief available in respect of earlier gifts and inheritances is as follows:-

Date of Gift or Inheritance	Agricultural Property	Threshold	Relief Gifts	Relief Inheritance
11.4.94 to 7.2.95	Farm land & buildings	£300,000	80%	65%
		Balance	30%	30%
	Other farm assets	All	25%	25%
8.2.95 to 22.1.96	Farm land & buildings	£300,000	80%	65%
		Balance	50%	50%
	Other farm assets	All	50%	50%
23.1.96 to 22.1.97	All farm assets	All	75%	75%

It should be noted that where the reliefs applying between 8.2.95 and 22.1.96 are more beneficial, they may be claimed instead of the 75% reduction.

FA91 s114;
FA94 s141;
FA95 s158;
FA96 s122;
FA97 s134

A farmer is an individual who is domiciled in the State and 80% of whose gross property in possession is, after the taking of the gift or inheritance, agricultural property, livestock, bloodstock and farm machinery.

Agricultural property is defined as meaning agricultural land, pasture and woodland in the State and crops and timber grown thereon, together with houses and other buildings appropriate to the property. It also includes with effect from 11 April 1994, livestock, bloodstock and farm machinery.

For gifts or inheritances taken before 23 January 1996, the relief claimed in respect of agricultural property is clawed back if the property is sold or compulsorily acquired within six years of the date of the gift or inheritance, and not replaced within one year by other agricultural property.

In the case of gifts or inheritances taken on or after 23 January 1996, the clawback period has been extended from 6 to 10 years. However, where the sale or compulsory acquisition occurs outside 6 years but within 10 years after the gift or inheritance the relief clawed back will be the difference between the relief granted under this section and that granted under the previous legislation. In the case of gifts or inheritances taken on or after 23 January 1997, the relief clawed back will be restricted to the amount of relief granted under the 1996 and 1997 Finance Acts.

Capital Acquisitions Tax

5.1.16 **Valuation of Shares in Private Companies**

FA93 s125;
FA96 s121

Shares in private companies, regardless of whether they are trading or non-trading companies, are, with effect from 24 February 1993 valued on a market value basis for CAT purposes. There are also certain specific valuation rules set down in respect of controlling interests as follows:-

(a) The valuation of shares in private companies is to be determined on the basis of an apportioned part of the market value of each class of share;

(b) Apportionment as between shares of a particular class is to be by reference to the nominal amount (ie the total value is spread equally over each single share with no regard being had to the size of a particular holding);

(c) Apportionment as between different classes of share is to have due regard to the rights attaching to each of the different classes (ie discounting the market value for entitlement or otherwise to voting rights).

5.1.17 **Valuation of Dwellings taken from Brother/Sister**

FA91 s117;
FA94 s144;
FA97 s138;
FA98 s126

A special relief from inheritance tax is provided in a case where a house or a part of a house is inherited from a disponer brother or sister. The successor must have attained the age of 55 years, have resided in the house (or in another house which the house replaced) with the disponer continuously for a period of not less than 5 years ending on the date of death of the disponer and must not be beneficially entitled in possession to any other house. If these conditions are complied with, the market value of the house for inheritance tax purposes is reduced as follows:-

Inheritance taken	*Market value reduced by the lesser of:-*
Up to 10.4.94	50% or £50,000
11.4.94 - 9.5.97	60% or £60,000
10.5.97-2.12.97	60% or £80,000
3.12.97 onwards	80% or £150,000

The relief does not apply to a dwelling house which is part of agricultural property taken by a successor "farmer" which gets the benefit of Section 19. The relief is extended to other "Class II" beneficiaries who have lived with the disponer for not less than 10 years.

Chapter 5

5.1.18 **Business Relief**

FA94 PtVI Ch1 — Provision is made for relief from CAT for business property acquired by gift or inheritance or on the termination of a life interest. The features of this relief are as follows:-

FA95 s162-163

1. The relief available in respect of all qualifying assets is as follows:-

Date of Gift or Inheritance	Threshold	Relief
11.4.94 to 7.2.95	250,000	50%
	Balance	25%
8.2.95 to 22.1.96	All	50%
23.1.96– 22.1.97	All	75%
23.1.97– onwards	All	90%

FA96 s125, 126

2. The business must be carried on wholly or mainly in the State.

FA97 s140, s141;
FA98 s128

3. The relief applies to business property as follows:-

    (a) property consisting of a business or an interest in a business;

    (b) unquoted shares or securities of an Irish company subject to certain conditions;

    (c) land, buildings, machinery or plant owned by the disponer but used by a company controlled by the disponer or by a partnership in which the disponer was a partner;

    (d) quoted shares or securities of an Irish company which were owned by the disponer prior to their becoming quoted.

4. The business carried on must not consist wholly or mainly of dealing in land, shares, securities or currencies or of making or holding investments, although shares or securities in an Irish holding company which wholly or mainly holds shares in a qualifying subsidiary are eligible for relief.

5. The relevant business property must have been owned by the disponer, or by the disponer and his spouse, for at least 5 years prior to the transfer, or for at least 2 years where the transfer gives rise to an inheritance taken on the disponer's death. There are provisions for modifying the 5 year and 2 year periods where business property is replaced by other business property.

6. Certain assets as set out below are ignored in valuing relevant business property for purposes of the relief. These are:-

    (a) agricultural property (See 7 below).

(b) assets not used wholly or mainly for the business concerned within the appropriate 5 year or 2 year periods prior to the transfer.

7. With effect from 12 April 1995 agricultural property owned by a company may be taken into account for the purposes of calculating relief on the shares in that company.

8. For gifts or inheritances taken before 23 January 1996, the relief is clawed back if, at any time within a period of 6 years commencing on the valuation date of the gift or inheritance, the business property is sold or otherwise disposed of and is not replaced by other qualifying business property.

In the case of gifts or inheritances taken on or after 23 January 1996, the clawback period has been extended from 6 to 10 years. If the clawback event occurs outside 6 years but within 10 years after the valuation date, the relief clawed back will be the difference between the relief granted at 75 per cent, and that granted at 50 per cent. In the case of gifts and inheritances taken on or after 23 January 1997, the relief clawed back will be restricted to the amount of the additional relief granted under the 1996 and 1997 Finance Acts.

The death of the donee or successor does not give rise to a clawback.

5.1.19 Valuation of Limited Interests

CATA76 Sch1 Limited interests in property are taxed by reference to the capital in which the interest subsists but the taxable value is arrived at by taking the appropriate percentage as provided in the First Schedule. The percentage takes into account the age and sex of the donee or successor or the period of time for which the interest is to last.

5.1.20 Free Use of Property

CATA76 s31 Where a person is allowed to have the use, occupation or enjoyment of another person's property free or for less than market value, this constitutes a gift under the CAT Act.

5.1.21 Companies

FA93 s34, s129 A disposition by or to a private controlled company may give rise to a gift or inheritance which will be received by or disposed of by the beneficial owners of the shares of the company in the same proportions as the market value of each person's shareholding. All acts, omissions and receipts of the company are deemed to be as those of the beneficial owners of the shares.

Chapter 5

5.1.22 Joint Accounts

FA86 s61, s110

Where a sum of money in excess of £5,000 was lodged or deposited (other than in a current account) in the joint names of two or more persons and one of such person dies, the banker concerned cannot make payments to the survivor(s) until he is furnished with a certificate by the Commissioners that there is no outstanding claim for inheritance tax in connection with the deceased. This provision does not apply where a husband and wife have a joint deposit account and one of them dies on or after 30 January 1985.

5.1.23 Exemptions

FA85 s59

The following are some of the exemptions from CAT:

FA90 s127; FA95 s165

(a) (i) An inheritance taken on or after 30 January 1985 by a successor, who is at the date of the inheritance the spouse of the disponer, is exempt from inheritance tax.

(ii) A gift taken on or after 31 January 1990 by a donee who is at the date of the gift the spouse of the disponer, is exempt.

(iii) An inheritance taken by a parent from a child on the death of the child. This exemption applies where the child had taken a non-exempt gift or inheritance from either or both of its parents within the period of 5 years immediately prior to the death of the child.

(b) S60 Policies

FA88 s60; FA89 s84; FA90 s130; FA91 s119

The proceeds of a qualifying insurance policy effected by the insured person will be exempt from inheritance tax in so far as such proceeds are used to pay such tax arising on the insured person's death or within a year of his death under dispositions made by him. Initially the "Section 60" policy was restricted to a policy effected on the life of a single individual.

The Finance Act 1989 extended the Section 60 policy concept to a policy effected for the joint lives of spouses and the life of the survivor.

The Finance Act 1991 extended cover to exposure to gift tax or inheritance tax arising under an inter vivos disposition made by the insured within one year after the appointed day. The appointed day is defined as meaning a date occurring not earlier than 8 years after the date on which the relevant insurance policy is effected, or a date on which the proceeds of a relevant insurance policy become payable either on the critical illness or the death of the insured.

The Finance Act 1996 extended the scope of the exemption granted to cover a policy effected by a life tenant for the purpose of paying an inheritance tax liability arising on the life

		tenant's death under a disposition made by someone other than the life tenant.
		Gift tax or inheritance tax payable on an appointment out of an inter vivos discretionary trust set up by the insured are not covered by a relevant insurance policy.
CATA76 s53	(c)	The first £500 of the total value of all gifts received from any one disponer in any year to 31 December. The amount is increased to £1000 with effect from January 1999. This exemption does not apply to inheritances, except in the case of a gift which becomes an inheritance on the death of the disponer within two years of the relevant disposition.
FA87 s50	(d)	Gifts or inheritances taken for public or charitable purposes shall be exempt where the Revenue Commissioners are satisfied that it has been, or will be, applied to purposes which are, in accordance with the law of the State.
CATA76 s55; FA95 s160; FA97 s137	(e)	Works of art, scientific collections, libraries, houses or gardens etc provided that they are of national, scientific, historic or artistic interest, are kept permanently in the State and are open to public viewing. The exemption may be lost if the objects are sold within six years after the valuation date.
CATA76 s56	(f)	Superannuation benefits payable to an employee.
CATA76 s58	(g)	Certain compensation payments or damages, winnings from lotteries or prizes.
FA95 s166	(h)	A gift or inheritance of shares in a company holding heritage property - see (e) above. The relief will be clawed back in certain circumstances
CATA76 s58	(i)	Certain normal and reasonable payments received in the disponer's lifetime by members of his family for support, maintenance or education, or by a dependent relative for support or maintenance.
FA78 s38	(j)	Government securities and unit trusts holding Government securities where any such security forms part of a gift/inheritance on condition that the donee/successor is neither domiciled nor ordinarily resident in the State at the date of the gift/inheritance and the disponer was the beneficial owner from 14 April 1978 to the date of the gift/inheritance, or for the three years prior to the gift or inheritance.
FA89 s85	(k)	With effect from the passing of the 1989 Finance Act any gift or inheritance which comprises UCITS at the date of the gift or inheritance and at the valuation date shall be exempt from tax and shall not be taken into account in computing tax on any gift or inheritance taken by the donee or successor provided at the date of the disposition
		(i) the disponer is neither domiciled nor ordinarily resident in the State

Chapter 5

or

    (ii) the proper law of the disposition is not the law of the State and at the date of the gift or inheritance the donee or successor is neither domiciled nor ordinarily resident in the State.

FA93 s133   (1) Certain life assurance policies issued to non ordinarily resident and non domiciled persons or where the "proper law" is Irish by companies located in the International Financial Services Centre.

FA96 s123   (m) A gift or inheritance taken exclusively for the purpose of discharging the medical expenses of a permanently, incapacitated individual.

FA99 s205   (n) Moneys raised by public subscription for permanently incapacitated individuals provided that these moneys are held in a qualifying trust. This applies with effect from 6 April 1997.

FA99 s206   (o) Any balance in an "approved retirement fund" or in an "approved minimum retirement fund" which passes on the death of a pensioner or of his spouse will be exempt from inheritance tax in certain circumstances.

5.1.24 Self Assessment

FA84 s36, s41, s43, s45, s106, s107;
FA89 s74;
FA95 s164;
FA96 s129

In order to introduce a self assessment system for Capital Acquisitions Tax a number of important changes were required in the Principal Act dealing particularly with Returns, Assessments, Payment of Tax, Interest and Penalties etc. The Self Assessment system took effect from 1 September 1989.

A person who is primarily accountable for CAT is obliged to deliver a return within four months of the valuation date where 80% of the class threshold limit is exceeded. The following must be shown on the Return:

(a) The gift or inheritance.

(b) The property comprised in the gift or inheritance.

(c) An estimate of the market value of the property.

(d) Any other particulars which may be relevant to the assessment of tax.

The taxpayer is obliged to make an assessment of the tax which to the best of his knowledge, information and belief ought to be paid and to pay that amount.

Provision is made for the payment of CAT by instalments and by the transfer of certain Government Securities.

Capital Acquisitions Tax

Persons who are secondarily accountable for CAT are obliged, if required in writing by the Revenue, to comply with the self assessment procedures.

An accountable person must, if required in writing by the Revenue, deliver a statement stating such particulars relating to the property and such evidence as they require as may be relevant to the assessment of tax.

The Revenue may authorise a person to inspect any property comprised in a gift or any books, accounts, etc relating to any property as may be relevant to the assessment of tax. Any person having the custody or possession of property, books, records etc must permit the authorised person to make the inspection at all reasonable times. The Revenue have power to require additional returns from the accountable person if the return made was materially defective and to make any consequent additional assessments.

If an accountable person who has made a return or additional return becomes aware that the return was defective in a material respect, he shall within three months of becoming aware of the defect in the original return make a new return, amend the assessment and pay the outstanding tax.

The tax due must accompany the return.

FA89 s75 — Notwithstanding the introduction of the self assessment system, the Revenue Commissioners retain the right to raise assessments, additional assessments and to correct assessments.

FA89 s76 — If an accountable person pays the self assessed tax within four months of the valuation date no interest will be charged.

If an accountable person makes a conditional or an incorrect tax payment, such payment will be treated as a payment on account.

5.1.25 Penalties

FA89 s77 — The following penalties are payable:

Self Assessment: Failure to make returns	£2,000
Obstruction of person inspecting property	£1,000
Fraudulent or Negligent Returns or Valuation Statements	*£5,000
Assisting or inducing incorrect returns	£1,000
If Court Judgement obtained for failure to make returns, a further penalty for each day the failure continues of	£25

* In the case of fraud, an additional penalty of twice the additional tax is payable.

Chapter 5

FA89 s78 — Accountable persons and persons with secondary accountability are obliged to comply with the Self Assessment provisions in relation to Discretionary Trust Tax.

5.1.26 Surcharge

FA89 s79 — Where an accountable person delivers a return which contains an estimate of the market value of a gift or inheritance which, when expressed as a percentage of the agreed value of that asset is within any of the percentages set out below, a surcharge will be applied as follows:

Percentage of Agreed Value estimated on Return	Surcharge
67% - 100%	nil
50% - 66%	10
40% - 49%	20%
0% - 39%	30%

Interest will be charged on any surcharge raised as per the provisions of Section 41 of the Principal Act.

An accountable person aggrieved by the imposition on him of a surcharge can appeal the imposition of the surcharge within 30 days of notification to him on the grounds that having regard to all the circumstances there were sufficient grounds on which he might reasonably have based his estimate of the market value of the asset. This is the only grounds for an appeal. The usual rights for the rehearing of the appeal by the Circuit Court and on a point of law by the High Court apply.

5.1.27 Delivery of Returns

FA82 s36, s37, s38, s101; FA89 s82 — The donee of a gift or the successor of an inheritance may deliver a return on Form GT1 or IT3 respectively or in a form delivered by electronic, photographic or other process where the form is approved by the Revenue Commissioners. Affidavits and accounts must be made on a form provided by or approved by the Revenue Commissioners.

No return is required where 80% of the threshold amount has not been exceeded.

Additional requirements arise on the occasion of inheritance. The Inland Revenue affidavit must be lodged with the Revenue Commissioners. In addition to giving details of all the chargeable assets, wherever situate, the affidavit should also provide the following information:

(a) Details of all gifts made by the deceased within two years of his death.

Capital Acquisitions Tax

(b) Details of the inheritances under the deceased's will, together with a copy of the will.

(c) Details of all other inheritances arising on his death.

(d) The names and addresses of the beneficiaries.

(e) Such other particulars as may be required for the purposes of the tax.

FA99 s200 The Finance Act 1999 imposes an obligation on a person to deliver a capital acquisitions tax return if requested to do so by the Revenue Commissioners even if no benefit has been received. This Act also imposes an obligation on the donor of a gift or a disponer in relation to a discretionary trust to make a return.

5.1.28 Interest

FA98 s133 With effect from 1 April 1998 interest on overdue tax is payable at a rate of 1% per month.

5.1.29 Accountable Persons

FA89 s81 In the majority of cases, the donee or successor will be primarily accountable.

The disponer and every trustee, personal representative, guardian, agent or other person in whose care the property is placed on or after the date of the gift or inheritance is secondarily accountable.

The 1989 FA extends the definition of accountable persons by making a disponer a secondarily accountable person for inheritance tax purposes, where

(a) the inheritance is taken on or before the date of death of the disponer and

(b) the date of the disposition is on or after 1 May 1989.

The limitation of liability to the value of the property is not applicable to disponers who are accountable persons.

5.1.30 Appeals

FA95 s51, s52, s159 There is the right to appeal to the Property Arbitrator where the taxpayer does not agree with the Revenue's valuation of real property. The normal appeal procedures which apply for income tax, broadly apply for CAT in relation to matters other than the valuation of real property. The Revenue Commissioners have the right however, to request the re-hearing of an appeal by the Circuit Court. In relation to gifts or inheritances taken after 11 February 1998 an appeal may only be lodged against a decision or assessment of the Revenue Commissioners if the taxpayer has lodged a self-assessed return and paid the tax in accordance with that return.

Chapter 5

5.1.31 Certificate of Discharge

FA84 s48, s113

The Revenue Commissioners may issue a certificate of discharge from liability for CAT on property to an accountable person. Such a certificate will discharge the property from liability to CAT in respect of the particular gift or inheritance to the extent specified in the certificate. The Finance Act 1984 enables the Revenue Commissioners to issue a certificate which will discharge from tax a person who is accountable but not primarily accountable for payment of CAT. Such an application may not be made until the expiration of two years from the valuation date, unless the Revenue Commissioners consent.

5.1.32 Clearance Certificate

FA94 s146;
FA96 s128

With effect from 23 May 1994, a CAT clearance certificate must be obtained in respect of applications for registration of title to land which are based on possession. Such applications will not be dealt with by the Land Registry unless the Revenue Commissioners have issued a certificate to the effect that they are satisfied that any liability to gift tax, inheritance tax and probate tax charged on the land, has been, or will be paid within a reasonable time.

The 1996 Finance Act relaxes the clearance certificate requirement by providing self-certification as an option for solicitors dealing with applications for registration of title to land which are based on possession. The relaxation may be availed of in cases where the solicitor is satisfied that the property in respect of which the application is being made is not part of a larger holding of property and that its market value does not exceed the following limits:-

— £15,000 in a case where the area occupied by the property does not exceed five hectares, or

— £100,000 in a case where the applicant is a statutory authority.

There are two exceptions to the rule that the property being registered should not be part of a larger property. The first exception is where the larger property is itself within the prescribed limit. The other exception is where the sole purpose of the application for registration is the rectification of the Register to take account of small mapping errors not exceeding 500 square metres in area or £2,000 in value.

5.1.33 Anti-Avoidance

FA89 s90;
FA93 s126

Capital Acquisitions Tax is payable where arrangements result in a shift of value from one class of share to another even though no actual transfer of shares has taken place. The tax payable is calculated based on the amount by which the value of shares has been reduced. These provisions are extended to situations where a benefit is conferred by the redemption of shares in a private company and no consideration is paid for the redemption.

5.2 PROBATE TAX

FA93 PtVI;
FA94 s137-s140
FA98 s127

Part VI, Finance Act 1993, imposed a probate tax of 2% on the estates of individuals dying on or after 18 June 1993. The main features of the probate tax are as follows: -

(a) Where the deceased was domiciled in the State all assets passing, wherever situate, are liable to Probate Tax - subject to certain exemptions.

(b) Where the deceased was not domiciled in the State, only assets situate in the State are liable.

(c) Debts owing at the time of death are deductible in arriving at the taxable value of the estate.

(d) Joint property which passes by survivorship is excluded from the tax.

(e) Estates with a taxable value of £10,980 or less are exempt in respect of persons dying in 1997 (See Chart 24 for previous limits). Marginal relief is available.

(f) Certain types of property are exempt. These include the family residence including normal contents (subject to certain conditions), property passing to charities, heritage property, superannuation benefits and certain exempt securities where the deceased was domiciled outside the State.

(g) The Finance Act 1993 provided that where there is a surviving spouse, the family residence is exempt irrespective of the share passing to the spouse (if any). Otherwise a portion of the family residence may be exempt if taken by a dependent child or dependent relative of the deceased residing in the house at the date of death. With effect from the passing of the 1994 Finance Act the family residence is exempt to the extent that it passes to the surviving spouse or to a dependent child or dependent relative. Where there is a surviving spouse any probate tax chargeable on the residence passing to a non-dependent need not be paid until 9 months after the date of death of that spouse.

(h) Section 140, Finance Act 1994 provides that the share in the estate passing to a surviving spouse is exempt from probate tax from its inception, 18 June 1993. Where the surviving spouse acquires a life interest in property, the tax on the settled property is not due and payable until the life interest ends. Such tax will be payable within 9 months of the termination of the life interest.

(i) Section 138 Finance Act 1994 provides for a 30% reduction in the market value of agricultural property for probate tax purposes with effect from 18 June 1993. "Agricultural property"

Chapter 5

has the same meaning as for CAT (See Page 252) but excludes farm machinery, livestock and bloodstock.

(j) Where a person requires a grant of probate or letters of administration it is necessary to deliver an inland revenue affidavit to the Revenue Commissioners. In the case of deaths on or after 18 June 1993 this affidavit must be accompanied by a self assessment probate form together with payment of any tax due except where postponement of the tax is allowed in situations of hardship.

(k) The personal representative is primarily accountable for payment of the tax. The tax will however, in effect, be borne proportionately by the beneficiaries to the extent that they take property which is not exempt. The beneficiary can claim his or her portion of the tax as an expense in calculating the value of the benefit for inheritance tax (if any).

(l) Where the tax remains unpaid 9 months after the date of death interest accrues at the rate of 1.00% per month. Where however the tax is paid earlier than 9 months from the date of death a discount of 1.00% per month is allowed.

(m) The proceeds of Section 60 policies are exempt to the extent to which they are used to pay probate tax and/or inheritance tax.

(n) For the purposes of probate tax the estate is treated as a deemed inheritance which allows for the application to the tax of the provisions of the Capital Acquisitions Tax Act 1976 with amendments and exclusions as necessary.

5.3 THE CAT/INHERITANCE TAX DOUBLE TAX AGREEMENT WITH THE UNITED KINGDOM

All references are to the Ireland-United Kingdom Double Taxation Agreement.

The Double Tax Treaty between Ireland and the United Kingdom (SI 279 of 1978) provides relief from double taxation in respect of taxes on estates of deceased persons and inheritances and on gifts and it came into force on 2 October 1978. Its provisions are retrospective to the introduction of CAT in Ireland and capital transfer tax (CTT) in the United Kingdom.

Inheritance Tax (IHT) was introduced by the UK Finance Act 1986 to replace CTT. The Treaty now applies to IHT in place of CTT.

5.3.1 Elimination of Double Taxation

Article 8

(1) If tax is paid in Ireland and in the United Kingdom on property which is situated in one country only, the country in which the property is not situated must give a credit for the tax paid in the other State where the property is situated. If both the Irish and the United Kingdom Tax Authorities disagree regarding the situation of property the country with subsidiary taxing rights must give the credit for the attributable tax paid in the other country.

(2) Where both Ireland and the United Kingdom tax property situated in a third territory, the country with subsidiary taxing rights gives a credit for the attributable tax paid in the other country, on the third territory doubly taxed property.

(3) Any credit given in Ireland under the above provisions will only be allowed if the gift/inheritance on which Irish tax is due, has been reduced by the payment of United Kingdom IHT.

(4) The tax attributable to any property is the United Kingdom or Ireland tax less any tax paid in a foreign territory on that property.

5.3.2 Time Limit for Credit or Repayment

Article 9

Any claim for a credit or a repayment under the Double Taxation Agreement shall be made within 6 years from the date of the event in respect of which the claim is made.

5.3.3 How to Determine the Country with Subsidiary Rights

Article 4(2)

The necessity to determine the country with subsidiary taxing rights generally only arises if both countries claim the domicile of the donor.

Chapter 5

To determine in which of the two countries an individual is or was domiciled for the purposes of the treaty the following series of tests is applied:

(a) Where has or had the individual his permanent home or the centre of his vital interest, or

(b) where has or had the individual his habitual abode, or

(c) of which State is or was the individual a national

If any one of the foregoing tests can be positively applied, then the domicile of the individual is determined as being in the particular country.

Should all these tests fail to produce a positive answer, the final decision is left to be agreed between the Revenues of each country.

Article 5(2) Having settled the question of domicile the rules for determining the country with subsidiary taxing rights are as follows:

(a) In relation to property, (other than settlement property) the State where he is not regarded as domiciled has subsidiary taxing rights.

(b) For settlement property:

(i) If at the date it was made the law of the settlement was the law of Ireland and the settlor's domicile (only United Kingdom claiming) was in the United Kingdom the country with subsidiary taxing rights will be the United Kingdom.

(ii) If the proper law of the settlement was not the law of Ireland and the undisputed domicile is the United Kingdom at the date the settlement was made, but at some time later the proper law of the settlement becomes Irish or the settlor's domicile becomes indisputably Irish then Ireland will have the subsidiary taxing rights.

(iii) If the proper law of the settlement was not the law of Ireland and the settlor's domicile is disputed and determined at the time the settlement was made under Article 4(2) the State where he is not domiciled will have subsidiary taxing rights.

CHAPTER 6   CAPITAL GAINS TAX

6.1 CAPITAL GAINS TAX

TCA97 s28

Capital gains tax is payable on chargeable gains arising on the disposal of assets after 5 April 1974.

6.1.1 Persons Chargeable

TCA97 s29

Individuals, trusts, unincorporated bodies etc are chargeable to capital gains tax. Capital gains of companies are chargeable to corporation tax.

An individual who is resident or ordinarily resident in the State for a year of assessment (year ended 5 April) is chargeable to capital gains tax on chargeable gains made on the disposal of assets wherever situated. An individual who is neither resident nor ordinarily resident in the State for a year of assessment is chargeable to capital gains tax only on chargeable gains made on the disposal of:

(a) Land or buildings in the State.

(b) Assets of a business carried on in the State.

(c) Minerals in the State.

(d) Exploration or exploitation rights in the continental shelf

(e) Unquoted shares deriving the greater part of their value from such assets as mentioned above at (a), (c) and (d).

An individual who is resident or ordinarily resident, but not domiciled in the State, is liable to capital gains tax on chargeable gains on the disposal of assets situate outside the State and the United Kingdom, only to the extent that the chargeable gains are remitted to the State. Losses accruing on the disposal of such assets are not allowable losses for capital gains tax purposes.

6.1.2 Assets

TCA97 s532

All forms of property are assets for the purpose of the Capital Gains Tax Acts, whether situated in the State or not, including options, debts and currency other than Irish currency.

Chapter 6

6.1.3 Disposal

TCA97 s534

A disposal takes place whenever the ownership of an asset changes and includes a part disposal. A disposal occurs even where no capital sum is derived from the change in ownership, eg gift or exchange.

6.1.4 Death

TCA97 s573

Death is not an occasion when disposal occurs. A person becoming entitled to an asset by reason of death is treated for capital gains tax purposes as having acquired the asset on the date of death and at its market value on that date.

6.1.5 Time of Disposal

TCA97 s542

The time of disposal is the time at which the contract is made. If the contract is conditional the time of disposal is the time when the condition is fulfilled. There are also provisions covering the time of disposal in the case of compulsory acquisition, hire purchase, capital sums derived from assets and certain life assurance policies and contracts for deferred annuities.

6.1.6 Husbands and Wives

TCA97 s1028

The chargeable gains of a married woman are assessed on the husband unless separate assessment is claimed.

Any unallowed loss of one spouse is deductible in computing the chargeable gains of the other.

A transfer of assets between husband and wife does not give rise to a disposal for capital gains tax purposes. The spouse who receives the asset is deemed to have acquired it on the date and at the cost at which the other acquired it.

6.1.7 Divorced Persons

TCA97 s1031

A charge to Capital Gains Tax will not arise when a person who has obtained a Decree of Divorce under the Family Law (Divorce) Act, 1996 disposes of assets pursuant to a Court Order under that Act to his or her former spouse.

The spouse acquiring the asset is deemed to have acquired it at the same time and the same cost as the other spouse.

This provision takes effect from 10 May 1997.

6.1.8 Separate Spouses

TCA97 s1030

A charge to Capital Gains Tax will not arise where a person disposes of an asset to his or her spouse and both spouses:-

(a) have been granted, or are treated as having been granted a judicial separation under the Family Law Act, 1995, or

(b) are parties to an order made under Part II of the Judicial Separation and Family Law Reform Act, 1989, on or following the granting of a decree of judicial separation where such order is treated, by virtue of Section 3 of the Family Law Act, 1995 as if made under the corresponding provisions of the Family Law Act 1995, or

(c) are parties to a deed of separation, or

(d) are the subject of a relief order within the meaning of the Family Law Act, 1995, made following the dissolution of marriage.

The spouse to whom the disposal is made will be treated as having acquired the asset on the same day and at the same cost as the spouse who had made the disposal.

6.1.9 Rates of Capital Gains Tax

TCA97 s28;
TCA97 s592

Up to 3 December 1997 there were two rates of capital gains tax as follows:-

(i) Reduced rate on the disposal of certain shares (see below)

(ii) 40% on all other chargeable gains

For disposals on or after 3 December 1997 the rate of capital gains tax is 20% except for:-

(a) sale of development land   40%*

(b) sales of foreign life assurance policies   40%

(c) sale of an interest in certain offshore funds when the capital gains of the fund are not subject to income tax   40%

TCA97 s649A

*The rate is 20% for gains on disposals of development land between 23 April 1998 and 5 April 2002 where the land has planning permission for residential development at the time of disposal. The 20% rate applies also to disposals of land zoned for residential development under a county development plan. This applies from 10 March 1999 to 5 April 2002.

FA99 s91

The 20% rate does not apply to disposals of development land between connected parties or to disposals of shares deriving value from development land. Such disposals are chargeable at the 40% rate.

Chapter 6

6.1.10 **Reduced Rate of CGT**

TCA97 s592

A reduced rate of capital gains tax applied for chargeable gains on disposals of certain shares made by individuals.

The reduced rates were:-

Disposals	Rate
6.4.94 - 5.4.97	27%
6.4.97 - 2.12.97	26%

For the reduced rate to apply, the shares being disposed of must be:-

(i) qualifying shares

(ii) in a qualifying company

(iii) held for at least five years before disposal in the case of disposals before 6 April 1996 and 3 years for disposals on or after 6 April 1996.

Qualifying shares were shares which were fully paid up and which carried no present or future preferential right to dividends or to the company's assets on a winding up and have no present or future preferential right to be redeemed.

A company was a qualifying company if:

(a) At the date of acquisition:

    (i) the company was unquoted

    (ii) the company was resident in the State and not resident elsewhere, and

    (iii) had an issued share capital, the market value of which did not exceed £25M.

(b) Throughout the five years before the date of disposal, in the case of disposals between 6.4.94 and 5.4.97 or three years in the case of disposals after 5.4.97, the company, has been resident in the State (and not resident elsewhere) and has carried on a business consisting:

    (i) wholly or mainly of a qualifying trade, or trades, or

    (ii) wholly or mainly of the holding of shares in one or more connected companies,

    or

    (iii) a combination of the two.

It must also be shown that at least 75% of the market value of the shares being disposed of was attributable to the carrying on of a qualifying trade(s) either by the company itself or by connected companies (including companies themselves connected with such connected companies).

Qualifying trade means all trading activities other than dealing in shares, securities, land, currencies, futures or traded options.

One company (the first-mentioned company) was connected with another company, if:-

(i) the company was unquoted at the date of acquisition of its shares by the first mentioned company,

(ii) it was resident in the State and not resident elsewhere,

(iii) the first-mentioned company was able to exercise at least 20% of the voting rights in the company.

The reduced rate also applied subject to certain conditions in cases where shares have been received in respect of a "paper for paper" transaction.

In respect of disposals made in the year of assessment 1995/96 only, the reduced rate was extended to disposals of non-qualifying shares which were acquired in exchange for qualifying shares under a reorganisation, takeover or amalgamation. The re-organisation etc must have taken place prior to 6 April 1994 and the original shares which were exchanged must have been capable of meeting all of the conditions applying to the reduced rate.

6.1.11 Computation of Chargeable Gains and Allowable Losses

Up to and including 5 April 1978 the computation of chargeable gains and allowable losses was made by comparing the proceeds of disposal with the original cost of the asset or its market value at 6 April 1974 where it was owned at that date.

6.1.12 Indexation

TCA97 s556

Relief is provided for the inflation content of chargeable gains accruing on the disposal, on or after 6 April 1978, of assets owned for more than twelve months prior to the date of disposal. Certain restrictions apply to the disposal of development land on or after 28 January 1982.

Inflation is measured by the increase in the Consumer Price Index, as compiled by the Central Statistics Office, in the period from mid-February in the year preceding the year of acquisition or in the year preceding the year in which further allowable expenditure was incurred to mid-February in the year preceding the year in which disposal takes place. All chargeable assets held on 6 April 1974 are deemed to have been acquired at their market value on that date with the result that the relief for inflation is calculated by reference to the level of the Consumer Price Index at mid-February 1974.

Chapter 6

The relief is granted by allowing the cost and, if applicable, additional expenditure on the asset to be adjusted by multiplying it by a figure as specified in Section 556. For disposals of assets taking place since 6 April 1981, the "multiplier" to be applied is shown at Chart 21.

The relief for inflation applies to all assets but certain restrictions apply to disposals of development land or shares deriving their value from such land on or after 28 January 1982.

TCA97 s650;
TCA97 s651

The application of the relief for inflation to the computation of chargeable gains arising on the disposal of development land or shares deriving their value from such land is as follows:

(i) Where the land or shares were acquired after 5 April 1974, the adjustment for inflation will only apply to that portion of the purchase price as reflects the current use value of the land at the date of purchase. The remainder of the purchase price is allowed as a deduction.

(ii) Where the land or shares were owned at 6 April 1974 the adjustment for inflation will only apply to that portion of the market value at that date as reflects the current use value of the land at that date. The remainder of the market value will be allowed as a deduction.

Development land is land in the State, the consideration for the disposal of which, or the market value of which at the date of disposal exceeds the current use value of that land at the date of disposal.

Current use value means the open market value of the land at a particular time, calculated on the assumption that it was at that time, and would remain, unlawful to carry out development, other than development of a minor nature.

Where the total consideration received by an individual from the sale of development land in a year of assessment does not exceed £15,000 no liability to "development land" capital gains tax will arise. The normal capital gains tax will apply.

6.1.13 Losses

TCA97 s546

Chargeable gains of a year of assessment are aggregated with allowable losses of the year for the purpose of computing the net amount assessable to capital gains tax. Losses brought forward from earlier years are also deductible. Losses are set off against gains chargeable at the highest rate of capital tax and so on in order. Allowable losses which remain unrelieved may be carried forward indefinitely.

Capital Gains Tax

TCA97 s651 Gains on development land may only be off set by losses on development land. Losses on development land may be set off against gains on disposals of other assets.

Inflation relief will not convert a monetary gain to an allowable loss or vice versa, nor will it increase a monetary gain or loss.

6.1.14 Part Disposals

In computing the chargeable gain or allowable loss on the disposal of part of an asset, the amount to be deducted from the proceeds of sale is restricted to the proportion of the original cost, or 6 April 1974 value of the asset, which the proceeds of sale bear to the value of what remains. The proportion is given by the following fraction:

$$\frac{A}{A+B} \text{ where}$$

A = The amount or value of the consideration for the part disposal.

B = The market value of that part of the asset which remains undisposed of.

6.1.15 Self Assessment

TCA97 s950-s959

The following are the main features of the self assessment system as applied to capital gains tax:

(a) Preliminary tax is payable on 1 November in the year after the year of assessment if the tax has not already been assessed. If the tax has been assessed before 1 November, the tax is payable on 1 November.

(b) Returns of capital gains must be made by taxpayers without being required to do so by an Inspector of Taxes.

(c) To avoid interest charges in the tax years up to and including 1997/98, the amount of preliminary tax paid must not be less than 90% of the final capital gains tax liability. For the tax years 1998/99 et seq, 100% of the final liability must be paid before 1 November in the year after the year of assessment.

(d) A return of chargeable gains must be made on or before 31 January in the year following the year of assessment.

(e) Failure to submit a return on time will result in a 10% surcharge being added to the basic capital gains tax liability.

(f) Where there is a liability to capital gains tax, an assessment will be made following the receipt of a return of chargeable gains. Where a preliminary tax payment of at least 90% is made, any additional capital gains tax payable on making an assessment will be due on 31 January following the preliminary tax payment date or, if later, within one month of the making of an assessment.

Chapter 6

(g) The existing provisions for the making of assessments during a year of assessment in the case of disposals by non-resident persons will continue to apply.

(h) The provisions relating to appeals and interest on underpayments/overpayments in the case of income tax also apply to capital gains tax.

6.1.16 Exemptions and Reliefs

TCA97 s1028 For the tax years 1998/99 et seq, the first £1,000 of chargeable gains of an individual is exempt. The exemption is not transferable between spouses.

TCA97 s593 Disposals of life assurance policies and deferred annuities by the original beneficial owner in respect of policies issued by an Irish life assurance company.

TCA97 s602 A gain accruing to an individual on the disposal of an asset which is tangible moveable property and not a wasting asset where the consideration does not exceed £2,000 is exempt. Where the consideration exceeds £2,000 marginal relief applies to restrict the tax payable to one half of the excess of the consideration over £2,000. Losses accruing on the disposal of such assets are restricted to the difference between cost and deemed proceeds of sale of £2,000.

This exemption does not apply to a disposal of commodities by a person dealing on a terminal market.

TCA97 s603 The disposal of an asset which is tangible moveable property and which is a wasting asset (a wasting asset means an asset with a predictable life not exceeding fifty years) is exempt.

The exemption does not apply to assets which have been exclusively used for the purpose of a trade or profession and have or could have qualified for capital allowances. Part use for the purpose of a trade or profession will cause part of the exemption to be lost.

The exemption does not apply to a disposal of commodities by a person dealing on a terminal market.

TCA97 s607 Irish Government securities and certain others.

TCA97 s608 A gain accruing on the disposal of investments held by a Superannuation Fund, exempt from income tax.

TCA97 s609 A gain accruing to a charity exempt from income tax, subject to certain conditions.

Gains accruing to:

TCA97 s610 (a) A registered trade union to the extent that its income is exempt from income tax.

(b) Registered and unregistered friendly societies whose income is exempt from income tax.

Capital Gains Tax

    (c)   A local authority.

    (d)   The Central Bank of Ireland.

    (e)   A health board.

    (f)   A vocation education committee established under the Vocational Educational Act 1930.

    (g)   A committee of agriculture established under the Agricultural Act 1931.

    (h)   Bord Failte and certain regional and other tourist organisations.

    (i)   Disposals on or after 5 December 1994 of assets by the Cork and Dublin District Milk Boards and their associated companies to an Interim Board and any subsquent disposal of the assets by the Interim Board.

    (j)   The National Rehabilitation Board

TCA97 s613 Gains on:

    (a)   National Savings Schemes.

    (b)   Prize Bonds.

    (c)   Compensation or damages for personal injury or wrong.

    (d)   Betting winnings.

    (e)   Payments under pension schemes.

    (f)   The disposal of a life interest under a settlement by the person for whose benefit the settlement was created or by any other person except where the interest was acquired for a consideration in moneys worth.

    (g)   Disposal of a work of art, valued at not less than IR£25,000 where it has been loaned to an approved gallery for a period of not less than 6 years for display to the public.

6.1.17 Private Residence

TCA97 s604 A gain accruing to an individual on the disposal of an interest in a private residence and grounds of up to one acre which has been occupied by him throughout the period of ownership as his only or main residence. Certain periods of absence are regarded as periods of occupation. These are:

    (a)   The last 12 months of ownership.

    (b)   Any period of absence throughout which the individual worked in a foreign employment.

    (c)   Any period of absence, not exceeding four years, during which the individual was prevented from occupying the residence because of local employment conditions.

Chapter 6

Periods of foreign or local employment will only qualify as periods of occupation if the individual occupies the residence both before and after the periods.

The gain arising on any portion of a private residence used exclusively for business purposes is not exempted.

For the purpose of the relief, an individual may not have more than one main residence at any one time. If an individual has more than one residence, he may agree with the Inspector of Taxes which is to be treated as his main residence by giving notice to the Inspector within two years of the beginning of the period of acquisition of the second residence. Spouses living together may only have one main residence for both.

The relief applies to a chargeable gain arising on the disposal by a trustee of an asset which was settled property and occupied as his only or main residence by an individual entitled to occupy it under the terms of the settlement.

The relief is extended to disposals on or after 6 April 1979 of a dwellinghouse which, during the period of ownership, was the sole residence rent free of a dependent relative. No more than one residence may qualify at any one time.

In the case of a married couple living together, relief may be claimed separately by each spouse in respect of a dwelling house owned by that spouse and occupied by a dependent relative.

The exemption is restricted where the consideration for the disposal is inflated because of development potential. Only such part of any chargeable gain as reflects the increase in the current use value of the property will be relieved from tax:-

Example

	£	£
Property sold 1994 - Proceeds		290,000
Market value - 6 April 1974		50,000
Current use value - 6 April 1974		8,000
Development value - 6 April 1974		42,000
Proceeds of sale		290,000
Less: Current Use Value Adjusted By Inflation		
8,000 x 5.754	46,032	
Development Value	42,000	
		88,032
Gain		201,968

6.1.18 Disposal of Business or Farm

TCA97 s598

A gain arising to an individual who has attained the age of 55 on the disposal of his business or farm or shares in his family company or holding company is disregarded where the consideration is less than

£250,000. Where the consideration is more than the limit, there is marginal relief which restricts the tax payable to one half of the difference between the consideration and the limit.

To qualify for the exemption, the individual must have owned the assets for a minimum period of 10 years ending with the disposal and where the farm or business is disposed of through shares in the family company, the individual must have been a working director for 10 years immediately prior to the disposal, of which 5 years must have been spent as a full time working director.

As respects disposals made on or after 6 April 1998 by a person who has participated in an EU Farm Retirement Scheme by way of leasing of land is not for that reason excluded from the relief.

6.1.19 Disposal within the Family of Business or Farm

TCA97 s599

For disposals on or after 6 April 1978, of assets as mentioned above at Section 598, an individual, meeting the conditions as for Section 598 and making the disposal to his children, is exempt from capital gains tax irrespective of the consideration. If the assets upon which exemption has been granted are disposed of within six years of having been acquired by the child, the capital gains tax which would have become payable, but for the exemption, becomes payable as well as any other capital gains tax which may be due on the disposal by the child.

For the purpose of the exemption "a child" includes a nephew or niece who has worked in the business substantially on a full time basis for the period of five years ending with the disposal.

The reliefs under Section 558 and Section 559 are not mutually exclusive.

6.1.20 Replacement of Business and Other Assets

TCA97 s597

A person engaged in a trade, business, profession or employment may defer gains realised on the disposal of certain business assets used solely for the trade etc throughout the person's period of ownership of them. The deferment is obtainable where the proceeds of disposal are reinvested in replacement assets for use exclusively in the trade etc. The chargeable gain arising at the time of disposal is deferred until the replacement assets cease to be used for the purpose of the trade etc. The following are the assets upon which the "roll over" relief may be claimed:

(i) Plant and Machinery.
(ii) Buildings.
(iii) Land (other than land held as stock in trade and development land) in certain circumstances.
(iv) Goodwill.

Chapter 6

The asset disposed of need not be replaced by a similar asset.

The relief is available in general where the old and replacement assets are used in the same trade. There is, however, provision to grant relief to a person who carries on two or more trades in different localities where the trades are concerned wholly or mainly with goods or services of the same kind.

Relief is also available where a person ceases to carry on a trade and starts a new trade within two years of the date of cessation provided that the old trade was carried on for at least ten years.

Normally, the replacement assets must be acquired within a period beginning twelve months before and ending three years after the date of disposal of the old assets. The Revenue Commissioners however, have power to extend these time limits.

If part only of the proceeds of sale of the old assets is reinvested in replacement assets, partial deferment will be allowed but only so long as the amount not reinvested is less than the chargeable gain. The relief for indexation is that applying at the date on which each disposal takes place.

6.1.21 Sale of Shares - Unquoted Company

TCA97 s591

If the consideration which an individual obtains for any material disposal of shares or securities in a trading company, is applied by him in acquiring shares in an unquoted trading company, the business of which consists wholly or mainly of qualifying trading operations including a profession, he is treated as if any chargeable gain accruing on the disposal did not accrue until he disposes of the new investment. For this purpose, dealing in shares, securities, land, currencies, futures or traded options will not be regarded as a qualifying trading operation. A trade will be regarded as consisting wholly or mainly of qualifying trading operations if not less than 75% of the total amount receivable by the company from all its trading operations in "the specified period" (the period throughout which the company must satisfy certain conditions) is derived from sales made or services rendered by the company in the course of the carrying on of the qualifying trading operations.

A material disposal occurs if throughout the 3 years ending with the date of disposal, or if shorter, the period during which the company traded, it was a trading or holding company, and the individual had been a working officer or employee of the company, or if the company is a member of a trading group, of one or more companies which are members of that trading group.

The conditions under which the relief may be claimed are:-

(a) the individual must have held at least 15% of the voting rights of the original company;

(b) the individual must have been an employee or officer acting in a managerial or technical capacity for a period of 3 years immediately prior to the disposal;

(c) the investment must be made within the period of 3 years following the disposal of the original shares;

(d) the individual must hold at least 5% of the ordinary share capital of the company within a period of 1 year following the disposal of the original shares;

(e) the individual must hold at least 15% of the ordinary share capital of the new company at any time in the period of 3 years from the date of disposal of the original shares;

(f) the individual must commence work with the new company within 1 year of the date of sale of the original shares and continue as a full-time working officer or employee of the company for a period of 3 years from the date of sale. As respects disposals made on or after 6 April 1996 this employment condition is amended to provide that the individual must commence employment within 3 years of the date of the sale of the original shares and remain so employed for a period of 2 years;

(g) the new company must not be a subsidiary of or under the control of another company, nor can it form a group with the original company.

The gain which is rolled over may be rolled over again where the new shares are disposed of and the proceeds re-invested in the foregoing manner.

Where part of the proceeds are not re-invested, the amount not re-invested is to be deducted from the gain and any balance is treated as not accruing until a disposal of the new shares is made.

Relief may be obtained where the individual was either a full-time or part-time employee or director of the company. Shares may be quoted or unquoted. There is no minimum voting rights requirement. The relief may be claimed on a disposal of shares in a company carrying on a profession and re-investment may be made in such a company. The individual must be a full-time employee or full-time director of the company in which the re-investment is made and the company must be unquoted.

The money raised by the company through the issue of the shares must be used for the purposes of qualifying trading operations.

A quote on the Developing Companies Market will not cause a crystallisation of the capital gains tax which has been deferred.

Chapter 6

6.1.22 Compulsory Purchase

TCA97 s605

Where certain assets situated in the State are disposed of under a compulsory purchase order and the proceeds are reinvested in assets within the same class as the original assets, there is no capital gains tax payable on the disposal, but the whole gain is assessed when the replacement assets are disposed of. Indexation relief is applied from the date of acquisition of the original assets and to the cost of those assets. There are two classes of assets for the purpose of this relief:

Class 1 - Plant or machinery used for the purpose of a trade and land or buildings used for the purpose of a trade (but excluding land or buildings held as trading stock) and goodwill.

Class 2 - Land or buildings held other than as trading stock, but not development land.

If part of the compensation monies is not reinvested, there will be a part disposal of the original assets.

The relief applies where the replacement assets are acquired in the period beginning twelve months before and ending three years after the disposal. The Revenue Commissioners, however, have power to extend these limits.

6.1.23 Compensation and Insurance Money

TCA97 s536

A person may claim that an amount received for compensation or damage to an asset which is not lost or destroyed may be treated as reducing the cost of the asset for capital gains tax purposes. To qualify for the relief, the amount received must be applied wholly or substantially in restoring the asset.

Any amount received as compensation or damages, and applied in restoring the asset, is to be deducted from the expenditure on restoration. Indexation is then applied to the net amount.

Where the asset is lost or destroyed, and the amount received in compensation is used within one year in replacing the asset, a person may claim that neither a gain nor a loss arises on the receipt of the compensation and as if the cost of the replacement asset were reduced by whatever amount which gives rise to no gain on the disposal of the old asset. The Revenue Commissioners have power to extend the time limit of one year.

If part only of the proceeds of the compensation is reinvested in a replacement asset, partial deferment will be allowed but only so long as the amount not reinvested is less than the monetary gain.

The relief under this Section does not apply to amounts received for wasting assets and thus excludes amounts received for plant and machinery.

Capital Gains Tax

6.1.24 Scheme for Retirement of Farmers

TCA97 s612

Any premium paid under the European Communities (Retirement of Farmers) Regulations 1974 is excluded from the consideration for the disposal of the farm.

6.1.25 Deductions

TCA97 s552

In computing chargeable gains or allowable losses the amounts to be deducted from the consideration received for an asset, excluding development land, include the following:

(a) The cost of acquisition as increased by the relief for inflation (indexation).

(b) Additional expenditure on the asset for the purpose of enhancing the value of the asset, as increased by the relief for inflation, calculated by reference to the date on which such expenditure is incurred.

(c) Incidental costs of acquisition and disposal.

No deduction is allowed for expenditure which is allowable for income tax purposes.

Where any of the expenditure, which is allowable as a deduction from the consideration received for an asset was incurred after the date of acquisition of the asset, and a chargeable gain arises to which tapering relief applies, the chargeable gain is attributed to the original and additional expenditure in the relative proportions of that expenditure as adjusted for inflation. The tapering relief is then applied to the chargeable gain by reference to the dates on which the expenditure was incurred.

6.1.26 Interest

TCA97 s552

Interest is not an allowable deduction for capital gain tax purposes except in certain circumstances where a company borrows money to defray expenditure on the construction of any building, structure or works.

6.1.27 Calls on Shares

TCA97 s582

Where there has been an issue of shares or debentures and a person gives any consideration on a date which is more than 12 months after the allotment of the shares or debentures, the consideration will be deemed to have been incurred on the date on which it was given. As a result, the relief for inflation applies from the later date.

Chapter 6

6.1.28 Rights Issues

TCA97 s584

Expenditure on a rights issue is deemed to have been incurred when the consideration was given. The relief for inflation is applied accordingly.

6.1.29 Identification of Shares Disposed of with Shares Purchased

Shares of the same class disposed of on or after 6 April 1978 are identified with purchases on a first in, first out basis. There are special problems, however, in relation to shares held at 6 April 1978, and acquired on or after 6 April 1974. Where some of these shares have been disposed of they have, up to and including 5 April 1978, been treated on a pool basis, ie treated as a single asset growing or diminishing on the occasion when shares were acquired or disposed of. The continuation of the pooling system for disposal of these shares on or after 6 April 1978 would not permit the inflation and tapering reliefs to be correctly applied. In order that the reliefs may be applied, it is provided that pools of shares existing at 6 April 1978 are to be unravelled by matching acquisitions and disposals in the period from 6 April 1974 to 5 April 1978 in the proportion which the number of shares disposed of bears to the total number of shares in the pool immediately prior to the disposal. The shares remaining at 6 April 1978 will then be identifiable by reference to both date of acquisition and cost.

The unravelling procedure will not affect computations of chargeable gains or allowable losses for periods up to 5 April 1978.

6.1.30 Options

TCA97 s540

Options are assets for capital gains tax purposes.

The granting of an option is a disposal separate from the asset to which it relates. If the option is exercised, the grant of the option ceases to be a separate transaction and becomes part of the overall transaction in which the asset is sold and acquired.

The abandonment of an option is a disposal but no allowable loss can occur.

6.1.31 Inheritances and Gifts

TCA97 s573

Assets acquired by inheritance or gift are deemed to have been acquired at market value at the date of death or gift.

6.1.32 Liquidations

TCA97 s571

The appointment of a liquidator does not give rise to a disposal for capital gains tax purposes. Any disposal of assets by a liquidator during the course of the liquidation or a distribution in specie of assets to the shareholders is a disposal by the company.

Capital Gains Tax

When the shareholders receive a distribution, either in cash or in specie, this is a disposal for capital gains tax purposes.

Capital gains tax arising on chargeable gains on disposals made by a liquidator, receiver, mortgagee or chargee ("accountable persons") is recoverable by means of an income tax assessment under Case IV of Schedule D, raised on the accountable person.

6.1.33 Reorganisations and Takeovers

TCA97
s583-s587

A share for share exchange in a takeover situation where the acquiring company obtains control, does not give rise to a disposal for capital gains purposes. The new shares are deemed to have been acquired at the cost and on the date on which the original shares were acquired. Similarly, there is no disposal where, under a capital reorganisation, shares are exchanged for new shares of either the same class or different classes.

If there is any payment of cash on either a takeover or a capital reorganisation, a part disposal will occur.

The relief will only apply where it is shown that the exchange was effected for bona fide commercial reasons and does not form part of any arrangement or scheme of which the main purpose or one of the main purposes is avoidance of liability to tax.

6.1.34 Acquisition by a Company of its Own Shares

(a) Unquoted company

TCA97
s173-s186

The changes introduced to company law (Part XI of the Companies Act 1990 - to enable a company acquire its own shares or those of its holding company) would have very severe consequences without consequent changes to tax legislation in view of the distribution rules in the Tax Acts. Section 130 provides that a premium payable on the redemption of a share shall be treated as a distribution. Under the provisions of Section 173-186 a person is liable to capital gains tax where the following conditions are satisfied:

1. The acquisition is made by an unquoted trading company or an unquoted holding company of a trading company. (See quoted companies below).

2. It is made wholly or mainly for the purpose of benefiting a trade carried on by the company or by any of its 51% subsidiaries.

3. It does not form part of a scheme or arrangement the main purpose of which is to avoid the treating of the receipt as a dividend.

283

4. The vendor (or his nominee if the shares are held by a nominee) is resident or ordinarily resident in the State for the period in which the purchase occurs.

5. The vendor is not connected with the purchaser, or any company which is a member of the same group as the purchaser, after the sale.

6. The shares have been owned by the vendor for 5 years prior to disposal. The period of ownership of a spouse living with the vendor is aggregated with that of the vendor, provided that they are still living together at the date of purchase. The period of ownership is reduced to 3 years where the vendor acquired the shares under a will or an intestacy.

7. The interest of the vendor and that of his associates if any in the company or the group immediately after the purchase has substantially reduced, i.e. the nominal value of issued share capital or entitlement to share of profits has reduced to at least 75% of its pre-purchase level.

The other major provisions are:-

(a) Where a company acquires shares from one of its shareholders such shares, where they are not cancelled, are deemed to be Treasury Shares. Treasury shares held by a company are deemed to be cancelled upon acquisition by the company. Such cancellation does not give rise to a chargeable gain or allowable loss. The re-issue by the company of Treasury shares is not treated as an issue of new shares.

(b) Dealers in shares will continue to be subject to tax under Case I and II of Schedule D on profits realised on the disposal of shares in this manner.

(c) For the purpose of this chapter associates include:

  (i) Husband and wife living together.

  (ii) A person under the age of 18 years and his parents.

  (iii) A person having a controlling interest in a company and that company.

  (iv) Two companies under common control.

(d) A person is connected with the company if he directly or indirectly possesses or is entitled to acquire more than 30% of the issued share capital or loan capital and voting rights of the company or is entitled to more than 30% of the assets of the company on a winding up.

(e) Any advance corporation tax payable on the purchase, redemption or repayment of shares which does not qualify for capital gains tax treatment is to be treated as though it was payable on a dividend.

(f) A group is defined as a company with its 51% subsidiaries. A company which has succeeded to a business previously carried on by a member of a group shall, together with this group of companies, be included as part of the group where that company commenced to carry on a business within 3 years.

(g) A company which makes a payment for shares is required to make a return on a prescribed form to the Inspector within 9 months of the end of the accounting period in which the purchase occurs. This requirement is amended to take account of the situation where an inspector requests in writing such a form; then the time limit in which the company must comply is not less than 30 days from the issue of such notice.

(b) Quoted Company

The redemption, repayment or purchase by a quoted company or a subsidiary of a quoted company of its own shares is not to be treated as a distribution received by the shareholders but instead will be treated as a capital gains tax disposal by the shareholder. This treatment is not subject to the numerous conditions for unquoted companies outlined above.

6.1.35 Assets which have Qualified for Capital Allowances

TCA97 s561

The majority of such assets would be wasting assets and but for express provision would be exempt from capital gains tax under the provisions of Section 603. Section 561 provides that where a gain arises on such assets, the computation disregards the fact that capital allowances have been granted. This is because the capital allowances will have been recovered by means of a balancing charge. The chargeable gain is computed by comparing cost with proceeds of sale. The indexation and, if applicable, tapering reliefs are granted in the normal way.

Where a loss arises on the disposal of such assets, that loss will not be allowed to the extent that it has been covered by capital allowances.

6.1.36 Grants

TCA97 s565

Where any part of the cost of an asset has been met directly or indirectly by any Government, by any Board established by statute or by any public or local authority, whether in the State or elsewhere, the grant or subsidy must be deducted in arriving at the cost of the asset for capital gains tax purposes. If the asset was owned on 6 April 1974 the cost will be the market value at that date and any grant or subsidy received before that date must be deducted from

Chapter 6

the market value. By this means the indexation is applied to the net amount after deducting the grant or subsidy.

6.1.37 Transfer of a Business to a Company

TCA97 s596-s600

Where an individual transfers a business to a company, together with the whole of the assets of the business, or the whole of the assets other than cash and the business is transferred in exchange for shares issued by the company to the individual, the chargeable gain arising is deferred until such time as the shares are disposed of.

Should the consideration for the transfer consist partly of shares and partly of cash, the gain is calculated on the basis of the total disposal of the business. The proportion referable to the shares is deducted from the cost of the shares and the balance, applicable to the proportion in which the consideration has been taken other than in shares, is taxable in the normal manner.

Transfers made on or after 24 January 1992 must be for bona fide commercial reasons and not form part of any arrangement or scheme for an avoidance of liability to tax.

6.1.38 Leases

TCA97 s566

A disposal of an interest in a lease which has more than 50 years to run is a normal disposal for capital gains tax purposes. Where a lease which has less than 50 years to run is disposed of, it is treated as a wasting asset and special rules apply as to the amount of the cost which is allowable as a deduction on disposal from the proceeds of sale. The rate at which the cost is assumed to be written off is in accordance with the table set out on page 289.

On disposal of a lease which has less than fifty years to run, the amount of the costs to be allowed is:

$$C - C \times \frac{P(1) - P(3)}{P(1)} \quad \text{where}$$

C = Cost

P(1) = the percentage derived from the table on page 289 for the duration of the lease at the beginning of the period of ownership.

P(3) = the percentage derived from the same table for the duration of the lease at the time of the disposal.

Where additional expenditure is incurred during the currency of the lease the amount of that expenditure allowable as a deduction is:

$$C - C \times \frac{P(2) - P(3)}{P(2)} \quad \text{where}$$

C = Cost

P(2) = the percentage derived from the table on page 289 at the date the additional expenditure was incurred.

P(3) = the percentage derived from the same table for the duration of the lease at the time of the disposal.

Where payment of a premium is required under a lease, there is a part disposal of the freehold or other asset out of which the lease is granted. Any part of the premium which is taxed under Case V of Schedule D is excluded from the consideration to be taken into account for capital gains purposes.

Table

Disposal of Short Lease

Years	Percentage	Years	Percentage
50 (or more)	100.00	25	81.1
49	99.7	24	79.6
48	99.3	23	78.1
47	98.9	22	76.4
46	98.5	21	74.6
45	98.1	20	72.8
44	97.6	19	70.8
43	97.1	18	68.7
42	96.6	17	66.5
41	96.0	16	64.1
40	95.5	15	61.6
39	94.8	14	59.0
38	94.2	13	56.2
37	93.5	12	53.2
36	92.8	11	50.0
35	92.0	10	46.7
34	91.2	9	43.2
33	90.3	8	39.4
32	89.4	7	35.4
31	88.4	6	31.2
30	87.3	5	26.7
29	86.2	4	22.0
28	85.1	3	17.0
27	83.8	2	11.6
26	82.5	1	6.0
		0	0.0

6.1.39 Trusts

TCA97 s574

The creation of a trust is a disposal by the settlor who will be charged to tax by reference to the market value of the assets placed in the trust.

Changes in investments effected by the trustees during the life of the trust will give rise to a charge to tax either by reference to the market value at the date the assets were placed in the trust or the cost of the assets where acquired by the trustees.

Where an asset leaves the trust by reason of a person becoming absolutely entitled as against the trustees, a charge to tax arises by reference to the market value of the asset at the date on which the person becomes absolutely entitled to the asset.

A charge to tax will not occur where the event which gives rise to the person becoming absolutely entitled is the termination of a life interest by the death of the person entitled to that interest. In these circumstances, the person becoming absolutely entitled acquires the asset at its market value at the date of death of the life tenant. This treatment only applies where no event giving rise to a charge has occurred since 5 April 1974.

Where a life interest terminates with the property remaining in the trust a charge to tax arises based on the market value of the assets at the date of termination.

A charge to tax does not arise where the asset in question is comprised in an inheritance taken on the death and is exempt from tax in relation to the inheritance under Section 55, Capital Acquisitions Tax Act, 1976. The charge to tax will crystallise should the assets cease to qualify for exemption from inheritance tax.

Where a trust is wound up either wholly or partly, any unallowed losses which have accrued on the property leaving the trust are treated as losses accruing to the beneficiary.

TCA97 s579 Section 88, Finance Act 1999 contains detailed provisions on the following:

(a) The attribution of chargeable gains of off-shore trusts, to beneficiaries who are resident or ordinarily resident in the State.

(b) The imposition of a charge to tax where the trustees of a trust cease to be resident and ordinarily resident in the State.

(c) The migration of a trust off shore because of the death of a trustee and the coming on shore of a trust for a similar reason.

(d) The imposition of a secondary liability on certain trustees where as a result of the trustees of a trust migrating off shore a capital gains tax charge arises, as at (b) above.

(e) The imposition of a charge where a trust ceases to be liable to Irish capital gains tax because of the provisions of any double taxation agreement.

TCA97 s613-s613A Section 90, Finance Act 1999 removes the exemption from capital gains tax for the disposal of an interest in a trust where the trust is or ever was an off shore trust or the trust is or ever was outside the charge to Irish capital gains tax by virtue of a double taxation agreement.

6.1.40 Anti Avoidance

There are provisions to prevent avoidance by means of the following:-

TCA97 s549	Sales to connected persons.
TCA97 s550	Assets disposed of in a series of transactions.
TCA97 s579	Dealings through non-resident trusts (see above).
TCA97 s589	Controlled companies transferring assets at undervalue.
TCA97 s590	Dealings through non-resident companies.

6.1.41 Time Limits

TCA97 s605 Replacement of Business and Other Assets and Compulsory Purchase. –

The replacement assets must be acquired in the period beginning twelve months before and ending three years after the date of disposal of the original assets.

TCA97 s536 Compensation and Insurance Money. –

The amount received for an asset which is lost or destroyed must be used within one year in acquiring the replacement asset.

6.1.42 Miscellaneous

TCA97 s914 The administration of the tax is under the care of the Revenue Commissioners. Returns must be made by those persons liable to capital gains tax.

Issuing houses, stockbrokers, auctioneers etc may be required to give particulars of transactions carried out on behalf of clients. In the case of transactions effected on or after 6 April 1995, involving assets which are tangible, movable property, only transactions with a disposal consideration in excess of £15,000 need be returned.

6.1.43 Clearance Certificates

TCA97 s980 Where any of the following assets is disposed of, the person by whom or through whom the consideration is paid must deduct capital gains tax at 15% from the payment:

(a) Land in the State.

(b) Minerals in the State.

(c) Exploration rights in a designated area.

(d) Unquoted shares deriving their value or the greater part of their value from assets at (a), (b) or (c).

Chapter 6

(e) Unquoted shares accepted in exchange for shares deriving their value or the greater part of their value from assets at (a), (b) or (c).

(f) goodwill of a trade carried on in the State.

(g) Goodwill of a trade carried on in the State.

The deduction is not required where the consideration does not exceed £150,000 or where the person disposing of the asset produces a certificate from the Revenue Commissioners authorising payment in full. A clearance certificate may be obtained by making application on form CG50 to the Revenue Commissioners supported by a copy of the agreement or contract for sale.

Clearance must be obtained before the consideration is paid. There is no exemption from the clearance procedure where the asset is held as trading stock or where the transaction is intra group and a capital gains tax liability does not arise. Failure to obtain the certificate will lead to the purchaser being assessed to capital gains tax for an amount of 15% of the consideration.

Where the consideration is of a kind from which the 15% deduction cannot be made and the vendor does not produce a clearance certificate the person acquiring the asset must within seven days of the time at which the acquisition is made:-

(i) notify the Revenue Commissioners of the acquisition by providing particulars of:-

   (a) the asset acquired

   (b) the consideration for acquiring the asset

   (c) the market value of that consideration

   (d) the name and address of the person making the disposal

(ii) pay to the Collector General, an amount of capital gains tax equal to 15% of the market value. This tax is payable without the making of an assessment. Any tax so paid is recoverable from the seller of the asset.

If the vendor obtains a clearance certificate in respect of the disposal, the capital gains tax withheld will be repaid to the purchaser.

Disposals of assets which do not involve the purchaser acquiring an asset are within the scope of these provisions.

TCA97 s980(9) The clearance procedures do not apply to the payment of insurance claims in respect of damage to property.

CHAPTER 7   RESIDENTIAL PROPERTY TAX

(Abolished from 5 April 1997)

7.1 RESIDENTIAL PROPERTY TAX

7.1.1 Charge

FA83 s96   With effect from 5 April 1983, all relevant residential property owned by an assessable person is charged to tax at a rate of 1.5% where the market value of the property exceeds an exemption limit and the income of the assessable person exceeds an income limit. (For 1993/94 "banding" applied. See Chart 26)

FA83 s97   A person who is domiciled in the State is liable on all his residential property wherever situate, whilst a person not domiciled in the State is liable to tax on his property situated in the State only.

Relevant residential property is any residential property in relation to which the assessable person is the owner and which is occupied by him as a dwelling or dwellings.

FA83 s95   Residential property is a building or part of a building used or suitable for use as a dwelling, and land which the occupier of a building or part of a building used as a dwelling, has for his own occupation and enjoyment with the building as its garden or grounds of an ornamental nature.

FA83 s95   An assessable person is the owner of a residential property if he:-

(a) owns the freehold, or

(b) occupies the property under a lease which exceeds 50 years, or

(c) is the owner or lessee at (a) or (b) subject to a mortgage, or

(d) occupies the property under a lease of 50 years or less or at will, and either pays no rent or a rent not at arm's length and the rent paid is less than 80% of the arm's length rent. Exceptions are made for persons:

    (i) who are chargeable to income tax on a benefit in kind in relation to the occupation, or

    (ii) where the property is chargeable to residential property tax in the hands of the landlord, or

    (iii) who are chargeable to tax under Section 96, Corporation Tax Act 1976 in respect of the provision of the property, or

    (iv) who occupy property under a caretaker agreement at arm's length.

Chapter 7

FA83 s95 — An assessable person is the occupier of a property if he has the use of it, whether used or not. He will be regarded as having the use of the property even though he does not have the use as a dwelling on 5 April if, for the greater part of the year ending on that date and for the greater part of the year commencing on the following 6 April, he has the use of the property as a dwelling.

7.1.2 Market Value

FA83 s98 — Market Value is the price which the unencumbered fee simple of the property would fetch on a sale in the open market.

FA83 s99 — Where residential property is jointly owned and occupied by two or more persons, the market value of the property is apportioned equally between them. There is no provision for apportionment by reference to the interest which the person holds.

7.1.3 Market Value Exemption Limit

FA83 s100 — The market value exemption limit is the aggregate of the unit exemption limits attributed to the various residential properties of the assessable person on 5 April in any year:

The unit exemption limit is the proportion of the general limit, determined by the formula:-

$$\frac{A \times G}{B} \quad \text{where}$$

A = market value (determined without regard to joint or common ownership) on 5 April of the unit comprised in the relevant residential property of the assessable person.

B = the aggregate of the market values (determined without regard to joint or common ownership) on 5 April of all the units comprised in the relevant residential property of the assessable person.

G = the general exemption limit of £101,000 for 5 April 1996 (see Chart 25 for previous limits).

7.1.4 Income Limit

FA83 s101 — Where an assessable person claims and proves that the aggregate income of himself and every relevant person does not exceed £30,100 for the year ended 5 April 1996 he is exempt from the tax (see Chart 25 for previous limits).

FA83 s95:
FA94 s115 — Relevant person means any person who, in the year ended on the valuation date, normally resided at any relevant residential property of the assessable person and who, or whose spouse, made no payment of rent or a payment of rent below arm's length rent in respect of such residence. Exceptions are made for:-

- individuals, other than the assessable person, age 65 or more on the valuation date;

- individuals, other than the assessable person, who by reason of mental or physical infirmity, are permanently incapacitated from maintaining themselves;
- individuals, other than the assessable person, where the owner/occupier is permanently incapacitated and the individual resides in the property as a consequence of that infirmity;
- individuals residing in the property as a consequence of a widowed assessable person having a qualifying child.

7.1.5 Income

FA83 s95;
FA94 s115

For the purposes of the income limit, income is defined as total income from all sources as estimated in accordance with the income Tax Acts. No account is taken of allowances, deductions and reliefs other than normal depreciation. Income includes any income arising inside or outside the State regardless of whether it is chargeable to income tax. Income is rounded down to the nearest £1,000.

The following are not regarded as income:

(a) Certain wound, disability and military service pensions.

(b) Scholarship income, bursaries etc.

(c) Social Welfare Children's Allowance.

(d) Redundancy payments.

(e) Payments re Thalidomide children.

(f) Military Service pensions - War of Independence.

(g) Income from savings certificates, savings bonds and national instalment savings.

7.1.6 Inflation Relief

FA83 s100;
FA83 s101

The general exemption limit is to be increased annually by the increase in the New House Price Index while the income limit is to be increased annually by the increase in the Consumer Price Index (see Chart 25)

7.1.7 Marginal Relief

FA83 s102;
FA94 s120

Marginal relief applies where the income exceeds the income limit by £10,000 or less. The tax is reduced to an amount arrived at by the formula -

$$T \times \frac{A - E}{10,000} \quad \text{where}$$

A = The amount of the income

E = The income limit

T = The tax payable before marginal relief

A claim to marginal relief must be made within two years of the valuation date. The excess is increased to £15,000 for those aged over 65.

7.1.8 Reduction for Children

FA90 s125

The tax payable is reduced by 10% for each child resident with an assessable person, in respect of which an entitlement to child allowance would have arisen.

7.1.9 Returns

FA83 s103

Returns must be submitted on or before 1 October after each valuation date.

7.1.10 Clearance on Sale of Certain Residential Property

FA93 s107

A person selling a residential property with a value in excess of the general exemption limit must provide the purchaser with a certificate issued by the Revenue Commissioners, certifying that all residential property tax has been paid. If the certificate is not produced, the purchaser must make a deduction from the purchase price and remit the amount to the Revenue Commissioners. The amount to be deducted is 1.5% of the value in excess of the general exemption limit multiplied by the number of years that the previous owner has owned the property subject to a maximum 5.

For disposals after 5 April 1999, a clearance certificate must be obtained where the sale proceeds exceed £200,000 (see Chart 25 for previous limits).

7.1.11 Assessment and Payment of Tax

FA83 s104;
FA94 s121

Tax is payable on 1 October after each valuation date and is payable without the making of an assessment. Payment may be made by instalments. Hardship cases are considered.

7.1.12 Interest on Overdue Tax

FA83 s105

Interest at the rate of 1.25% per month is payable on overdue tax up to 31 March 1998 and 1% per month thereafter.

If the tax is assessed because the Revenue Commissioners are dissatisfied with a return, interest is not due if the tax does not exceed £100. If the Revenue Commissioners raise an additional assessment and the tax charged by the additional assessment does not exceed 10% of the total tax due, interest will not be charged provided the additional tax and the tax in the original assessment are paid in time and the return was made on time.

7.1.13 Overpayment of Tax

FA86 s114

Tax overpaid is repaid with interest at 0.6% per month, or part of a month, from the date of payment to the date of repayment, up to 31 March and 0.5% thereafter.

7.1.14 Appeals

FA83 s109

In general, the provisions of the Income Tax Acts regarding appeals against assessments to income tax apply in relation to appeals against assessments to residential property tax. However, if a person appeals on the grounds that he is not an assessable person, the right of appeal may be exercised only on payment of 75% of the tax assessed. The minimum payment requirement does not apply where exemption is claimed on income grounds.

7.1.15 Penalties

FA83 s112

An assessable person who does not lodge a return or fails to comply with a notice is liable to a penalty of £1,000 and a further £50 for each day after judgement until compliance. A similar penalty will be imposed on the purchaser of residential property who, in the absence of a clearance certificate being furnished by the vendor, fails to deliver to the Revenue Commissioners a return of the consideration in a sale and the amount deducted therefrom. A person obstructing an authorised officer from inspecting property will be subject to a penalty of £1,000 also. Where a person fraudulently or negligently makes an incorrect return the penalties are:

(i) £2,000 and

(ii) the amount of the additional tax or in the case of fraud twice the additional tax.

A genuine error corrected immediately will go unpunished but if there is unreasonable delay in correcting the matter the penalties which apply in the case of negligence will apply. Any person assisting or inducing a person to make an incorrect return or valuation shall be liable to a penalty of £1,000.

The Revenue may also institute criminal proceedings.

The income tax procedural provisions as regards penalties apply.

Chapter 7

CHAPTER 8 STAMP DUTIES

8.1 STAMP DUTIES

The legislation on stamp duties is contained in the Stamp Act 1891 and in subsequent Finance Acts.

It is consolidated in "The Law of Stamp Duties", the second edition of which was issued in 1971. Subsequent revisions were issued in 1973, 1975 and in 1987, to incorporate the provisions of the Finance Acts 1972 to 1986 inclusive. The Stamp Act 1891, continues to be the main single piece of legislation on stamp duties and many of the subsequent amendments down through the years have been made to this Act.

Stamp duty is charged on instruments, i.e. written documents. Before the Finance Act 1991 stamp duty was unique among taxes in that, apart from a few exceptions, there were no statutory enforcement provisions. Taxpayer compliance was achieved in many indirect ways mainly by reason of conveyancing or commercial practice. However, under Finance Act 1991 in respect of instruments executed on or after 1 November 1991, stamp duty is compulsory and specific persons are made accountable for the duty. For example, in a sale, the accountable person is the purchaser, in a lease the accountable person is the lessee and in an instrument which operates as a gift, both the donor and donee are accountable persons.

The Stamp Act 1891 is drafted on the assumption that documents are stamped before execution. It is normal practice however to stamp after execution, and if a document is presented for stamping within 30 days of execution no penalty is payable. If a document is submitted for adjudication (formal system whereby the Revenue Commissioners give their opinion on the amount of stamp duty payable on a particular document), stamp duty does not have to be paid until 14 days after the notice of assessment by the Revenue Commissioners is received. Furthermore, if a document was executed outside the State and retained abroad, penalties would not run until the expiration of 30 days after the document was brought into the State. The new system makes no distinction between documents executed inside the State or outside the State. If the documents are not stamped within 30 days of execution, penalties are chargeable, and these new penalties apply also to all documents whenever executed which are unstamped or insufficiently stamped on 1 November 1991.

Chapter 8

8.1.1 **Amnesty**

Where an instrument which was executed prior to 1 November 1991 remained unstamped on 30 January 1992 it could be stamped free of interest and penalties if the duty was paid on or before 30 June 1992. If the instrument was stamped between 1 July 1992 and 30 September 1992 interest and penalties were charged only as if it had been executed on 1 June 1992.

8.1.2 **Charge**

Stamp duty is chargeable on certain instruments and on certain transactions. Stamps are impressed on or affixed to the instruments. Stamp duty may be divided into two categories as follows:

(1) Duty based on the value of the transaction (ad valorem duty).

(2) Duty of a fixed amount regardless of the value of the transaction.

The following are examples of the main items to which ad valorem duty applies and the rates applicable.

8.1.3 **Conveyance or Transfer on Sale of**

FA90 s110;
FA91 s94

FA91 s96;
FA91 s100;
FA97 PtIV

(a) Stocks or Marketable Securities - £1 per £100 or part of £100 of the consideration

(b) Other Property - From 1 September 1990, the following are the rates of duty

Amount of consideration Exceeding	Not Exceeding	Rate of Duty
–	£5,000	Not Liable
£5,000	£10,000	£1 per £100 or part of £100
£10,000	£15,000	£2 per £100 or part of £100
£15,000	£25,000	£3 per £100 or part of £100
£25,000	£50,000	£4 per £100 or part of £100
£50,000	£60,000	£5 per £100 or part of £100
£60,000		£6 per £100 or part of £100

(c) Residential Property - From 23 January 1997 the rates relating to certain residential property were increased as follows:-

Amount of consideration Exceeding	Not Exceeding	Rate of Duty
£150,000	£160,000	£7 per £100 or part of £100
£160,000	£170,000	£8 per £100 or part of £100
£170,000		£9 per £100 or part of £100

Stamp Duties

The higher rates of duty apply to all instruments executed on or after 23 January 1997. There is a transitional provision to the effect that where there is a contract evidenced in writing prior to 23 January 1997, then provided an instrument to give effect to the contract is executed prior to 1 May 1997, the higher rates do not apply.

Detailed provisions relating to apportionment between residential and non-residential property are included in the 1997 Finance Act.

(d) Residential Property 1998 - From 23 April 1998 the rates relating to certain residential property are amended as follows:-

Amount of consideration exceeding:	Not exceeding	Rate of duty
–	£60,000	Not liable
£60,000	£100,000	£3 per £100 or part of £100
£100,000	£170,000	£4 per £100 or part of £100
£170,000	£250,000	£5 per £100 or part of £100
£250,000	£500,000	£7 per £100 or part of £100
£500,000		£9 per £100 or part of £100

FA99 s146

The new rates of duty apply to certain conveyances and leases of residential property executed on or after 23 April 1998. Transitional arrangements apply to new residential property transferred to or leased by investors where there is a contract evidenced in writing prior to 23 April 1998 and the instrument is executed before 1 April 1999. A transfer of property which includes both residential and non-residential elements will be treated as that of 2 properties. The consideration will be apportioned on a just and reasonable basis and the residential portion will attract the new rates while the existing rates will apply to the non-residential portion.

FA99 s145

There is provision for surcharges in the case of both over-valuation and under-valuation of the residential element in the case of a mixed property. The existing exemption from stamp duty which applies to the purchase of a house or apartment not exceeding 125 sq metres in size will continue to apply in certain circumstances only. The purchase must be made by or on behalf of a person who will, among other things, occupy the property as his only or main place of residence for a 5 year period. The purchase of larger new houses or apartments will be chargeable to stamp duty on the total consideration paid for the site and building costs. In the case of a person occupying the property as his only or main residence for a period of 5 years, however, duty will be payable on the greater of (a) the site cost and (b) 25% of the total cost. If the conditions relating to the 5 year occupancy period etc are broken, the reliefs granted will be clawed back.

Chapter 8

8.1.4 The Crest System

FA96 Ch1 PtIV — The Finance Act 1996 imposes a stamp duty charge of 1% on the electronic transfer of shares. It adapts the stamp duty code to ensure that existing provisions apply notwithstanding the fact that there is no instrument which can be physically stamped.

8.1.5 Letters of Renunciation

FA86 s95 — Statutory Instrument No 152 of 1985 provided for the charging to stamp duty of a renunciation of a right under a letter of allotment to stocks or shares which are not quoted on the Stock Exchange. Such renunciations are charged at the rate applicable to securities. This provision came into effect on 11 June 1985 and was continued on by Section 95 Finance Act 1986.

8.1.6 Voluntary Dispositions Inter Vivos

FA10 s74; FA78 s34 — These are liable to the same rate of duty as conveyances or transfers on sale with substitution of the market value of the property in place of the consideration on sale. Up to 9 June 1983, however, where the disposition was in consideration of marriage it was exempt from duty provided it was for the benefit of a party to the marriage or of a party to and the issue of the marriage. This relief was abolished by Section 92 Finance Act 1983.

Surcharge

FA91 s103; FA94 s103 — The Finance Act 1991 introduced a surcharge as a penalty where the market value of the property has been understated by the accountable person.

With effect from 23 May 1994 the surcharge applies only when the submitted value is less than the ascertained value by more than 15% (previously 10%). The rates of surcharge (which apply to the total duty payable) are now as follows:-

Amount of Understatement	Surcharge %
More than 15% but not more than 30%	25
More than 30% but not more than 50%	50
More than 50%	100

8.1.7 Where Consideration cannot be ascertained

FA91 s104 — In the case of an instrument where the amount or value of the consideration cannot be ascertained at the date of the execution of the instrument, the Revenue Commissioners may charge ad valorem duty on the value of the property conveyed or transferred.

8.1.8 Valuation of Property Chargeable with Stamp Duty

FA91 s105;
FA94 s104

The provisions of Sections 15, 16 and 17 CAT Act 1976 in respect of the market value of property are applied to stamp duty in respect of instruments executed on or after 1 November 1991. With effect from 23 May 1994 only the provisions of Section 15 CAT Act 1976 apply.

8.1.9 Anti Avoidance

FA81 s47

(a) An anti avoidance measure introduced by the Finance Act 1981 deems certain conveyances involving sub purchasers to be voluntary dispositions inter vivos, thus rendering them liable to duty on the value of the property conveyed.

FA86 s96;
FA86 s99

(b) Statutory Instrument No 151 of 1985 which came into operation on 11 June 1985 contained anti avoidance provisions in relation to the stamp duty chargeable on certain instruments. The instruments affected are as follows:-

   (i) A conveyance or transfer on sale where the vendor of property enters into an agreement for a long lease, or grants rights in relation to the property. In this case, any conveyance or transfer subject to the agreement, of the property by the vendor shall be charged to stamp duty as a conveyance or transfer on sale of the property for a consideration equal to the value of the property and the value shall be determined without regard to the agreement.

   (ii) An instrument which evidences the surrender of a leasehold interest, or the merger of a leasehold interest in a superior interest. In this case, the instrument shall be charged to the same stamp duty as if it were a surrender of that leasehold interest.

   (iii) A declaration by deed to the effect that a term in land is enlarged in a case where the term was created by an instrument executed within six years of the date of the execution of the deed. In this case, the instrument shall be charged to stamp duty as a conveyance or transfer on sale of that land for a consideration equal to the value of the land and that value shall be determined without regard to the term or any part thereof.

(c) Where an instrument effects a transfer of immovable property in the State in consideration for any other property (wherever situated and whether movable or immovable) duty will be payable on the value of the relevant immovable property situated in the State thereby conveyed or transferred.

FA98 s199

(d) With effect from 27 March 1998 contracts for the sale of bearer shares are liable to stamp duty.

Chapter 8

8.1.10   **Deductions in relation to certain Conveyances and Transfers**

FA78 s34;
FA93 s105

Section 34, Finance Act 1978 restricts the deductions which can be made from the value of a property in relation to a conveyance or transfer operating as a voluntary disposition and in relation to a conveyance in contemplation of sale made with a view to a possible later sale to the transferee. Following the passing of the 1993 Finance Act duty must be determined without regard to the following deductions:

(a) any power on the exercise of which the property may be revested in the person from whom it was conveyed or transferred;

(b) any annuity or other periodic payment reserved out of the property or any part of it, or any life or other interest so reserved, being an interest which is subject to forfeiture;

(c) any right of residence, support, maintenance, or other right of a similar nature which the property is subject to or charged with, except where such rights are reserved in favour of the transferor or the spouse of the transferor and in any such case regard shall be had to such rights only to the extent that their value does not exceed 10% of the unencumbered value of the property.

8.1.11   **Transactions between Related Persons**

FA82 Sch4;
FA92 s114

In the case of a conveyance or transfer on sale or in the case of a conveyance or transfer operating as a voluntary disposition inter vivos where the instrument contains a certificate to the effect that the parties to the transaction are related, the duty payable thereon is restricted to 50% of the duty that would otherwise be payable. A person is related to another if he is his lineal descendant, parent, grandparent, step parent, brother or sister of a parent or brother or sister, or lineal descendant of a parent, husband or wife or brother or sister. Transactions between spouses are exempt.

8.1.12   **Transfers between Associated Companies**

FA52 s19;
FA80 s85;
FA82 s95;
FA90 s116;
FA95 s143

The rate of duty payable on certain instruments relating to such transactions was £1 per £50 or part of £50 of the amount of the consideration for the sale. Duty on such transactions was abolished with effect from 8 February 1995. To qualify for this relief certain conditions must be satisfied as follows:

(a) The transferor was entitled to the entire beneficial interest in the relevant property and this becomes vested in the transferee.

(b) At the time of the transfer one of the companies owns directly or indirectly at least 90% of the issued share capital of the other, or at least 90% of the issued share capital of each is owned directly or indirectly by a third company. The provisions of Section 156 Corporation Tax Act 1976 apply in determining indirect ownership. The 1990 Finance Act extends the 90% relationship to being entitled to not less than 90% of the profits and not less than 90% of the assets on distribution, in the event of the company being wound up.

(c) There is no arrangement whereunder the consideration is provided directly or indirectly by a person outside the prescribed 90% relationship.

(d) Without prejudice to the generality of the previous condition an arrangement shall be treated as being in existence if it is one whereunder the transferor or the transferee, or a body corporate associated with either is to be enabled to provide any of the consideration, or is to part with it, by or in consequence of the carrying out of transactions involving, or any or them involving, a payment or other disposition by a person other than the body corporate so associated.

(e) There is no arrangement whereunder the property was previously transferred directly or indirectly by a person outside the prescribed 90% relationship.

(f) The transfer must not be made in pursuance of or in connection with an arrangement whereby the transferor and the transferee are to cease to be associated in the prescribed 90% relationship.

(g) The relief will be lost where the prescribed 90% relationship ceases to exist within a period of two years from the date of the conveyance or transfer.

(h) Adjudication by the Revenue Commissioners is necessary.

8.1.13 Leases

Ad valorem duty is payable on the granting of a lease on the amount of the consideration (other than rent) moving to the lessor. The rates are similar to those charged under the head of charge "conveyance or transfer on the sale of any property other than stocks or marketable securities", including the higher rates on residential property, except that there is no consanguinity relief as given in the latter head of charge. Duty is also payable on that part of the consideration which consists of rent and the rates of duty in this case depend on the length of the term of the lease in question. Under Section 75, Stamp Act 1891, an agreement for a lease for any term not exceeding 35 years is to be charged the same duty as if it were an actual lease made for the term and consideration mentioned in the agreement.

Chapter 8

The duty on rent is:-

£1 per £100 of the average annual rent where term does not exceed 35 years or is indefinite.

£6 per £100 of the average annual rent where term exceeds 35 years but does not exceed 100 years.

£12 per £100 of the average annual rent where term exceeds 100 years.

These rates apply to instruments executed on or after 1 September 1990.

Domestic leases with annual rent of less than £6,000 and where the term is indefinite or is less than 35 years are not liable.

8.1.14 Mortgage, Bond, Debenture, Covenant, charged on property within the State

FA90 s110;
FA91 s90

(a) Being the only or principal or primary security (other than an equitable mortgage) for the payment or repayment of money

Amount secured not exceeding £20,000	Exempt
Amount secured exceeding £20,000	£1 per £1,000 or part of £1,000 of the amount secured

(b) Being an equitable mortgage

Amount secured not exceeding £20,000	Exempt
Amount secured exceeding £20,000	50p per £1,000 or part of £1,000 of the amount secured

(c) Transfer, assignment or disposition of any mortgage, bond, debenture, or covenant (except of a marketable security)

Amount secured not exceeding £20,000	Exempt
Amount secured exceeding £20,000	50p per £1,000 or part of £1,000 of the amount transferred, assigned etc.

(d) Being the only or principal or primary security for any annuity

    (i) For a definite and certain period, so that the total amount to be ultimately payable can be ascertained -

where the total amount does not exceed £20,000	Exempt
where the total amount exceeds £20,000 for every £1,000, or any fractional part of £1,000 of the amount secured,	£1.00

    (ii) For the term of life or any other indefinite period -

for every £100 or any fractional part of £100 of the annuity or sum periodically payable	£2.50

In each of the above cases, the maximum duty payable is £500.

8.1.15 Life Insurance Policies for periods exceeding 2 years

SA1891 Sch1

Sum insured not greater than £50	Exempt
Sum insured over £50 up to £1,000	10p per £100 or part of £100
Sum insured over £1,000	£1 per £1,000 or part of £1,000

8.1.16 Settlements

SA1891 Sch1

Any instrument whereby certain property is settled or agreed to be settled attracts duty @ 25p for every £100 or fractional part of £100 of property involved.

8.1.17 Companies' Capital Duty

FA73 s67-s75; FA79 s51; FA95 s145

This is a duty payable on the issue of, or increase in a capital company's share capital and on certain other transactions. The rate of duty is 1% of the actual value of the new assets contributed to a company in consideration of the issue of shares, provided that the minimum amount on which the duty is payable is the nominal value of the shares allotted. The duty is payable where, at the date of a transaction or as a result thereof, the effective centre of management or the registered office of the capital company is in the State. Any scrip issue of shares does not give rise to liability and a deduction may be claimed against the amount of capital duty payable in respect of a sum proportionate to the duty already paid (if any) on the nominal share capital of the company.

The definition of a capital company is extremely wide, but the most usual type of body falling within the definition is a limited company incorporated in a member state of the EU or a company whose shares can be dealt in on a stock exchange.

Chapter 8

FA73 s72;
FA79 s52;
FA90 s119

Certain reconstructions and amalgamations of companies involving the issue of shares in one company to the shareholders in another company attract a zero rate of duty. The conditions to be satisfied are:

(a) Both companies must be capital companies. (The relief is however available in a situation where the body being acquired is considered to be a capital company in another member state of the EU notwithstanding that it might not be so regarded in this State).

(b) Either the effective centre of management or the registered office of the target company must be in a member state of the EU.

(c) After completion of the transaction the acquiring company must own at least 75% of the issued share capital of the target company.

(d) The consideration for the acquisition must consist of the issue of shares in the acquiring company with or without a payment in cash so long as the payment in cash does not exceed 10% of the nominal value of the shares issued in the acquiring company.

(e) The acquiring company must retain for five years all the shares which it held after the transaction in the target company and, for the duration of that period, these must comprise at least 75% of the issued share capital of the target company. Exceptions to this rule are:

  (i) The liquidation of the acquiring company.

  (ii) A transfer of the shares in the target company forming part of a transaction which would, of itself, qualify for relief from capital duty.

Where the acquiring company issues shares to another company as consideration for the undertaking of that company the same relief from duty applies provided that conditions broadly similarly to those mentioned above are fulfilled.

8.1.18 Levy on Section 84 Loans

FA86 s94

Section 94, Finance Act 1986 imposes by way of stamp duty a levy on interest arising from Section 84 loans. The duty is charged at the rate of 12% on statements showing the amount of interest which must be furnished to the Revenue Commissioners half-yearly.

8.1.19 Ad Valorem Duty - Exceptions

FA65 s31;
FA89 s70
FA90 s117;
FA95 s144;
FA96 s116

The following transfers are exceptions to the general rule relating to the charge to ad valorem duty.

(a) Transfers on Delivery - The property in chattels, eg stock in trade, plant and machinery (other than fixed plant and machinery), motor vehicles, cash, bank balances, generally passes by delivery without documentation. Accordingly no liability to stamp duty arises if there is no documentation. If the chattels, however, form part of a larger transaction with other property which is liable to duty on conveyance it is aggregated with the other property for the purpose of determining the rate of duty which applies to the conveyance of that other property. If the chattels are included in the conveyance, they are liable to stamp duty. Under Section 59, Stamp Act 1891, certain chattels are liable to stamp duty at contract stage if included in a contract for sale.

(b) Liquidations - Transfers on liquidation of a company where the shareholders receive distributions in specie of the property of the company involve duty of £5.

(c) Reconstructions and Amalgamations - Certain reconstructions and amalgamations of companies involving the transfer of shares in one company to another attract a zero rate of duty. The conditions to be satisfied are:

   (i) There must be a scheme of reconstruction or amalgamation effected for bona fide commercial reasons and not having as a main purpose the avoidance of tax.

   (ii) The acquiring company must be a limited company.

   (iii) The acquiring company must issue new shares in exchange for 90% or more of the shares in the target company.

   (iv) The shares being issued in the acquiring company must represent at least 90% of the value of the shares in the target company.

   (v) The acquiring company must retain its beneficial ownership of the shares in the target company for at least two years unless it loses this as a result of a reconstruction, amalgamation or liquidation.

   (vi) The relief applies where the acquiring company is registered in the State or in another EU State, while the target company may be registered anywhere in the world.

   (vii) Adjudication by the Revenue Commissioners is necessary within 12 months of the transaction.

Chapter 8

The same relief from duty applies where the undertaking of one company is transferred to another provided that, in general, similar conditions are fulfilled.

8.1.20   Fixed Rate of Duty

The following are examples of the main items to which a fixed rate of duty applies:

Bill of exchange, cheque or promissory note drawn in the State.	7p
Appointment of a new trustee	£10
Declaration of trust	£10
Revocation of trust	£10
Life insurance policies for less than 2 years	£10
Conveyance or transfer not specifically charged and relating to Irish immovable property and marketable securities.	£10
Duplicate or counterpart of any instrument chargeable (max)	£10
Surrender of any property, or of any right or interest in any property not chargeable with duty as a conveyance on sale or a mortgage	£10

8.1.21   Young Farmers

FA94 s112; FA97 s126

Relief by way of a two thirds reduction in the duty payable will be granted as respects instruments executed in the period 7 January 1994 to 31 December 1999. The features of this relief are as follows:-

(a) The relief applies in respect of stamp duty on the transfer of agricultural land (including buildings) to young trained farmers.

(b) The relief applies to sales and gifts where no power of revocation exists.

(c) A young trained farmer is a person under 35 years of age at the date of transfer who meets certain training requirements.

(d) The instrument of transfer must contain a certificate stating that the provisions of the section apply.

(e) The young trained farmer must furnish a written declaration to the Revenue Commissioners confirming that for a period of 5 years after the date of transfer he intends to spend not less than 50% of his normal working time in farming the land and that he will retain ownership of the land.

Stamp Duties

(f) Where all the training conditions have not been satisfied at the date of transfer it is possible to apply for a refund of stamp duty paid provided the conditions are satisfied within 3 years of the date of execution of the instrument.

(g) The Revenue Commissioners must adjudicate all instruments where relief is claimed.

(h) The Revenue Commissioners have power to claw back the relief if the land is disposed of within the 5 year period and is not replaced within 1 year with other agricultural land.

8.1.22 Transfer on Divorce

There is a total stamp duty exemption for transfers between spouses. This section incorporates into the Finance Act, provisions already included in the Family Law Act 1995 and the Family Law (Divorce) Act 1996. These provide that where under any order of the Family Law or Family Law Divorce Acts, property is transferred on the dissolution of a marriage, the stamp duty exemption applies.

However, this exemption will not apply where the property, although transferred under a Family Law Order, is conveyed to a person other than one of the parties to the marriage. Thus transfers to children are not exempt.

8.1.23 Exemptions from Stamp Duties - General

FA79 s50

FA90 s114;
FA90 s120;
FA91 s93;
FA92 PtIV;
FA93 s101

FA93 s106;
FA94 s105;
FA94 s106

FA94 s111;
FA95 s148

FA95 s150;
FA96 s111

FA96 s116
FA99 s141

(a) Transfer of shares in

    (i) Irish Government or Oireachtas stocks, the payment of the interest on which is guaranteed by the Minister for Finance, or any loan stock of the ESB, RTE, ICC plc, Bord Telecom Eireann, Bord Gais Eireann or Irish Tele- communications plc, where the interest is not so guaranteed.

    (ii) UK Government stocks which are registered in the books of the Bank of Ireland in Dublin.

    (iii) Transfers of stocks or securities to which S92 FA 1973 applies.

(b) Instruments for the sale or transfer either absolutely or by way of mortgages of ships or aircraft.

(c) Wills.

(d) Sales of certain new houses and apartments up to 125 sq metres in size.

(e) Bills of exchange (including cheques) and promissory notes drawn outside the State.

(f) Conveyances, transfers or leases of land and houses for charitable purposes in Ireland to bodies of persons or trusts which have been established for charitable purposes only.

(g) Transfers between spouses whether separately or jointly except in sub-sale situations.

(h) Any instrument under which any land, easement, way-leave, water right or other right whatsoever over or in respect of the land or water is acquired by the Dublin Docklands Development Authority.

(i) Instruments securing the advancement of moneys by the Housing Finance Agency plc to housing authorities.

(j) Leases for an indefinite period or any term not exceeding 35 years, of any dwelling house, part of a dwelling house or apartment at a rent not exceeding £6,000 per annum.

(k) Commercial woodlands where such woodlands are sold or leased with land. (Stamp Duty applies to the land.)

(l) A licence or a lease granted by the Minister for Energy in respect of oil exploration or the sale, assignment or transfer of any such licence or lease or any right or interest therein.

(m) Conveyance or transfer of units in a collective investment undertaking and units in certain unit trusts.

(n) Conveyance or transfer of stocks or marketable securities of a company which is not registered in the State provided that such conveyance does not relate to:

   (i) any immovable property situated in the State, or any right over or interest in such property, or

   (ii) any stocks or marketable securities of a company having a register in the State.

(o) Certain instruments used predominantly in the financial services industry including the following:-

   (i) a debt factoring agreement.

   (ii) a swap agreement.

   (iii) a forward agreement.

   (iv) a financial futures agreement.

   (v) an option agreement.

   (vi) a combination of any two or more of the instruments specified under (i) to (v) above.

   (vii) a transfer of, or agreement to transfer, any instruments specified under (i) to (v) above or a combination of any two or more such instruments or an American depositary receipt.

(p) Foreign immovable property provided the instrument of transfer does not relate to Irish immovable property or shares.

(q) Instruments executed by or on behalf of the National Treasury Management Agency and similar instruments executed by or on behalf of the Minister for Finance.

(r) Instruments relating to the acquisition of property in the Temple Bar area by Temple Bar Properties Limited or any of its subsidiaries.

(s) Shared ownership leases of houses and for any subsequent instrument whereby the lessee acquires the remaining interest of the lessor in the property. The shared ownership lease must have been granted by an "appropriate person" as defined.

(t) The issue and transfer of specified categories of marketable debt instruments including certain types of corporate bonds and mortgage backed securities.

(u) Transfers of foreign government securities.

(v) Certain transfers of unquoted loan stock.

(w) Certain stock borrowing and stock return transactions.

(x) The transfer, sale or assignment of mortgages by a housing authority to a designated body or the transfer of securities issued by a designated body.

8.1.24 Appeals

FA94 s109
FA99 s173
FA99 s174

Up to the date of passing of the 1994 Finance Act any person aggrieved by a decision or determination of the Revenue Commissioners, had the right to appeal to the Appeal Commissioners, High Court or Property Arbitrators depending on the circumstances. As regards instruments executed after 23 May 1994 appeal provisions similar to those which apply for income tax apply for stamp duty purposes (See page 46). In the case of appeals against the value of land, these are heard by the Land Values Reference Committee

8.1.25 Payment of Stamp Duty on Instruments

FA90 s113;
FA94 s108

This section enables the Revenue Commissioners to enter into agreements at their discretion for the payment of stamp duty under an agreement whereby, at regular intervals, stamp duty is paid in one sum equal to the total duty which would have been payable had each instrument been stamped individually. The 1994 Finance Act confirms that the duty is payable on the VAT exclusive consideration in the case of a conveyance, transfer or lease of property.

8.1.26 Interest

FA98 s124

The 1998 Finance Act amends with effect from 1 April 1998 the following rates of interest:-

(a) payable on overdue capital duty and stamp duty - reduction from 1.25% to 1.0% per month.

(b) payable on refunds of companies capital duty - reduction from 9% per annum to 6% per annum.

(c) payable on refunds of stamp duty under Section 112, Finance Act 1990 - reduction from 1% per month to 0.5% per month.

CHAPTER 9 VALUE ADDED TAX

9.1 VALUE ADDED TAX

9.1.1 Legislation

The principal pieces of Irish legislation governing the value added tax system are as follows:-

Value Added Tax Act 1972 (Principal Act) - PA

Value Added Tax (Amendment) Act 1978 - VAT (A)A

Value Added Tax Regulations - R

Significant changes were included in Part III of the 1992 and 1993 Finance Acts to reflect the establishment of the Single Market within the European Union and the abolition with effect from 1 January 1993 of frontier checks and controls on trade between the Member States of the Union.

9.1.2 European Union Directives

The EU Council issues VAT Directives to the Member States and the Member States must modify their VAT legislation accordingly. EU law takes precedence in the event of an inconsistency. The most important Directives are the Sixth, Seventh and Eight VAT Directives and the Second Simplification Directive.

9.1.3 Charge

PA s2;
VAT(A)A s3;
PA s8;
FA94 s94;
FA95 s124

Value added tax is chargeable on the supply of goods and services within the State by a taxable person in the course or furtherance of any business carried on by him, and on goods imported into the State from outside the EU. Taxable persons account for VAT on their outputs and they are allowed credit against this liability for tax borne on business purchases and other inputs as evidenced by correctly prepared VAT invoices. Taxable persons must be registered with the Revenue Commissioners for VAT purposes. A detailed definition of "taxable person" is included in Section 8 of the Value Added Tax Act 1972 as amended.

9.1.4 Supply and Self Supply of Goods

PA s3
VAT(A)A s4;
FA89 s54
FA92 s167;
FA95 s120

The term "supply" includes:

(a) The transfer of ownership of the goods by agreement, whether or not accompanied by a transfer of possession.

(b) The handing over of possession of goods under a hire purchase contract. In the case of repossessed goods VAT is chargeable on their resale only where the original customer was entitled to an input credit.

FA96 s89
(c) The sale of movable goods pursuant to a contract under which commission is payable on purchase or sale by an agent or auctioneer who concludes agreements in his own name but for the account of another.

(d) Compulsory acquisition or statutory seizure.

(e) The application by a taxable person for the purpose of any business carried on by him of goods which he has acquired, except where a full input credit would be allowable to him in respect of the application of the goods.

(f) The appropriation by a taxable person of goods, on which an input credit was wholly or partly deductible, for a non business purpose, or the disposal of such goods free of charge.

(g) Intra-Community transfers (with certain exceptions).

(h) Where a liquidator, receiver or trustee in bankruptcy sells business assets in satisfaction of a debt of a taxable person or in the course of the winding up of a company, the sale is deemed to be a supply of goods by the taxable person in the course of business.

9.1.5 Amount on which Tax is Chargeable

PA s10;
FA95 s125;
FA97 s102
FA99 s124

Broadly speaking this is the total consideration which the person becomes entitled to receive in respect of a supply of goods or services, including all taxes, commissions, costs and charges whatsoever, but not including VAT chargeable in respect of the supply. The main exception to this relates to certain supplies of immovable goods. The 1995 Finance Act prohibits the deduction for the trade-in value of goods received in exchange which had applied heretofore. It also provides that the taxable amount of goods sold under a hire purchase agreement is the open market price of the goods or the total amount received by the person supplying the goods, whichever is the greater. The 1997 Finance Act provides that a person who gives a reduction or discount to a customer cannot adjust his VAT liability until a proper VAT credit note has been issued to the customer. It also provides that where goods are exchanged for vouchers, the sum on which VAT is chargeable is the sum actually received on the sale of the vouchers, regardless of their face value.

The 1999 Finance Act provides that, in accordance with the Sixth VAT Directive, tax should be based on cost price rather than open market price for certain transfers of goods to other Member States. It also provides that cost price should be used to establish the tax due in the case of certain intra-community acquisitions following transfers in other EU countries.

Value Added Tax

9.1.6	**Intra-Community Acquisitions – Registered Persons**
FA95 s121; PA s3A; FA97 s97	Where a trader who is registered for VAT in Ireland makes an intra-community acquisition from a trader in another Member State, the VAT implications are as follows:-

    (i) the goods are liable in Ireland to tax on the intra-community acquisition at the VAT rate applicable here;

    (ii) the VAT payable is accounted for through the normal periodic VAT return, and

    (iii) the tax payable is simultaneously deductible.

    (iv) Where goods have been subject to VAT under the margin scheme, the auction scheme or the special scheme for second-hand means of transport in another Member State, they are not treated as an intra-community acquisition on arrival in the State and are not subject to Irish VAT, unless re-sold.

9.1.7   Intra-Community Acquisitions – Unregistered Persons

Traders who make an intra-community acquisition but who are not registered for VAT in Ireland because their turnover is below the registration threshold are not taxable in the State if the annual value of their intra-Community acquisitions remains below £32,000. Instead, VAT is payable in the Member State of purchase (ie the country of origin) at the VAT rate applicable there. Where the threshold in respect of intra-Community acquisitions is exceeded, the trader must register for VAT in the State and will then be covered by the system already described in the preceding paragraph.

9.1.8   Non-Taxable Entities

In relation to non-taxable entities such as Government Departments or exempt businesses such as insurance companies or banks that acquire goods in other Member States, an intra-Community acquisition arises. As in the case of small traders, such intra-Community acquisitions are not taxable in Ireland if the annual value of acquisitions remains below the £32,000 threshold already referred to above. VAT is instead payable in the Member State where the goods were purchased at the VAT rate applicable there. Where a non-taxable entity or exempt business exceeds the intra-Community acquisition threshold, it must register for VAT and is liable to tax in Ireland on its intra-Community acquisitions.

9.1.9   Private Individuals

As regards goods purchased by individuals in other Member States (other than a new means of transport or purchasing goods by way of mail order or distance selling) VAT is payable in the Member State of purchase at the rate of VAT applicable there and no intra-Community acquisition arises. Private individuals are therefore free to purchase goods at VAT-inclusive prices in other Member States and are not liable to an additional Irish VAT charge provided the purchases are for personal and not business use.

9.1.10   New Means of Transport

The intra-Community acquisition of new means of transport (including motor vehicles, boats and aircraft) is always taxable in the Member State of arrival. Special arrangements apply in respect of the payment of VAT on new means of transport acquired by private individuals or by traders not entitled to a deduction. A transfer by an entity in the State to the territory of another Member State is an intra-Community supply.

9.1.11   Mail Order and Distance Selling

A new rule has been introduced regarding the place of supply in the case of mail order and distance selling (ie where the supplier arranges for the goods purchased to be transported to a private individual or to any other non-taxable person in another Member State). Where a mail order or any other type of distance selling business, located in another Member State, sells goods with a value in excess of £27,515 in Ireland in any one year, the goods are taxable in Ireland rather than in the Member State where the seller is located and the seller is obliged to register and to account for VAT in Ireland.

9.1.12   Supplies by VAT-Registered Traders in Ireland

Where a taxable person in the State supplies goods to a VAT-registered trader in another Member State, the supply is zero-rated in Ireland and is liable to VAT as an intra-Community acquisition in the other Member State. However, the Irish supplier must ensure the purchaser in the other Member State is registered for VAT before zero-rating the supply of goods.

9.1.13   Telecommunications Services

FA97 s99

Significant changes are included in the 1997 Finance Act. These came into force on 1 July 1997 and their effects are as follows:-

(a) A user, other than a private individual, purchasing telecommunications services from outside the EU, must self-account for and pay the VAT on those services.

(b) The same applies where a user, other than a private individual, purchases the services from another member state.

(c) Where a non-EU service provider supplies services to private individuals in the State, the service provider must register for VAT here.

Value Added Tax

9.1.14 Transfer of Business

PA s3;
FA91 s75;
FA98 s105

The transfer of ownership of goods in connection with the transfer of a business or part of a business to another taxable person is not a supply of goods, and therefore, no VAT is payable on such a transfer. If, however, the goods are diverted to non-business use, this is treated as a self-supply. A deduction is allowed in respect of VAT borne on services (eg auctioneer's fees) directly related to the transfer of a business from one taxable person to another.

9.1.15 Taxable Periods

PA s1

Taxable persons must make returns and payment of VAT between the 10th and 19th days following the end of a taxable period. Each taxable period is a period of two months beginning on the 1st day of January, March, May, July, September or November. Failure to make the returns and payments can give rise to interest charges and/or penalties. If the aggregate of deductible inputs exceeds the VAT payable on outputs for a taxable period the Revenue Commissioners will make a repayment of the excess.

9.1.16 Annual Accounting for VAT

PA s10;
FA89 s58;
FA95 s134

Section 58, Finance Act, 1989 enables the Collector General to authorise persons to make an annual VAT Return and pay their VAT on an annual basis. The features of this provision are as follows:

(a) The Collector General may determine that Returns be submitted for any number of taxable periods not exceeding 6.

(b) The taxable person may continue to operate VAT on a two-monthly basis if he so wishes.

(c) The period covered by the authorisation is defined as the accounting period.

(d) VAT Returns and payment must be submitted between the 10th and 19th days of the month following the end of the accounting period.

(e) The Collector General must consider certain factors before issuing an authorisation, and the authorisation may be issued conditionally or unconditionally.

(f) The Collector General may terminate the authorisation, having taken account of certain factors.

(g) The taxable person has the option to align the date of his annual VAT Return with his commercial accounting period.

(h) There are provisions for a deemed termination of authorisation on cessation of trading, or liquidation, bankruptcy or death of the taxable person as appropriate.

(i) Where the deemed termination arises on the death of a taxable person, his personal representative is deemed to be the taxable person.

9.1.17 Tax Deductible

PA s12;
FA94 s96;
FA95 s129;
FA98 s106
FA99 s128

Provided that the goods and services to which such tax relates are used for the purpose of the taxable supply of goods and services, or for the purposes of qualifying activities abroad, VAT paid on the following inputs is deductible in computing liability.

(a) Tax charged to a taxable person by other taxable persons on supplies of goods and services to him

(b) Tax paid or payable by the taxable person on goods imported by him.

(c) Tax payable on self supplies of goods or services.

(d) Tax payable on purchases from flat rate farmers.

(e) Tax on imported Fourth Schedule services.

(f) Residual VAT in relation to a supply of second-hand means of transport or agricultural machinery.

(g) Tax payable by a lessee in accordance with the provisions of Section 93, Finance Act 1994.

(h) Tax payable on certain purchases of second hand goods as provided in Regulations.

(i) Tax payable on the intra-community acquisition of goods.

(j) Where not previously allowed, any residual VAT contained in the value of goods transferred from a branch of a business within the State to a branch of the same business in another member State.

(k) Post-letting expenses of a landlord who has made a long lease of commercial property.

9.1.18 Margin Scheme

FA95 s126
FA99 s125

The Seventh VAT Directive includes measures for the elimination of double taxation in relation to the sale of second-hand movable goods, works of art, collectors items and antiques. The margin scheme allows a dealer to account for VAT on resale of the goods, on his profit margin at the appropriate rate of VAT. This scheme is optional. Agricultural machinery which benefits from the new special scheme for agricultural machinery is excluded from the margin scheme.

9.1.19 Agricultural Machinery

FA99 s131

A new scheme for agricultural machinery will come into effect from 1 September 1999. It provides that where a dealer in agricultural machinery buys machinery from an unregistered farmer the dealer can claim back the residual VAT contained in the price.

9.1.20 Auction Scheme

FA95 s127

A scheme similar to the margin scheme has been introduced for auctioneers where the auctioneer's commission is the basis for calculating the profit margin.

9.1.21 Second-Hand Means of Transport

FA95 s130

A taxable dealer may claim a deduction for "residual VAT" where he purchases or acquires second-hand means of transport from certain categories of persons - broadly those not in a position to supply a VAT invoice.

9.1.22 Tax Not Deductible

VAT(A)A s10;
FA87 s41;
FA95 s129

No deduction is allowed in respect of tax paid on expenditure on the following:

(a) The provision of food, drink, accommodation or other personal services supplied to the taxable person, his agent, or his employees.

(b) Entertainment expenses incurred by the taxable person, his agent or his employees.

(c) The acquisitions, hiring or leasing of motor vehicles other than as stock in trade or for the purposes of a business which consists in whole or part of the hiring of motor vehicles or for use in a driving school business for giving instruction.

(d) The purchase of petrol otherwise than as stock in trade.

(e) Expenditure incurred on food, drink, accommodation or other entertainment services as part of an advertising service is not deductible in the hands of the person providing that advertising service.

(f) Any VAT incurred by a taxable person in a transaction where the margin or auction schemes apply.

9.1.23 Bad Debts

PA s10;
FA94 s95

Sub-Section 3(c) of Section 10, PA provides for relief from VAT for bad debts incurred. An amendment contained in the 1994 Finance Act removes the relief where the bad debt occurs in the case of the long-term letting of immovable goods. This operates with effect from 23 May 1994.

Chapter 9

9.1.24   **Place where Goods Supplied**

PA s3

The place where goods (other than goods sold by mail order or distance selling) are supplied is deemed to be:

(a) Where the supply requires their transportation, the place where the transportation begins.

(b) In any other case the place where the goods are located at the time of the supply.

(c) With effect from 1 January 1993 in the case of the intra-community acquisition of goods, where the dispatch or transportation ends. This is modified, however, so that where the person acquiring the goods quotes his VAT registered number the acquisition is deemed to be within the territory of the Member State which issued that number.

9.1.25   **Place where Services Supplied**

PA s5;
FA95 s123;
FA97 s99
FA99 s121

In general the place of supply of services is where the business of the supplier of the services is located or where he has his fixed establishment. Problems can arise, however, in the case of the supply of international services and the following are general guidelines in this regard.

Immovable Goods - The place where services connected with immovable property are supplied is the place where the property is situated.

Transport Services - These are deemed to be supplied where the transport takes place. The 1992 Finance Act, however, amended the position relating to intra-community goods transport services. The changes provided that, where a customer is registered for VAT, supplies of intra-Community goods transport and related ancillary and agency services are treated as being supplied in the Member State of issue of the customer's VAT number.

Where a customer is not registered for VAT, the place of supply is deemed to be the place of departure in the case of transport and transport agency services and the place where the services are physically performed as regards ancillary services and associated agency services.

Telecommunications Services - These are deemed to be supplied in the State in cases where they are supplied to private individuals in the State by non-EU suppliers

Means of Transpot – where a means of transport, supplied by a lessor in Ireland is used outside the EU, the place of supply is deemed to be outside the EU.

VAT(A)A s27

"Fourth Schedule" Services - These include advertising services, consultancy, legal and accounting services, data processing services, banking, financial and insurance services, the provision of staff, transfers and assignments of copyright patents, licences, trade marks and similar rights, hiring out of movable goods (other than means of transport) and telecommunication services. There are complicated provisions determining the place of supply of these services and this will vary according to the place of residence or establishment of the customer and according as to whether or not the services are supplied for business purposes (See Chart 27). It should be noted that any person within the State acquiring a Fourth Schedule Service for business purposes from a foreign supplier is chargeable to Irish VAT as if he himself had supplied the service to another person. The amount on which the tax is payable is the consideration for the service supplied. Such tax is available for deduction, as a tax borne on inputs in the normal way. Although vehicle leasing is not a Fourth Schedule Service, an Irish trader leasing a vehicle from a foreign supplier will be chargeable to Irish VAT as if he himself had supplied the service to another person. These provisions will apply in situations where no VAT is effectively payable in the supplier's country.

9.1.26 Rates

VAT(A)A s9

Exempt - Details are set out in the First Schedule to the Principal Act (See Chart 28). Those carrying on exempted activities cannot, with some minor exceptions, register for VAT.

Zero Rate - Details of goods and services taxable at this rate are set out in the Second Schedule to the Principal Act (See Chart 29).

4% Rate - This rate applies to livestock which includes live cattle, sheep, pigs, goats, deer, horses and greyhounds.

10% Rate - Details of goods and services taxable at this rate are set out in the Third Schedule to the Principal Act (See Chart 30).

12.5% Rate - Details of goods and services taxable at this rate are set out in the Sixth and Eight Schedules to the Principal Act (See Chart 31).

21% Rate - All goods and services which do not fall into the categories mentioned above are liable to VAT at this rate (see Chart 32).

9.1.27 Immovable Goods

PA s4;
VAT(A)A s8;
FA95 s122

Certain activities involving immovable goods (land and buildings together with all fixtures attached thereto) are liable to VAT at 12.5%. This rate applies in cases where the value of any movable goods supplied as part of the contract does not exceed 2/3 of the full contract price.

Chapter 9

VAT(A)A s10
FA95 s122;
FA97 s98

The activities involved are as follows:

(a) The development of land including drainage and reclamation, the installation of fixtures in building and the repair and decoration of buildings in the course of business.

(b) The development of land or buildings and the disposal of a freehold interest in them.

(c) The granting of a lease of land or building for a period of at least 10 years or the disposal of a leasehold interest under a lease which, at the time it was created, was for a term of at least 10 years (or if less than 10 years contained an option to extend it to 10 years or more).

(d) The disposal of an undeveloped site in connection with which another taxable person enters into a contract with the purchaser to carry out development in relation to the site.

R19
FA94 s93

It should be noted that the activities mentioned at (b) and (c) above do not attract liability to VAT unless all of the following conditions are satisfied:

(i) The property must have been developed wholly or partly after 31 October 1972.

(ii) The vendor must have disposed of a taxable interest in the course of business. Such an interest would be either the freehold or leasehold interest mentioned at (b) or (c) above.

(iii) The vendor must have been entitled to a tax credit in respect of any tax suffered on the development of the property or on the acquisition of his interest in the property.

Where the activity involves the granting of a lease of land or buildings for a period of at least 10 years VAT is payable on the capitalised value of the rent reserved. In making this calculation it is open to the tax payer to provide evidence of what the value should be. In the absence of such evidence leases under which the rent cannot be increased earlier than the end of the fifth year after the interest was created are valued at the lower of the amounts arrived at by the following formulae

(i)
$$R \times \frac{3}{4} \times N \quad \text{where}$$

R = The annual amount of the rent

N = The number of complete years for which the rent has been created

(ii)
$$R \times \frac{100}{Y} \quad \text{where}$$

R = The annual amount of the rent.

Y = The yield to redemption on the last Government security issued before the creation of the rent for subscription in the State and which is redeemable not less than five years after the date of issue.

Where a person creates a lease of ten to twenty years he is disposing of his interest for the period of the lease but retaining his right of reversion at the end of the period. This gives two elements to the transactions as follows:

(a) The creation of the lease, any VAT on which will be chargeable to the tenant.

(b) The retention of the reversion, any VAT on which is a self-supply to the landlord and is irrecoverable.

Section 93 Finance Act 1994 provides that, subject to approval by the Revenue Commissioners, where the lessee is entitled to a repayment of all the VAT charged it will not be necessary for the lessor to charge VAT on the capitalised value of the lease. Instead, the lessee will be liable to pay the tax as if he had supplied the goods in the course or furtherance of business and he will also be in a position to claim a simultaneous input credit, thus removing the need to finance the VAT charge. A joint application for this treatment, if required, must be supplied by the lessor and lessee along with such further information as may be required by the Commissioners. Where approval has been received from the Commissioners the invoice issued by the lessor must include an endorsement specifying the lessee's accountability for the VAT liability arising on the transaction. This provision has effect from 7 July 1995.

1997 Finance Act Provisions

FA97 s96, s98, s102

Detailed amendments to the provisions on the taxation of leasehold interests are included in the 1997 Finance Act and came into effect on 26 March 1997. The main amendments are summarised as follows:

(a) The definition of the disposal of a leasehold interest is extended to include a surrender or assignment of a lease.

(b) The surrender or assignment of a lease will be valued in the same way as the creation of a lease, ie the capitalised value of the lease is added to any sum payable on the surrender or assignment of the lease.

(c) A surrendered or assigned lease is taxable in the hands of the new leaseholder ("reverse charge"). This applies where the new leaseholders are taxable persons, the State or local authorities and most exempt persons. It does not apply to private individuals nor to those involved in the medical, dental, educational and sporting fields. Taxable persons are entitled to an input credit for the tax paid.

(d) To avoid the possibility of lease values being reduced artificially it is specified that rental values for the purposes of calculating the capitalised value of a lease are to be based on the unencumbered open market rents.

Chapter 9

VAT(A)A s24;
FA97 s101

Rents receivable under leasehold interests which when created, are for a term of less than 10 years are not liable to VAT unless the recipient elects to be taxable. If he so elects he becomes taxable on all rents which in the absence of such election would have been exempt. An exception to this treatment arises where under the 1997 Finance Act amendments a short term letting follows the taxable surrender of a leasehold interest. It is possible to waive the exemption in this situation without affecting the exempt status of other rents. A further amendment contained in the 1997 Finance Act provides that where a person cancels his election, there is a claw-back of input credits to the extent that the input credits exceed the VAT charged on the rents. Rents receivable from the following activities are always liable to VAT:

(a) Letting of machinery or business installations when let separately from any other immovable goods of which such machinery or installations form part.

(b) Letting in the course of carrying on a hotel business.

(c) Provision of parking accommodation for vehicles by the operators of car parks.

(d) Hire of safes.

9.1.28 Option not to Register

VAT(A)A s6;
F(No 2)A81 s11

The following persons are not obliged to register for VAT unless they otherwise elect:

(a) A farmer (see definition below).

(b) A person whose supplies of taxable goods or services consist exclusively of the following

    (i) supplies to taxable persons of unprocessed fish caught by him in a sea fishing business, or

    (ii) supplies of the kind mentioned at (i) along with either or both of the following:

        (1) supplies of machinery, plant or equipment which have been used by him in the course of a sea fishing business, and

        (2) supplies of other goods and services the total consideration for which has not exceeded and is not likely to exceed £20,000 per annum.

(c) Persons whose receipts do not exceed £40,000 per annum, provided that 90% of their total receipts arises from the supply of taxable goods. This does not apply, however in the case of persons supplying goods chargeable at the 21% rate where these goods were produced or manufactured by the taxable person wholly or mainly from materials chargeable at the zero rate.

(d) Persons whose receipts do not exceed £20,000 per annum and to whom (a), (b) or (c) do not apply. Where two or more persons, one of whom controls one or more of the others, supply goods or services of a similar nature, the total consideration for such supplies will be aggregated to determine if the £20,000 exemption limit is exceeded.

9.1.29 Farmers

VAT(A)A s6

A farmer is defined as a person who engages in at least one Annex A Activity and whose supplies of taxable goods and services in the course of business consist exclusively of:

(a) Supplies of agricultural produce (ie goods produced by the farmer in the course of an Annex A Activity).

(b) Supplies of agricultural services (ie any Annex B Service supplied by the farmer with his own or his employees' labour and using his farm machinery) excluding insemination services, stock minding and stock rearing, the total consideration for which has not exceeded and is not likely to exceed £20,000 per annum.

(c) Supplies of agricultural services (i.e. any Annex B service supplied by the farmer with his own or his employees' labour and using his farm machinery) excluding insemination services, stock minding and stock rearing which, in addition to supplies by retail of horticultural produce and supplies of bovine semen, the total consideration for whcih has not exceeded and is not likely to exceed £20,000 per annum.

(d) Supplies of race horse training services the consideration for which has not exceeded and is not likely to exceed £20,000 per annum.

(e) Supplies of other goods and services the consideration for which has not exceeded and is not likely to exceed £20,000 per annum.

(f) Supplies by retail of horticultural produce or supplies of bovine semen or a combination of both, the total consideration for which has not exceeded and is not likely to exceed £40,000 per annum.

Annex A Activities - These relate to agricultural production activities such as crop production, stock farming and cultivation, forestry and fisheries. (See page 330 for further details).

Annex B Services - These relate to the supply of agricultural services which normally play a part in agricultural production. (See page 331 for further details.)

As stated above farmers are not obliged to register for VAT purposes.

9.1.30 Flat Rate Farmer

VAT(A)A s11

A flat rate farmer is a farmer who is not a taxable person. Where such a farmer supplies agricultural produce or agricultural services to a taxable person the taxable person is entitled to an input credit of 4% of the tax exclusive consideration for the supply. An invoice must be prepared by the taxable person showing the tax exclusive price and the VAT. The rate of 4% applies as and from 1 March 1999.

9.1.31 Farm Buildings, Land Reclamation and Land Drainage

PA s20

A flat rate farmer who has borne tax on expenditure on the construction or improvement of farm buildings or on land reclamation may reclaim the tax provided the expenditure qualifies for certain specified grants from the Department of Fisheries.

9.1.32 Repayments to Foreign Traders

PA s13;
FA98 s113

There are provisions for the repayment to such traders of tax borne on services supplied to them within the State and on goods purchased within the State or imported for business purposes. These provisions apply broadly speaking to a person who satisfies the Revenue Commissioners that he carries on business outside the State and that he supplies no goods or services within the State.

9.1.33 Retail Export Scheme

PA s13;
FA97 s106, s109, s111;
FA99 s132

Detailed provisions are contained in the VAT (Export of Goods) Regulations 1992 as amended by the 1997 Finance Act to allow for the zero-rating of goods purchased by non-EU visitors.

9.1.34 Supplies to certain Taxable Persons

FA93 s90;
FA95 s95

The 1993 Finance Act provided for the zero-rating of supplies to taxable persons whose output is mainly supplied to other EU states or exported out of the EU. A "qualifying person" is a taxable person whose turnover from supplies of goods (including certain contract work) either supplied outside the EU or dispatched or transported to a registered person in another EU state amounts to 75% of his total annual turnover from the supply of goods and services. The effect of this provision is that traders authorised for this purpose will no longer have to pay VAT to their suppliers and subsequently reclaim it from the Revenue Commissioners. Authorisation will be granted by the Revenue Commissioners on application by the appropriate persons and will be valid for a certain period only. An authorised person must notify the Revenue Commissioners if he is no longer a "qualifying person". The authorised person is obliged to provide a copy of the authorisation to all his suppliers in the State. This ensures that such suppliers will be aware of his authorised status. There is an obligation on the supplier in the State to quote the relevant authorisation number on the invoice on making a zero-rated supply.

9.1.35 Cash Basis

PA s14;
FA92 s177;
FA94 s97;
FA95 s131

With effect from 1 July 1994 the following have the option to account for VAT on the basis of cash received in a taxable period rather than on the basis of sales.

(a) A person who satisfies the Revenue Commissioners that taking one period with another, not less than 90% of his turnover is derived from taxable sales to unregistered persons.

(b) A person who satisfies the Revenue Commissioners that the total consideration which he is entitled to receive in respect of his taxable supplies has not exceeded and is not likely to exceed £250,000 in any continuous period of twelve months. The limit of £250,000 has been increased to £500,000 with effect from 1 July 1997.

9.1.36 Group Registration

VAT(A)A s6;
FA91 s79

Where the Revenue Commissioners are satisfied that it would be in the interests of efficient administration and that no loss of tax would be involved, they may treat a group of persons such as a number of interlinked companies, as a single taxable person. In these circumstances only one member of the group will submit VAT returns for the taxable period and such returns will cover the activities of all the members of the group. However all parties to the group registration are jointly and severally liable for all the VAT obligations of the other group members. In addition the necessity of issuing tax invoices in respect of inter-group transactions is avoided.

To qualify for group registration the Revenue Commissioners must be satisfied that:-

(1) The persons seeking the group registration are all established in the State.

(2) They are closely bound by financial, economic and organisational links.

(3) That it would be expedient in the interest of efficient administration of VAT to grant the group registration.

The granting of group registration is at the discretion of the Revenue Commissioners and there is no right of appeal. It should be noted that prior to the Finance Act 1991, group registration was at the

Chapter 9

request of the taxpayer. The Finance Act 1991 gives the Revenue the power to group register persons compulsorily.

Parties to a group registration do not have to be legally related and need not be taxable persons. The Finance Act 1991 provides that any person established in the State can be part of a group registration even where that person is engaged in the supply of non-taxable goods or services.

The Revenue Commissioners may defer payment of VAT where the business activities of one or more persons are so interlinked that group registration could be imposed and one or more of the persons has not made VAT returns or remitted VAT due.

9.1.37 Appeals

PA s25;
FA95 s137;
FA97 s109

Any person aggrieved by a determination of the Revenue Commissioners in relation to VAT may lodge an appeal against such a determination. The same rights attach to such an appeal as attach to appeals against income tax assessments. (See Page 46)

9.1.38 Bankruptcy and Winding Up

FA76 s62

Unpaid VAT is a preferential debt in cases of bankruptcy or company winding up. The tax which ranks as a preferential debt is confined to that due for taxable periods ending not more than 12 months before commencement of bankruptcy or winding up proceedings.

9.1.39 Unjust Enrichment

FA98 s114

S114 FA 1998 provides that a taxable person will be entitled to a refund of tax overpaid by him as a result of a mistaken assumption. This is subject to the person not being unjustly enriched by the refund. There are detailed provisions contained in the legislation concerning the question of what constitutes unjust enrichment.

9.1.40 Time Limits

FA98 s114
FA98 s115

The time limits for claiming refunds of VAT and for making an estimation or assessment by the Revenue are reduced from 10 years to 6 years.

9.1.41 Documentation

FA92 PtIII

Arising from the 1993 changes, certain VAT registered traders are required to complete the following returns and statements.

FA95 s132, s133

(i) Intrastat Return - to be completed monthly by any trader who imports more than £100,000 per annum from, or exports more than £500,000 per annum to, other EC Member States. (Commencement date 1 January 1993).

(ii) VIES – to be completed either quarterly or monthly by traders who export to a VAT registered trader in another EC Member State. (Commencement date 1 November 1992).

(iii) Upon request by an authorised officer a taxable person must give details to the Revenue Commissioners of any gifts or promotional items given in connection with taxable supplies and services.

Chapter 9

9.2   **ANNEX A ACTIVITIES**

I. Crop Production

1. General agriculture, including viticulture.
2. Growing of fruit (including olives) and of vegetables, flowers and ornamental plants both in the open and under glass.
3. Production of mushrooms, spices, seeds and propagating materials; nurseries.

II. Stock Farming together with cultivation

1. General stock farming
2. Poultry farming
3. Rabbit farming
4. Beekeeping
5. Silkworm farming
6. Snail farming

III. Forestry

IV. Fisheries

1. Fresh water fishing
2. Fish farming
3. Breeding of mussels, oysters and other molluscs and crustaceans
4. Frog Farming

V. Where a farmer processes using means normally employed in an agricultural, forestry or fisheries undertaking, products deriving essentially from his agricultural production, such processing shall be regarded as agricultural production.

9.3 ANNEX B SERVICES

Supplies of agricultural services which normally play a part in agricultural production shall be considered the supply of agricultural services, and include the following in particular:

- field work, reaping and mowing, threshing, baling, collecting, harvesting, sowing and planting

- packing and preparation for market, for example drying, cleaning, grinding, disinfecting and ensilage of agricultural products

- storage of agricultural products

- stock minding, rearing and fattening

- hiring out, for agricultural purposes, of equipment normally used in agricultural, forestry or fisheries undertakings

- technical assistance

- destruction of weeds and pests, dusting and spraying of crops and land

- operation of irrigation drainage equipment

- lopping, tree felling and other forestry services.

Chapter 9

CHAPTER 10   TAX AMNESTIES 1993

10.1 TAX AMNESTIES 1993

The Waiver of Certain Tax / Interest and Penalties Act 1993 provides for a main and a general amnesty.

10.1.1 Main Amnesty

The main amnesty covers income tax, sur-tax, capital gains tax, income levy, health contribution and employment and training levy, for the period up to and including 5 April 1991 which has not been paid by individuals (companies are excluded from the main amnesty).

Excluded from the scope of the main amnesty are:-

- Tax already at enforcement stage on 25 May 1993.
- Tax which had been under appeal at 25 May 1993.
- Tax on income and gains derived from illegal sources.
- Tax not paid by virtue of a tax avoidance scheme which would have been payable on or before 25 May 1993.
- Individuals under investigation in respect of tax liability up to and including 5 April 1991.

To qualify for the amnesty, the individual must, on or before 30 November 1993, give to a Chief Special Collector, a full declaration of the amounts coming within the terms of the amnesty and must then remit 15% of that amount to the Chief Special Collector by 14 January 1994. He must also declare that the amounts do not arise from any illegal source or activity.

The Chief Special Collector will issue a certificate of receipt.

The Revenue will be precluded from commencing an investigation into the tax liability of an individual for any period up to and including 5 April 1991 which is paid to the Chief Special Collector if the individual produces a certificate of receipt. An investigation may proceed if the declarations made to the Chief Special Collector are shown not to be full and true declarations.

The Special Collectors, who will administer the amnesty are precluded from disclosing any information obtained in the course of their duties.

10.1.2 General Amnesty

The general amnesty applies to all taxpayers and provides for an amnesty from the payment of interest in respect of arrears of certain taxes up to and including 5 April 1991.

The taxes in question are the same as those covered by the main amnesty plus PAYE, corporation tax, corporation profits tax, VAT, capital acquisitions tax, stamp duty and residential property tax. In order to avail of this amnesty, the full amount of tax arrears must be paid by 14 January 1994. Where arrears of VAT are being paid by an individual, who is availing of the main amnesty, the VAT may be remitted to the Chief Special Collector.

The benefits of both amnesties will be withdrawn if:-

- in the case of an individual, a correct return for 1992/93 is not submitted on time and for companies, a correct return for any accounting period ending in the year to 31 December 1993;
- a declaration given to the Chief Special Collector is found to be false;
- the amount remitted under the general amnesty was less than the full amount of arrears.

New penalties are provided for failure to comply with or abuse of the terms of the amnesty and for future non-compliance. An individual who abuses or ignores the amnesty by failure to make the appropriate declarations or by falsely making such declarations and who has failed to make returns or has submitted false returns for any years covered by the amnesty will be liable to specified penalties which will consist of financial penalties or terms of imprisonment or both.

The ability to mitigate certain fines and penalties is to be restricted. From now on, it will only be possible to remit penalties to the extent of 50%. In cases where the amnesty has been abused or ignored no mitigation will be allowed.

In certain circumstances, the Revenue Commissioners may obtain from financial institutions, details of the accounts and certain ancillary financial information of a taxpayer resident in the State. The circumstances are that:

- the taxpayer has filed a return and the Inspector feels that it is unsatisfactory;
- the Inspector has reasonable grounds to believe that the taxpayer has an undisclosed account or that the financial institution has information which would establish that the taxpayer's return is materially false;
- the Appeal Commissioners issue a determination that the Inspector is justified in seeking details of accounts held by the taxpayer with a financial institution.

APPENDIX IRISH TAX CASES, INDEX TO

1 IRISH TAX CASES, INDEX TO

The sources for the material included are as follows:

Reports of Irish Tax Cases - Vol. 1 (1.ITC)
Reports of Irish Tax Cases - Vol. 2 (2.ITC)
Reports of Irish Tax Cases - Vol. 3 (3.ITC)
Irish Tax Case Leaflets (ITL)
Unreported High Court (HC) and
Supreme Court (SC) Written Judgements

1.1 Appeals

Appeal Commissioner's right to change his decision	The State -v- M Smidic	2 ITC 188
Appellate Court - Function	Browne -v- Bank of Ireland Finance Ltd	SC 1991
Appeal to High Court	A & B -v- WJ Davis	2 ITC 350
Case stated	The State (Multiprint Label Systems) -v- Neylon	HC 1983
Judicial Review	Michael Wiley -v- Revenue Commissioners	HC 1989
Jurisdiction	Inspector of Taxes -v- Arida Limited	HC 1995
Mandamus	The King -v- Special Commissioners	1 ITC 227
Question of Law	O'Srianain -v- Lakeview Ltd	ITL 125
Rehearing of appeal from Special Commissioners	The King -v- Special Commissioners	1 ITC 71
Re opening of settled appeal	Bolands Ltd -v- CIR	1 ITC 42

1.2 Capital Acquisitions Tax

Settlement - persons becoming entitled in possession	Jacob -v- Revenue Commissioners	HC 1981
Valuation of shares in private company	Revenue Commissioners -v- Young	HC 1996

335

Appendix

1.3	**Capital Allowances**		
	Industrial Buildings	O'Conaill -v- Waterford Glass Ltd	HC 1982
		Patrick Monahan (Drogheda) Limited -v- O'Conaill	ITL 122
	Plant	Airspace Investments Ltd -v- Moore	HC 1994
		Breathnach -v- McCann	ITL 121
		Dunnes Stores (Oakville) Limited -v- M C Cronin	HC 1988
		O'Srianain -v- Lakeview Ltd	ITL 125
		O'Culachain -v- McMullan Bros	SC 1995
1.4	**Capital Gains Tax**		
	Agricultural use	JC McMahon -v- Albert N Murphy	HC 1988
	Avoidance	Patrick W McGrath -v- J E MacDermott	SC 1988
	Certificate of Exemption	The State -v- O'Ceallaigh	HC 1983
	Chargeable gain accruing after date of liquidation	Revenue Commissioners -v- Donnelly	SC 1981
	Clearance Certificate	The State (Melbarien Enterprises) -v- Revenue Commissioners	HC 1985
	Compulsory Acquisition	In re Heron	HC 1985
	Debt on a Security	Mooney -v- McSweeney	HC 1997
	"Rollover" Relief	EP O'Coindealbhain -v- Kieran N Price	HC 1988
1.5	**Case III**		
	Deduction for interest paid	WF Phillips -v- Limerick County Council	1 ITC 96
	Double Tax relief on U.K. employment	Travers -v- O'Siochain	HC 1994
	Foreign trade	M O'Conaill -v- R	3 ITC 167
	Payment on signing of lease of United Kingdom property	JM O'Sullivan -v- P Ltd	3 ITC 355
	Pension from UK Company	T McHugh -v- A	3 ITC 355
		M P Cronin -v- C	ITL 106

Pension under British National Insurance Act	MJ Forbes -v- GH Dundon	3 ITC 365
Remittances arising from compulsory sale of dollar balances to the State	JM O'Sullivan -v- Administratrix of Evelyn H O'Brien (Dec)	2 ITC 352
Transfer of assets to son	G Hewson -v- JB Kealy	2 ITC 286
Wife's income - basis of assessment	JD Mulvey -v- RM Kieran	2 ITC 179

1.6 Corporation Profits Tax

Accounting Period	Revenue Commissioners -v- R Hilliard & Sons Ltd	2 ITC 410
Building society business	Property Loan and Investment Company Limited -v- Revenue Commissioners	2 ITC 312
"Business" for purposes of CPT	City of Dublin Steam Packet Company -v- Revenue Commissioners	1 ITC 118
"Company" for purposes of CPT	CIR -v- Bank of Ireland	1 ITC 74
Control of company	Associated Properties Ltd -v- Revenue Commissioners	3 ITC 25
Distribution of profits precluded by constitution	TJ Wilson -v- Dunnes Stores (Cork) Ltd	HC 1974
Dividend received from another company	Kellystown Company -v- Hogan	HC 1982
Excess CPT	Revenue Commissioners -v- Orwell Ltd	3 ITC 93
	Revenue Commissioners -v- Switzer Limited	2 ITC 290
Interest to person in control	Revenue Commissioners -v- Associated Properties Ltd	3 ITC 293
Irish Profits of foreign company	Cunard Steam Ship Company Limited -v- J Herlihy	1 ITC 373
Liquidation - CPT on company in	City of Dublin Steam Packet Company (in liquidation) -v- Revenue Commissioners	1 ITC 285
Mutual trading	JP Kennedy -v- Rattoo Coop Dairy Society Limited	1 ITC 282
	Revenue Commissioners -v- Y Ltd	3 ITC 49

Appendix

	"Railway" company exemption	Great Southern Railways Company -v- Revenue Commissioners	1 ITC 298
	"Trade" business or similar	CIR -v- Dublin & Kingstown Railway Company	1 ITC 131
1.7	**Corporation Tax**		
	Associated company	Bairead -v- Maxwells of Donegal Limited	ITL 134
	Double Taxation Agreement	Murphy -v- Asahi Synthetic Fibres (Ireland) Limited	HC 1985
	Exchange Losses	Brosnan -v- Mutual Enterprises Ltd.	HC 1995
	Income of Branch	Murphy -v- Data Products (Dublin) Ltd	HC 1988
	Interest on repayment of tax	Navan Carpets Limited -v- O'Culachain	HC 1987
	Management services provided gratis	Belville Holdings -v- Cronin	HC 1984
	Overpayment - Interest on	Texaco (Ireland) Ltd -v- Murphy	SC 1992
1.8	**Dispositions, Estates, Trusts**		
	Appointment by parent in favour of child	EG -v- PT MacSamhrain	3 ITC 217
	Disposition of income - deed of trust in favour of charitable object	HPC Hughes -v- Miss Greta Smyth & Others	1 ITC 418
	Relatives taken into partnership	JM O'Dwyer -v- Caffola & Company	2 ITC 374
	Repayment of Tax	Revenue Commissioners -v- HI	ITL 126
	Section 434 Income Tax Act 1967	Estate of Teresa Downing (Owner)	2 ITC 103
		John EH Colclough and others -v- Colclough and Robb	ITL 103
	Trust for expenditure of monies upon property beneficially occupied by life tenant	Frances Elizabeth Sarah Marchioness Conyngham -v- Revenue Commissioners	1 ITC 259
1.9	**Export Sales Relief**		
	Deposit interest	J G Kerrane -v- N Hanlon (Ireland) Limited	HC 1987

	Income calculation	Cronin -v- Youghal Carpets (Yarns)	ITL 129
	Intervention sales	Cronin -v- IMP (Midleton) Limited	HC 1985
1.10	**Land Dealing & Developing**		
	Capital sum paid for annuity	McCabe -v- South City and County Investment Company Ltd.	HC 1995
	Isolated transaction - application of Section 17 Finance (MP) Act 1968	J Mara -v- Hummingbird Ltd	SC 1977
	Land sold - whether in trade or adventure in the nature of trade	Spa Estates Ltd -v- L O'hArgain	HC 1974
	Site fines and capitalised value of ground rents - tax treatment of	A G Birch -v- Denis Delaney	2 ITC 127
		Edward Connolly -v- A G Birch	2 ITC 127
		R D Swaine -v- V E	3 ITC 389
	Trading Stock - appropriation of land as	L O'hArgain -v- Beechpark Estates Limited	ITL 116
	Trading Stock - Calculation of value	Cronin -v- Cork & County Property Company Ltd	SC 1986
		O'Connlain -v- Belvedere Estates	HC 1983
1.11	**Liquidations & Receiverships**		
	Appropriation of Payments	Bernard Uniake -v- Collector General	HC 1988
	Arrangement	In re MFN Construction Co Ltd (in liquidation)	SC 1988
	Chargeable gain accruing after date of liquidation	Revenue Commissioners -v- Donnelly	SC 1981
	CPT on company in liquidation	City of Dublin Steam Packet Company (in liquidation) -v- Revenue Commissioners	1 ITC 285
		In re A Noyek & Sons Ltd. (in liquidation)	SC 1988
	"Double Preference"	In re H. Williams (Tallaght) Ltd. (in receivership and liquidation)	HC 1996
	Interest earned by liquidator	In re Hibernian Transport Companies	HC 1970

Appendix

		Irish Provident Assurance Co Ltd (in liquidation) -v- W P Kavanagh	1 ITC 52
	Interest earned by receiver	Wayte (holdings) Limited -v- Edward N Hearne	HC 1986
	Preferential claim in receivership	Attorney General -v- Irish Steel Ltd & Vincent Crowley	2 ITC 40
	Surcharge on Undistributed income	Rahinstown Estates -v- Hughes	HC 1986
1.12	**Manufacture of Goods**		
	Advertising film	O'Culachain -v- Hunter Advertising Ltd	HC 1988
		Saatchi and Saatchi Advertising Ltd -v- McGarry	HC 1996
	Assembly of agricultural machinery	Irish Agricultural Machinery Ltd -v- O'Culachain	SC 1989
	Cultivation of Chrysanthemums	Brosnan -v- Leeside Nurseries Ltd	HC 1994
	Processing of milk	Cronin -v- Strand Dairy Limited	ITL 135
	Ripening of bananas	Charles McCann Limited -v- O'Culachain	HC 1984
	Unaltered Cloth	O'Laochdha -v- Johnson and Johnson (Ir) Ltd	HC 1991
1.13	**Married Persons**		
	Aggregation of income	Gilligan -v- C.A.B	HC 1997
		Gerard Muckley and Ann Muckley -v- Attorney General	HC 1982
		Francis Murphy and Mary Murphy -v- Attorney General	SC 1979
	"Married woman living with her husband"	T Donovan -v- C G Crofts	1 ITC 126
		D Ua Clothasaigh -v- P McCartan	2 ITC 367
	Tax Treaty with U.K.	Travers -v- O'Siochain	HC 1994
1.14	**Miscellaneous**		
	Annual Returns	McLoughlin -v- Tuite	HC 1983
		Downes -v- D.P.P.	HC 1987
	"Discovery" of inadmissible deductions	W Ltd -v- T J Wilson	ITL 110

Ex gratia payment	W S McGarry -v- E F	3 ITC 103
Income Tax exemption for agricultural society	Trustees of the Ward Union Hunt Races -v- H P Hughes	2 ITC 152
Interest earned by liquidator	Irish Provident Assurance Company Ltd (in liquidation) -v- W P Kavanagh	1 ITC 52
Limited partnership	MacCarthaigh -v- Daly	ITL 127
Management expenses	Howth Estate Company -v- W J Davis	2 ITC 74
	W J Casey -v- Monteagle Estate Company	3 ITC 313
Market gardening	L -v- W S McGarry	3 ITC 111
	W S McGarry -v- J V A Spencer	2 ITC 297
Overpayment - Interest on	Mooney -v- O'Coindealbhain	HC 1992
Patent Income - Whether income from patent rights disregarded for income tax purposes	Pandion Haliaetus Limited -v- Revenue Commissioners Osprey Care Ltd -v- Revenue Commissioners Osprey Systems Design Ltd -v- Revenue Commissioners	HC 1987
Preferential claim in receivership	Attorney General -v- Irish Steel Limited & Vincent Crowley	2 ITC 402
Promoting amateur games	Revenue Commissioners -v- O'Reilly	SC 1982
Rates - whether assessable to tax	Moville District Board of Conservators -v- D Ua Clothasaigh	3 ITC 1
Residence and domicile	Captain R H Prior-Wandesforde -v- Revenue Commissioners	1 ITC 248
	Earl of Iveagh -v- Revenue Commissioners	1 ITC 316
Validity of PAYE Regulations	Kennedy -v- Hearne	HC 1987
Withholding Tax – judicial review	Daly -v- Revenue Commissioners and Attorney General	HC 1995

1.15 Rental Income

Authorised deduction	Stephen Court Ltd -v- Browne	ITL 120

1.16 Residential Property Tax

Constitutional validity	Madigan -v- Attorney General	SC 1984

Appendix

1.17 Schedule E Expenses

Miscellaneous expenses	H F Kelly -v- H	3 ITC 351
	S P O'Broin -v- S McGiolla Meidhre	3 ITC 235
	S P O'Broin -v- F Pigott	3 ITC 235
Travelling expenses	J P Mac Daibheid -v- D S A Carroll	ITL 115
	Phillips -v- Keane	1 ITC 69

1.18 Schedule E Income

Amount accrued due but not received	M J J MacKeown -v- P J Roe	1 ITC 206
Benefit in kind - Car	Browne -v- Attorney General	HC 1991
Benefit in kind from rented House	J F Connolly -v- D McNamara	3 ITC 341
Charge on property of estate in favour of son	G O'Reilly -v- W J Casey	2 ITC 220
Deferred Gratuity	O'Siochain -v- Morrissey	HC 1992
Ex gratia payment	W S McGarry -v- E F	3 ITC 103
Grant to a president of a college on retirement	J D Mulvey -v- D J Coffey	2 ITC 239
Health grounds payment	S Shea -v- Mulqueen	HC 1995
Interest on overpayment	O'Rourke -v- Revenue Commissioners	HC 1996
Jockey receiving present from employer	M A Wing -v- H J O'Connell	1 ITC 170
Nun Employed as school teacher	J D Dolan -v- "K" (National School Teacher)	2 ITC 280
Office or employment within the State	W J Tipping -v- L Jeancard	2 ITC 360
PAYE - operation of regulations	S P Bedford -v- B Hannon	ITL 105
Service - contract of	J E MacDermott -v- P Loy	ITL 118
	EP O'Coindealbhain -v- Thomas B Mooney	HC 1988
Widows pension	EP O'Coindealbhain -v- Breda O'Carroll	HC 1988
	O'Siochain -v- Neenan	HC 1997

1.19	**Service Company**		
	Meaning of	P MacGiolla Mhaith -v- Brian Cronin Associates	ITL 124
1.20	**Stock Relief**		
	Assembly of agricultural machinery	Irish Agricultural Machinery Ltd -v- O'Culachain	SC 1989
	Excess Profits Duty	J W Green & Co (Cork) Limited -v- Revenue Commissioners	1 ITC 142
	Progress Payments	O'Laoghaire -v- Avonree Buildings	HC 1982
	Separate Trades	P McElligott and Sons Ltd -v- Revenue Commissioners	ITL 123
1.21	**Stamp Duty**		
	Conveyance - Legal estate	Viek Investments Ltd -v- The Revenue Commissioners	HC 1992
	Deed of Release – whether a sale	Cherry Court -v- Revenue Commissioners	HC 1995
	Lease – whether a sale	O'Sullivan -v- Revenue Commissioners	SC 1949
1.22	**Trading Deductions**		
	Compensation for loss of rights as regards light and air	W J Davis -v- X Ltd	2 ITC 320
	Corporation Profits Tax - deduction in Case 1 computation	J M O'Dwyer -v- Dublin United Transport Company Ltd	2 ITC 437
	Exclusivity agreements - payments under	J D Dolan -v- A B Company Ltd	ITL 109
	Holding Company expenses in connection with formation of	J B Kealy v O'Meara (Limerick) Limited	2 ITC 265
	Irish trading operation of foreign company - expenditure attributable to	Revenue Commissioners -v- L & Co	3 ITC 205
	"Know how" payments	S Ltd -v- J M O'Sullivan	ITL 108
	Legal costs	W J Casey -v- A B Ltd	ITL 104
	Loss in value of goods before delivery	Revenue Commissioners -v- Latchford & Sons Limited, Tralee	1 ITC 238

Appendix

Loss on sale of investments	Alliance and Dublin Consumers Gas Co -v- R G Davis	1 ITC 114
Lump sum paid on execution of lease	W Flynn -v- Blackwood & Co (Sligo) Limited	3 ITC 79
Mill sanitation - expenditure on	J B Vale -v- Martin Mahony & Bros Limited	2 ITC 331
"Obsolescence" - meaning of	J P Evans & Co -v- W F Phillips	1 ITC 38
Promoting Bill in Parliament – cost of	W S McGarry -v- Limerick Gas Committee	1 ITC 405
Re building of business premises	M D Curtin -v- M Limited	3 ITC 227
Removal of top soil from quarry surface	Milverton Quarries Limited -v- Revenue Commissioners	3 ITC 279
Re organisation of share capital	W J Davis -v- Hibernian Bank Limited	2 ITC 111
Replacement of weighbridge	J T Hodgins -v- Plunder & Pollak (Ireland) Limited	3 ITC 135
Restoration of destroyed premises under covenant to repair	Martin Fitzgerald -v- CIR	1 ITC 100
Scientific expenditure	Texaco (Ireland) Ltd -v- Murphy	SC 1992
Trees - Forestry operation	J M Wilson-Wright -v- J F Connolly	SC 1976

1.23 Trading Losses

Carry forward	Molmac Limited -v- P MacGiolla Riogh	3 ITC 376
Cessation	Cronin -v- Lunham Brothers Limited	HC 1984

1.24 Trading Miscellaneous

Business carried on by Charity	P J Beirne -v- St Vincent de Paul Society	1 ITC 413
Commencement of new trade	H A O'Loan -v- M J Noone & Co	2 ITC 430
Current Cost Accounting	Carroll Industries PLC -v- O'Culachain	HC 1988
Capital allowances - diminishment	IAWS Ltd -v- J E MacDermott	ITL 112
Discontinuance of trade	Bolands Ltd -v- W J Davis	1 ITC 91

Hospital - whether carrying on a trade	R G Davis -v- Mater Misericordiae Hospital	2 ITC 1
Leasing of premises - whether a trade	E S Pairceir -v- EM	ITL 107
Levies on course betting	Racing Board -v- O'Culachain	HC 1988
Occupation of land	M O'Conaill -v- George Shackleton & Sons Ltd	ITL 111
Partnership - cessation of trade	A B -v- J D Mulvey	2 ITC 345
Professional examinations - conduct of	Pharmaceutical Society of Ireland -v- Revenue Commissioners	2 ITC 157
Statutory body - whether carrying on a trade	Exported Livestock (Insurance) -v- T J Carroll	3 ITC 67
	Veterinary Council -v- F Corr	3 ITC 59
Stock Relief - Excess Profits Duty	J W Green & Co (Cork) Limited -v- Revenue Commissioners	1 ITC 142
Trustees of will carrying on trade	Executors & Trustees of A C Ferguson (Decd) -v- T Donovan	1 ITC 214
Valuation of stocks and shares held by finance company	A B Ltd -v- P MacGiolla Riogh	3 ITC 301

1.25 Trading Receipts

Bad Debt recovered	W H Bourke -v- Lyster & Sons Limited	3 ITC 247
	C D -v- J M O'Sullivan	2 ITC 422
Compensation paid by Government for compulsory detention of ship	Alliance & Dublin Consumers Gas Company -v- O J McWilliams	1 ITC 199
Compensation paid by Government to parent company on termination of contract with subsidiary	J M O'Dwyer -v- Irish Exporters and Importers Limited (in liquidation)	2 ITC 251
Ex gratia payment by British Government	W A Robinson (James Pim & Son) -v- JD Dolan	ITC 25
Grants - training	Jacob International -v- O'Cleirigh	ITL 128
Illegal trade	C Hayes -v- R J Duggan	2 ITC 269
	D Collins & M Byrne -v- J D Mulvey	3 ITC 151

Appendix

Loss of profits policy	F Corr -v- F E Larkin	3 ITC 13
Lump sum paid on execution of lease	W Flynn -v- John Noone Limited	3 ITC 79
Pig rearing	Inspector of Taxes -v- P J Kiernan	ITL 117
	Knockhall Piggeries -v- Kerrane	HC 1983
Race horse sold	P MacGiolla Riogh -v- G Ltd	3 ITC 181
Realisation of Investments	Agricultural Credit Corporation Limited -v- J B Vale	2 ITC 46
	JA Browne -v- Bank of Ireland Finance Limited	HC 1987
Requisition of stocks	Arthur Guinness, Son & Co Ltd -v- CIR	1 ITC 1
Sale of subsidiary company	Guinness & Mahon Ltd -v- Browne	ITL 133
Services - contract for	J E MacDermott -v- P Loy	ITL 118
Stallion fees	Cloghran Stud Farm -v- A G Birch	2 ITC 65
Sweep Tickets	HH -v- Forbes	ITL 114
Whiskey sold in bond	Reps of P J McCall (Decd) -v- CIR	1 ITC 31

1.26 **Value Added Tax**

Attachment	O. -v- Revenue Commissioners	HC 1994
Copyright	Phonographic Performance (Ireland) Ltd -v- Somers	HC 1992
Credit Cards	Diners Club Ltd -v- Revenue Commissioners	HC 1988
Instalment of Fixtures - TV aerial	Maye -v- Revenue Commissioners	HC 1984
Leases – expenses on	Erin Executor and Trustee Company Ltd -v- Revenue Commissioners	HC 1994
Registration	WLD Worldwide Leather Diffusion Ltd -v- Revenue Commissioners	HC 1994
Retailers' Scheme	D.H. Burke & Son Ltd -v- Revenue Commissioners	HC 1997
Services supplied by Solicitor	JJ Bourke -v- WG Bradley & Sons	HC 1988
Television - electricity	Brosnan -v- Cork Communications Ltd	HC 1991
U.K. Restraint Order	Bank of Ireland -v- Meeneghan	HC 1994

INDEX

A
Accounting Periods...177
    Corporation Tax...177
Advance Corporation Tax...212
Age Allowance...56
Age Exemption...64
Agricultural and Fishery Co Operatives...216
Agricultural Property
    Capital Acquisitions Tax...252
Airports...132
Alarm Systems...61
An Bord Pinsean...216
Anti Avoidance...229
    Bond Washing...230
    Capital Distribution Treated as Dividend...231
    Exchequer Bills...230
    Friendly Societies...229
    Industrial and Provident Societies...229
    Limited Partnerships...230
    Property Transactions...229
    Transactions to Avoid Liability to Tax...231
    Transfer Abroad...229
Appeals...46
    Capital Acquisitions Tax...262
    Corporation Tax...175
    Income Tax...46
    Residential Property Tax...295
    Stamp Duty...311
    Value Added Tax...328
Approved Profit Sharing Schemes...117
Assessment
    Joint Assessment...52
    Separate Assessment...52
    Separated Spouses...52
    Single Assessment...52
Assessment – Basis of
    Case I and II...71
    Case III...76
    Case IV...77
    Case V...88
    Schedule E...111

Index

Assets
    Transfer Abroad...229
Attachment – Power of...49

B

Benefit-in-Kind Exemptions...115
    Bus/Train Passes...115
    Childcare Services...116
    Works of Art...115
Benefits-in-Kind...112
    Accommodation...114
    Cars...112
    Interest Paid at a Preferential Rate...114
    Vans...114
BES...154
Blind Persons' Allowance...57
Bond Washing...230
Book Debts – Fixed Charge...51
Branch Profits...210
Building Societies...216

C

Capital Acquisitions Tax...245
    Accountable Persons...261
    Agricultural Property...252
    Appeals...261
    Business Relief...254
    Certain Dwellings...253
    Certificate of Discharge...262
    class thresholds...31
    Class Thresholds...246
    Clearance Certificate...262
    Disclaimer...251
    Discretionary Trusts...247
    Double Aggregation...249
    Exemptions...256
    Free Use of Property...255
    Gifts...249
    Indexation...247
    Joint Accounts...256
    Joint Tenants...251
    Limited Interests...255
    Marriage Settlements...251
    Nephew or Niece of the Disponer...250
    Penalties...259
    Prior Tax...249

rates...27
Returns...260
Revised Class Threshold...246
S60 Policies...256
Self Assessment...258
Shares in Private Companies...253
Surcharge...260
Surviving Spouses...250
Territorial Limit...251
Threshold Amount...247
Capital Allowances...127
Airports...132
Balancing Allowances...128
Balancing Charges...128
Childcare Facilities...134
Dredging...131
Holiday Camps...132
Holiday Cottages...132
Hotels...132
Industrial Buildings...129,...130
Lessors...130
Motor Vehicles...128
Multi-Storey Car Parks...131
Nursing Homes...133
Park and Ride Facilities...135
Patent Rights...131
Plant and Machinery...127
Private Convalescent Facilities...134
Rental Income...86
Restrictions...139
Room Ownership Scheme...133
Scientific Research...131
Significant Buildings...137
Student Accommodation...134
Third Level Institutions...135
Wear and Tear Allowance...127
Writing-Down Allowance...129
Capital Gains Tax...267
Anti Avoidance...289
Assets...267
Business – disposal of...276
Capital Allowances...285
Chargeable Persons...267
Clearance Certificates...289
Compensation and Insurance Money...280
Compulsory Purchase...280
Computation...271
Death...268

Index

    Deductions...281
    Disposal...268
    Disposal – Time of...268
    Divorced Persons...268
    Exemptions and Reliefs...274
    Farm – disposal of...276
    Grants...285
    Husbands and Wives...268
    Inheritances and Gifts...282
    Interest...281
    Leases...286
    Liquidations...282
    Losses...272
    Miscellaneous...289
    Options...282
    Part Disposals...273
    Private Residence...275
    Rates...269
    Reduced Rate...270
    Reorganisations and Takeovers...283
    Retirement of Farmers...281
    Rights Issues...282
    Roll-Over Relief...277
    Self Assessment...273
    Separate Spouses...269
    Shares – Acqusition by a Company of its Own...283
    Shares – Calls on...281
    Shares – Identification...282
    Shares – Sale of...278
    Time Limits...289
    Transfer of a Business to a Company...286
    Trusts...287
CAT/IT DTA with the UK...265
Charges on Income...182
Charities – Eligible...221
Childcare Facilities...134
Clearance Certificates
    Capital Acquisitions Tax...262
    Capital Gains Tax...289
    Liquor Licences...244
    Other Licences...244
Close Companies...200
    Distributions...202
    Participators and Associates...200
    Section 84 Loans...203
    Surcharge on Undistributed Income...201
College
    Fees...60

Company – Acquisition of its Own Shares...283
Corporation Tax
    Accounting Periods...177
    Appeals...175
    Charges on Income...182
    Doubt – Matters of...179
    Late Returns...178
    Losses / Management Expenses...180
    Payment...179
    Preliminary Tax...179
    Pre-Trading Expenses...180
    Rates...175
    Residence...176
    Restriction of Allowances and Reliefs...178
    Returns...178
    Section 151 Assessments...182
    Self Assessment...177
    Surcharge...178
Cross Border Workers...170

D

Deeds of Covenant...124
Dependent Relative Allowance...57
Deposit Interest Retention Tax...78
Designated...221
Directors...46
Discretionary Trusts...247
Distributions...231
    Capital Distribution Treated as Dividend...231
    Manufacturing Profits...204
    Matters to be treated...202
    Section 84 Loans...203
Dividend withholding tax...206
Dividends
    Non Resident Subsidiary...209
Divorce Persons
    Stamp Duty...309
Divorced Persons
    Capital Gains Tax...268
    Income Tax...53
Domicile...170
Donations/Gifts
    Tax Relief...61
Double Rent Allowance
    Designated Area / Street...96
    Temple Bar...93
Double Taxation Agreements...223

Index

Double Taxation Agreements – Rep. of Ire and UK...224
Doubt – Matters of...44
Dredging...131
Dublin Docklands Development Authority...217

E

EC Directives...227
Employed Person Taking Care of Incapacitated Individual...57
Employee Allowance...58
Employee Share Ownership Trusts...119
Employee Share Schemes...116
Employers
    Double Deduction...220
Employment Related Payments...219
Energy (Renewable) Generation...221
Enterprise Trust Limited...220
Entertainment Expenses...70
Euro...209
Exemptions...149
    Age...64
    Artists...149
    Forests...152
    Greyhound Stud Fees...152
    Haemophilia HIV Trust...152
    Hepatitis C Compensation...153
    Income...64
    Patent Royalties...149
    Personal Injuries...152
    Stallion Services...151

F

Farming...141
    Income Tax...141
    Value Added Tax...325
Films...165
First Step Limited...222
Foreign Exchange Transactions...208
Forests...152

G

Gifts...61,...249
Greyhound Stud Fees...152
Group Relief...195
    "Loss Buying" of trading losses...197
    Anti-Avoidance...196
    Company entering a Group...197

Index

Company leaving a Group...196
Depreciatory Transactions...197

H
Haemophilia HIV Trust...152
Hepatitis C Compensation...153
Holiday Camps...132
Holiday Cottages...132
Hotels...132
    Room Ownership Scheme...133
Housing Finance Agency plc...217

I
Incapacitated Child Allowance...56
Income Exemption...64
Income Tax
    Assessments...45
    Attachment – Power of...49
    Doubt – Matters of...44
    Interest on Overdue Tax...49
    Payment...45
    Preliminary Tax...45
    Pre-Trading Expenses...70
    Returns...44
    Surcharge...44
Indexation
    Capital Acquisitions Tax...247
    Capital Gains Tax...271
    Probate Tax...263
    Residential Property Tax...293
Industrial Buildings...129,...130
Injuries – Personal...152
Interest on Overdue Tax...49
Interest Payable...65
    death duties...65
    mortgage interest...65
    non residents...66
    paid net...66
    Restrictions – Case V...85
Investment in Corporate Trades...154
Investor Compensation Company Limited...218
Irish Horse-Racing Authority...217
Irish Tax Cases...335

J
Joint Assessment...52

Index

L
Limited Partnerships...230
Losses
    10% Companies...190
    Capital Gains Tax...272
    Case I and II...73
    Case V...88
    Corporation Tax...180
    Manufacturing Companies...190
    Restrictions...139

M
Management Expenses...180
Marginal Relief...64
Married Allowance...54
Medical Expenses...57
Medical Insurance...58
Mining Taxation...198
    Exploration Expenditure...198
    Rehabilitation Expenditure...199
Motor Expenses...70
Multi-Storey Car Parks...131

N
National Lottery...217
National Treasury Management Agency...217
Nitrigin Eireann Teoranta (NET)...218
Nursing Homes...133

P
Park and Ride Facilities...135
Participators and Associates...200
    Expenses for...200
    Interest Paid to...200
    Loans to...200
Patent Rights...131
Patent Royalites...149
Payments in Connection with
    Retirement or Removal from an Employment...122
    the Commencement of Employment...121
Permanent Health Benefit Schemes...58
Personal Allowances
    Age Allowance...56
    Alarm Systems...61
    Blind Persons' Allowance...57
    Dependent Relative Allowance...57

Index

    Donations/Gifts...61
    Employed Person Taking Care of Incapacitated Individual...57
    Employee Allowance...58
    Fees paid for Training Courses...60
    Fees paid to EU Colleges...60
    Fees paid to Private Colleges...60
    Incapacitated Child Allowance...56
    Long Term Unemployed...59
    Married Allowance...54
    Medical Expenses...57
    Medical Insurance...58
    Permanent Health Benefit Schemes...58
    Rents Paid by Certain Tenants...59
    Retirement Annuities...61
    Seafarers Allowance...59
    Service Charges...60
    Single Allowance...55
    Single Parent Allowance...55
    Widowed Allowance...54
Petroleum Companies...199
Power of Attachment...49
Preliminary Tax
    Capital Gains Tax...273
    Corporation Tax...179
    Income Tax...45
Private Convalescent Facilities...134
Private Residence...275
Probate Tax...263
PRSI Rates & Levies...6

R
Remuneration
    Unpaid...121
Rental Income
    Capital Allowances...86
    Expenses...85
    Farm Land...88
    Interest Restrictions...85
    Leases...87
    Non Residents...88
    person aged 55 years or more...59
    Premiums...87
    rent relief...59
    Section 23...86
Reporting Requirements...237
    Foreign Accounts...238
    Information from Ministers...240

Index

    Non Resident Companies...239
    Off-Shore Funds...238
    Returns of Certain Information...237
    Show Tax Reference...240
Research and Development...193
Residence...168
    Companies Changing...211
    Corporation Tax...176
    Cross Border Workers...170
    Deduction for Foreign Earnings...169
    Domicile...170
    Ordinary Residence...168
    Seafarer Allowance...170
    Split Year Residence Relief...168
Residential Property Tax...291
    Appeals...295
    Assessment...294
    Charge to RPT...291
    Clearance...294
    Income...293
    Income Limit...292
    Inflation Relief...293
    Interest on Overdue Tax...294
    Marginal Relief...293
    Market Value...292
    Market Value Exemption Limit...292
    Overpayment...295
    Payment...294
    Penalties...295
    rates from 6th April 1994...33
    Returns...294
Resignation of Professional Advisors...243
Restriction of Capital Allowances/Losses...139
Retirement Annuities...61
Revenue Commissioners...43
Revenue Offences...241
    Revenue Offences Made Public...242
Revenue Powers...232
    Application to Appeal Commissioners – financial institutions...235
    Application to Circuit Court or District Court – financial institutions...236
    Application to High Court – financial institutions...235
    Authorised officers and Garda Síochána...235
    DIRT...234
    General...232
    Information from third parties – Application to High Court...233
    Information to be furnished by Financial Institutions...235

Inspection of documents and records...234
Inspector's right to make enquiries...232
PAYE...233
Power to obtain from certain persons particulars...233
Power to require production of accounts and books...232
Production of books and records – Application to High Court...233
Statement of Affairs...236
Subcontractors...233
Roll-Over Relief...277
Round Sum Expense Allowances...112
Rural Renewal Scheme – 1998...109

S

Save As You Earn (SAYE) Share Scheme...121
Schedule C...68
Schedule D – Case I and II...69
Schedule D – Case III...76
Schedule D – Case IV...77
Schedule D – Case V...85
Schedule E...111
    Deductions...111
    Exemptions...123
Schools – Designated...221
Scientific Research...131
Scientific Technological Educational and (Investment) Fund...222
Seafarers Allowance...59,...170
Securitisation of Assets...172
Seed Capital Investment...163
Separate Assessment...52
Separated Spouses...52
Service Charges...60
Shannon Airport...192
Share Subscription Schemes...116
Significant Buildings...137
Single Allowance...55
Single Assessment...52
Single Parent Allowance...55
Social Welfare Benefits...111
Special Investment Policies (SIP)...82
Special Investment Products – Limits...84
Special Investment Schemes (SIS)...82
Special Portfolio Investment Accounts (SPIA)...83
Special Savings Accounts...78
Stallion Services...151
Stamp Duties...297
    Ad Valorem Duty...307

Index

    Amnesty...298
    Anti Avoidance...301
    Appeals...311
    Associated Companies – Transfers Between...302
    Bond...304
    Capital Duty – Companies...305
    Charge...298
    Consideration Cannot be Ascertained...300
    Conveyance...298
    Covenant...304
    Debenture...304
    Deductions...302
    Exceptions...307
    Exemptions...309
    Fixed Rate of Duty...308
    Leases...303
    Letters of Renunciation...300
    Life Insurance Policies...305
    Mortgage...304
    Payment...311
    Related Persons – Interactions Between...302
    Section 84 Loans...306
    Settlements...305
    The Crest System...300
    Transfer on Sale...298
    Valuation of Property...301
    Voluntary Dispositions Inter Vivos...300
    Young Farmers...308
Stamp Duty
    Divorce...309
    Divorce, transfers on...309
    Residential Property – From 23 January 1997...298
    Residential Property 1998 – From 23 April 1998...299
    Stocks or Marketable Securities...298
Standard Capital Superannuation Benefit...122
Student Accommodation...134
Sub-Contractors...144
Surcharge...44
    Capital Acquisitions Tax...260
    Capital Gains Tax...273
    Corporation Tax...178
    Income Tax...44
    Stamp Duty...300
Surcharge on Undistributed Income...201
    Trusts...174

Index

T

Tax Clearance Certificates...244
    Liquor Licences...244
    Other Licences...244
Temple Bar...92
Termination Payments...122
Tourism Facilities...100
Training Courses – Fees...60
Trustee Savings Banks...218
Trusts and Settlements...173

U

Unemployment – Long Term...59
Unilateral Relief...210
Urban Renewal...89
    1986 Scheme...89
    1998-1999 Scheme...107
    Customs House Docks Area...89
    Dublin Docklands...105
    Enterprise Areas...98
    from 1st August 1994 – Designated Area/Street...94
    Islands...104
    Resort Areas...100
    Tallaght (Dublin)...89
    Temple Bar Area of Dublin...92

V

Value Added Tax...313
    Annex A Activities...330
    Annex B Services...331
    Annual Accounting for VAT...317
    Appeals...328
    Auction Scheme...319
    Bad Debts...319
    Bankruptcy and Winding Up...328
    Cash Basis...327
    Charge...313
    Distance Selling...316
    Documentation...328
    European Union Directives...313
    Farmer – Flat Rate...326
    Farmers...325
    Foreign Traders – Repayment to...326
    Group Registration...327
    Immovable Goods...321
    Intra-Community Acquisitions – Registered Persons...315

Index

    Intra-Community Acquisitions – Unregistered Persons...315
    Legislation...313
    Mail Order...316
    Margin Scheme...318
    Non-Taxable Entities...315
    Place where Goods Supplied...320
    Place where Services Supplied...320
    Private Individuals...315
    Rates...321
    Register – Option not to...324
    Retail Export Scheme...326
    Self Supply...313
    Supply of Goods...313
    Tax Deductible...318
    Tax Not Deductible...319
    Taxable Periods...317
    Telecommunications Services...316
    Transfer of Business...317
    Transport – New Means of...316
    Transport – Second-hand Means of...319
VAT
    Unjust Enrichment...328

W

Widowed Allowance...54
Withholding Tax
    Professional Services...74

Publishing Programme

The Institute of Taxation in Ireland is committed to the publication of taxation titles which provide a valuable up-to-date reference source for tax consultants and students. Books are written by eminent tax consultants who are specialists in their particular area of taxation. Many of the publications are the sole comprehensive publication on the relevant tax in Ireland. These publications are available at discount prices to Institute members and subscribers.

The Institute publishes twenty one taxation titles:

- Taxation Summary, Republic of Ireland
- Income Tax
- The Taxation of Capital Gains
- Corporation Tax
- The Law of Stamp Duties
- Valuation of Shares in Private Companies
- Capital Acquisitions Tax
- Value Added Tax
- VAT on Property
- Finak
- PRSI & Levy Contributions
- Tax Implications of Marital Breakdown
- Double Taxation Agreements
- Case Law for the Tax Practitioner
- Pensions: Revenue Law & Practice
- Trust & Succession Law: A Guide for Tax Practitioners
- Taxes Consolidation Act, 1997: The Busy Practitioner's Guide
- Direct Tax Acts
- Seminar & Conference Papers
- Law of Capital Acquisitions Tax
- Capital Allowances